# RUNNING

# Microsoft® Windows NT®
# Server 4.0

## The Essential Guide for Administrators, Systems Engineers, and IS Professionals

*Charlie Russel and*
*Sharon Crawford*

PUBLISHED BY
Microsoft Press
A Division of Microsoft Corporation
One Microsoft Way
Redmond, Washington 98052-6399

Library of Congress Cataloging-in-Publication Data pending.

Printed and bound in the United States of America.

3 4 5 6 7 8 9    QMQM    2 1 0 9 8

Distributed to the book trade in Canada by Macmillan of Canada, a division of Canada
Publishing Corporation.

A CIP catalogue record for this book is available from the British Library.

Microsoft Press books are available through booksellers and distributors worldwide. For
further information about international editions, contact your local Microsoft Corporation
office. Or contact Microsoft Press International directly at fax (206) 936-7329.

**Acquisitions Editor:** David J. Clark
**Project Editor:** Sigrid Anne Strom
**Technical Editor:** Jim Fuchs

# Contents

# Acknowledgments

A book can be a wonderful thing—informative, enlightening, educational. To the extent that this book succeeds at being any of these, it's because of the talented and hardworking people involved in the project from the first. We owe heartfelt thanks to many, especially David J. Clark, Acquisitions Editor at Microsoft Press, who gave us a chance and offered continual help and support every step of the way.

But there are many others to whom we owe gratitude:

Gino Marnoni for his sage advice on many subjects and, specifically, for his helping us work out the intricacies of WINS and TCP/IP.

US Mach, Inc., of Fremont, California, for the lengthy loan of an Alpha server to test and for many years of hardware support.

Dave Kearns, networker *extraordinaire*, who supplied the chapter on security planning and the material on Novell NetWare.

Joseph M. Salmeri, who not only wrote the excellent chapter on the difficult subject of the Registry but made it understandable, too—quite an achievement.

Gene Baucom of Microsoft for his many insights into the workings of Disk Administrator and for his outstanding help in getting us through some serious hard drive problems.

At Microsoft Press itself, there are a host of other people to thank:

Our editor, Sigrid Strom, and technical editor, Jim Fuchs, for their hard work and grace under pressure; Pam Hidaka for the elegant internal design of the book; electronic artists Michael Victor and Lori Campbell for the beautiful (and accurate) illustrations; and William Teel, Dail Magee, Jr., Sandra Haynes, Patricia Masserman, and Deborah Long for their editorial contributions and technical support during the production of this book.

Special thanks to Mary DeJong, who offered just the right words of reassurance and encouragement at just the right time.

# INTRODUCTION

Sometimes it seems that every book on each new operating system starts out with the declaration that a new era has begun. Aside from the humorous aspects of these frequent avowals, they are not all outsized exaggerations. The qualification that's usually left out is that eras are not what they used to be.

In the computer business, anything prior to 1981 is practically Pleistocene, and new eras start every few months. Everything you learn this week will be null and void by next week, as some are fond of saying. Of course, it could not be otherwise in an area of technology that is in a state of maximum ferment and that spews forth "breakthroughs" at a maniacal pace. One of the main occupations of those who watch the computer business is debating which breakthroughs are genuine and which are dead ends, and they have to arrive at an opinion in a hurry before events overtake them.

Microsoft Windows NT Server version 4, if not an actual revolution, is a marked advance in the quest for powerful, rock-solid networking software that can accommodate client machines of various types and that does not require a genius for an administrator. It doesn't *hurt* to be a genius, but patience, good sense, and equanimity will serve an administrator better than any particular flashes of brilliance.

## Is This Book for You?

Our approach in writing this book was to try to provide a bridge to Windows NT Server version 4 for several categories of people. One category is administrators of networks using Microsoft Windows NT Server 3.*x*. These administrators will find an easy guide to installing the new version of Windows NT Server and plenty of material on how to use the new tools as "the old tools with new interfaces." If you're unacquainted with the Microsoft Windows 95 interface, you'll find a guide to the interface in Appendix A.

Another category is power users who, while not full-fledged administrators, perform administrative tasks and need to be brought up to speed on the features of Windows NT Server version 4 without delay. Power users can quickly locate the chapters that cover their particular administrative duties, such as backups or printer management.

A third category is people who are new to Windows NT Server but who are not necessarily new to the concept of networking. This group is likewise accommodated with chapters on planning for installation, as well as detailed information on the installation itself.

Although we make occasional references to the differences between Windows NT Server version 4 and earlier versions of Windows NT, we assume no detailed knowledge of Windows NT 3.*x* on the part of the reader.

## What's in the Book?

*Running Microsoft Windows NT Server 4.0* is divided into five parts, each roughly corresponding to a different layer of development in a Windows NT Server network.

◆ **Part One: Preinstallation Planning** You've heard of Edison's famous quote: "Genius is one percent inspiration and ninety-nine percent perspiration." Modify that statement slightly, and you have a good motto for network building: "A good network is one percent implementation and ninety-nine percent preparation." That's why this book begins with five chapters of planning. The first chapter is an overview of the new features in Windows NT Server version 4. The other four chapters cover domain and trust relationship configurations, appropriate hardware choices, appropriate levels of security for your system, and the best file system for your Windows NT network.

◆ **Part Two: Installation and Setup** In Part Two, we take you first through the process of installing Windows NT Server. Then in subsequent chapters, we cover setting up network protocols (and how to decide which protocols to use) and the use of Disk Administrator to set up hard drive storage that is fault tolerant and ultimately safe.

◆ **Part Three: Domain Administration** Part Three covers the basic building blocks of a Windows NT network: setting up users and groups, installing and sharing printers, and setting file and directory permissions. You'll also find chapters on day-to-day chores, such as applications and messaging services and using Windows NT Server tools on a Windows 95 computer.

◆ **Part Four: Enterprise NT** Administrators who have responsibility for company-wide networks will find much that's useful in this section. There are chapters on managing multiple domains, setting up and running remote access and the Internet information server, and a chapter on coexisting with Novell NetWare networks and Macintosh computers. You'll also find a chapter to help demystify TCP/IP so that you can set up Domain Name System services and other tools with ease.

◆ **Part Five: Tuning, Maintenance, and Troubleshooting** This final section covers crucial material on network health. There's a chapter on that most basic element of preventive medicine—backups. Other chapters cover disk maintenance, auditing, and the registry and registry tools. And if, in spite of your best efforts, your network falters, we conclude with a chapter on disaster recovery.

At the end of the book, you'll find a glossary and three appendixes. Appendix A is a guided tour around the new Windows NT interface. If you're not familiar with the Microsoft Windows 95 interface, Appendix A can save you from a lot of wasted time and many fruitless mouse clicks. Appendix B is a list of keyboard shortcuts for those who prefer the keyboard to mouse clicks. Appendix C is a brief discussion of the Open Systems Interconnection (OSI) reference model, a model for networking protocols that can help you understand some network basics. You'll need to know about the OSI reference model some day when we're all sitting around at the Old Geeks Home swapping lies about Altair machines and punch cards.

We intend this book to be an easy reference for solving the everyday problems and questions of a system administrator. You should be able to find answers quickly here, but occasionally you may need a deeper or more arcane knowledge. In that case, you should consult the *Microsoft Windows NT Server Resource Kit*.

## NOTE

*Most chapters will include some notes like this that present alternate ways to perform a task or that highlight some additional pertinent information.*

Tip

*Shortcuts or other helpful bits of information will show up in these Tip boxes.*

◆ Special Information

Elaboration on a particular theme or background information is set off in sidebar boxes like this one.

# Talk Back! We're Listening

We've done our best to make this book as accurate and complete as a single-volume reference can be. However, given that Windows NT Server is such a large and complex system, we're sure that alert readers will find omissions (and even errors). If you have suggestions or corrections, please write to us:

c/o Microsoft Press
The Running Series Editor
One Microsoft Way
Redmond, WA 98052

We really do appreciate hearing from you.

# Part One

## Preinstallation Planning

# CHAPTER 1

Overview of Windows NT

# CHAPTER 1

# Overview of Windows NT

Since its release in 1993 as Windows NT 3.1, the Microsoft Windows NT operating system has shown promise as a standard setter for network operating systems. As superficially inauspicious as that first version was, the improvement from then on in the operating system's features and functionality has been continuous. While the hoopla has been focused on Microsoft's *really* famous operating system, Windows 95, new features and new functions have steadily, if not noisily, been added to Windows NT in successive iterations. People who specialize in networking software have been aware of this progress, reporting the gains with each new iteration but never quite ready to declare Windows NT a leader in network operating systems. With the advent of Windows NT version 4, that has changed.

Version 4 of Windows NT represents a tremendous advance in network operating systems, not only because it incorporates the easy-to-use graphical interface from Windows 95 but also because it provides solutions to problems of how to connect users in disparate geographical locations—both around the corner in the neighborhood and around the world. Then after it connects all of these users, it provides new and *powerful* tools for sharing information that can enhance or even revolutionize how people work.

What's more, all of the technological machinery is more easily controlled and configured than ever before. Version 4 of Microsoft Windows NT Server is a big step toward painless administration. We're not there yet—if we were, you wouldn't need this or any other book—but the mysteries are fewer and less like the proverbial Gordian knot in nature.

In the following sections of Chapter 1, we describe the differences between a server operating system, such as Windows NT Server, and a client operating system, such as Microsoft Windows NT Workstation or Microsoft Windows 95. We also provide lists of the new features and the older-but-continuing-to-improve features that are part of this latest Windows NT Server iteration. A list of the hardware required for installing and using Windows NT Server version 4 rounds out the chapter.

# Server and Client Operating Systems

The Windows NT network uses a centralized network operating system, which is usually called a *client/server architecture*. The central computer, where most of the network operating system runs, is called the *server*. A computer that uses the resources managed by the server is called a *client*. All computers on such a network are designated as either servers or clients: servers provide services, and clients use services. It's as simple—and as complicated—as that.

Every computer requires an operating system, of course; but the needs of a network server are generally quite different from the needs of a network client. In addition to the functions normally handled by an individual PC operating system, the server also must manage these processes:

◆   Remote file systems

◆   Running of shared applications

◆   Input and output to shared network devices

◆   CPU scheduling of networked processes

◆   Network security

A network server uses an operating system designed to handle the added network functions of a server—a network operating system. Because a server has to supply print, file, and other services to dozens or even hundreds of users, the network operating system must be high-powered and robust. Many users will be relying on the server to get their work done, so you not only don't want frequent system failures—you don't even want to have to reboot!

A network client uses a workstation operating system because the client operating system doesn't have to be as sturdy as the server operating system. Rebooting a workstation can be a pain for the user, but it usually doesn't disrupt anyone else's work. Nor does a client require a built-in security system because its security is provided by the network operating system. On a Windows NT Server network, clients can run just about any operating system, including MS-DOS, Microsoft Windows 3.1, Windows 95, Windows NT Workstation, UNIX, Macintosh OS, and OS/2. However, the more advanced a client operating system is, the better it is at "cooperating" with the network operating system in the areas of security and information sharing over the network.

# Features of Windows NT Server Version 4

Although its look is completely new and its capabilities are greatly expanded, Windows NT version 4 isn't starting from ground zero. Its new look and new capabilities are built on a foundation of features established in earlier versions of Windows operating systems.

## Features from Previous Versions of Windows NT

The bedrock on which Windows NT version 4 is built consists of basic features introduced in the earlier versions of Windows NT: hardware independence, support for multiprocessors, multitasking and multithreading, security, RAID support, and the NT file system.

### Hardware independence

Hardware independence, also known as *portability* or architecture independence, means that Windows NT was not designed for just one type of processor. In fact, its first implementation was on a reduced instruction set computing (RISC) chip, the MIPS R4000. You can install version 4 of either Windows NT Server or Windows NT Workstation on computers with the following types of processors:

◆   Intel 80486, Pentium, PentiumPro

◆   DEC Alpha RISC

◆   MIPS RISC

◆   PowerPC


The parts of Windows NT that are written for a specific processor are isolated in a small portion of the software called the *hardware abstraction layer* (*HAL*). To port the operating system to a new chip, the engineers at Microsoft recompiled the C code and wrote a new HAL—not as easy as it sounds but not all that difficult either. The result is that you can choose the hardware that gives you the balance between cost and performance that best fits your particular situation.

### Support for multiprocessors

Windows NT Server also supports computers with symmetric multiple processors; it can be installed on a computer that has up to four processors. Windows NT Workstation is limited to machines that have no more than two processors.

## Multitasking and multithreading

Multitasking is a bit of smoke and mirrors to persuade you that several things are happening all at once. But, in fact, what's happening is that the processor is switching very quickly among several tasks. On a fast computer with an operating system that handles it well (such as Windows 95), multitasking produces a very convincing illusion that several things are happening at the same time. Windows NT also handles multitasking well, and it carefully isolates each of the tasks from the others. This is essential to prevent one stumbling program from bringing the whole system down. A crashed application can be closed without affecting either the other tasks or the system itself.

However, Windows NT also can take advantage of applications that perform multithreading. Multithreading is the process by which an application can execute multiple paths of execution (called *threads*). When operating on a multiprocessor computer, two threads can execute simultaneously. In other words, multithreading actually does what multitasking only appears to do.

## Security

Windows NT Server comes with a host of security features that can be configured by the administrator for any type of network. Information on a network is valuable and must be protected; the larger the network, the more critical security becomes. Opportunities for system failure and user problems proliferate. The network must keep each user's data safe from hardware and software failures. It also must keep unauthorized users out and prevent authorized users from doing what they shouldn't.

Security is such a continuing theme throughout the book that you'll find discussions of different aspects of security in several different chapters.

### For More Information

*Making decisions about which security policies to implement is covered in Chapter 4.*

*Protecting your data on the hard drives is the focus of Chapter 8.*

*Security issues around user access are covered in Chapters 9 and 12.*

*Printer security is discussed in Chapter 11.*

*Security issues related to connecting your network to the outside world are discussed in Chapters 17, 18, and 19.*

### RAID support

RAID (redundant array of inexpensive disks) technology improves the *fault tolerance* of hard drives. In most cases, you can only take advantage of RAID by buying special hardware. Windows NT Server comes with software support for RAID that requires only SCSI hardware and standard hard drives.

### NT file system

The NT file system (NTFS) was designed specifically for use with Windows NT Server and Windows NT Workstation. It's a very different file system from the file allocation table (FAT) or VFAT systems you might have worked with previously and is much better suited for a network environment. NTFS includes these features:

◆ Support for filenames of up to 255 characters (including spaces) and for multiple extensions.

◆ Automatic generation of short MS-DOS–compatible filenames.

◆ A hot-fix feature. Data in a bad disk sector is automatically moved to a good sector, and the bad sector is removed from service.

◆ Built-in security that lets you specify permissions on files and folders.

◆ Fault tolerance in the form of a log file that can be used to restore files in the event of disk failure.

> **For More Information**
>
> *The advantages and disadvantages of NTFS are discussed in more detail in Chapter 5.*

## Features New to Windows NT Version 4

Windows NT version 4 adds a variety of features that were not present in previous versions of Windows NT. Some features are entirely new; some are borrowed from Windows 95.

### Microsoft Windows 95 user interface

The most obvious and important change in version 4 of Windows NT is the adoption of the Windows 95 user interface. The new interface makes opening programs and finding files easier than ever. Most of the administrative tools and utilities also have a new look that makes them easier to use.

**For More Information**

*For help in navigating the new interface, see Appendix A. It's worth reading because the interface is a very simple one to use—once you learn a few of its tricks.*

## Microsoft Internet Explorer version 3

The latest and slickest version of Internet Explorer is built into Windows NT. Internet Explorer is a simple and fast Internet browser that's totally integrated with the operating system.

## Microsoft Internet Information Server

An integral part of Windows NT Server version 4, Internet Information Server (IIS) lets you set up and administer World Wide Web, ftp, and Gopher services. IIS works with the new Peer Web Services, which is included with Windows NT Workstation version 4 and allows users to create their own personal Internet server.

**For More Information**

*Chapter 19 explains how to install and use Internet Information Server as well as how IIS works with Windows NT Workstation's Peer Web Services.*

## Microsoft Exchange

Microsoft Exchange is a built-in messaging center that accommodates Internet mail and Microsoft Mail. You can send and receive files embedded in messages. Add Exchange Server to your network, and you'll have a complete messaging and information-sharing system for local and worldwide networks.

**For More Information**

*The basics of Microsoft Exchange as well as Microsoft Exchange Server and Microsoft Exchange Client are discussed in Chapter 13.*

## Telephony API

The new Telephony API (TAPI) technology is used by the Windows messaging subsystem (Exchange E-Mail Client), fax applications, and Internet Explorer.

## Protocol improvements

Included with Windows NT Server version 4 is the Microsoft Point-to-Point Tunneling Protocol, a new technology that permits remote users secure access to their networks across the Internet. You'll also find improved TCP/IP features, including support for BOOTP forwarding. Another new feature is the DHCP Relay Agent, which improves the routing of BOOTP and the Dynamic Host Configuration Protocol (DHCP).

### For More Information

*Networking protocols and their related features are described in Chapters 7 and 17. Chapter 17 focuses specifically on TCP/IP.*

## And more features...

These are other new features you will find in Windows NT Server version 4:

◆ **DNS Name Server**

Now Windows NT Server can be a Domain Name System (DNS) name server, which means it can be configured to use WINS for host name resolution. The Universal Naming Convention (UNC) now supports DNS names.

◆ **Multiprotocol Routing**

Multiprotocol routing (MPR), part of a Windows NT Server 3.51 service pack, is now integrated into version 4.

◆ **DirectX**

Windows NT now has full API support for DirectDraw version 2, DirectSound version 1, and DirectPlay version 1.

◆ **Remote Booting of Windows 95 Desktops**

Remoteboot service simplifies using "diskless" Windows 95 desktops.

◆ **Remote Administration**

Remote Administration is a set of new tools for performing administration tasks from a Windows 95 desktop.

◆ **Connectivity with Novell NetWare**

Windows NT users can access Novell NetWare 4.*x* servers running NetWare Directory Services (NDS). Shared objects on a NetWare server are organized into easy-to-use hierarchical trees.

# Hardware Requirements
# for Windows NT Server

Windows NT Server version 4 is a powerful operating system, so it's not surprising that it needs a powerful computer. Some kinds of servers will need hardware that is a bit more or a bit less brawny. Chapter 3 offers some guidance on choosing hardware to fit different network tasks.

Here are the basic hardware requirements for a server:

◆ An Intel 80486/66 or higher, an Intel Pentium, or a supported RISC processor, such as the MIPS R4x00, Digital Alpha AXP, or PowerPC. Windows NT Server supports computers with up to four microprocessors. Although an 80486/25 is the minimum specified for a processor running Windows NT Server, a computer in the role of a domain controller or file server should have at least a Pentium microprocessor. The 80486/66 is the realistic minimum for any other computer running NT Server.

◆ A hard drive with a minimum of 123 MB of free disk space on the partition that will contain the Windows NT Server system files. For RISC-based computers, at least 159 MB of free disk space should be available on the hard drive partition.

◆ A VGA or better monitor.

◆ A supported CD-ROM drive for any computer not installing over a network. For Intel x86–based computers, a high-density 3.5-inch floppy drive in addition to the supported CD-ROM drive.

◆ A minimum of 12 MB of RAM for x86–based computers; 16 MB recommended; 32 MB much better. A minimum of 16 MB of RAM for RISC-based computers; 32 MB preferred (if you actually intend to *do* anything).

◆ A mouse or other pointing device.

◆ A supported network card.

The term *supported* means that the hardware is on the Windows NT 4.0 Hardware Compatibility List included on the Windows NT Server CD-ROM. You often can get unsupported devices to work; but on a server that's crucial to network operations, it's very risky. If the hardware becomes erratic or fails, both Microsoft and the hardware manufacturer will gently but firmly point out to you that neither of them promised the device in question would work with Windows NT Server. And you will be up the proverbial creek. Prevention is the key. Make sure that every piece of hardware on a server is on the hardware compatibility list.

## POINTS TO REMEMBER

♦ A network operating system performs the usual tasks of an operating system and in addition can extend these capabilities to remote machines.

♦ On a client/server network, servers provide file, application, print, and other services to clients; clients use the services.

♦ Clients on a Windows NT network can run almost any workstation operating system, including Windows NT Workstation, Windows 95, Windows 3.11, MS-DOS, UNIX, Macintosh OS, and OS/2.

♦ Windows NT Server and Windows NT Workstation are platform independent and can be installed on machines with x86, RISC, and PowerPC microprocessors.

♦ It is essential that you choose server hardware from the Windows NT 4.0 Hardware Compatibility List.

## WHAT'S NEXT?

Because Windows NT Server is both a powerful and a complex operating system, setting up a Windows NT network is akin to designing a building. First you must understand the elements of the structure, and then you must decide how to use these elements to meet your particular network needs. Our next subject is *domains*—the basic Windows NT network building blocks—and how domains operate in specific situations.

# CHAPTER 2

**Domains and Trust Relationships**

# CHAPTER 2
# Domains and Trust Relationships

The concept of a *domain*, the underlying structural principle in a Microsoft Windows NT Server version 4 network, and the concept of *trust*, the basis of interdomain relationships in a complex Windows NT Server network, grew from the increasingly sophisticated demands on network systems. In its initial network offerings, Microsoft introduced the concept of a *workgroup* in Microsoft Windows for Workgroups. A workgroup is a logical grouping of several computer users whose information needs or work activities are related and who want to share their file resources with one another. Usually, all of the computers in a workgroup are equal; there is no central computer in which resources are concentrated because there is no advantage to having a central resource. This is why such setups are referred to as *peer-to-peer networks*.

## Workgroups vs. Windows NT Server Networks

Workgroup networks are appealing because they are easy to set up and maintain. Individual users manage the sharing of their resources by determining what will be shared and who will have access. A user can allow other users to share a printer, a CD-ROM drive, a hard drive, or only certain files or directories. The difficulties arise when the network becomes very large or when the level of access to resources needs to be differentiated for each user or group of users.

Size alone can limit the efficacy of a workgroup. When there are many users and the usual corresponding increase in number of resources, users might find it difficult to locate the resources they need. Also, the informal nature of workgroups means that there is no central administration or control. In a large group, the time and effort required to maintain and administer the system becomes daunting because everything has to be configured computer by computer.

When it becomes necessary to distinguish among users (that is, to allow different levels of user access to specific resources), passwords can be and are used to restrict access. But as a peer-to-peer network gets larger, passwords proliferate and the system becomes increasingly complicated. Users who are required to have many different passwords to gain access to various parts of the system start using the same password over and over or choose passwords that are easy to remember—and, therefore, easy to guess. Security, such as it is on this system, falls apart. In addition, if the system has dial-up connections and someone leaves the organization to work for the company's largest competitor, all of the passwords will have to be changed; users in the workgroups will have to be notified of their new passwords—again, a daunting prospect for the system administrator as well as for users.

For these reasons, peer-to-peer networks are not particularly satisfactory for large networks or for networks that require centralized control. The domain structure that is built into Windows NT Server offers more flexibility and a simplified method of administration that works well for large or complex systems.

# Planning Your Network

Every project begins with planning. Unless you know exactly, and in detail, what you want to accomplish *before* you start, errors will abound and time will be wasted (and everyone involved will end up with a bad attitude). The last place you want to be is in the middle of a network of disgruntled users—much better to think things through at the beginning, before connecting cable to machine. In the following sections of this chapter, we will discuss the basic concepts underlying Windows NT Server and some of the choices you will have to make initially in setting up your system.

# Defining Domains

The basic unit of Windows NT Server, the domain, is a group of computers that share a database and have a common security policy. A domain consists of a computer that functions as the *primary domain controller* (also known as a PDC), at least one computer that functions as a *backup domain controller* (also known as a BDC), and at least one workstation. There might be additional backup domain controllers and servers as well as additional workstations.

## NOTE

*A server on a Windows NT Server network is a computer that is running Windows NT Server but is not a domain controller.*

It can be said that the domain is a type of workgroup that includes a server. It continues to be a logical grouping of users who are connected by more than the cables between their computers, in other words, users who share a common set of information needs or work activities. The goal still is to allow users to share resources within their group and, thus, make it easier for members of the group to work together and to work productively. The key difference in a domain is the existence of a server on the network, which allows for a single point of network administration and control.

A Windows NT Server network can consist of a single domain, or it can consist of many interconnected domains, such as a corporate-wide network that has thousands of individual workstations all over the world. In the latter case, the individual workstations are grouped into specific domains with specific access requirements. The real beauty of the domain concept is that it easily scales up or down to support network domain models at either end of the spectrum and all combinations and permutations in between.

**NOTE**

*A Microsoft network domain is not the same as a TCP/IP network domain, which is the domain concept used on the Internet. In this book, we'll use the word "domain" only in the Microsoft Windows network sense of the word. If we are talking about a domain on the Internet, we'll point that out.*

# Advantages of the Windows NT Domain Model

The advantages of the Windows NT network domain model include the following characteristics:

- Flexible design configuration

- Centralized network administration

- Flexibility in adding new users and changing access restrictions

- A single database for user accounts

- One unified security system for the entire domain

- Discretionary access control of files and directories

The machine-by-machine administration that is required to maintain a peer-to-peer network severely limits the effective maximum size of a workgroup. In the Windows NT Server system, the limitations are determined solely by what divisions make sense in your business. An entire company—even a large one—can be managed as a single Windows NT Server domain. Even if your company has all of its users under one roof and has no particular need to segregate groups of users according to which resources they may access, you can have as many computers as you like on the network, but you'll still have a single point of administrative control. In addition, all users, even the newest, can have access to their resources from any computer on the domain. Permission for access to files and directories is granted to individual users (or groups of users), not to individual computers.

In a domain-configured network, you as the system administrator can make changes to the system from any of the computers on the network. You simply log on to any Windows or Windows NT Server computer in the domain and make the desired change. You can even add or delete users or change access restrictions this way. All changes are made to the single point of administrative control—the primary domain controller—and they are then implemented immediately across the entire domain as Windows NT Server automatically synchronizes the user accounts database across the domain. This greatly reduces the headaches of the system administrator, who will not have to revise the database machine by machine.

In the Windows for Workgroups network, you are limited in your options for making a computer's resources available to the other members in the workgroup. At the simplest level, the user at a workstation can either share the computer's resources with other users or not share them. At the next level, you can assign a password that allows access to that computer. This provides a limited ability to control individual user access to specific machines. It means, however, that virtually none of a computer's resources are physically accessible to someone who is not given a password for that computer. In addition, if each user requires a password to access his or her files, some users will have to remember several different passwords.

Windows NT Server has increased the flexibility of the network system to provide what is called discretionary access control. In this system, the level of access for each user to another user's resources can be specified precisely. You can set user access for an individual file, for files within a directory, or for an entire directory. Windows NT Server lets you make selections that are as detailed or as broad as needed. It requires only one password for each user. One example of a Windows NT Server system with user access control is a domain in which some users can make changes to an existing document, some users can only read the document, and other users can't even see the document.

# Domain Components

A typical domain configuration might look like the one illustrated in Figure 2.1 on the following page, with a mixture of operating systems, servers, and workstations. Let's take a look at each of these network domain components and see how they fit into the overall picture.

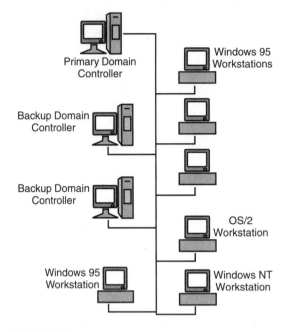

**FIGURE 2.1**

*Example of a network domain*

## Primary Domain Controller

The primary domain controller is the most important computer in a domain. It enforces the security policies for the domain and is the main repository for the accounts database. It also might be the primary holder of the shared resources of the domain; however, it isn't necessary, and might not even be desirable, to have the primary domain controller fulfill this function.

Changes to the user account database are made only on the primary domain controller and then propagated automatically to the backup domain controllers, where read-only copies of the database are maintained. When you're logged on as the administrator, all of your changes are made to the primary domain controller's database whether or not you're actually working at the primary domain controller. The tool you use for administering user accounts is User Manager for Domains (Figure 2.2). When you run User Manager for Domains, you don't choose which server to log on to, but only which domain you want to administer.

If the primary domain controller isn't present on the network, users will continue to be able to log on to the network if you have created one or more backup domain controllers and if at least one of them is present. However, you won't be able to make changes to the user or group accounts in the domain, add new users and groups to the domain, or remove users and groups from the domain until the primary domain controller is back on line or until you change one of the backup domain controllers to a primary domain controller.

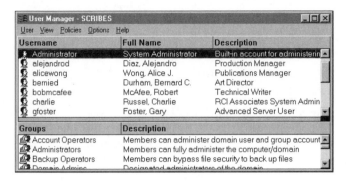

**FIGURE 2.2**

*User Manager for Domains*

**For More Information**

*Creating a primary domain controller is covered in Chapter 6.*

# Backup Domain Controller

The Windows NT Server domain can, and in most cases should, have one or more backup domain controllers. Each backup domain controller contains a copy of the accounts database and can validate users when they log on to the system and authorize user access to resources. This makes it fairly easy to provide redundancy of critical shared resources in the system in case there is a catastrophic failure of the primary domain controller. One of the backup domain controllers can be changed to a primary domain controller, and the network will continue to function normally (except for access to resources that were physically located on the failed server). In a small domain with a limited number of users, a backup domain controller isn't absolutely essential, but it is still a good idea. If there is only a primary domain controller on the network, the entire network will be disabled when—not if—that server isn't available.

A computer running Windows NT Server can be the primary domain controller or a backup domain controller or neither. It's usually better to use an operating system other than Windows NT Server for a computer that will function as a workstation. The workstation will be faster and easier to use.

**For More Information**

*The steps for changing a backup domain controller to a primary domain controller are described in Chapter 16.*

## Workstation

Workstations can run MS-DOS, OS/2, Microsoft Windows 3.*x*, Windows for Workgroups, Microsoft Windows 95, Microsoft Windows NT Workstation, and Macintosh OS. You'll need client licenses (and networking software) for MS-DOS, OS/2, Macintosh OS, and Windows 3.*x*. The others include the necessary networking software as part of the base operating system. In this book, we assume that, in general, workstations are running Windows 95. The overhead and hardware requirements for Windows 95 are substantially less than for Windows NT Workstation, and Windows 95 is far better behaved and more stable than earlier versions of MS-DOS or Windows. Other workstation operating systems are touched upon in our discussions when a workstation's needs dictate the use of another system.

**For More Information**

*Chapter 3 has information about how to determine hardware requirements for both present and future network configurations.*

One exception to using Windows 95 is in the case of workstations that are used primarily for software development. These workstations will benefit from the increased stability and process isolation of Windows NT Workstation. They typically have a substantially greater memory and greater processing power than the minimum required for Windows 95. And although Windows 95 is better than earlier versions of Windows at protecting other processes from an ill-behaved process, an unruly program still can bring the entire system down. Windows NT Workstation is much less likely to fail in such a situation. (This concern doesn't apply to those who write code that always works the first time.)

Some kinds of workstations on your network do not need to be a part of the domain, but they still can be part of a workgroup. Windows 95, Windows NT Workstation, and Windows for Workgroups all permit a user to be part of either a workgroup or a domain. But to take advantage of the domain, these computers must be configured to log on to the domain. Although they function as part of a workgroup, they won't have access to the user accounts database of the Windows NT server or to the resources controlled by the user accounts database.

# Trust Relationships

In a network that consists of two or more domains, each domain acts as a separate network with its own accounts database. Even in the most rigidly stratified organization, some users in one domain will need to use some or all of the resources in another domain. The usual solution to configuring user access levels among domains is what's called a *trust relationship*. Windows NT Server provides all the tools needed to set up a multiple-domain network with trust relationships between domain controllers that protect sensitive resource areas, while freeing users from the burden of having to cope with detailed procedures and multiple passwords.

## Non-Trusting Domain Relationships

It's certainly possible to have multiple domains without trust. For example, an individual user could have a separate account for each domain on a multiple domain network. Figure 2.3 shows a two-domain network; one domain is named Marketing and the other Finance. Margaret is a user who has an account on each of the domains. She is called Mag on the Finance domain and Meg on the Marketing domain. The account names are completely arbitrary in this example. When domains are not connected by trust relationships, a user could have the same user name on each domain.

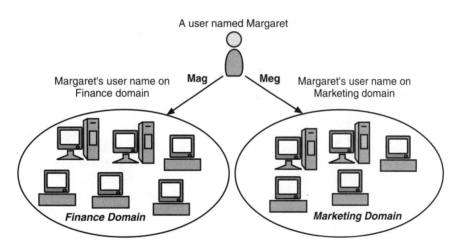

**FIGURE 2.3**

*Domains with no trust relationships*

When Margaret logs on to Marketing, she has access to the resources there as defined by the administrator but she has no access to the Finance domain. When she logs on to the Finance domain, she has no access to the Marketing domain. To move back to the resources on the Marketing domain, Margaret must log off Finance and log on again to Marketing.

The problem with this approach is that a user who needs access to more than one domain usually needs simultaneous access, which isn't possible in this setup. All of the logging off and logging on is inefficient and frustrating. The situation rapidly turns into a nightmare for the administrator as well. Any network big enough to need more than one domain will have many users, and many of them will have accounts on more than one domain. Every time a password needs to be changed or a set of permissions needs to be altered, the administrator has to traipse around from domain to domain, logging on and making the changes at each one. This gets very tiresome very quickly.

## One-Way Trust Relationships

To accommodate a user who needs access to both the Marketing domain and the Finance domain as described above, a one-way trust relationship can be established between the domains. Figure 2.4 shows this simplest type of trust relationship. Finance is the *trusting* domain; Marketing is the *trusted* domain.

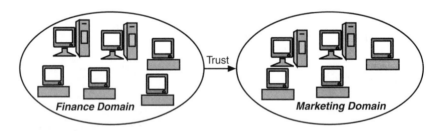

**FIGURE 2.4**

*One-way trust relationship*

If the user is able to log on to the Marketing domain successfully, Finance trusts that the user has been properly authenticated. It *doesn't* mean that the user has automatic access to Finance's resources; that permission must be granted by Finance's administrator. It also doesn't mean that users who log on to Finance directly have access to Marketing, the trusted domain. For that to happen, a separate one-way trust relationship has to be established in which Marketing is the trusting domain and Finance the trusted domain.

*The mechanisms for establishing trust relationships are discussed in Chapter 16.*

Usually, a one-way trust relationship cannot adequately address the necessary interactions on a multiple domain network. At least one two-way trust relationship will be needed to accommodate users' needs.

## Two-Way Trust Relationships

Two-way trust relationships allow greater flexibility in user access to resources and make network administration substantially easier. In a two-way trust relationship, a user who logs on successfully to one of the domains will be considered authentic by the other domain. The user would then have access to resources on either domain to the extent granted the user by the administrator. A two-way trust relationship is created by setting up two one-way trust relationships, one in each direction, as shown in Figure 2.5. The two-way arrow indicates that Finance trusts Marketing and Marketing trusts Finance. Always keep in mind that the real relationship is two separate one-way trust relationships. If circumstances require that you modify the trust relationships, you'll need to remember that there are actually two relationships involved.

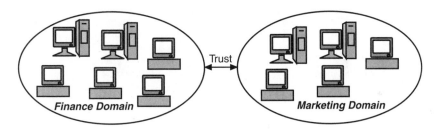

**FIGURE 2.5**

*Two-way trust relationship*

A major advantage to having two-way trust relationships is that you will need to create user accounts only once, preferably in the "home" domain. They will be recognized in all trusting domains across the enterprise. This makes administration of the network much easier. It also allows for decentralized system administration; each department can manage its own affairs without having to propagate every change in user accounts to all of the other domains.

## Nontransferability of Trust

It's important to know as you design your Windows NT Server network that each trust relationship has to be established separately. Or to put it another way, trust does not *flow through* a domain to encompass any other domain. Figure 2.6 shows an example of a network with three domains. Marketing trusts Finance, and Finance trusts Marketing. The third domain, Editorial, has a two-way trust relationship with Finance. However, Editorial and Marketing will not trust each other until a separate trust relationship is set up between them. Editorial's trust relationship with Finance does not flow through Finance to include Marketing. Likewise, the two-way trust relationship Marketing has with Finance does not flow through Finance and encompass Editorial.

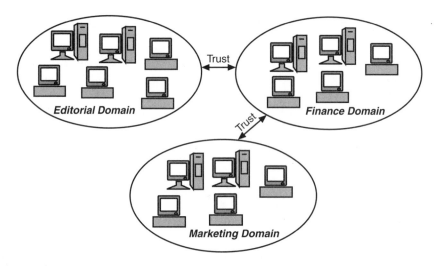

**FIGURE 2.6**

*Multiple domains with separate trust relationships*

If we wanted to allow a user in either the Editorial or the Marketing domain to have access to resources in the other domain, we'd need to create a separate trust relationship between Editorial and Marketing to close the relationship loop. Now our trust diagram would look like the one in Figure 2.7, assuming we stuck with two-way relationships.

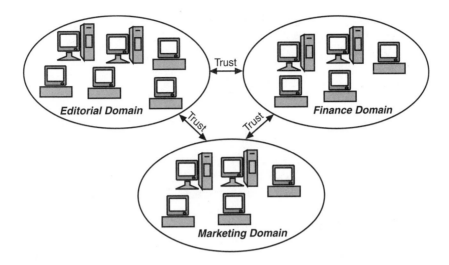

**FIGURE 2.7**

*Multiple domains with fully trusted relationships*

As you can see from this last example, creating a full set of trust relationships can require a bit of planning and thought. Before you start, it's a good idea to do the necessary research and then draw your trust relationship diagrams. This will not only make your job easier but also lay the groundwork for clear network documentation, which you (and maybe your successor) will be glad to have in the future.

# Domain Models

Windows NT Server has four domain trust relationship models. Consider the options carefully, and plan your networking strategy in advance. This can greatly improve both the ease of maintenance and the ease of expanding your network as it grows. We'll take a look at each of these models, the business situations each meets best, and the advantages and disadvantages of each.

These are the domain models you can use:

◆ Single domain

◆ Single-master domain

◆ Multiple-master domains

◆ Fully trusted domains

Your network might end up being an exact match of one of these models, a variation of one, or even a mix of two or more models in different areas of the network. But the basic building blocks will remain the same.

## Single Domain Model

This is the simplest domain model; all servers and clients are in a single domain. Local groups and global groups are the same, and all administrators can administer all servers. With a single domain, there are no trust relationships to administer.

The single-domain network is an effective model and a useful model for a small business that doesn't have a large number of servers or users. What's a large number in this context? Unfortunately, there's no simple answer. It depends on what hardware is being used and on the overall number of resources available. If everyone in your business uses basically the same set of resources, if the resources are all in the same physical area, and if it doesn't take an unacceptably long time to browse the network for resources, you're probably at a good comfort level for the single domain model.

It's time to move beyond the single domain model if any of the following circumstances apply to your business:

◆ You have users who are working with different sets of resources and have different needs.

◆ Your business has branched out to include another building, another floor, or other physically separate location.

◆ Browsing for resources on your current network seems to take forever.

| ADVANTAGES OF A SINGLE DOMAIN MODEL | DISADVANTAGES OF A SINGLE DOMAIN MODEL |
|---|---|
| Simpler administration | No departmental or other logical groupings of users |
| Central management of user accounts | Performance degradation as number of resources grows |
| No trust relationships to define or manage | No logical groupings of resources |
| Local groups defined only once | Browsing slower as number of servers grows |

# Single-Master Domain Model

The single-master domain model provides central administration of users together with logical groupings of department resources. This model includes one or more department-level domains (*secondary domains*) that each trust the same *master domain*. The single-master domain model is an obvious extension of the single domain model; it is a good choice for an organization with relatively few users and obvious logical groupings of resources where the number of resources is growing. All user accounts as well as all *global groups* are created at the master domain level. But each department-level domain can have its own *local groups*. Figure 2.8 shows a diagram of the single-master domain model.

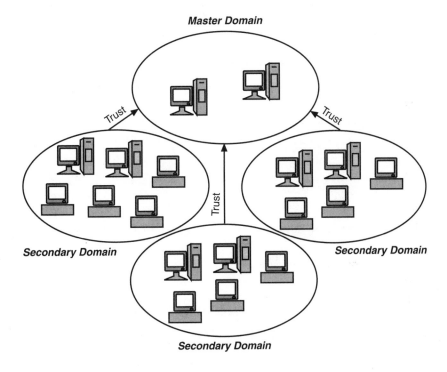

**FIGURE 2.8**

*Single-master domain model*

**For More Information**

*See page 201 of Chapter 10 for descriptions and discussions of local groups and global groups.*

The master domain's primary function is to be the central account management hub. It's imperative that the master domain have at least one backup domain controller because all user account databases for the entire network are kept only on the primary and the backup domain controllers of the master domain. Each of the other domains (secondary domains) functions primarily as a resource manager. Each secondary domain has its own set of resources, which are available to the entire network but which can be locally administered. Users in a secondary domain initially will see only their own resources, which simplifies and speeds up browsing. Resources can be managed at the departmental level at the same time accounts are managed centrally.

The single-master domain model makes a lot of sense as a natural growth path from the single domain model. The original single domain, which contains the existing user accounts, becomes the new master domain. The resources are moved to the new secondary domains and organized there in logical groupings. The model breaks down, however, if the number of users grows too large. Performance is substantially degraded because each account authorization must go to the master domain.

### ADVANTAGES OF A SINGLE-MASTER DOMAIN MODEL

Central management of user accounts

Necessary to define global groups only once

Department-level administration of resources

Only one trust relationship necessary for each secondary domain

### DISADVANTAGES OF A SINGLE-MASTER DOMAIN MODEL

Performance degradation as number of users and groups grow

Central point of failure

Necessary to define local groups for each secondary domain

## Multiple-Master Domain Model

If the number of users has grown beyond a comfort and performance level that can be supported easily in a single-master domain but you still want to administer user accounts centrally, your network is a candidate for a multiple-master domain configuration. The multiple-master domain model is a good choice for an organization with a large number of users and a centralized administrative structure. It provides central administration across two or more master domains, with resources distributed across secondary domains (Figure 2.9).

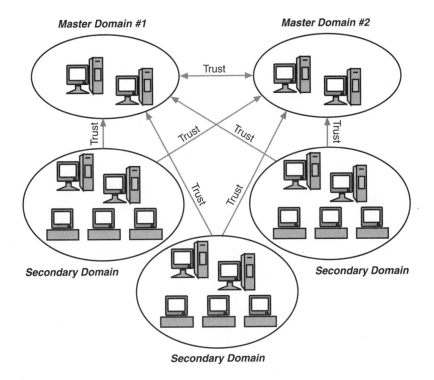

**FIGURE 2.9**

*Multiple-master domain model*

In this model there are a small number of master domains, each of which trusts all of the other master domains. User accounts are located on the master domains and are distributed across them relatively evenly. Each user account is located on only one master domain, however. Each secondary domain trusts each of the master domains, but the secondary domains do not necessarily trust one another. Resources, such as printers and files, are provided and administered at the secondary domain level.

If you use the multiple-master domain model, you'll have to decide early in the network design process how you will distribute users' accounts. The division of user accounts among the master domains can be done according to logical groupings of users or on a purely arbitrary basis, such as the alphabetical order of user names. If your organization is relatively flexible, with users frequently changing departments and responsibilities, you might well find it awkward to group users in a logical way. If you use an arbitrary distribution method, such as alphabetical order to group them, you'll have substantially more work in creating and administering global groups but you won't have to make changes as users move around or change job responsibilities.

| ADVANTAGES OF A MULTIPLE-MASTER DOMAIN MODEL | DISADVANTAGES OF A MULTIPLE-MASTER DOMAIN MODEL |
|---|---|
| Central management of user accounts | No single point of administration of users and groups |
| Scalable as needs and size grow | Necessary to define local and global groups more than once and to modify them in more than one place |
| Department-level administration of resources | |
| Logical groupings of resources | Increasingly complex trust relationships |

## Fully Trusted Multiple-Master Domain Model

The fully trusted multiple-master domain model makes sense if you prefer the distributed administration of users and resources but your organization has a strong, centralized administrative structure. Every domain trusts every other domain, and a user account is created in the domain to which the user will log on by default. (The domain in which a user account is located is known as the *home domain*.) Secondary domains are responsible for managing their own users and global groups, and these users and global groups are accessible across the network. (See Figure 2.10.)

The fully trusted multiple-master domain model makes good sense in relatively small organizations that have outgrown the single domain model, but it breaks down if the number of domains gets too large. Each domain must have a two-way trust relationship with every other domain. Therefore, the number of trust relationships grows exponentially as the number of domains grows. The number of trust relationships required for $n$ domains in a fully trusted domain model is $n*(n-1)$. If you have five domains, you have twenty trust relationships; adding a single additional domain will require ten additional trust relationships.

A word of caution about the fully trusted domain model: all trust relationships are two-way, which means you're granting users access to resources in one domain on the basis of trust in the administrative practices of another domain. If you establish user access that is based on global groups, you are giving an unauthorized user added by an administrator in another domain the same permissions in all domains as the authorized users.

## ADVANTAGES OF A FULLY TRUSTED MULTIPLE-MASTER DOMAIN MODEL

Logical groupings of resources and users

Department-level control of both resources and users

Scalable as needs and size grow

## DISADVANTAGES OF A FULLY TRUSTED MULTIPLE-MASTER DOMAIN MODEL

No single point of administration of users and groups

Necessary to define local and global groups more than once and to modify them in more than one place

Very complex trust relationships

Requires confidence in the administrators of other domains

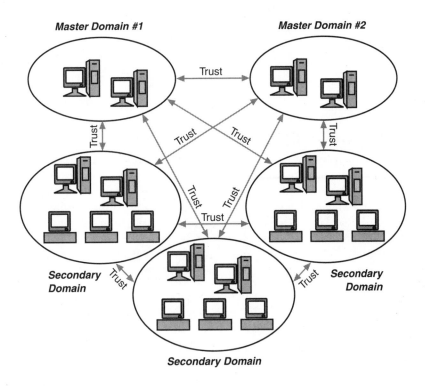

**FIGURE 2.10**

*Fully trusted multiple-master domain model*

# The Basics of User Accounts

Everyone who uses a Windows NT Server network must have a user account in one of the domains. If the user's account is not in the domain he or she is trying to log on to, access to the domain will be allowed only if the domain has a trust relationship with the domain where the user's account is stored. A user account includes a name, a password, and restrictions on how the user can use the network. The account actually is created with a hidden security identifier (SID) that is unique across the entire network; Windows NT Server uses the SID, not the user's name, to identify a user.

Users can be grouped into local or global groups with similar sets of access rights and permissions. Organizing users by group allows you to change the rights and permissions for the entire group in one operation.

### For More Information

*Chapter 9 contains the information that is necessary to create user accounts.*

# Management of Users as Groups

Windows NT Server comes with a set of built-in global and local groups that provides an excellent starting place for managing the users on your network. You can easily manage large numbers of users at a time by taking advantage of this *user group* function. There are basically two types of user groups, local groups and global groups. A local group exists and retains its permissions only within the domain in which it is created, whereas a global group resides in one domain but retains its permissions across all trusting domains. You can easily create custom local and global groups that have the sets of permissions you want and need.

Once you set up a group and the necessary permissions for the group, you can quickly add new users or adjust the permissions for the group. If, for example, you create a group of users that handle the payroll database and the printing of checks, you can add a new payroll clerk to the group very easily; the clerk will automatically have all of the necessary permissions and access for the domain or domains in which resources are located.

### For More Information

*How to create and maintain groups is covered in Chapter 10.*

A well-thought-out group structure can save administrative time as well as prevent unwanted access. The built-in groups provide you with a group structure that's already very complete. Don't get too anxious to start adding groups of your own until you feel adept with Windows NT Server.

## POINTS TO REMEMBER

♦ The domain, a group of computers that share a common database and a common security policy, is the basic organizational unit of a Windows NT Server network.

♦ The choice of domain model and trust relationships will determine how your network functions in the present as well as its ease of expansion in the future.

♦ Windows NT Server's groups are necessary tools for the efficient administration of large numbers of user accounts.

♦ After you've planned *everything*, plan some more.

## WHAT'S NEXT?

Now that you have a general idea of the possible structures in a Windows NT Server network, we'll move on to hardware. The focus in the next chapter is on the hardware that is necessary to obtain optimal performance for each kind of machine on the network.

# Planning and Placing Hardware

# CHAPTER 3

# CHAPTER 3

# Planning and Placing Hardware

Hardware for a network has to be selected more carefully than hardware for a single workstation. Workstations usually can be connected to a network regardless of their internal configuration, but, to give the best performance, servers and controllers have to be designed with their network roles in mind. Although a poorly configured or designed workstation will be an annoyance for the individual using that workstation, a server that isn't configured and designed with its role on the network in mind will cause suffering for all of the users on the network.

The first rule is: Don't even think about using a server or controller not made up entirely of hardware from the Microsoft Windows NT 4.0 Hardware Compatibility List. There are two reasons for this. First, you have an excellent chance of everything working properly if the most important machines on your network are all "officially" compatible. Second, if you have difficulty with a computer or other equipment on the list, you can call Microsoft with your problem and someone there will try to help you fix it. If you use equipment that is not designated as compatible, you're on your own. It will not matter how sure *you* are that the problem is not hardware related. So always be sure to pick components from the hardware compatibility list, no matter how attractive the specs are for that new whiz-bang network card. Although Microsoft Windows NT is a lot fussier about hardware than are other versions of Microsoft Windows, such as Microsoft Windows 95, the list of compatible hardware grows longer with every version of Windows NT. Restricting your choices to the hardware compatibility list should not be a hardship.

If you are going to deploy a large number of systems and if you believe you absolutely have to consider using a hardware part that is not on the hardware compatibility list, it might be well worth your hardware supplier's time and money to submit the item to Microsoft for inclusion on the list. If you have a big enough stick to encourage this, both of you will benefit in the long run. You will have the assurance that the hardware really is compatible; and your supplier will get this part on the next version of the list, which will make it easier for the product in question to gain acceptance in other venues.

# Designing the System

When you design your Microsoft Windows NT Server version 4 system, there are three important factors to consider and balance in your decision making:

◆ The type of domain model you've chosen for your network

◆ The initial size vs. the expected growth of the system

◆ The locations of the resources in your organization

## Domain Model

Whatever your domain model ultimately will look like, start with a single domain and stay there until the kinks are worked out of the system. This allows you to become familiar with the Windows NT server tools, identify potential problems in your installation, make sure that the hardware choices are wise ones, and generally work through the system bugs and user interface issues that inevitably crop up even in a controlled environment. You'll run into enough new problems when you scale up the network without having to worry about the ones you should have caught in the test environment. Spend as much time in this phase as necessary. Although you might be tempted to push ahead quickly, taking extra time now will smooth the overall process of installing and implementing the system.

After you have the initial primary domain controller up and running, get the influential users in the organization involved in the process. Make them a part of the whole startup operation, allowing them to help make decisions about domains, types of global and local groups, and implementation schedules. Getting a key group of users involved at the very beginning will make implementation of the system *infinitely* easier by creating allies who feel a sense of ownership for the whole process. They can be your best and most influential advocates. And as anyone who has ever implemented a major network project knows, you need advocates.

This core group will have another equally important role. They can be your very own canaries in the coal mine; that is, when there are problems during the installation (notice that we didn't say "if"), they'll be your early warning system, giving you a chance to respond immediately before a problem gets out of hand. They will have a firm grasp of what to expect of the new environment from their work with you during the testing phase and will be able to quickly spot performance degradation or anomalies that occur as your project grows from its small prototype environment to its full size and complexity.

## Initial Size vs. Expected Growth of the System

It is important that you take into account the difference between your initial network size and the expected growth of your system. This will not necessarily require psychic ability, although that certainly wouldn't be an unwelcome skill to have at your disposal. For example, you might be setting up a network in one department of a large company with every expectation that the system will expand to include the rest of the company. Or your small company has been growing rapidly, and there's reason to believe that this growth will continue at the same pace for some time to come.

Choose a domain model that will fit the projected future circumstances of your company, not just your current situation. It's a lot harder to change your domain model later if your initial design doesn't take into account the company's future needs. For example, if your organization has a strong, centralized information systems department, you don't want to design your domain architecture around a fully trusted model. Instead, a master domain or multiple-master domain model will be more appropriate. If, on the other hand, your information systems department has played primarily a support role, with each division or department in the organization generally being responsible for its own resources, a fully trusted multiple-master domain model will probably make the most sense. But even in this case, if you expect your enterprise to grow beyond a few departments and a single location, you'll want to go with a master or multiple-master domain model. Maintaining the complex trust relationships of a fully trusted multiple-master domain model is just too much grief at some point—when that is will depend on a variety of factors, but it's almost always at the time your business goes to multiple locations.

You'll also want to plan your network topology and addressing. The gory details of network topologies and the design decisions that need to be made with respect to these issues are beyond the scope of this book, but we will make one suggestion. Over the years, we've seen a variety of networks. Some have had names that made sense, and others have had names that were cute. Still others have had names that were arbitrary and capricious. Of the available possibilities, we recommend that you make an effort to give your domains quickly identifiable names. In other words, if you don't want to alienate your users quickly and at almost no extra cost, don't give your servers names such as "B7_A32."

If you intend to have relatively few servers—each server performing multiple functions—you'll need high-end machines. If your resources are more distributed, with several servers helping the domain controllers, not every machine needs to be a powerhouse. But even if you will have relatively distributed resources, leave yourself room for growth. You'll benefit now by giving your users a quality product, and you'll benefit later by being able to support their ever-increasing demands. Keep in mind the following key areas as potential growth areas:

- Memory
- Processing power
- Hard drive capacity, flexibility, and speed
- Network bandwidth

In each of these areas, it's easy to leave yourself room for expansion without breaking the bank during the initial network setup phase.

### Memory

One of the tricks we've learned the hard way is to always choose our memory modules to take up the minimum possible number of slots for a given amount of memory. For example, you could easily use four or even eight slots to give yourself 64 MB of RAM on a server. But you don't want to do that if you can avoid it. By planning ahead, it's easy to avoid cramping your style later. Choose the maximum memory module size that will give you the result you need. In most cases on newer Pentium or PentiumPro motherboards, that will be two slots, leaving six slots for future memory. Don't choose a motherboard that will not support more than 128 MB. That might sound like a lot of memory initially, and it might well be enough. But if you need more memory later on, it's really annoying to have to find a way to recycle your old RAM because your new application or database server needs 256 MB of RAM to run well and your computer is maxed out.

All domain controllers and servers on a Windows NT network (except print servers and remote access servers) will benefit from having at least 32 MB of RAM. Of course, memory prices being what they are, you might not be able to afford that much RAM on every machine. A controller can get by with as little as 16 MB of RAM; but every 4 MB makes a difference, so go to 20 MB or 24 MB as soon as you can do so.

In general, the disbursement of resources across your network is a good idea, but only if you're not going to be short of RAM or processing power. You're better off having fewer servers, each with the most RAM you can manage, than having a large number of machines with less RAM.

### Processing power

Consider starting out with a server that can support additional processors. Even if your original systems don't need the extra power, having a design that will support additional CPUs lets you scale up your capacity rapidly and easily if your needs grow quickly beyond what you had expected. Although you'll pay a premium price for a server that can support more than one CPU, the cost really won't be all that much. Most systems that can support more than one CPU are already designed to scale up easily in other key areas as well.

## Hard drives

The same considerations apply to hard drives. You can be sure that sooner or later, probably sooner, you will have to add additional hard drive capacity to the servers. It's one of Murphy's immutable laws that the need for storage will always exceed your current capacity—and quickly. If you have designed your storage subsystem around multiple drives, it's much easier to add additional space without having to disrupt either your users or your configuration. For example, you can add storage to a "type 5" Redundant Array of Inexpensive Disks (RAID 5 array) fairly easily, and the hard drive will continue to appear as a single drive to the users. If you have only one humongous hard drive, you'll have an awkward time adding capacity when it runs out of space. Plus, of course, you're in big trouble if your single drive suffers a catastrophic failure.

### For More Information

*Skip ahead to Chapter 8 to find out how RAID works.*

## Network bandwidth

The last area to keep in mind as a potential system growth bottleneck is the networking subsystem. Windows NT Server supports the NetBEUI, IPX/SPX, and TCP/IP networking protocols, as well as others, but you'll definitely want to use TCP/IP as much as possible. NetBEUI is just not up to the job of handling a large and busy network. You also can't divide up your network into segments with NetBEUI because it can't be routed. The default protocol in earlier versions of Windows NT is IPX/SPX, which is used primarily by Novell NetWare networks. It is easier to set up and configure than TCP/IP, but the future of networking is going to be TCP/IP. You'll find it substantially easier to set up TCP/IP with the tools in Windows NT than to figure it out and set all the gory details the old-fashioned way. If you have legacy MS-DOS or Windows machines that you can't upgrade to Windows 95 or Microsoft Windows NT Workstation, you might choose to connect these machines to the server with NetBEUI. Windows 95 machines already have an excellent built-in TCP/IP, and you can easily add TCP/IP to your Microsoft Windows for Workgroups 3.11 clients.

Like your hard drive host adapter, your network card needs to be in your system's fastest bus. In addition, you might want to choose a network card that will support higher speed networks easily if you decide to upgrade later.

**For More Information**

*Chapter 5 and Chapter 7 have more information on networking protocols and how to choose the protocol or protocols most appropriate for your network.*

## Resource Locations

Another aspect of your network that you'll want to think about carefully during the planning process is what resources you'll be providing on the network and where on the network you want those resources to reside. You might want to centralize most of your resources on one or two servers in each domain, or you might want to spread them out across several servers, depending on the size and the primary function of your network. Generally you'll benefit from spreading your resources over as many servers as possible. For example, if you'll be using one of your servers primarily as a database server, you don't want to load it down by also having it support large numbers of user applications. Likewise, your primary application server probably shouldn't be your print server. By spreading these functions across the network, you will maximize the processing power and bandwidth for each function. But this will mean planning preconfigured alternatives for these functions. If you need, for example, to take down the print server, you don't want your entire network suddenly to be without printers. A little planning here can make for a much happier user community.

# Selecting Suitable Hardware

As you might suspect, there isn't much of a role for low-end computers as servers on a Windows NT Server network. However, it's not necessary to break the budget on every machine. Evaluate each machine on the basis of what it has to do and how its relative speed will affect the rest of the network.

## Hardware for Controllers

Domain controllers, whether primary or backup, require hardware that suits their role. Because controllers provide logon verification for users and also verify file access requests, you'll want a fast network card (PCI or EISA) and a fast hard drive to speed up these processes.

Because the controller is not going to be used as a workstation, you don't need any more than the minimum VGA video card and VGA-compatible monitor. Neither is a superprocessor called for because not much processing takes place. A Pentium 90 or 100 is the minimum, however. Any of the RISC-based machines also should be up to the job.

Consider some basic design alternatives, such as using multiple smaller disks rather than one huge one, and choose server hardware that will easily support additional hard drives. Even though Windows NT Server will support EIDE hard drives, they have no place on a server. You need a SCSI bus to off-load as much of the processing of hard drive requests as possible so that the bus and the hard drive can handle multiple requests simultaneously. Put the SCSI host adapter on the fastest bus your system supports (either EISA or PCI) because this is a potential bottleneck in system performance. Disk mirroring and RAID require SCSI disk subsystems to work properly. When buying SCSI systems, don't economize by going with unproven equipment from a little-known company. Stick with a well-known name such as Adaptec.

Windows NT Server only comes on CD-ROM now, so you'll need a CD-ROM drive to install the software. Be sure the drive is SCSI-based and not proprietary or IDE-based. Consult the hardware compatibility list for a compatible CD-ROM drive.

## Hardware for File Servers

File servers have to receive requests and answer them very quickly. To accomplish this, they need a reasonably fast processor (Pentium 120 or better) and a fast network card (PCI or EISA). The requests are for files from the hard drive; therefore, fast hard drives and fast hard drive controllers are a must. On a busy network, a single computer might have multiple hard drives and hard drive controllers.

### NOTE

*Windows NT Server also has methods of organizing disk storage so that multiple hard drives can appear as a single hard drive to an application, speeding up access considerably. (See Chapter 8.)*

## Hardware for Application Servers

Application servers also need a fast hard drive and a PCI or an EISA network card. In addition, an application server needs as fast a processor as you can get (and afford). If applications are to be kept on a server, a slow processor will annoy your users past the limits of their patience.

## Hardware for Remote Access Servers

A remote access server is a suitable place for an older computer with an 80486 processor; a not-especially-speedy network card is also fine to use for such a server.

There's no point in wasting expensive hardware on a remote access server because the computer can't go any faster than the dial-up connection, which is slower than the slowest computer. Only if your RAS is handling a lot of users at the same time will you need to crank up your requirements for this machine.

## Hardware for Print Servers

Here's where you can deposit the slowest computers in your hardware inventory. The bottleneck in printing is the printer itself, not the computer or the network card. Printers are slow beasts (relative to computers), so almost any computer can find a home as a print server. Neither RAM nor fast hard drives are a big concern here either. You will, however, want to be sure that you have sufficient free hard drive space to handle the necessary spooling files.

## Hardware for Workstations

Workstations need only the hardware appropriate for the tasks they'll be performing. Here's where to spend the money on good video cards and monitors for the benefit of users. Hard drives need to be fast and large only if all the workstation work is being done locally. If the files and applications are out on the network, the local hard drive can be small, but the network card needs to be fast and efficient.

### POINTS TO REMEMBER

- Make sure all components of a server or controller are on the Microsoft Windows NT 4.0 Hardware Compatibility List.

- When installing Windows NT Server, start out with a core group of computers and expand slowly.

- Select equipment so that controllers and servers have hardware suitable for their roles on the network.

- When you think your plan is complete, go over it again.

### WHAT'S NEXT?

One of the major issues on any network is security. In Chapter 4, we help you find that delicate balance between lax policies that open you up to trouble and draconian measures that interfere with productivity.

# CHAPTER 4

Security Planning

# CHAPTER 4

## Security Planning

Almost all network users believe, in the abstract, that security is a Good Thing—that is, until they forget a password, are denied access to documents they want, have to walk down the hall for print output instead of printing to the printer nearest their desks, or can't install the latest, coolest bit of software they downloaded from the Internet. At that point, security becomes a roadblock and they Can't Do Their Jobs. Alternatively, users will complain bitterly about Lax Security when it's *their* files that have been accessed and maybe changed or even destroyed. As a network administrator, you need to be aware that people will tend to speak to you as if all their words began with capital letters. They will do this while protesting about too much security or too little security, perhaps both at the same time.

Ideally, you want your security to be so thorough that no one can access anything without specific permission, and at the same time have the enforcement of that security so transparent that no one notices it's occurring. In this chapter, we will help you plan security so that you come as close to this ideal as possible.

## Network Administration Models and Security Issues

The administrative model you've chosen for your network can affect what types of security measures you need to implement. Network administration can be organized in one of four basic configurations:

◆ Centrally for the whole enterprise

◆ Locally by department or group ("distributed" administration)

◆ By operating system

◆ Some combination of the above

Surprisingly, the administrative models can be similar for both small systems and large, complex systems. They would differ in scale and degree but not in basic concept. We'll look at three of the models and the security issues for each model.

*When domain administration is divided up by operating system, the security issues vary substantially, depending on what operating systems are involved. For example, if you have separate administrators for Microsoft Windows NT Server, Novell NetWare, and UNIX systems, the administrator for each system will have to deal with the mechanics of making that system secure. But you'll always need someone to arbitrate differences of opinion among the various administrators when problems arise. Decide early on who that someone will be.*

## Central Administration

In a *central administration model*, one person, group, or department administers all of the networks, users, and resources within the organization. (See Figure 4.1.) The model works well for small to medium-size organizations, but it can be slow or inefficient for a large or geographically scattered enterprise. From the standpoint of security, however, central administration is the best model. It ensures that system policies and procedures are uniform throughout the organization. Administrators can both change the locations of users and resources within the network and make the necessary changes to user profiles and user access quickly.

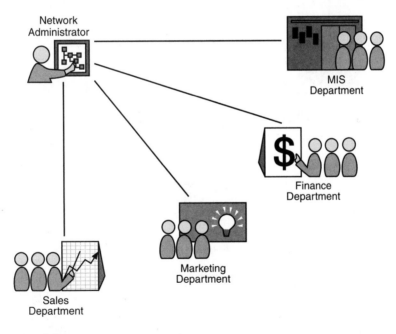

**FIGURE 4.1**

*Central administration model*

# Distributed Administration

In a *distributed administration model*, the network is managed at the department or workgroup level. (See Figure 4.2.) Although administration at these local levels can facilitate fast responses to user needs, this response time is often achieved at the expense of network security. With several department-level or workgroup-level administrators on a network, system policies will differ from workgroup to workgroup. The more groups that exist in a system, the more multiple trust relationships will be required—which increases the possibility that an intruder could infiltrate one system and exploit the trust relationships to gain access to a high-security system.

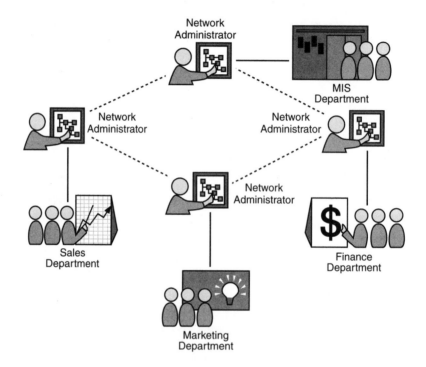

**FIGURE 4.2**

*Distributed administration model*

# Mixed Administration

The *mixed administration model* features elements of both the central and distributed administration models. (See Figure 4.3.) A central administrator (or group) ensures that system policies are enforced throughout the enterprise, while department-level or workgroup-level administrators handle users' day-to-day needs. This generally requires a greater investment in staff than smaller organizations can afford, so the mixed administration model is usually limited to larger organizations.

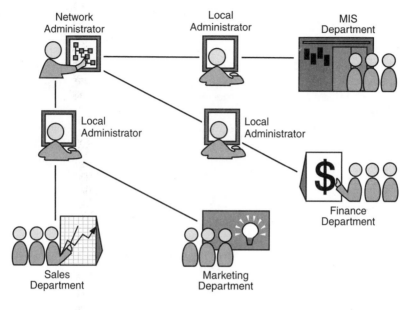

**FIGURE 4.3**

*Mixed administration model*

**For More Information**

*Chapter 16 has much more information about administration models.*

# Types of Network Security

Network security can be broken down into four basic categories. We'll discuss each of these categories and then help you put together a coherent network security plan. There are four basic categories of network security:

◆   Physical security

◆   User security

◆   File security

◆   Intruder security

No matter how large or how small your network, you need to be knowledgeable about all of these categories, although the relative emphasis on one or another of them will change as the size of your network changes.

## Physical Security

Any computer, whether it's a network server, a desktop workstation, a portable notebook, or a public access terminal in a shopping mall kiosk, needs to be physically secure. Unless the case has a self-destruct mechanism (and we've never seen this except in spy movies), if someone can physically walk away with your computer, he or she can gain access to your data. This doesn't mean, however, that you have to bolt down all of your computers or lock your server away in a vault. A workstation sitting in an open area of your office actually can be more secure than one shut away in a closet because people can see what's happening to it. As long as the office is locked during nonbusiness hours when no one's around, this is relatively safe. Network servers, though, deserve a little more thought when you are deciding where they will be located. You'll want quick access to them during the business day, protection from accidental loss of power and reboots, and a means of locking them away during nonbusiness hours. Many network and server administrative tasks can be performed from your desktop workstation, so there's no need to keep the servers in your office. However, you'll want them nearby to prevent a lot of trekking about. A well-ventilated, well-lit room with a door that locks should do just fine.

## User Security

User security has two aspects:

◆   Facilitating the users' access to the resources they need.

◆   Keeping from them—and even hiding from them—resources that aren't necessary for them to do their jobs. These resources include both your company's most confidential information and other users' personal property.

As much as possible, you want users to have to remember only one password, which they have to enter only once to gain access to the network and its resources. Conversely, having to enter a second password to access highly sensitive resources can reinforce their confidential nature. Use this procedure sparingly, though. People can remember two or three passwords fairly easily. Beyond that, they either will write their passwords down and tape them to the computer monitor or will choose similar or related passwords—easy to remember but also easy to guess.

Planning the logical layout of your network along with its physical layout can save you lots of security and administrative headaches further down the road. Plan the layout so that domains contain logical groupings of people and objects rather than simply those in proximity to each other. Figures 4.4 and 4.5 show the difference between physically grouped users and logically grouped users. Acme Advertising has four departments: account executives, copywriters, illustrators, and media buyers. The office is designed so that all of the people who use the same physical resources (office supplies, reference materials, specialized equipment) sit near each other. The company's work practice, though, is for one account executive, one illustrator, one copywriter, and one media buyer to work together as a permanent team for projects. In Figure 4.4, each network domain is configured to include all users in the same physical location. In Figure 4.5 on the following page, each domain is configured to include the members of a single project team.

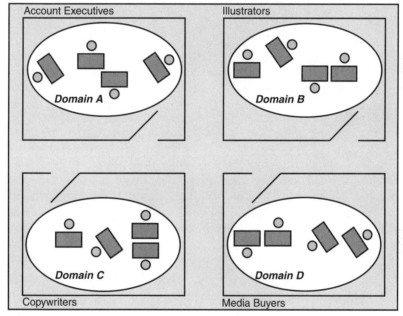

*Acme Advertising, Inc.*

**FIGURE 4.4**

*Example of domains defined by physical location*

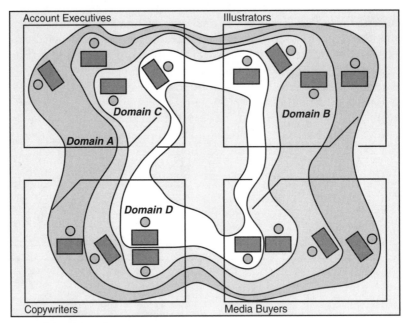

Account Executives

Illustrators

Domain C

Domain B

Domain A

Domain D

Copywriters

Media Buyers

*Acme Advertising, Inc.*

## FIGURE 4.5

*Example of domains defined by logical functional groups*

In practice, a small office like this probably would have only one domain, in which everyone was included. This fact notwithstanding, it saves time and frustration down the road to expend the extra effort initially and set up domains according to logical functional groupings. Then you can enlarge your network later with very little time and effort and still keep it secure. Access to physical resources, such as printers and modems, can be handled through the use of global groups. Be sure, however, to place printers near their users.

In our example, if the members of the project groups at Acme Advertising were changed for each new project, a different type of logical domain grouping would have to be used. Otherwise, you—the administrator—would be constantly moving users from one domain to another or, more likely, would give all users access to everything. The latter scenario might facilitate the users' access to resources, but it would also result in a system with poor security.

## File Security

There are also two aspects to maintaining file security:

◆ Controlling access to the file

◆ Protecting the integrity of the file

Both data files and document files contain data in a structured format, but document files are usually human-readable, whereas data files must be interpreted by a program. (The one exception is word processor files, which are best read within the word processor but are conventionally referred to as "documents.") We'll look at security considerations for each type of file.

Microsoft Windows NT Server version 4 allows you to control user access at both the folder level and the file level. So it's possible for someone to have full access to a folder but not to a file within that folder, or vice versa. This is only possible, however, if you've chosen to install the NTFS file system. (Chapter 5 has a full discussion of the file systems that can be installed.) Table 4.1 lists the *permissions* that can be applied to directories and files. Note that there are two permissions listed for each Directory Permissions entry in Table 4.1. The first permission applies to the directory itself; the second applies to the files in the directory. Under Windows NT, permissions are actually combinations of attributes that can be assigned to any file. These are the individual *file attributes*:

- Read (R)
- Write (W)
- Execute (X)
- Delete (D)
- Change Permissions (P)
- Take Ownership (O)

You also should consider auditing sensitive or confidential files to ensure that no one is attempting unauthorized access.

**Table 4.1**
**Standard Permissions for NTFS Directories and Files**

| Directory Permissions | Explanation |
| --- | --- |
| No Access (None) (None) | The user cannot gain access to the directory at all, even if he or she is a member of a group that, as a whole, has been granted access to the directory. |
| List (RX) (Not Specified) | The user can list the files and subdirectories in this directory and can change to a subdirectory of this directory. He or she cannot gain access to files created in the directory by others. |
| Read (RX) (RX) | The user can read the contents of the files and can run applications in the directory. |

*(continued)*

*Table 4.1* *continued*

| Directory Permissions | Explanation |
| --- | --- |
| Add (WX) (Not Specified) | The user can add files to the directory but cannot read the contents of current files or change them. |
| Add & Read (RWX) (RX) | The user can read and add files but cannot change files. |
| Change (RWXD) (RWXD) | The user can read and add files and can change the contents of current files. |
| Full Control (All) (All) | The user can add, read, and change files; can change permissions for the directory and its files; and can take ownership of the directory and its files. |
| *File Permissions* | *Explanation* |
| No Access (None) | The user cannot gain access to the file at all, even if he or she is a member of a group that, as a whole, has been granted access to the file. |
| Read (RX) | The user can read the contents of the file and can run it if it is an application. |
| Change (RWXD) | The user can read, change, and delete the file. |
| Full Control (All) | The user can read, change, delete, set permissions for, and take ownership of the file. |

## Program files

Program files and the folders that contain them should almost always be set to Read because users rarely need to write to them. A Read access also prevents users from either deliberately or inadvertently deleting or overwriting the files or introducing viruses. However, it's not enough to merely set all the files to Read because a user with a Change Permissions (P) access to a folder can change the access for any individual file in the folder.

## Library files

Handle library files in the same manner as program files, especially when the library files are in the same folder as the program that uses them. When many library files are shared among applications, however, as is often the case in a Microsoft Windows environment, the library file most likely will be located in the user's %SYSTEMROOT% or %SYSTEMROOT%\SYSTEM folder. Users do not need more than Read access to the %SYSTEMROOT%\SYSTEM folder unless they install their own software. %SYSTEMROOT%, however, can hold data or document files to which applications write. There's little you can do to protect these files from being removed, changed, or corrupted except to educate the users. Virus protection, or "scanning," software should be used to safeguard files from a virus infection.

## Data and document files

Obviously, users need full access to their personal data and document files. This need is best accommodated by creating a folder specifically for each user in which no program or library files are kept. Give each user All permission to his or her own folder and None permission to everyone else's folders.

Create separate folders for user groups to use as a shared repository. Depending on the structure of the group, each member might have an All access, or only a small number of members might have an All access and the rest of the group a Read or Change access. Again, do not use these folders for program or library files.

Another common type of folder is one that contains documents that should be made available to all or a large number of users as Read access and to just one user as All access. For example, a NOTICES folder, in which company policy documents are located, would be Read accessible to everyone on the network but All accessible only to the user responsible for maintaining the files. Figure 4.6 shows a typical folder arrangement including Group, User, and Public Access folders.

**FIGURE 4.6**

*Example of a typical folder arrangement*

# Intruder Security

Keeping out the "bad guys," or intruder security, is what usually comes to mind when the topic of security is raised. In fact, far more damage usually is done by people inside the enterprise than by people outside the enterprise. Nevertheless, there are a few steps you should take to ensure that risk to the system from intruders is minimized.

All users on your system should have well-chosen passwords and should be required to change these passwords periodically. Passwords should be chosen according to the guidelines presented under "Rules for Choosing Good Passwords." Users should not reuse a particular password immediately; set up the accounts to require a minimum "lag time" before someone can reuse a password. Accounts also should be set to lockout when invalid passwords are entered. (Three attempts should be permitted, however, to allow for typographical errors.)

## For More Information

*See Chapter 9 for information on how to set password policies.*

If your network users will be dialing into the network from their homes or other remote sites, you might want to implement more security measures than just domain-level password authorization. One option is to configure your remote access server so that it calls back a predetermined number when a user dials in; as long as the user will be calling from the same place every time, this works well. Another option is to place a third-party security device between the remote client and the remote access server. An example of a third-party device is the so-called "smart card," which authenticates the user by means of a card reader on the remote machine that is linked to a security device on the host network. The remote user is allowed to access the network only if this card is valid.

As a systems administrator, you should have two accounts on the system—an administrative account and a regular user account. You should use the administrative account only if you are performing administrative tasks. Administrative accounts are a prime target for intruders because of the permissions associated with them.

## NOTE

*If your network is connected to the Internet, there are many additional steps you should take to protect your system from intruders. Which of these options you will want to implement will depend on what Internet services you are providing (for example, NNTP, SMTP, ftp, TELNETD). Although security for Internet services and protocols is beyond the scope of this book, there are books available that focus on Internet security, which you can consult for specific information.*

A good password has the following characteristics:

◆ It is not a rotation of the characters in a logon name. (How many brain cells would it take to figure out such a password?)

◆ It contains at least two alphabetic characters and one nonalphabetic character.

◆ It is at least six characters long.

◆ It isn't the user's name or initials, the initials of his or her children or significant other, or even any of these items combined with other commonly available personal data such as the user's birth date or phone number.

Some of the best passwords are alphanumeric abbreviations of phrases that have some deeper meaning for the user. As an example, we have a joke in our family that is derived from the old advertising slogan, "I can't believe I ate the whole thing." So, for awhile, we used the initial letters of the words in the slogan, *Icbiatwt2* (the 2 represents "twice"), as a password.

It pays to educate your users about passwords and password privacy, but most of all, it pays to heed your own advice. Make sure you initially select a good password and change it frequently. These simple procedures will help you avoid the disastrous consequences of having someone break into your system and wreak havoc in your very own kingdom.

## POINTS TO REMEMBER

◆ Networks and servers need to be physically secure. If you can't watch it, lock it up.

◆ Require passwords, but limit the number of passwords per user. Otherwise, it becomes impossible for the user to remember them. Wherever possible, a single password should control a user's access to all of his or her resources.

◆ Wherever possible, use a logical domain layout rather than a physical domain layout. Group people by their access needs rather than by job title or by department.

◆ Group files by type. Keep the executable program files in folders separate from the data and document files that users will be manipulating.

- Grant only the minimum number of folder and file permissions that are required.

- Require users to change their passwords periodically. Do not allow users to reuse passwords more often than every six months.

- Use your administrative account sparingly. Create a standard user account for your everyday needs.

- Install an additional layer of security for remote users.

- Use the central administration model. If this is not possible, use a mixed model that allows security concerns to be addressed globally.

## WHAT'S NEXT?

Now that you've decided which security measures to implement for your system—at least the preliminary ones—there are a few other decisions that still need to be made before installation of the network can begin. These decisions involve choices of file systems, partitions, and network protocols, all of which are reviewed in Chapter 5.

# CHAPTER 5

More Planning for Network Installation

# CHAPTER 5

# More Planning for Network Installation

Yes, here we are all the way to Chapter 5, and we're still talking about *planning!* But there's no getting around it. The data structures used by Microsoft Windows NT Server version 4 provide great value in terms of security, but they also can prevent some changes to the system once it's installed. The administrator's lot is not always a happy one, so make things easier for yourself by taking the time to plan carefully so the system can be installed correctly the first time.

In this chapter, we'll cover some of the decisions it is advisable to make *before* the installation is proceeding pell-mell, decisions such as which file system to use, how you will want your hard drive(s) partitioned, and which network protocol to use.

## Selecting a File System

You have two network file system options when you install a Windows NT network, FAT (file allocation table) or NTFS (NT file system). You can install the network on a partition that is already formatted as either FAT or NTFS. You also can format a partition as FAT or NTFS as you install the system. Or you can convert a FAT partition to an NTFS partition without data loss at the time of installation.

Although FAT has lower overhead than NTFS, FAT is not an appropriate choice for a server. It lacks the security and recoverability features built into NTFS. Several features of NTFS make it the preferred file system for Windows NT.

◆ Protections can be assigned to either directories or individual files. Files can retain their permissions even when moved.

◆ No one can gain unauthorized access to an NTFS system by booting from a floppy disk.

◆ The system can recover in the event of a failure because the logging of transactions is completed before the transactions are carried out. Disk repair utilities aren't necessary.

◆ NTFS constantly monitors its disk areas; if it finds damage, it takes the bad area out of service and moves the data from that area to another area. This is called a *hot fix,* and it's invisible to any running application.

◆ Fragmentation is less of a problem on an NTFS partition because the system always attempts to locate a contiguous block of hard drive space large enough to hold the file being stored.

You will need a FAT partition on machines with RISC processors, but only a very small one for boot purposes. (A partition size of 5 MB is the minimum recommended.) The rest of the hard drive should be formatted as NTFS.

If you are in an environment where convenience, not security, is the major concern, you might want to consider using at least a small FAT partition, even on Intel-based servers. It's definitely not as secure and in many ways not as robust a configuration. But it sure is a lot easier to deal with some system administration chores, such as running EISA configuration utilities, if you have a small FAT partition on your hard drive. You can load all your hardware utilities on it, and, even if your system crashes or has major problems, you'll be able to boot off a floppy and get to the utilities. Of course, this won't work if the hard drive itself has crashed, so you'll need to keep floppy versions available in a secure but accessible place. But having a small FAT partition certainly will make life easier in most other situations.

In an environment where security is a serious concern, however, do not use a FAT partition. In this situation, you'll want to keep your entire storage system configured for NTFS—except, as we mentioned above, on RISC machines, where you need a 5-MB to 10-MB FAT partition.

Although only computers running Windows NT can use NTFS files directly, network users can access files on NTFS partitions without difficulty, even if they're using MS-DOS, OS/2, UNIX, or any flavor of Microsoft Windows (Windows 3.1, Windows for Workgroups, Windows 95).

# Planning Disk Partitions

As you set up your server, you will need to make decisions about how to divide up the server's available disk space. You'll need to play the old game of balancing huge, single partitions and multiple, small partitions.

Conceptually, it's always easier to deal with large, monolithic partitions, but using large partitions is not always the most efficient way of configuring a system. One consideration to keep in mind is the overall stability of the system. If you expect your overall configuration to be stable, with a fairly fixed group of applications and a stable user population, you can opt for largish partitions that match those needs.

As OS/2 slips slowly, slowly out of sight on the operating system horizon, High Performance File System (HPFS) is joining it. Until now, you could install Windows NT on a partition formatted with HPFS. Earlier versions of Windows NT recognized HPFS partitions so that applications running on early versions of OS/2 could be run on Windows NT as well. This is no longer true. An HPFS partition will have to be reformatted as FAT or NTFS *before* Windows NT Server is installed. If you have an HPFS partition, these are your choices:

◆ On an earlier version of Windows NT, run the Convert utility to convert the HPFS volume to FAT or NTFS. Do this *before* installing Windows NT version 4.

◆ Under OS/2, back up the partition, reformat it as a FAT partition, and restore the files. If the partition is your OS/2 boot partition, you'll have to reinstall OS/2 after the restoration. (The FAT partition can then be turned into an NTFS partition using the Convert utility that comes with Windows NT version 4.)

Admittedly, it is a pain to have to do either of these things, but it's unavoidable if you have HPFS.

If your server will function primarily as a database server, you won't have to do much in the way of making decisions. You'll want to put your database's core program files on a single partition with enough room for reasonable growth. But you'll almost certainly want to keep everything else off this partition to keep speed to a maximum, so size the partition accordingly. How the data files themselves generally will be arranged will depend in great part on your database, but the files either will be spread across multiple partitions or drives or will be stored on a special "raw" partition that is entirely under the control of the database application. In either case, you'll find that you need to allow *lots* of room for the database to grow. A database server is also an obvious place for using either a software or a hardware RAID solution that will let you spread your database across multiple hard drives using striping or arrays. This not only allows for unlimited growth but also has the advantage of letting you expand your hard drive space cautiously because you can simply add an additional drive to your array when you need more file space. This is a relatively easy thing to do.

**For More Information**

*You can find more about RAID in Chapter 8.*

On the other hand, if the nature of your business will require fairly frequent changes in the system, with users being added and removed on a regular basis and a variety of different programs being added, removed, or changed to meet production needs, you might find it makes sense to use smaller hard drive partitions so that you can create a partition for a particular project easily. When the project is done, it's only necessary to archive the data, and the partition is wiped clean, ready for the next project.

The big plus of NTFS is that it will allow you to have large, single partitions without the enormous amounts of wasted space you would have if you were using FAT. Generally, we suggest you go with separate partitions—for the system itself, for your applications, and for your user files. The system partition will be fairly stable and should be sufficiently large that you won't have to worry about suddenly having to "grow" it. For a typical installation, given that hard drive space is cheap these days, somewhere around 500 MB should do nicely on a typical server. The size of the user and application partitions will, of course, depend entirely on your particular environment. But you don't have to leave quite as much room for them to grow because it's easy to simply add another drive or partition when you need to add new users or applications, usually without having to do much with the old partitions.

Another thing to keep in mind as you plan your disk partitions is what kind, if any, of RAID or other method of drive access you'll be using. If you have a choice, we strongly urge you to consider using either a special RAID controller or a software RAID solution. There's an adequate, though hardly extravagant, software RAID solution built into the Windows NT Disk Administrator. We'll cover use of the Disk Administrator in detail in Chapter 8, but a quick comment or two about it makes sense here.

There certainly are advantages to using the built-in tools of Disk Administrator to build a disk array or mirror. The most obvious one is, of course, cost because the cost isn't any more than the cost of the lost drive space. But there are other advantages as well, including portability and compatibility. Disk Administrator is an integral part of the operating system; therefore, you can easily configure it the same way for either an Intel-based server or a RISC-based server. This allows you to maintain a similar configuration across a diversified network easily, where some computers have different processors, according to their needs. You also won't need to worry about subtle compatibility problems because Disk Administrator is designed into the operating system.

On the other hand, there are some serious limitations to using Disk Administrator. It supports only three basic types of RAID—mirroring (RAID 1), striping (RAID 0), and striping with parity (RAID 5). Although these are the best known and most common types of RAID, they are hardly the only possible RAID options and might not suit your needs. There also can be definite advantages in terms of both speed and flexibility to moving the handling of your disk arrays onto a separate hardware subsystem. For one thing, most of the hardware RAID solutions allow you to replace failed hard drives ("hot swapping") without shutting down the server at all, which is a definite plus in a production environment.

With the cost of hard drive space shrinking almost hourly and the needs of users and applications growing at an even faster rate, we believe that some sort of RAID solution definitely makes sense in most server environments. Where many of us chose not to spend the extra money on RAID in the past, we now see the economics of the situation changing. You'll want to consider your situation carefully as you plan your network.

# Selecting Network Protocols

Windows NT Server is largely protocol independent. It can do its job using any of the standard protocols, and it ships with all the major protocols "in the box":

◆   IPX/SPX: the protocol for Novell NetWare networks and the default protocol for Windows NT Server

◆   TCP/IP: the protocol of the Internet and the preferred protocol for wide area networks

◆   NetBEUI: the protocol used by Microsoft LanManager networks and Microsoft Windows for Workgroups networks

◆   AppleTalk: the protocol used by Macintosh computers

◆   SNA DLC: the protocol for mainframe access

Few of us really want to have to support all of these protocols at once, and there isn't really a need to do so. Your basic choices probably will boil down to two, IPX/SPX or TCP/IP.

IPX/SPX is a fast, flexible network protocol that has been used successfully in NetWare networks for years, and it is easy to set up and configure. It's the default protocol for a local area network and a good choice if you don't plan on connecting beyond that level. It is also the preferred protocol if you're going to be in a mixed environment with NetWare servers.

TCP/IP is also a fast, flexible network protocol. Originally created for the Internet, TCP/IP is a widely accepted protocol that runs on virtually any hardware or operating system you are likely to encounter. As such, it is the preferred protocol for your network if you'll be connecting to a wide area network or the Internet. TCP/IP has had a reputation, not unjustified, as a protocol that is hard to configure and maintain; but with the tools in Windows NT Server, you'll find the task of configuring and maintaining TCP/IP less onerous than in the past.

NetBEUI was developed originally in the early days of local area networking. It is small and relatively fast in some circumstances and is the protocol used by the LanManager and Windows for Workgroups networks. It has reached the end of its useful life, however, and its limitations outweigh its benefits in the current diverse networking environment.

AppleTalk and SNA DLC are included in Windows NT Server to facilitate connecting to Macintosh and mainframe environments, respectively. If your network includes either of these platforms, you'll probably need to add the appropriate protocol. DLC is a useful protocol for talking to Hewlett-Packard printers. (DLC is discussed in Chapter 11.) However, in either case you might well find that you can (and should) use TCP/IP instead. There are excellent TCP/IP solutions for both of these environments, and it is likely that both will move to TCP/IP more and more in the future. However, you might need to support a legacy environment, and Windows NT Server includes the tools you'll need to do that.

## For More Information

*The uses and limitations of various protocols are covered in more detail in Chapter 7.*

## POINTS TO REMEMBER

- Although you can install Windows NT Server on a FAT partition, NTFS is much preferred for its higher security and fault tolerance.

- NTFS also has the advantage of remaining relatively unfragmented for long periods of time.

- Plan your disk partitions with recovery from disaster in mind. (See Chapter 8 and Chapter 25 for help.)

- Make your protocol plans early, too. (Check Chapter 7.)

## WHAT'S NEXT?

By this time, you should have a notebook or two full of planning notes for your network. Now we move to the actual process of installation and walk through it step-by-step.

# Part Two

## Installation and Setup

# CHAPTER 6

# CHAPTER 6

# Installation of Windows NT Server

In previous chapters, you've been presented with the questions you need to answer and the problems you need to solve before you start the process of setting up your system. There is one last preparatory step.

## Preinstallation Checklist

During installation, Microsoft Windows NT Server version 4 will ask you for a lot of specific information about your planned network system. Many of the questions require more than a simple "Yes" or "No" answer. Table 6.1 is a checklist of the critical things you should know before starting your Windows NT Server installation. We strongly recommend that you take the necessary time to complete this checklist. Otherwise, you can get quite far into the installation process only to discover that you are missing a critical piece of information and can't proceed without it. Even worse, you might have to abort the installation to find the answer to one of the questions and then have to start the process all over again.

**Table 6.1**
**Windows NT Server version 4 Preinstallation Checklist**

| Question | Answer |
| --- | --- |
| What type of hard drive controller are you using? | |
| Is a special boot driver required from the manufacturer? | |
| Which partition will be your primary boot partition? | |
| Which partition will be your system partition? | |
| What file system will you use? | |
| Is there at least 150 MB of free space on the system partition? | |

| Question | Answer |
|---|---|
| What license mode (per server or per seat) will you use? | |
| What is the name of this computer? | |
| What will be the role for this server (primary domain controller, backup domain controller, stand-alone)? | |
| What is the administrative account name of the primary domain controller and the account password? | |
| Are you installing an Internet Information Server? | |
| What is each network card's brand and model? | |
| What is each network card's IRQ, address, and type of connection? | |
| What network protocols (TCP/IP, IPX/SPX, NetBEUI, other) are you installing? | |
| What network services are you installing? | |
| Will you use an IP address or a DHCP server? | |
| What subnet mask will you use? | |
| What default gateway(s) will you use? | |
| Will there be a separate host name? | |
| What is the Internet domain name (if there is one)? | |
| What is the DNS server address (if it exists)? | |
| What is the WINS server (if there is one)? | |
| What is the Novell NetWare gateway (if there is one)? | |

## NOTE

*There are two versions of the Setup program, WINNT.EXE and WINNT32.EXE. If your operating system is MS-DOS, Microsoft Windows 3.x, or Microsoft Windows 95, run the program WINNT.EXE, which is in the I386 folder on the CD-ROM. If you're running a previous version of Windows NT Server on an Intel processor, run WINNT32.EXE, which is also in the I386 folder. For other processors, use WINNT32.EXE in the appropriate directory for your hardware platform.*

# Installation Options

Finally we arrive at the actual installation of your system. There are several ways of installing Windows NT Server. Which method you choose depends on whether you're performing an upgrade or a new installation, whether you're installing over the network, and what operating system (if any) currently is on the server. We'll try to cover most of the scenarios by looking first at a generic installation and then pointing out the differences for other installation options. There are four basic installation options:

◆ New Installation: Setup Floppy Disks and Local CD-ROM Drive

Probably the single most common type of installation is the use of a retail package of Windows NT Server, which includes three 1.44-MB floppy disks and a CD-ROM. The server will have a local CD-ROM drive and a floppy disk drive.

◆ New Installation: No Setup Floppy Disks and Local CD-ROM Drive

Many servers will not have a local floppy disk drive at all, for security reasons; in other cases, administrators simply will choose not to use the floppy disks.

◆ New Installation: Floppy Disk Drive and Network CD-ROM Drive

Not every machine will have a local CD-ROM drive, although it sure makes life easier at the server to have one.

◆ Upgrade Installation

The choices here are pretty much the same as for a new installation. The exception is that some installation decisions have already been made by Windows NT Server, and you won't have the need or the opportunity to make them yourself.

There are undoubtedly other possible installation scenarios, but any others would for the most part be variations of these.

# Windows 95 Considerations

If you're installing Windows NT Server on a machine that currently has Microsoft Windows 95 installed on it, the first thing to do is ask yourself, "Why am I doing this?" The two operating systems have very different roles in the enterprise, and it's hardly likely that one machine would be using both systems. It makes sense to install Windows NT Server on a Windows 95 machine only if you're upgrading from an existing peer-to-peer network to a Windows NT domain network, and this machine is to function as a server on the network.

The main thing to keep in mind if you do install Windows NT Server over an existing Windows 95 installation is that you *must* start from scratch. Windows NT Server has to be installed in a completely new directory; you can't install it into the directory in which Windows 95 is installed. You'll also have to reinstall most of your applications because they won't be properly registered with Windows NT Server.

By default, Windows NT Server will install itself into a dual-boot configuration that would allow you to reboot the server into Windows 95 if you wanted to do so. Personally, we think this is a major hole in server security. We recommend that you disable the dual-boot capability when the Windows NT Server installation is complete. Remove the line from the BOOT.INI file that reads something like the following:

```
C:\="Microsoft Windows"
```

Also delete the entire Windows 95 subdirectory structure, not only to recover the space but to prevent someone from booting off a floppy disk and re-enabling the Windows 95 boot.

An alternative to deleting the Windows 95 subdirectory structure is simply to convert the machine to NTFS. This will get rid of any lingering Windows 95 problem because Windows 95 can't see an NTFS formatted drive. This is a much more secure solution anyway because even with a floppy disk boot, the hard drive is normally not accessible—which also makes for more grief because you can't, for example, store hardware configuration utilities on the hard drive. But we can think of several reasonable ways around the latter problem, including the use of a portable, external drive (such as a ZIP drive) that has all of your hardware utilities on it for emergency situations.

### ◆ Creating Setup Floppy Disks

Windows NT Server comes with three Setup floppy disks plus a CD-ROM. If you're doing multiple installations of Windows NT Server, it's important that the set of three Setup floppy disks always be available locally to a machine running Windows NT Server; they'll be needed in the case of a serious server failure. Fortunately, it's easy to make installation floppy disks using your current operating system and the CD-ROM.

To install the system without making floppy disks, add the /B switch to the command you use to start the Setup program. For more on Setup floppy disks, see "New Installation Using a Local CD-ROM Drive but No Setup Floppy Disks" on page 78.

# New Installation Using Setup Floppy Disks and a Local CD-ROM Drive

This is the basic Windows NT Server installation method and the one used by most folks. We'll use it as our generic installation model.

◆ Insert the Windows NT Server Setup boot disk (the first of three Setup floppy disks) into the A: drive, and turn on the power. Once the machine goes through its POST (power-on self test), it should boot off the floppy disk in the A: drive. However, the BIOS in some modern computers lets you disable booting from the A: drive. If your machine isn't allowing you to boot from a floppy disk, you might need to go into the BIOS and change that setting.

◆ After a certain amount of noise, while the machine slowly reads the floppy disk, the Setup program will eventually ask you to insert the second disk of the Setup floppy disk set. The specific message is:

```
Please insert the disk labeled

Windows NT Server Setup Disk #2

        into Drive A:

  * Press ENTER when ready.
```

Pop out the first boot floppy disk, pop in the second Setup floppy disk, and press Enter.

◆ While the Windows NT Setup program grinds slowly away on that second floppy disk, it's a good time to put the CD-ROM in the CD-ROM drive.

◆ Finally another lovely blue screen pops up. This time it's called the Welcome To Setup screen. From here, you have four choices:

  ◆ To learn more about Windows NT Setup before continuing, press F1.

  ◆ To set up Windows NT now, press Enter.

  ◆ To repair a damaged Windows NT version 4.0 installation, press R.

  ◆ To quit Setup without installing Windows NT, press F3.

If you really want to see five screens of Help information, press F1. Otherwise, you can just press Enter and get on with it. This will take you to the first of the hardware detection screens.

**NOTE**

*The installation program refers to hard drives and CD-ROM drives as* mass storage devices.

◆ Setup automatically detects floppy disk controllers and standard ESDI/IDE hard disks without user intervention. However, on some computers, detection of other types of mass storage devices (for example, SCSI adapters and CD-ROM drives) can cause the computer to become unresponsive or to malfunction temporarily. For this reason, you can bypass Setup's mass storage device detection and manually select SCSI adapters, CD-ROM drives, and special disk controllers (such as drive arrays) for installation.

To let the Setup program do all the hard work, press Enter. It will start by telling you to insert the third Setup floppy disk into the drive. When Setup's search is finished, it will show you a list of the devices it found. You can accept the list as is, or you can add more items to it. Press Enter to accept the list; press S to select additional items manually.

**Tip**

*It's generally a good idea just to let the Setup program detect the drives by itself. If you have problems and the machine hangs during the hardware detection process, or if you're in a hurry and you know exactly what the Setup program is looking for, feel free to bypass the automatic detection. You can add the specific SCSI controllers and non-SCSI CD-ROM drives you have manually. Press S at the first hardware detection screen instead of Enter, and select your hardware from a list of manufacturers and their controllers.*

◆ When you're satisfied that the Setup program has found or been told about all of the controllers, move to the next screen by pressing Enter.

◆ The next screen is the Microsoft Windows NT Licensing agreement, which contains all sorts of tedious legal language. Read all the text, pressing PgUp to scroll up or PgDn to scroll down. When you get to the bottom of the agreement you'll see you have exactly two choices— accept the Microsoft agreement, or not.

If the agreement violates some deeply held principle of yours, simply press Esc, and the whole process is over. You're done. You'll see a fatal error message indicating that you have elected not to accept the Microsoft Windows NT Licensing agreement. Then the system will reboot, and you'll have to go find another operating system (and another book, too, we're afraid).

Assuming you're willing to accept the Microsoft Windows NT Licensing agreement, press F8. The Windows NT Server Setup program will continue, and you'll see a list of basic hardware that Setup detected. Change any items that Setup detected incorrectly, then move the highlight to "The above list matches my computer" and press Enter.

◆   If there's a previous version of Windows NT on the machine, Setup will suggest that you install Windows NT Server version 4 in the directory of the earlier version of Windows NT, which results in an upgrade installation. (See "Reinstallation or Upgrade of Windows NT" on page 84 for more information on upgrade installations.)

However, if you want to perform a *new* installation because you are changing the role of the machine in the domain, for example, or if you just want to have your old version of Windows NT around to fall back on, do not press Enter at this screen. Press C to change the directory, and type a new directory name.

◆   If there are no previous versions of Windows NT on the machine, Setup will present you with a list of the available space on each hard drive, which might be a single partition or a long list of partitions, depending on the equipment in your system. In any case, choose the location for your system files now.

### Tip

*Try to keep your system partition fairly small and focused, and do not put your applications and user files on the system partition. This makes system recovery and repair simpler and less stressful.*

◆   Select the partition for your system files.

◆   Tell the Setup program what kind of file system to put on the partition. The choices are FAT or NTFS. If you have an existing formatted file system on the partition, you can elect to do one of the following:

- Maintain the existing formatted file system.

- Convert it to NTFS, if it's currently FAT.

- Simply reformat the partition.

On a new hard drive, you might not even have a partition, just unused space. In this case, you can elect to create partitions as part of the installation process.

## For More Information

*For the lowdown on NTFS vs. FAT, see Chapter 5.*

- After you've selected a file system, Setup will ask if you want to do a quick or an exhaustive check of your hard drives. We advise taking the time to do the exhaustive check. It doesn't take a great deal of time for most hard drives (and not that much longer than the "quick" version), and it is some assurance that the hard drive is working correctly.

- The Setup program will run its tests of the hard drive(s). When the tests are completed, Setup will ask permission to reboot. Remove the floppy disk from the A: drive.

## WARNING!

*If your computer has a BIOS that supports booting from the CD-ROM, you also must remove the Windows NT Server CD-ROM from the drive before the system tries to reboot. Otherwise, your system will simply hang, without any comment or warning whatsoever. If you're not sure what kind of BIOS you have, remove the CD-ROM from the drive anyway.*

- Click OK to reboot.

- After the system reboots, Setup will begin the graphical portion of the installation. From this point on, the installation process is quite similar regardless of whether you're using a local CD-ROM drive or a network CD-ROM drive to install the system. The role you choose for the server and the type of installation (new or upgrade) will determine the differences in installation process from here on out. So jump ahead to "Graphical Installation" on page 85 for the rest of the story.

# New Installation Using a Local CD-ROM Drive but No Setup Floppy Disks

If your server has a local CD-ROM drive and if you already have an operating system on it that can see the CD-ROM, you can install Windows NT Server without going through the process of either creating the floppy disk Setup or using the floppy disks that came with your package. This can save a substantial amount of time.

## WARNING!

*This procedure makes perfect sense if you already have the set of three Setup floppy disks and are simply trying to save some time. It is not a good idea to install the system this way if the three Setup floppy disks are not available. It is also not a good idea if there are only a limited number of Setup disks and if they won't be available at the site where the server ultimately will be installed. In these situations, you definitely will want to make another set of Setup disks because they will be needed for recovery in the event of a catastrophic failure of the server.*

◆ Run the Setup program appropriate to your processor type. For example, if you have an Alpha system with Microsoft Windows NT 3.51 installed and the local CD-ROM drive as the E: drive, you'd run:

```
E:\ALPHA\WINNT32.EXE /B
```

If you have an Intel processor machine with Windows 95 installed and the local CD-ROM drive as the D: drive, you'd run:

```
D:\I386\WINNT.EXE /B
```

◆ Setup will search your local hard drives to verify that there's enough free space on at least one of them to install the system. You need at least 150 MB of free hard drive space to install Windows NT Server.

◆ The Setup program will create a temporary source subdirectory on one of your local hard drives and then copy the necessary Setup files there. When it has finished all of the copying, it will prompt you to reboot.

**NOTE**

*Although Windows NT Server takes a great deal of space to install—150 MB is a safe amount to allow—the final installation takes up less space, usually less than 100 MB, depending on which options you've selected.*

◆ After the computer has rebooted, you'll see the same blue screen that you'd see if you were using the Setup floppy disks. However, in this case, the program will have already completed the first step of hardware recognition. It should show your CD-ROM drive (or the SCSI adapter that it's on, if you have a SCSI CD-ROM drive). Make the appropriate choices for your server as the system prompts you, and add any necessary SCSI adapters or other specialized hard drive adapters when it offers you the option.

◆ When you're satisfied that the Setup program has found or been told about all of the controllers, move to the next screen by pressing Enter.

◆ The next screen is the Microsoft Windows NT Licensing agreement, which contains all sorts of tedious legal language. Read all the text, pressing PgUp to scroll up or PgDn to scroll down. When you get to the bottom of the agreement you'll see you have exactly two choices—accept the Microsoft agreement, or not.

If the agreement violates some deeply held principle of yours, simply press Esc, and the whole process is over. You're done. You'll see a fatal error message indicating that you have elected not to accept the Microsoft Windows NT Licensing agreement. Then the system will reboot, and you'll have to go find another operating system (and another book, too, we're afraid).

Assuming you're willing to accept the Microsoft Windows NT Licensing agreement, press F8. The Windows NT Server Setup program will continue, and you'll see a list of basic hardware that Setup detected. Change any items that Setup detected incorrectly, then move the highlight to "The above list matches my computer" and press Enter.

◆ If there's a previous version of Windows NT on the machine, Setup will suggest that you install Windows NT Server version 4 in the directory of the earlier version of Windows NT, which results in an upgrade installation. (See "Reinstallation or Upgrade of Windows NT" on page 84 for more information on upgrade installations.)

However, if you want to perform a *new* installation because you are changing the role of the machine in the domain, for example, or if you just want to have your old version of Windows NT around to fall back on, do not press Enter at this screen. Press C to change the directory, and type a new directory name.

◆ If there are no previous versions of Windows NT on the machine, Setup will present you with a list of the available hard drive space, which might be a single partition or a long list of partitions, depending on the equipment in your system. In any case, choose the location for your system files now.

## Tip

*Try to keep your system partition fairly small and focused, and do not put your applications and user files on the system partition. This makes system recovery and repair simpler and less stressful.*

◆ Select the partition for the system files.

◆ Tell the Setup program what kind of file system to put on the partition. The choices are FAT or NTFS. If you have an existing formatted file system on the partition, you can elect to do one of the following:

   ◆ Maintain the existing formatted file system.

   ◆ Convert it to NTFS, if it's currently FAT.

   ◆ Simply reformat the partition.

On a new hard drive, you might not even have a partition, just unused space. In this case, you can elect to create partitions as part of the installation process.

## For More Information

*For the lowdown on NTFS vs. FAT, see Chapter 5.*

◆ After you've selected a file system, Setup will ask if you want to do a quick or an exhaustive check of your hard drives. We advise taking the time to do the exhaustive check. It doesn't take a great deal of time for most hard drives (and not that much longer than the "quick" version), and it is some assurance that the hard drive is working correctly.

- The Setup program will run its tests of the hard drive(s). When the tests are completed, Setup will ask permission to reboot. Remove the CD-ROM from the CD-ROM drive. Click OK to reboot.

- After the system reboots, Setup will begin the graphical portion of the installation. From this point on, the installation process is quite similar regardless of whether you're using a local CD-ROM drive or a network CD-ROM drive to install the system. The role you choose for the server and the type of installation (new or upgrade) will determine the differences in installation process from here on out. So jump ahead to "Graphical Installation" on page 85 for the rest of the story.

# New Installation Using a Floppy Disk Drive and a Network CD-ROM Drive

If your server doesn't have a local CD-ROM drive but you have a network installed, you can install Windows NT Server using a CD-ROM that is shared over the network. Map one of the CD-ROM drives on the network to a drive letter, and then install the system. You can choose to create or not create the floppy disks as you prefer.

## Tip

*When installing the system using a network CD-ROM drive, opt for not making the floppy disks (unless you don't already have a set for the computer on which you're installing Windows NT Server). If something breaks down and you have problems during the installation, you'll probably have to restart the installation from scratch anyway.*

- Run the Setup program appropriate to your processor type. For example, if you have an Alpha system with Windows NT 3.51 installed and the network CD-ROM drive as the E: drive, you'd run:

```
E:\ALPHA\WINNT32.EXE /B
```

If you have an Intel processor machine with Windows 95 installed and the network CD-ROM drive as the D: drive, you'd run:

```
D:\I386\WINNT.EXE /B
```

- Setup will search your local hard drives to make sure that there's enough free space on at least one of them to install the system. You need at least 150 MB of free hard drive space to install Windows NT Server.

- The Setup program will create a temporary source subdirectory on one of your local hard drives and then copy the necessary Setup files there. When it has finished all of the copying, it will prompt you to reboot.

## NOTE

*Although Windows NT Server takes a great deal of space to install—150 MB is a safe amount to allow—the final installation takes up less space, usually less than 100 MB, depending on which options you've selected.*

- After the computer has rebooted, you'll see the same blue screen that you'd see if you were using the Setup floppy disks. However, in this case, the program will have already completed the first step of hardware recognition. It should show your CD-ROM drive (or the SCSI adapter that it's on, if you have a SCSI CD-ROM drive). Make the appropriate choices for your server as the system prompts you, and add any necessary SCSI adapters or other specialized hard drive adapters when it offers you the option.

- When you're satisfied that the Setup program has found or been told about all of the controllers, move to the next screen by pressing Enter.

- The next screen is the Microsoft Windows NT Licensing agreement, which contains all sorts of tedious legal language. Read all the text, pressing PgUp to scroll up or PgDn to scroll down. When you get to the bottom of the agreement you'll see you have exactly two choices—accept the Microsoft agreement, or not.

  If the agreement violates some deeply held principle of yours, simply press Esc, and the whole process is over. You're done. You'll see a fatal error message indicating that you have elected not to accept the Microsoft Windows NT Licensing agreement. Then the system will reboot, and you'll have to go find another operating system (and another book, too, we're afraid).

  Assuming you're willing to accept the Microsoft Windows NT Licensing agreement, press F8. The Windows NT Server Setup program will continue, and you'll see a list of basic hardware that Setup detected. Change any items that Setup detected incorrectly, then move the highlight to "The above list matches my computer" and press Enter.

◆ If there's a previous version of Windows NT on the machine, Setup will suggest that you install Windows NT Server version 4 in the directory of the earlier version of Windows NT, which results in an upgrade installation. (See "Reinstallation or Upgrade of Windows NT" on page 84.)

However, if you want to perform a *new* installation because you are changing the role of the machine in the domain, for example, or if you just want to have your old version of Windows NT around to fall back on, do not press Enter at this screen. Press C and type a new directory name.

◆ If there are no previous versions of Windows NT on the machine, Setup will present you with a list of the available hard drive space, which might be a single partition or a long list of partitions, depending on the equipment in your system. In any case, choose a location for your system files now.

## Tip

*Try to keep your system partition fairly small and focused, and do not put your applications and user files on the system partition. This makes system recovery and repair simpler and less stressful.*

◆ Select a partition for your system files.

◆ Tell the Setup program what kind of file system to put on the partition. The choices are FAT or NTFS. If you have an existing formatted file system on the partition, you can elect to do one of the following:

◆ Maintain the existing formatted file system.

◆ Convert it to NTFS, if it's currently FAT.

◆ Simply reformat the partition.

On a new hard drive, you might not even have a partition, just unused space. In this case, you can elect to create partitions as part of the installation process.

## For More Information

*For the lowdown on NTFS vs. FAT, see Chapter 5.*

- After you've selected a file system, Setup will ask if you want to do a quick or an exhaustive check of your hard drives. We advise taking the time to do the exhaustive check. It doesn't take a great deal of time for most hard drives (and not that much longer than the "quick" version), and it is some assurance that the hard drive is working correctly.

- The Setup program will run its tests of the hard drive(s). When the tests are completed, Setup will ask permission to reboot. Remove any floppy disks from the A: drive. Click OK to reboot.

- After the system reboots, Setup will begin the graphical portion of the installation. From this point on, the installation process is quite similar regardless of whether you're using a local CD-ROM drive or a network CD-ROM drive to install the system. The role you choose for the server and the type of installation (new or upgrade) will determine the differences in installation process from here on out. So jump ahead to "Graphical Installation" on page 85 for the rest of the story.

# Reinstallation or Upgrade of Windows NT

When you reinstall Windows NT Server over an existing installation of Windows NT version 4 or upgrade an earlier version of Windows NT, you're presented with far fewer choices than when you install the system from scratch. For one thing, you won't be able to change the server's role in the domain. An upgrade or reinstallation to the same directory will always assign the same role to the server as the previous installation did. There is no way to change the server role without installing to a completely new directory. In most situations, this isn't likely to be an issue; but there might be a time when you would wish you could convert a stand-alone server to a domain controller.

Personally, we think it's a major bummer not to be able to change the server role without reinstalling the whole system, but that could be because we've had to install Windows NT Server so many times in so many different ways. For example, suppose you have deliberately installed a database server as a stand-alone server so that it won't have to carry the overhead cost of being a controller. This is a reasonable option. But then your only backup domain controller goes out for an extended lunch, and you're seriously concerned about the domain's continued ability to operate in case of a second failure, this one on the primary controller. Unfortunately, you're out of luck. You can't turn your stand-alone server into a backup domain controller—not even by reinstalling Windows NT Server over the existing version. You'll have to completely reinstall Windows NT Server *and all your applications*. Not fun.

To perform an upgrade installation, follow any of the installation scenarios discussed in previous sections of this chapter, depending on whether the CD-ROM drive is a local drive or a network drive. As the Setup program progresses through the installation of the new system, it will detect the existing Windows NT installation and suggest that you upgrade it by placing the new installation in the directory of the existing version. Select this option, and the installation will become a system upgrade. This will reduce the number of choices you need to make later because the Setup program is smart enough to simply take many of the settings from the earlier version and plug them into the appropriate places in version 4. When the *upgrade* of the previous installation is complete, Setup will begin the graphical part of the installation.

# Graphical Installation

When the text-based portion of the Setup program is complete (whether a new or an upgrade installation) and the system has rebooted, you'll be in the graphical portion of the Setup process. From here on, there are a few choices you will still need to make, depending on what the role of the server is on your network and on whether you're doing an upgrade or a new installation.

At any point during this process, you can go back and change your mind about something you've answered earlier. Just click Back at the bottom of the dialog box. Feel free to do this as often as you think it's necessary.

### WARNING!

> *Going back to change domain names, computer names, or the role of Windows NT Server in a domain is fraught with peril. See Chapter 16 before attempting any of these changes.*

Enter your name and your organization's name. You can skip the organization name; but you must enter something for your name, or the Setup program won't continue.

## Software Licensing

Decide what licensing mode you're going to use on your server. There are two basic types of licensing:

◆ **Per Server**  Each simultaneous connection to the server must have a separate client license.

◆ **Per Seat**  Every computer that accesses any server on the network has to have its own individual client license.

So what does this mean in the real world? Is your decision irrevocable? Well, the answer to the second question depends on what type of licensing you choose, so let's look at the choices first.

If you choose Per Server licensing, your licenses are counted by how many different machines connect to this server *at the same time*. In other words, if you have 100 Windows 95 machines on the network but no more than 25 of them ever use this server at any one time, you'd need 25 licenses for the server.

If you choose Per Seat licensing, your licenses are counted by the total number of clients on your network, not by how many of them are connected to your server. So you'd need 100 licenses to cover your 100 Windows 95 machines.

"OK," you think. "That's simple enough. We'll use Per Server." But not so fast; there's more to the story. Suppose there are five servers on your network overall. One server is used by as many as 50 of the Windows 95 clients at a time, whereas the other servers are used about as much as the server that you are installing—up to 25 clients at a time. Obviously, some of your clients are using more than one server at a time, which is by no means uncommon. We now have a total of 150 connections, or $(25 \times 4) + (1 \times 50)$. If you use Per Server licensing, you'll need a total of 150 licenses on the network. If you use Per Seat licensing, you'll need a total of only 100 licenses. With Per Seat licensing, you'll need a license for each client on the network, but each client can connect to as many different servers as it wants to for the same price.

Therefore, you must evaluate your network and its usage patterns before you can make an intelligent decision. You can use either of the two following general rules of thumb for your decision making:

◆ If you have only one server, definitely choose Per Server licensing because it can be changed later.

◆ If you have multiple servers and if the total number of clients with access to one or more servers at one time is equal to or greater than the number of computers on the network, Per Seat licensing is the better option.

If you're unsure of the usage patterns, select the default choice (Per Server); you can always change it to Per Seat later.

> ### Tip
>
> *You have a one-time, one-way, no-charge chance to change your licensing from Per Server to Per Seat. So start with Per Server; if you decide later that you're pushing up against the license count because of your usage patterns, that's the time to make the change to Per Seat. The conversion option is available only for Windows NT Server, Microsoft Exchange Server, Microsoft SQL Server, and Microsoft SNA Server.*

When you have finished entering your licensing choices, return to the initial installation scenario. (This is page 74 for setup floppy disks and local CD-ROM drive, page 78 for local CD-ROM drive and no floppy disks, and page 81 for floppy disk drive and network CD-ROM drive.)

## Computer Name

Each computer must have a unique name on the network. Give the server you are installing a name that is up to 15 characters long. Take a few moments to think about your options in naming conventions before you go and commit to one. There are lots of different ways to come up with network server names—from the cute to the arbitrary to the sensible. We've seen them all. Try to resist the desire to be cute in your machine names. And avoid at all costs the arbitrary names based on some formula that only you know how to crack. The names might be easy to generate, but they just frustrate users and make them angry.

Frankly, we think the tendency, more often than not, is to choose a naming convention that meets the needs of the system administrator rather than the needs of the users. This is a poor idea. It's easy enough for you to keep a map of what and where the different clients and servers are on your network; you won't have to worry about it that often anyway. But what about your users, who also have to remember which server is what and where—on a daily basis? If you make life hard on your users, you'll end up paying in the long run. So naming your primary domain controllers after Norse, Roman, or Greek gods and your clients after characters from Shakespeare might make sense to you. And it does, at least, have the virtue of consistency. But unfortunately, it isn't going to do a thing to help your users figure out that LOKI is the server in Legal and ODIN is the server in Production. On the other hand, if you use a server name such as LEGAL_SERVER_1 for the primary domain controller in Legal, it might not appeal to anyone's aesthetic sense, but it does tell your users immediately which machine it is.

## Server Role on the Domain

If this is a new installation, you will have to specify what kind of server this machine will be. You have three choices:

◆ Primary domain controller

◆ Backup domain controller

◆ Stand-alone server

If you are new to Windows NT, be sure you have read the section "Domain Components" in Chapter 2 before you choose your server role on the domain.

### WARNING!

*Consider your options carefully. Once you have installed Windows NT Server in a particular server role, the only changes you can make in the assigned role are changes from primary domain controller to backup domain controller and vice versa. If you want to change a stand-alone server to a domain controller (or vice versa), you will have to reinstall the software from scratch in a new directory. For more information about changing server roles on the network, see Chapter 16.*

## Software Components

Next you will be asked whether you want to make an Emergency Repair Disk. Say "Yes," by all means. You can and should make new versions of this disk periodically, but you also should make one now.

### Tip

*After you make an Emergency Repair Disk, label it clearly with the date, the server's name, and the version of Windows NT Server, and put the disk in a safe place. And then make a good faith effort to remember where you put it.*

The next step is choosing which software components to install. By default, the Windows NT games and the Microsoft Exchange client are not installed. We tend to agree on the exclusion of the games because this is a server after all. But even if you're not going to be installing Microsoft Exchange Server right away, install the client program now. Also, live it up; go into Accessories and add Mouse Pointers to the list of selected software components (only one set of mouse pointers is installed by default). Even system administrators need to go a little wild sometimes.

# Network Hardware and Software Installation

Now that you've made all of your selections, Windows NT Server Setup is ready to install the networking portion of Windows NT Server. This means installing the necessary drivers for your network card(s), installing the protocol stacks to be used on the network, and configuring the network software.

**NOTE**

*What network and protocol choices you have and when you make these choices are the subject of this chapter. If you have questions about what a choice will mean for your network or why you should choose one protocol or service over another, see Chapter 7.*

The first question that is asked in this part of the installation program is how your server will be attached to the network—by a direct connection, by modem, or both. For servers, the usual answer is direct connection. In any case, select the appropriate answer and click Next.

## Internet Information Server

You now get to decide whether this server will run the Microsoft Internet Information Server (IIS). You can postpone installing the IIS if you're not sure whether you will use it or not. However, if you even think you're likely to want to use the server for either Internet or intranet services (Chapter 19), you might as well install the IIS now and get it over with. Click the check box if you don't want it. The default is to install the IIS.

## Hardware Detection and Selection

Now comes the fun part. Windows NT Server can search your machine and find any network cards you have installed. Amazingly, it succeeds most of the time, although it can get fooled on occasion. So let the Setup program figure out what you have on your machine unless the following conditions apply:

◆   You know that your network card is not on friendly terms with Windows NT Server, *and*

♦ You know exactly what network card you have on this computer *and what resources it's using.*

## Protocols

Next select the network protocols you'll be using. These protocols are the default choices:

♦ TCP/IP

♦ NWLink IPX/SPX Compatible Transport

♦ NetBEUI

NetBEUI is disabled by default. If you don't need to worry about legacy Microsoft Windows 3.1 and MS-DOS machines, it's probably just as well to leave it disabled. In addition to the default protocols, you also can add these protocols manually:

♦ Data Link Control

♦ Point to Point Tunneling

♦ Streams Environment

But unless you're sure you need additional protocols, wait to install them until you have the system up and running.

**For More Information**

*For details about the networking protocols and the pros and cons of each, see Chapter 7.*

## Network Services

Next choose which network services you'll want to install. The services listed below have already been selected as default services:

◆ RPC Configuration

◆ NetBIOS Interface

◆ Workstation

◆ Server

◆ Internet Information Server, if you've opted to install it

◆ Remote Access Service, if you've said that your server will be connecting to the network via modem

In addition to these default services, you can add other services, such as DHCP Server, DNS Server, TCP/IP Printing, and others. Take the default choices now, and add the others as you need them.

**For More Information**

*For information about other options, check out Chapter 7.*

Once you've chosen your network services, you're ready to install them. Click Next, and Setup will start the process. One of the first things it will request is information about the resources your network card uses. If your card is an EISA or a PCI card, the chances are Setup will get it right. But if your card is an ISA or a PCMCIA card, you'll probably have to tell Setup what resources are being used. If the I/O port address, IRQ, and transceiver type are not the defaults for these cards, the Setup program often will identify them incorrectly.

If you've made any changes to what Setup proposes, you'll get a rather rude warning about the parameters not being verifiably correct. But if you know you've got them right, just blow on by the message. Of course, if this is a backup domain controller you're installing, you absolutely must get this right. If you don't, Setup won't be able to find the primary domain controller to complete the Setup process and you're stuck.

The next question is about the DHCP. If you're using this on your network with a DHCP-configured server, by all means use DHCP on this machine. If you're not using DHCP at this time, add your TCP/IP address, gateway, subnet mask, and so forth to configure TCP/IP on the server.

## Remote Access Setup

Next configure your remote access setup, if you have either selected a modem connection to the network or specified that this machine will be a remote access service (RAS) server. Because there's much more information about remote access servers in Chapter 18, we'll focus here on the minimum you need to know to get RAS installed.

The first step is for the Setup program to install a remote access device. You haven't added a modem yet, so you will need to do so now. Setup will offer to try to detect your modem. By all means, let it try. If Setup finds a modem, you're usually in better shape than if you had to configure all of the stuff by hand, and it's certainly easier. Setup then will ask for your area code and whether you dial a number to get an outside line. Then the remote access device is pretty much ready to go. Save any additional tweaks for later. For now, accept the defaults unless you know for sure that something needs to be changed.

Finally, Setup gives you one last chance to check out the network bindings before the network gets started, and after you've looked at those or simply accepted them, Setup is ready to start the network.

## Setting Up the Administrator Account

Setup will request you to provide administrative information about the server with respect to its designated role on the network.

### Primary domain controller

If you have specified that you want to create a primary domain controller, Setup will ask you for the name for the domain. Type the domain name in the Domain text box. Setup then will search the network to make sure this name is not duplicated anywhere else. You can proceed only if the domain name is a new one on the network.

Setup provides a built-in administrator account for the primary domain controller in the domain so you'll have someplace to start after the install. You'll be asked to provide the initial password for the account. The password must be entered twice for confirmation. Write this password down and keep it in a safe place.

### WARNING!

*If the password for the administrator's account is lost before your other administrative accounts are created, you'll have to reinstall Windows NT Server and start over.*

### Backup domain controller

If you have specified that you want to create a backup domain controller, you must have your network connections in place because Setup must be able to find the primary domain controller on the domain. If it is not able to do so, Windows NT Server either will fail to install or will insist on installing this computer as the primary domain controller. You should have at hand the domain name and the password for an administrative-level account on the domain to which the backup controller is to be assigned. Type the name of the domain in the Domain text box and the administrative account name and password in the Administrator Name and Administrator Password text boxes.

If the network isn't working correctly, you won't be authenticated on the domain and the Setup program won't be able to finish. If this happens, back up through the steps, especially the hardware configuration of the network card, to make sure that you haven't made a mistake. Check very carefully that you've selected the right type of network transceiver for your network cabling and that the IRQ and I/O Port Address are correct. Then work your way forward through the steps, and try again.

### Stand-alone server

If you have specified that this server is to be a stand-alone server, tell Setup whether the server will be participating in a domain or will simply be part of a workgroup. If it's going to be part of a domain, even if it isn't a domain controller, you'll need to provide a password and an administrative-level account name so that the server can be added to the domain. If the server is to be part of a workgroup, type the name of the workgroup in the text box. If you're not sure whether the computer will be part of a domain or just part of a workgroup, select workgroup for the moment. You can always go back and change this choice, even though it'll require rebooting the system.

## Internet Information Server

Now you need to configure the basics of Internet Information Server—specifically, what portions of Internet Information Server will be used, where on your hard drive it will reside, and what its home directories will be. For the moment, stick with the defaults. They seem needlessly deep in the directory tree, but there's no compelling reason for changing them. It's always easier to troubleshoot when you take the default settings.

## Time Zones and Display Parameters

Finally, a few more questions—and you're done. Configure the time zone for your computer. The starting point is Greenwich mean time, which is five hours ahead of eastern standard time and eight hours ahead of Pacific standard time. Select the correct time zone for your location; double-check that the clock and date are correct. You've only one thing left to do: set the default display parameters. Make sure you test the parameters you select.

The Setup program will now copy the necessary files into the correct places and reboot the machine.

## POINTS TO REMEMBER

♦ If you don't have the Setup floppy disks, you should make them.

♦ If you do have the Setup floppy disks, you can install faster using the /B switch.

♦ If you want to change the role of a server in the domain, you'll have to do a new installation. You can't just do an upgrade.

♦ If the machine currently has Windows 95 on it, you can't preserve any of the existing settings.

## WHAT'S NEXT?

Installation is just the beginning of configuration, so now we move on to networking protocols. Windows NT Server can support many protocols, but only some of them will be useful on any given network.

# Network Configuration

# CHAPTER 7

# CHAPTER 7

# Network Configuration

As you install Microsoft Windows NT Server version 4, you'll have to address the initial setup and configuration of the network. After all, there's not much point to running Windows NT Server if there's no network. In this chapter, we'll discuss the choices you'll be asked to make during installation. For situations in which you might need additional information, we'll refer you to later chapters in this book that provide more in-depth coverage. For most situations, however, the material in this chapter will be sufficient for you to make appropriate decisions.

## Protocol Options

To start the discussion, let's look at your protocol options. During installation, the Setup program will ask you to choose one or more of the three core protocols included in Windows NT Server for communicating with other computers on your network or in your enterprise. The core network protocol options for Windows NT Server are these:

◆ **TCP/IP** A default protocol and the preferred protocol for connecting a Windows NT server to a network

◆ **IPX/SPX** Also a default protocol and the protocol used by Novell NetWare

◆ **NetBEUI** The protocol used by Microsoft Windows for Workgroups, Microsoft LanManager, and earlier versions of Microsoft Windows NT

In addition to the core protocol choices, you might, depending on your situation, also want or need to add one of the following protocols to your networking soup:

◆ **AppleTalk** A protocol that allows a Windows NT server to communicate with Macintosh computers

◆ **DLC (Data Link Control)** A protocol that allows a Windows NT server to communicate with IBM mainframes and Hewlett-Packard network printers

- **PPTP (Point-to-Point Tunneling Protocol)** A new Microsoft protocol that supports virtual private networks over the Internet

- **Streams Environment** An encapsulating layer derived from UNIX System V that's used primarily by developers porting other protocols to Windows NT

As you can see, Windows NT Server supports a wide range of networking protocols, which allows you to connect your server to a variety of networks. In addition, there are third-party network protocols available to meet communication or network needs that aren't met by the default choices. One example is the Network File System (NFS), which is used primarily by UNIX systems to share file systems and printers. There are several implementations of NFS available for Windows NT Server, if you need this functionality.

Given the choices available, which protocols should you install? And why? What do the protocols do? What are the significant advantages or disadvantages of each protocol? Well, let's take a look at the choices.

# TCP/IP

TCP/IP is a term that is tossed around a lot lately, primarily because it's the underlying protocol of the Internet. We'll go into quite a bit more detail about some of the new (new to Windows NT Server) features and options of TCP/IP later in Chapter 17. But for the moment, let's take a quick look at what TCP/IP is and why you would want to use it on your network.

TCP/IP stands for Transmission Control Protocol/Internet Protocol. "What's this?" you say. "Two protocols together?" Actually, TCP/IP is a whole suite of protocols that work together to accomplish the task of connecting your computers. In some ways, TCP/IP is very much like an office suite of applications programs. But instead of a word processor, spreadsheet, and presentation package, it has various protocols and applications. Each protocol and application is designed to do part of the job of connecting your computers to one another. Let's take a brief look at the major pieces of the TCP/IP pie.

## Internet Protocol (IP)

The Internet Protocol (IP) is the underlying protocol that provides packet delivery for the other members of the TCP/IP suite. It yields a "best-effort" attempt to deliver the packets to the correct machine. It provides for a checksum as part of the packet to ensure the integrity of the packet header, but it does not ensure the integrity of the data itself. It also does not provide any guarantee of correct delivery sequence or even that the packets will arrive at the intended destination—that's the responsibility of one of the suite members using the IP.

### Transmission Control Protocol (TCP)

The Transmission Control Protocol (TCP) is in many ways the primary protocol of the suite. It is a *connection-based* protocol. This means that when a packet is sent between machines, it goes specifically to the destination machine and its arrival, correct sequence, and content integrity are assured. If the receiving machine doesn't receive the packet or if it gets the packet out of order, TCP is smart enough to recognize this and request that the correct packet be re-sent; it does this without any intervention on the part of the user or any extra work by the programmer who writes the program.

Obviously, TCP makes the most sense as the default protocol for most of what you would do with TCP/IP. It's fast, dependable, and easy to work with from the programmer's point of view. Of course, programmers don't generally have to worry about the nitty-gritty details of the particular protocol they're using; that's the specialized job of those folks writing network-specific applications. Users don't really have to worry about it, either. But as a system administrator, it's important for you to understand, at least in a general sense, what's going on "under the hood."

So which of the standard TCP/IP suite of applications use TCP? Well, actually, most of them. The ftp (file transfer protocol) program, for example, uses the TCP protocol. The less commonly used application, tftp (trivial file transfer protocol), however, uses the User Datagram Protocol (UDP) instead. (This application is not included with the standard Microsoft TCP/IP suite.)

## User Datagram Protocol (UDP)

Like TCP, the User Datagram Protocol (UDP) is a basic network packet, but it's a *connection-less packet*. This means that when a program sends a UDP packet, the packet is sent to the entire network on the chance that it will get to where it's going and that it will get there in the correct sequence. It's faster than TCP because there's less overhead in terms of determining whether the packet actually arrived or when it arrived. But the onus is on the programmer of the application to make sure that the proper error checking and confirmation are done.

UDP is used for protocols such as BOOTP and DHCP, which do general broadcasts, hoping that someone will answer them. It's sort of like standing up in the middle of a theater and yelling, "Yo, Larry," on the chance that your brother might be there. You *might* get his attention if he's there; but you'll also get a lot of looks from everyone else, including a few other Larrys, and perhaps some complaints as well about the amount of noise you're making.

UDP also is used for protocols such as NFS, where the intent is not a general broadcast; the application's designers decide in this case to pay the extra programming costs of additional error checking and tracking in the application to take advantage of the extra speed and reduced overhead of UDP.

# IP Addresses

In addition to providing the underlying packet delivery for other protocols, IP is also the "street address" that TCP/IP uses to identify each machine on the Internet. The address is written in the form *w.x.y.z*, where each variable is a number from a range of values from 1 to 254. Two additional values in each range (0 and 255) are reserved for specific Internet addresses. For example, the IP address of the machine on which this book is being written is 205.158.231.34. The IP address number must be unique for each machine. You can't just arbitrarily pick an IP number unless you know, unequivocally and irrevocably, that the machine is never going to be connected to the Internet. If there's any possibility that the computer will *ever* be connected to the outside world, you must get an official IP address for it.

The problem is, of course, that official IP addresses are getting to be in short supply. When the numbering convention for the Internet was created in the late 1960s, the range of values seemed more than large enough to accommodate all of the computers that were ever likely to exist in the world. (Ah, don't you love those assumptions? Sort of like assuming that 640 KB would be *more* than enough for conventional memory.) Realistically, though, we can't fault the designers much. After all, the numbering convention provided a sufficient number of unique addresses to accommodate some 4 billion computers, give or take a few hundred million—which is an awful lot of computers, when viewed from the perspective of the 1960s. However, with the explosion of the Internet over the last several years, it's become clear that there needs to be a change in the addressing scheme. We'll touch on that subject in more depth in Chapter 17; so stay tuned.

## Address Resolution Protocol (ARP)

The Address Resolution Protocol (ARP) is used by TCP/IP to get from the machine IP address to the actual physical hardware address. Every network interface card (NIC) ever made has a unique, 48-bit number assigned to it by the manufacturer. This physical address is called a media access control (MAC) address. TCP/IP uses ARP request packets to get the physical address of each device on the network, and then it maps the physical location to the IP address. When a packet needs to be sent to a particular IP address, the packet is mapped to the MAC address of the device for actual delivery.

## Internet Control Message Protocol (ICMP)

The Internet Control Message Protocol (ICMP) is used primarily by the Ping utility. ICMP packets are encapsulated within IP packets; they allow two nodes on a network to share IP status and error information. This is used by Ping in the form of *echo request* and *echo reply* messages to determine whether a particular IP address is present on the network.

# IP Addressing

As we mentioned in the preceding section about the Internet Protocol, the IP address is the street address of the TCP/IP suite, which allows a protocol to find the right machine and deliver the mail (data packets) to it. But like all addressing schemes that have to deal with billions of addresses, the IP needs some help in limiting the number of actual machines it has to look for. And it has to have a way to know where to look for these machines. If IP didn't have either a way to limit the number of machines it had to look for or a road map to find the machines that weren't close by, finding the correct machine would be a hopeless task. And mail delivery would be way too slow to be useful.

The designers of TCP/IP, who were spending mostly tax dollars of United States taxpayers, actually put the money to good use. They created a system that not only makes it easy for a machine to find other machines located on the same or nearby "streets" but also makes it easy, if not quite as fast, for a machine to find other machines located across the world.

## How IP Addresses Are Assigned

The number (or range of numbers) for an IP address is assigned to you. If you're part of a large corporation, the corporation might have a central authority that controls IP addressing; in this case, you'll need to consult the person with this authority. If you're in a smaller company, where you're just putting in your first set of IP addresses, you'll need to get the addresses either from your Internet Service Provider (ISP), if you already have selected one, or directly from the Internet Network Information Center (InterNIC) at http://www.internic.net. Whatever the source, you'll have a range of addresses that you can use.

## Netmask

A *netmask* is the principal way that TCP/IP limits the number of possible addresses a machine has to deal with at any given time. As the name implies, a netmask is a way of masking or hiding portions of the network from other portions of the network. It's sort of like having a map that shows all of your city's streets but leaves out the streets from the rest of your state or province. The netmask for your address determines how much of the number that makes up the IP address will actually be seen by other machines as a "local" address. For this reason, it's important that all computers on one local portion of the network use the same netmask. If you're installing on an existing network, use the same netmask number as the other machines that are already on the network. If you don't already know the appropriate netmask for your network addresses, ask the ISP or InterNIC what the appropriate netmask number would be or jump ahead to Chapter 17 for details on how to determine the netmask number.

## Gateway

When your server needs to talk to a machine that is not in the same portion of the IP address range, it will have to use a *gateway* to get there. This gateway can be a *router*, or it can be another Windows NT machine that is operating as a router.

No gateway is needed when one computer is communicating with another computer in the same portion of the IP address range; the two computers simply pass their packets back and forth. But when a computer needs to communicate outside of its local range of IP addresses, it has to know how to find the other machine. A specialized device known as a router was developed to move a packet of data from one section of the network to another; it functions as a gateway between sections of the network. It will have at least two IP addresses, each for a different portion of the IP address range and each physically connected to a different segment of the network. The router grabs the data packet sent by one computer and shuffles it to the other side of the network, sending it on its way to the other computer. Now, your computer does not have to know how to find every other computer in the world. All it needs to know is the address of the gateway; the rest of the gory details are handled by the gateway.

## Fixed vs. Dynamic IP Addresses

In a world with a limited number of available IP addresses and an ever increasing demand for addresses, not everyone can have as many IP addresses as he or she might want. This means that you might have to consider using a shared pool of IP addresses, especially for intermittently connected machines, such as laptops. It is certainly easier and requires less administration to simply give every machine that might ever be connected to your network a fixed IP address, but that might not be either practical or feasible. It's for this reason that DHCP was devised.

Using DHCP, you can easily accommodate a group of laptops or remote users who are connected only occasionally to the network with a substantially smaller pool of IP addresses; the addresses are allocated only as needed and only for as long as needed. Before the advent of DHCP, this would have been an essentially impossible task; but with DHCP, you simply determine the most likely maximum number of devices that will be connected and allocate that number of IP addresses (plus a few extra, just in case, of course).

### Tip

*If you know that you already have enough IP addresses for all of the devices you're likely to connect to your network, you don't have to configure for DHCP. And we don't suggest it. But if you will have intermittently connected users but you are short of available IP addresses, using DHCP would make sense.*

There is another important advantage to using DHCP that might make it a good choice, even when you know you have more than enough IP addresses. All of the configuration and parameter settings for addresses are controlled at the DHCP servers. This makes it much easier for less experienced administrators to add new machines to the network. They don't really need to know a whole lot about TCP/IP because the decisions have already been made for them at the DHCP server.

**For More Information**

*For all of the details on setting up and maintaining Windows NT Server as a DHCP server, see Chapter 17.*

## Multiple IP Addresses

There are some situations in which your server will have more than one IP address. This will be the case if you have multiple network cards in the server, for example, and are using Windows NT Server as a router or gateway between two (or more) networks or subnets. If you need to do this, you should refer to the *Microsoft Windows NT Server Resource Kit*: *Windows NT Networking Guide* and suitable texts on TCP/IP and routing.

# Name Resolution

As we've seen, TCP/IP provides a mechanism for identifying every computer on your network—or, in fact, the entire Internet—with a unique number. That's great, but it's a lot easier on your users if they don't have to worry about knowing the IP address of each and every computer with which they need to communicate. Windows NT Server provides several mechanisms for mapping numbers to names. We'll look briefly at the various mechanisms used by Windows NT Server and how they interact. The goal is to provide a unique name and number for each and every computer on the network.

## NetBIOS

Microsoft Windows networking relies on a single-part naming convention known as NetBIOS. This was an adequate naming convention when networks were relatively simple and when few of the computers on a Windows-based network also were on the Internet. A single-part name becomes inadequate very quickly, however, when you have to deal with hundreds or thousands of computers, much less the millions of computers currently on the Internet. The single-part NetBIOS name therefore needed to map to something that would scale to handle millions or billions of computers if we were to have a solution. Because the Internet has to deal with those kinds of numbers, you'd expect to find a solution there; and sure enough, one exists. It's known as the Domain Name System.

*As we mentioned in Chapter 2, an Internet domain is not the same as a Windows networking domain, although some very similar terms are used for the two types of domains.*

## Domain Name System (DNS)

The Domain Name System (DNS) was adopted in 1984 as the naming convention on the Internet that would be used to map individual IP addresses to machine names. It was designed by Paul Mockapetris and was published originally in Request for Comments (RFC) 882 and RFC 883 (now replaced by RFC 1034 and 1035), where it is described as a hierarchical, distributed database of names that could be maintained by a series of name servers. This hierarchical or tree-shaped structure is unlike the essentially flat naming space of NetBIOS and can grow as required.

The first part of the DNS name is usually the NetBIOS name. (Although the NetBIOS name can be changed, don't do it. This stuff is confusing enough without making your life harder by adding more potential confusion.) For example, if the NetBIOS name of a machine is rci1, this is the name used on the local network to find the computer. But its DNS name would be rci1.scribes.com, the name by which it identifies itself to the outside world, including the Internet.

Although the DNS name for a particular computer might be rci1.scribes.com, this name is more properly referred to as the machine's *fully qualified domain name*. It would be a nuisance to have to type the complete DNS name each time we wanted to communicate with another computer within a local network; so even with DNS names we usually can refer to just the first part of the machine name, in this case rci1, when we communicate with other local machines. The rest of the name is actually the Internet domain name and is the same for all of the fully qualified domain names of computers on the local network.

The DNS hierarchical structure starts with the *root domain,* sometimes designated as a single dot ("."), as shown at the top of the inverted tree structure in Figure 7.1 on the following page. Below the root domain are the top-level domains, which now include the original seven top-level domains plus a whole bunch of domains that were added later to accommodate the various geographic regions. The original seven top-level domains were decidedly U.S.-centric, as you can see here:

◆ **com** Commercial organizations, such as Hewlett-Packard (hp.com) and Microsoft (microsoft.com)

◆ **edu** Educational organizations, such as the University of California at Berkeley (berkeley.edu) and Stanford University (stanford.edu)

◆ **gov** Government units, such as the Office of the President of the United States (whitehouse.gov)

- **mil** Military organizations, such as the United States Department of the Navy (navy.mil)

- **net** Networking organizations, such as the InterNIC (internic.net)

- **org** Noncommercial organizations, such as National Public Radio (npr.org)

- **int** International organizations, such as NATO (nato.int)

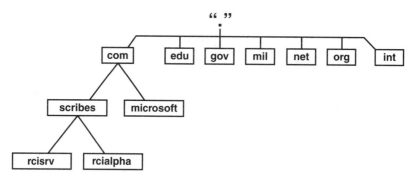

**FIGURE 7.1**

*Hierarchical name space of the Domain Name System*

The names for various geographical areas that were added to these top-level domains are in the format *uk* for Great Britain, *au* for Australia, and so forth.

The one problem with DNS is that it's essentially a static naming convention. One of its big strengths is that it is a distributed database; the downside is that any changes made to this database take a long time to get to all of the places where they need to go. When it was devised originally, there weren't portable laptop computers that moved around from place to place and, consequently, had to have different IP addresses depending on where they were plugged in. So something was needed to make the existing naming convention dynamic, in much the same way that DHCP made IP addressing dynamic to accommodate these mobile computers. Enter WINS, the Windows Internet Naming Service.

## Windows Internet Naming Service (WINS)

WINS was designed to provide a flexible name-to-number mapping system that would allow computers to communicate across router boundaries and would easily map NetBIOS names to IP addresses. When WINS is combined with DNS, it provides dynamic name resolution ability. If you will be using DHCP on your network, you'll probably find that it is a good idea to have at least one, and probably more than one, of your Windows NT servers running as a WINS server. If your network crosses router boundaries and if your primary protocol is TCP/IP, you will need a WINS server on both sides of the router unless you want to cope with the time, effort, and administrative overhead of manually maintaining and updating text files for the network.

**For More Information**

*Setting up a WINS server and the technical details of how WINS and DNS work together are covered in Chapter 17.*

## HOSTS and LMHOSTS Files

If you have a small Windows NT Server network, if you don't expect your network to grow very quickly, and if you don't plan on connecting to the Internet anytime soon, you can bypass all the fun and games of setting up DNS and WINS servers and set up the IP address to NetBIOS name mapping with a couple of text files. These files are known as the HOSTS file and the LMHOSTS file, and they are located in the %SYSTEMROOT%\SYSTEM32\DRIVERS\ETC folder. Sample versions of these files are installed there when you install Windows NT Server. These text files allow you to enter the name and corresponding IP address for each computer on your network and for any other machines with which you connect regularly, although you'll have to edit the files manually. If you have a fairly static network and if it isn't a terribly big network, you can probably get away with editing these files manually. How big is too big? Well, it varies according to your personal tolerance level for manually maintaining these things; but if your network has more than a dozen or so computers, you'll probably find it annoying to have to update files manually every time something on the network is changed.

## DHCP and BOOTP Forwarding

We've talked about DHCP already, but what's *BOOTP*? BOOTP is short for Bootstrap Protocol. It's a well-established and still quite popular way of allowing relatively unintelligent devices to boot off your TCP/IP network. A device doesn't need any more built-in intelligence than to know its own hardware address and how to send a simple UDP broadcast message to the network. All of the computers on the network can receive the message; if a computer both supports BOOTP *and* has information about the device, it will answer by downloading the necessary code to the requesting device, which allows the device to wake up and do its thing.

When a device uses BOOTP, it must download from the answering server almost everything that it might need to perform its function on the network, including its IP address, the TCP/IP parameters it will be using (such as netmask, gateway, and so forth), and all of the binary code necessary to perform its function. Examples of typical BOOTP devices are graphical X-terminals and printers.

Unfortunately, BOOTP still is not supported directly by Windows NT Server; but at least Windows NT Server will forward BOOTP requests when you are using your Windows NT server as a router. This allows another server further along the network, such as a UNIX box, to answer the request. There are also third-party and freeware versions of BOOTP servers available for Windows NT Server.

DHCP requests also can be forwarded by Windows NT Server when it's acting as a router, in much the same way as are BOOTP requests. So if you're setting up DHCP on your network, you don't necessarily have to have a DHCP server on every segment of the network. However, if you have more than just a few DHCP devices, we'd recommend you have a DHCP server on each network segment to keep network traffic and loading down.

# IPX/SPX

IPX/SPX, more properly known on Windows NT Server as the NWLink IPX/SPX Compatible Transport, is the native protocol of NetWare networks. If your network must interact with a NetWare network, you'll need to install the NetWare-compatible IPX/SPX protocol when you install Windows NT Server. In addition, you can have your Windows NT server act as a gateway to the NetWare network, providing access to and support of NetWare servers to your Windows networking clients without the requirement that NetWare client software be loaded on the client machines.

**For More Information**

*For additional information about setting up a Windows NT server as a NetWare gateway, see Chapter 20.*

You should add IPX/SPX to your Windows NT Server protocols whenever you know you'll need to provide connectivity to an existing, legacy NetWare network. You'll also need to include gateway (and client) services for NetWare in order to provide NetWare client services on your Windows NT server, even if you don't expect to use the server as a gateway.

It might also make sense to choose IPX/SPX for your Windows NT server when you have a substantial number of Windows 95 clients and don't have any particular need or desire to install TCP/IP. This is probably the simplest way to get these clients up and connected because Windows 95 clients install the IPX/SPX protocol stack by default. However, we believe that in the long run the slightly extra overhead of setting up and configuring TCP/IP in addition to IPX/SPX will pay substantial benefits. The future of networking, at least in the near term, is definitely in the direction of TCP/IP. And if you also install DHCP, setting up client machines results in much less grief and overhead.

## Configuring IPX/SPX

There's really nothing to setting up IPX/SPX in most cases. You can almost always just accept the default settings, which results in automatic frame detection and network number configuration. If you need to use your Windows NT server as an IPX/SPX router or if you will be installing File and Print Services for NetWare, you might have to make adjustments to the default settings. See Chapter 20 for details.

## Routing

IPX/SPX is a routable protocol, which allows you to divide up your network into logical segments. Your Windows NT server can act as an IPX/SPX router and can forward routing information packets to other routers on the network. For more information on setting up, configuring, and maintaining routing IPX/SPX in a Windows NT Server environment, see the *Microsoft Windows NT Server Resource Kit version 4.0: Windows NT Networking Guide*.

# NetBEUI

NetBEUI is short for NetBIOS Extended User Interface protocol. That doesn't tell you a whole lot, does it? NetBEUI was the preferred Microsoft networking protocol for many years, and it works well in small workgroup or departmental networks. It's easy to set up and configure and fairly fast for small tasks. But it doesn't scale well to a larger enterprise network. It is limited to 254 sessions (connections to other computers) for each process. This is an improvement over previous versions, which had a limit of 254 sessions for all processes. More important is the fact that NetBEUI cannot be routed from one network segment to another. This makes it unsuitable for large networking environments in which routers are used to connect the various segments of the network.

You should choose NetBEUI only when you need to maintain connectivity to existing legacy networks that require the use of this protocol. Some examples of NetBEUI-based networks include Microsoft LanManager 2.*x*, IBM's OS/2 Lan Server, and Windows for Workgroups 3.*x* networks.

## Configuring NetBEUI

There isn't much to configure with NetBEUI; but if some of the parameters need fine-tuning, you'll have to go into the registry with your favorite registry editor and muck around on your own. The registry entries that can be changed are under HKEY_LOCAL_MACHINE\SYSTEM\CurrentControlSet\Services\Nbf. Refer to the *Microsoft Windows NT Server Resource Kit: Windows NT Networking Guide* for details about the various entries. Rather than retaining the NetBEUI protocol, we really believe that you should think about how to move the existing NetBEUI-based clients to TCP/IP. You might be able to change the legacy system to support TCP/IP, even with these clients.

## Changing NetBEUI Clients to TCP/IP

In many cases, you can change your existing NetBEUI clients from NetBEUI to TCP/IP by adding a TCP/IP stack to them. The clients that can be changed most easily to TCP/IP are your existing Windows for Workgroups 3.11 clients. You can download a 32-bit Microsoft TCP/IP stack for Windows for Workgroups 3.11 from Microsoft's Ftp server at:

```
ftp.microsoft.com/peropsys/windows/public/tcpip
```

If you add this stack to existing Windows for Workgroups clients that can't be changed to Microsoft Windows 95 or Windows NT Workstation version 4, you will have one less set of NetBEUI clients to worry about. In addition, most LanManager servers can be configured to use TCP/IP as their protocol, although it probably makes more sense to move these LanManager servers to Windows NT Server or the appropriate versions of Advanced Server for UNIX.

# Remote Access

One of the things that Windows NT Server does really well is set itself up as a remote access server. You don't need to know very much at all about modems or about any of the other ugly details that you'd expect to have to know about in order to set up remote access service (RAS) on Windows NT Server. You can do the setup either when you install Windows NT Server or at any time thereafter.

## Initial Configuration

To configure RAS, you'll have to have the Windows NT Server CD-ROM available, but that's hardly a surprise. The Windows NT Server Setup program takes you through all of the steps for setting up RAS for incoming or outgoing connections. We'll start from the Network dialog box shown in Figure 7.2, which lets you add or configure the various services and protocols on your Windows NT server. You'll see this dialog box during the installation process; you also can get to it anytime after you have installed Windows NT Server by double-clicking the Network icon in Control Panel or by right-clicking the Network Neighborhood icon on your desktop and choosing Properties.

However you get to the Network dialog box, click the Services tab. Then click Add to bring up the Select Network Service dialog box shown in Figure 7.3. Select Remote Access Service, and click OK. You'll be prompted to insert the original Windows NT Server CD-ROM in the drive.

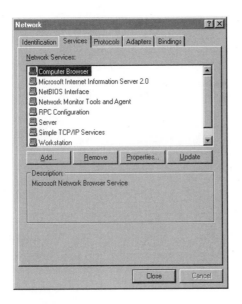

**FIGURE 7.2**

*The Network dialog box Services tab*

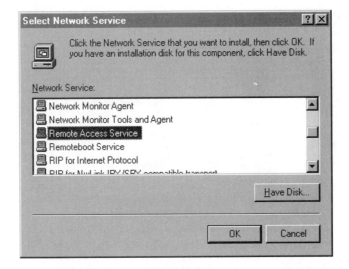

**FIGURE 7.3**

*Select Network Service dialog box*

If you haven't yet installed a modem or other remote access hardware device, you'll get prompted to do so before you go any further, as shown in Figure 7.4. You must install a remote access–capable device before you can use remote access services.

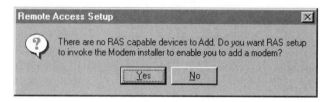

**FIGURE 7.4**

*Remote Access Setup dialog box*

Click Yes, and the Install New Modem wizard (shown in Figure 7.5) will walk you through the steps for adding a modem to your system. You can choose to add your modem manually or to let Windows NT Server try to find it for you. Generally we think it's a good idea to let Windows NT Server first do its best to find the modem. If Windows NT Server gets it right, and it usually does, you're pretty much assured that there are no problems. If you have to add the modem manually, you certainly can do so; but save this option for the times when it's really necessary.

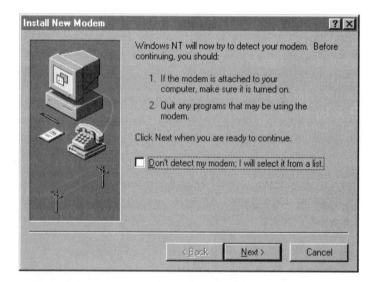

**FIGURE 7.5**

*Install New Modem wizard dialog box*

If Windows NT Server locates your modem, you're all set. But if it doesn't find your modem or if it finds the wrong one, you still have a chance to correct it manually before you proceed. When Windows NT Server's best guess with respect to the identity of your modem doesn't match the modem you actually have, click Change (Figure 7.6) and select the closest approximation to the modem you have from the list that appears. If all else fails, select one of the generic types of modems.

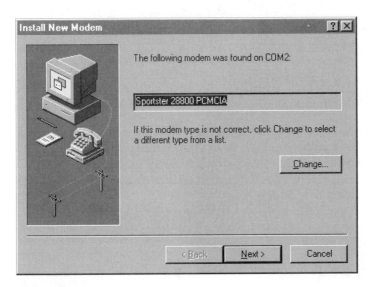

**FIGURE 7.6**

*Install New Modem dialog box showing "found modem" message*

After you have installed the modem, you have to tie it to RAS by adding it as a RAS device. You might be prompted once again to insert the original Windows NT Server CD-ROM into the drive, but after Setup has installed all of the necessary files, the message will disappear and the dialog box shown in Figure 7.7 on the following page will appear. From here, you can add a second modem or an X.25 pad by clicking the appropriate button; or you can proceed directly to add the modem you've already chosen to your RAS configuration.

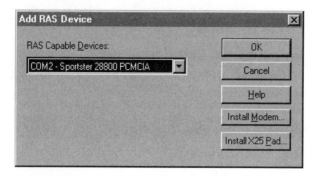

**FIGURE 7.7**

*Add RAS Device dialog box showing the selected device*

Click OK. You'll see the Remote Access Setup dialog box shown in Figure 7.8. You finally get to actually configure RAS. From this dialog box, you can also click Add if you want to add another remote access–capable device, click Remove if you want to remove a device, or click Clone if you want to duplicate an existing entry as a way of adding a new device.

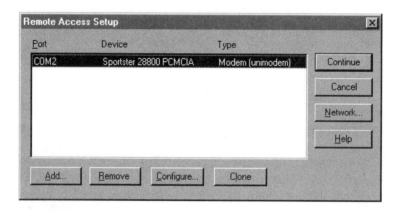

**FIGURE 7.8**

*Example of a Remote Access Setup dialog box*

Click Configure to bring up the Configure Port Usage dialog box, which is shown in Figure 7.9. You'll have to configure your new RAS port for either incoming or outgoing calls or for both. The Windows NT Server default setting is to receive calls only; but if you have remote sites that are running Windows NT Server locally, you'll want to change the setting to support outgoing calls as well.

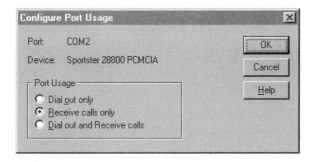

**FIGURE 7.9**

*Configure Port Usage dialog box showing default setting*

After you've configured the RAS port, you'll have to decide which networking options you want to support. Click Network to bring up the Network Configuration dialog box shown in Figure 7.10. Depending on whether you chose incoming calls only or incoming and outgoing calls, you will see different sets of options enabled. You can decide what protocols your RAS server will use, as well as determine what level of encryption the connection will require.

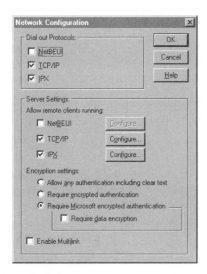

**FIGURE 7.10**

*Network Configuration dialog box for RAS*

If you selected dial-out capability for the port, you can now select the protocols that will be used. If your purpose is to connect only to the Internet or other TCP/IP network, you need choose only TCP/IP. But if you will be connecting to NetWare networks as well, select the IPX option also.

You'll also have to decide what clients you are going to accept on your network and how much access to the network they will be allowed to have. You can configure these things protocol by protocol, if you want, so that you could, for example, allow IPX clients to see any machine on the network but limit TCP/IP clients to the server.

## Configuring RAS for IPX

If you're going to allow your remote access clients to log on using the IPX protocol, click the IPX check box. Then click the IPX Configure button to bring up the RAS Server IPX Configuration dialog box (Figure 7.11), where you can configure several important options for your remote IPX clients, the most important one being the level of access these clients will have to the network.

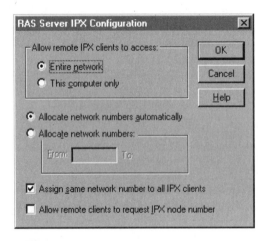

**FIGURE 7.11**

*RAS Server IPX Configuration dialog box*

You can choose to limit remote computers using IPX by restricting their access to only the server, thus locking them out of the rest of the network; or you can allow these remote computers to access the entire network. You cannot, however, limit access to specific machines on the network. It's an all-or-nothing option, unfortunately.

You also can manually assign network numbers from this dialog box. You can assign all remote IPX clients the same network number or you can assign them a range of network numbers. And you can decide whether you want to allow IPX clients to request a specific network node number or you want to assign client network node numbers without regard to the client's preference.

# Configuring RAS for TCP/IP

If you're going to allow your remote access clients to log on using the TCP/IP protocol, click the TCP/IP check box in the Network Configuration dialog box. Then click the TCP/IP Configure button to bring up the RAS Server TCP/IP Configuration dialog box (Figure 7.12), where you can configure the options for your remote TCP/IP clients, including how they'll be assigned an IP address and what level of access they'll have to the network.

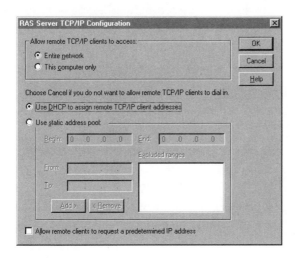

**FIGURE 7.12**

*RAS Server TCP/IP Configuration dialog box*

You can limit remote computers using TCP/IP to have access only to the server and not to the rest of the network, or you can allow them access to the entire network. Like the IPX configuration, however, this is an all-or-nothing proposition. You can't limit access to specific machines on the network.

You'll also have to decide whether your remote clients will be using DHCP or will have preassigned (and, therefore, fixed) IP addresses. Obviously, this is an ideal situation for using DHCP. But even if you're not running a DHCP server and if you don't really want to set one up, you can assign a pool of TCP/IP addresses for the use of remote clients. RAS will assign addresses from that pool.

If you have clients that cannot yet support a dynamic IP address, click the check box at the bottom of the window, which will allow the TCP/IP client to ask for its own address. This should be sufficient for older clients that are fussy, although we think you'll want to upgrade these clients as soon as it's convenient to do so to reduce the nuisance of dealing with a fixed remote user IP address.

After you've made all your choices, click OK; you'll be returned to the main Remote Access Setup dialog box. Click Continue to complete the installation of remote access services on your server.

If you've selected IPX as one of your protocols, you might see an informational message about enabling NetBIOS Broadcast Propagation. Leave it disabled unless one of your clients is using NwLink IPX to connect to the server; if this is the case, you'll have to enable the option in order to let the client connect properly.

After you've completed the installation of your remote access services, you'll have to go to either the User Manager application or the Remote Access Admin application to assign specific rights to specific users. For more on assigning dial-in rights to users, see Chapters 9 and 18.

## POINTS TO REMEMBER

◆ The default network protocol for Windows NT Server is now TCP/IP.

◆ Use DHCP to simplify later client configuration changes.

◆ Install IPX/SPX if you're going to coexist with a NetWare network.

◆ Install remote access services to enable either dial-in or dial-out capability on the server.

## WHAT'S NEXT?

In this chapter, we covered the basics of setting up your network's communication protocols. Now that your computers can exchange data, we will move on in Chapter 8 to discuss how you make sure the data stays safe and is protected against hardware failure.

# CHAPTER 8

# CHAPTER 8

# Disk Configuration

What does a server really *do* on a network? Probably the single most important service to users is storing files and then making them available on demand. File services are *the* area that will get you, the system administrator, into the most hot water if there is a failure. It's your job to make sure these conditions are met for your network:

◆  There is sufficient hard drive space available.

◆  All of the files are backed up.

◆  Procedures are in place to recover files in the event of a system failure.

◆  Security procedures are sufficient to prevent unauthorized access to files but don't create hardship for normal users.

All of these are important parts of providing quality file services; and, if you've done your job correctly, they'll go completely unnoticed, barring some natural disaster. (If you're looking for glory, you're probably in the wrong job.)

In this chapter, we'll discuss configuring your storage subsystem using the built-in Disk Administrator application of Microsoft Windows NT Server version 4. With Disk Administrator, you can easily manage your disk storage to provide a flexible, fast, and dependable file system for your users.

## Disk Administrator

Disk Administrator (shown in Figure 8.1) is your tool for managing the hard disk subsystem, which includes any removable hard drives, such as Bernoulli, ZIP, and Syquest drives. You can use it to create, modify, or remove partitions; to format drives; to assign hard drive letters to specific volumes; and to create fault tolerant arrays of hard drives that will protect you from drive failure. If your Disk Administrator screen doesn't look like the one in Figure 8.1, it's probably just showing a different view. Choose Disk Configuration from the View menu to switch to the Disk Configuration view.

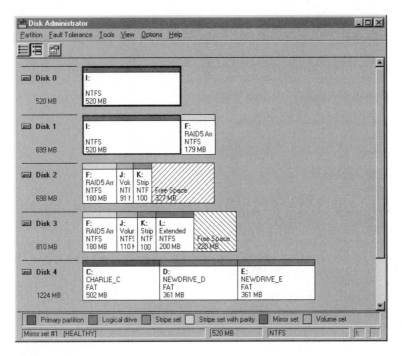

**FIGURE 8.1**

*Disk Administrator window showing disk configurations*

Any time you're in Disk Administrator, you can point at a portion of the disk with the mouse cursor and right-click to open a menu. When you right-click in an existing partition, you'll see this menu:

When you right-click on an area of free space, you'll see this menu:

Both menus provide shortcuts to many of the functions described later in this chapter.

# Terminology

Before we go into the details of using Disk Administrator, let's review the terms we'll be using in this discussion to make sure that we're all using the same words to mean the same things.

- **Physical drive** The actual hard drive itself, including case, electronics, platters, and all that stuff. Not terribly important to Disk Administrator.

- **Partition** A portion of the hard drive that acts as a single unit. In many cases, this might well be the entire hard drive space, but it needn't be.

- **Primary partition** A portion of the hard drive that's been marked as a potentially bootable unit by an operating system. MS-DOS is able to support only a single primary partition, but Windows NT Server can support multiple primary partitions. There can be only four primary partitions on any hard drive.

- **Extended partition** A nonbootable portion of the hard drive that can be subdivided into logical drives. There can be only one extended partition per hard drive, but this partition can be subdivided into several logical drives.

- **Logical drives** A section or partition of a hard drive that acts as a single unit. For example, an extended partition might be divided into several logical drives.

- **Volume set** Portions of unused hard drive space that are collected into a single unit and formatted like a single drive. A volume set can have a drive letter assigned to it, but it actually spans several physical drives. It doesn't provide any fault tolerance—it actually increases your risk of failure—but it does permit you to make more efficient use of the available hard drive space.

- **RAID (Redundant Array of Inexpensive Disks)** The use of multiple hard drives in an array to provide for larger volume size, fault tolerance, and increased performance. RAID comes in different levels, such as RAID 0, RAID 1, RAID 5, and so forth. Higher numbers don't indicate greater performance or fault tolerance, just different methods of doing the job.

- **Stripe set** Like a volume set, but uses special formatting to write to each of the portions equally in a stripe to provide for increased throughput. It also doesn't provide any fault tolerance and actually increases your risk of failure. A stripe set is often referred to as RAID 0, but this is a misnomer because plain striping includes no redundancy.

- **Stripe set with parity** Like a regular stripe set, but writes parity information for each stripe onto a separate portion of a disk, which provides the ability to recover files in the event one drive fails. This method is called RAID 5.

- **Mirror set** A pair of hard drive partitions that contain exactly the same data and appear to the world as a single entity. Disk mirroring can use two drives on the same hard drive controller, or it can use separate controllers, in which case it is sometimes referred to as *duplexing*. In the event either hard drive fails, the second hard drive can be split from the failed drive and continue to provide complete access to the data stored on the drive, which provides a high degree of fault tolerance. This technique is called RAID 1.

- **SLED (Single Large Expensive Disk)** A strategy for maximizing hard drive performance that is used less often than RAID and is, in fact, the opposite of RAID. Rather than using several cheap hard drives and using redundancy to provide for fault tolerance, you buy the best hard drive you can afford and bet your entire network on it. If this doesn't sound like a good idea, you're right. It's not.

# Partitions

A physical hard drive can be divided into as many as four partitions, of which one can be an extended partition. However, if you attempt to use Disk Administrator to create more than a single primary partition, you'll get a warning like the one in Figure 8.2 on the following page, which tells you that what you're about to do isn't supported by MS-DOS. This is pretty much irrelevant information because you're not likely to be running MS-DOS very much on your server. If you're following our advice and using NTFS for all but your first rather small partition, you wouldn't be able to see the NTFS partitions from MS-DOS anyway. This is just as it should be—if only for security reasons.

**NOTE**

*All of the advanced capabilities of Disk Administrator, such as creating stripe, mirror, and volume sets, are unsupported by other operating systems, such as MS-DOS and Microsoft Windows 95. If your server needs to be booted into one of these operating systems for some reason, any drive that uses one of these advanced features will be invisible to the operating system. Personally, we think this is a definite plus; it certainly shouldn't be a reason for not using the Disk Administrator tools on a server. A Microsoft Windows NT Workstation can only take advantage of volume sets and simple striping. But if the server is set up to dual boot, you might need to consider the consequences of using Disk Administrator to create stripe, mirror, and volume sets.*

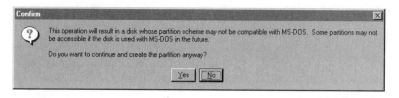

**FIGURE 8.2**

*Multiple partitions warning message*

You can create a second partition on a hard drive, however, that would be supported and accessible from MS-DOS (or Windows 95, or whatever) by using Disk Administrator to create a single primary partition (which would need to be a FAT partition so that other operating systems could see it) and then creating an extended partition. The extended partition will have multiple drive letters associated with it if you assign logical drive letters in the extended partition. Disk 4 in Figure 8.1 on page 119 shows an example of this, where C:, D:, and E: are the assigned drive letters and drives D: and E: are the logical drive letters in the extended partition.

An extended partition allows you to divide a drive into multiple drive letters for logical grouping. This can be useful for organizing your available drive space into different functions; but in the long run the more drive letters you have, the more administrative time and effort is required. This additional time and effort should be weighed against the problems inherent in having a single, humongous drive with everything on it—the primary one being the difficulty of finding anything on it. Your individual situation will dictate the best balance. We generally have found the best combination to be a small FAT partition as the boot partition, on which you have stored some basic utilities and your hardware configuration programs, a mirrored NTFS partition with the main Windows NT Server directory, and a pair of stripe sets with parity for applications programs and user file space.

## Primary Partitions

To create a primary partition with Disk Administrator, follow these steps:

1. Click on the free space that will contain the partition, and choose Create from the Partition menu. This will bring up the Create Primary Partition dialog box, as shown in Figure 8.3.

2. After you have created the primary partition, Disk Administrator will assign a drive letter to it immediately. Your Disk Administrator window now will look like the one in Figure 8.4.

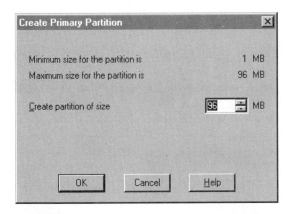

**FIGURE 8.3**

*Dialog box for creating a primary disk partition*

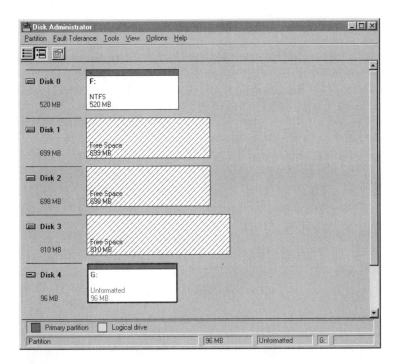

**FIGURE 8.4**

*Disk Administrator window showing the drive letter (G) for a new partition*

This new drive letter, however, doesn't really mean anything or exist until you've actually committed to the change you just made. You can't, for example, format the new partition. Disk Administrator won't let you.

3. Choose Commit Changes Now from the Partition menu. Disk Administrator will give you one last chance to back out before it makes the new partition permanent, as shown in Figure 8.5.

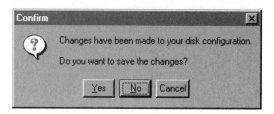

**FIGURE 8.5**

*Confirmation request for changes to disk configuration*

When you've completed step 3, you'll get an acknowledgment and some sage advice from the program, as shown in Figure 8.6. Disk Administrator will suggest that you update your Emergency Repair Disk with the new partition information. As we'll see later in Chapter 25, this is very good advice because it will make it easier to recover information in the event of a catastrophic system failure.

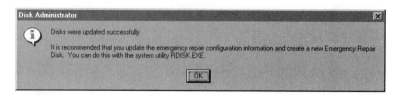

**FIGURE 8.6**

*Emergency Repair Disk update message*

4. Now choose Format from the Tools menu. The dialog box shown in Figure 8.7 will appear. Choose a volume label for the new drive, and choose either the FAT or NTFS format. The default is NTFS, so you can simply type in a label if you want to do so and then click OK. You'll get one last-minute warning that any data on the volume will be overwritten (which isn't hard to figure out).

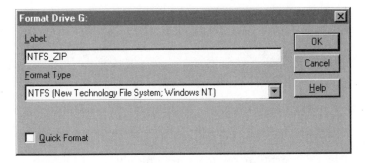

**FIGURE 8.7**

*Dialog box for formatting a disk partition*

5. Click OK again, and the formatting will begin. Disk Administrator shows your progress while formatting a partition, as shown in Figure 8.8.

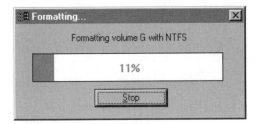

**FIGURE 8.8**

*Format progress message*

6. When the formatting is complete, you'll get a message telling you how many bytes of disk space the formatted partition actually contains, as shown in Figure 8.9. If there were any errors, they too will be seen in the message box.

**FIGURE 8.9**

*Partition format confirmation message*

## Extended Partitions

A single extended partition can be created on the hard drive and can range in size from 1 MB to all of the contiguous free space that is available on the drive. If you do create an extended partition, the maximum number of primary partitions you can create on the drive is reduced from four to three.

The steps you take to create an extended partition are much like the ones used to create a primary partition.

1. Open Disk Administrator; click on the free space that will contain the partition.

2. Choose Create Extended from the Partition menu.

3. A dialog box will open. Select the size of the partition you want (you don't have to use all of the available free space), and click OK.

## Logical Drives

Once you've created an extended partition, you have the option of creating one or more logical drives.

1. Click in the extended partition to select it; then choose Create from the Partition menu.

2. Type the size of the logical drive you want to create in the Create Logical Drive dialog box.

3. Click OK, and the drive is set up.

When you exit Disk Administrator, you'll be asked whether you want to save the changes you've made to your disk configuration. This is your last chance to backtrack. Click No, and the changes you've made will be erased. Click Yes, and the system will shut down and restart, with the changes you've made incorporated on the disk.

# RAID

RAID is a term you'll be hearing a lot in the future. As recently as five years ago, RAID was basically an unheard-of concept. Until recently, most server systems have relied on expensive, high-quality hard disks that were backed up frequently. Backups are still crucial, but now you can use a form of RAID to provide substantial protection from hard drive failure—and for a lot less money than what the big server drives cost.

RAID can be implemented at a software or hardware level. If RAID is implemented at the hardware level, it is the responsibility of the hardware vendor to provide an interface that administers the arrays and drivers that support the various operating systems under which the hardware will be used. There certainly are advantages to using a hardware RAID solution, although it's not an inexpensive solution.

Windows NT Server includes a perfectly reasonable software RAID solution in the Disk Administrator, which includes a fully functional software implementation of RAID levels 0, 1, and 5. These are not all of the possible RAID solutions, by any means, but they certainly are sufficient for most purposes.

There are, however, some limitations you'll need to keep in mind when using Disk Administrator to implement RAID.

◆ Because Disk Administrator RAID is a software feature, it will generate overhead expense. For a simple stripe (RAID 0) or mirror (RAID 1), the overhead expense is fairly minimal because there isn't much calculating that needs to be done. For a stripe set with parity (RAID 5), each write requires the CPU to calculate parity information. It's not a huge overhead expense, but it's one you need to know exists. In a hardware RAID system, this processing would be off-loaded to the controller.

◆ You won't be able to replace a failed drive without powering down the system. Disk Administrator doesn't support hot swapping or even online "hot spares" that can be instantly substituted for a failed drive. This is a fairly serious limitation. The reason for having any sort of RAID solution is to provide maximum uptime and availability of the system. If you have to bring the system down to replace a failed drive, it's at best an inconvenience. In an environment where the system is expected to be up and available 24 hours a day, 7 days a week, this kind of downtime would be unacceptable. If your organization requires 24-hour availability, you definitely should consider a hardware rather than software RAID system.

◆ In these days of inexpensive, removable drives, such as Syquest's EZ-Drive and Iomega's Jaz, ZIP, and Bernoulli drives, it would make sense if removable drives were supported for more than a single, primary partition by Disk Administrator, but they're not. Disk Administrator only supports primary partitions on removable disks. If you try to give a removable drive even a simple extended partition, much less include it as part of a stripe or volume set, you'll see an error message like the one shown in Figure 8.10.

**FIGURE 8.10**

*Disk error message for removable media*

## ◆ Hardware RAID

Hardware RAID solutions are available from a number of vendors. They range from simple RAID controllers to fully integrated, stand-alone subsystems. Their features vary, as does their cost, but all claim to provide superior performance and reliability compared with a simple software RAID solution, such as the one included in Disk Administrator. And, in general, they do. Some of the advantages that hardware RAID solutions offer include the following:

◆ Hot swap and hot spare drives, which allow virtually instantaneous replacement of failed drives

◆ Integrated disk caching, which provides improved disk performance

◆ Improved performance, with all processing handled by a separate, dedicated processor

◆ Increased flexibility and additional levels of RAID

Not all hardware RAID systems provide all of these features, but any of them can improve the overall reliability and performance of your hard drive subsystem. You should definitely consider using them with any mission-critical server on your network.

# Volume Sets

Most server disk management programs will allow you to create volume sets, even though they are not a RAID tool. A volume set takes all of the unused space on one or more drives (up to 32 drives per volume set) and combines it into a single, large entity that is recognized by the system as a drive. Volume sets were more necessary in the past, when you wanted to be able to use every last scrap of expensive and scarce hard drive space. As hard drives have gotten larger and cheaper, the need for volume sets has declined. Nevertheless, if you have some older, smaller hard drives hanging around that don't really provide enough space on their own to be useful, you can create a volume set out of them easily.

## Creating a Volume Set

To create a new volume set, follow these steps:

1. Open Disk Administrator; click on the first area of free space that you want to include in the volume set. Hold down the Ctrl key, and click on the other areas of free space you want to include in the set.

2. When you have all the pieces selected, choose Create Volume Set from the Partition menu. The dialog box shown in Figure 8.11 will appear. You can use the maximum size shown or enter some smaller size. Click OK.

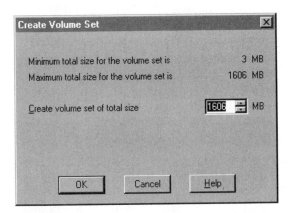

**FIGURE 8.11**

*Dialog box for creating a volume set*

3. Disk Administrator will highlight in bright yellow the areas on the various drives that make up the volume set. Choose Commit Changes Now from the Partition menu, which will bring up the confirmation dialog box shown in Figure 8.5 on page 124.

**4.** To accept the changes, click OK. You can't format the volume set until you commit the change to your configuration.

## WARNING!

*When you select OK in the confirmation box for creating a volume set, Disk Adminis-trator might warn you that this change requires a reboot of your system. Click Yes; Windows NT Server starts the shutdown procedure. You'll want to be very sure you're really in a position to shut down your server before you click Yes.*

**5.** After you've restarted Windows NT Server (if that was required), you still have one task left before you can use the new volume set. The new volume set must be formatted before it can be used. Start Disk Admin-istrator again. Click the volume set you've just created; it will be high-lighted in yellow (unless you've changed the default colors for Disk Administrator, of course) and will display either "Unknown" or "Unformatted" as the format type, as shown by drive L: in Figure 8.12.

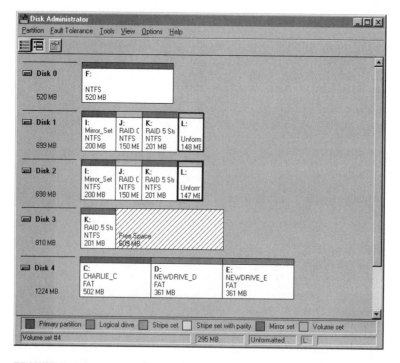

**FIGURE 8.12**

*Disk Administrator window showing new volume set prior to formatting*

Choose Format from the Tools menu. Add a label if you want. You also can format the volume set as a FAT partition, but it makes no sense to do this unless you're not using NTFS at all. You won't have access to the partition from MS-DOS or Windows 95 anyway. After you confirm that you really want to format the volume set, Disk Administrator will format the set. It will also assign the next available drive letter to the set, which is fine for most situations. But there might be a time when you need to use a specific drive letter for the set. In this case, simply choose Drive Letter from the Tools menu and change the default drive letter that has been assigned by Disk Administrator.

Once you've formatted the volume set, it will be available to use immediately. To your applications, the volume set appears as just another drive letter, no different from any other. And it is treated exactly the same as any other drive for sharing to the network.

## CAUTION

*If any drive of a volume set fails, the entire volume set becomes unavailable. So instead of being more reliable than a standard drive, a volume set is actually less reliable because the entire volume set is toast if any portion of it fails.*

## Extending a Volume Set

One of the most important benefits of volume sets is that they allow you to provide additional drive space to your users quickly, without having to worry about changes to drive letter assignments or about having to delete the original set first and losing the data that was on it. After you've created a volume set, you can extend it easily to add additional drives or portions of drives. You simply add the additional disk and then extend the volume set to include the new disk.

The process of extending a volume set takes one or two reboots of the system, however, so plan accordingly. The first time you reboot you'll need to shut the system down to physically add the new drive, unless you're merely using more of the free space from existing drives, in which case, you'll be spared the necessity of shutting down the system at this time. A reboot will be required, however, later in the process.

To extend (add to) an existing volume set, follow these steps:

1. Open Disk Administrator; click in the volume set that is to be expanded.

2. Hold down the Ctrl key, and click on each area of free space that you want to add to the volume set. A black border appears around the selected areas.

**3.** Right-click on one of the selected areas of free space; choose Extend Volume Set from the pop-up menu. (See Figure 8.13.) The Extend Volume Set command is also available on the Partition menu.

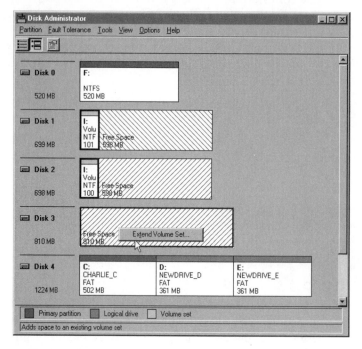

**FIGURE 8.13**

*Disk Administrator window showing the Extend Volume Set pop-up menu*

**4.** A dialog box will appear. The box shows the minimum amount of space (the current volume set plus 1 MB) and the maximum amount of space (the current volume set plus *all* of the available free space you've selected) that you can choose. Type in the *total* amount of space you want the volume set to contain. Click OK.

**5.** Right-click in the new volume set; choose Commit Changes Now from the pop-up menu shown below.

*You can also use the pop-up menu to assign a drive letter other than the default letter to a volume set.*

6. Provide all of the information requested in the various dialog boxes, and reboot the server.

This reboot will take a bit longer than usual. The new piece of the volume set needs to be formatted, which can take a while. Because this is all done before the logon prompt, it can be a bit unnerving. But don't worry, Windows NT Server will format the additional piece automatically and append it to the existing volume set without disturbing the existing data.

**CAUTION**

*Even though Disk Administrator should be able to extend a volume set without losing any data on the existing set, make sure you have at least one verified backup (preferably two) before doing any disk reconfiguration. Never forget Murphy's Law!*

Although you can make a volume set larger without having to delete it first, you can't make it smaller without the drastic action of completely deleting and then recreating the set, which means losing any data that might have been in it.

## Deleting a Volume Set

To delete an existing volume set, click in any portion of the set; choose Delete from the Partition menu. This will bring up the dialog box shown in Figure 8.14, which warns you that all data in the volume set will be lost.

**FIGURE 8.14**

*Confirmation message for deleting a volume set*

Click Yes, and the volume set will be deleted. But you'll still be asked whether you want to commit the changes before this action becomes final.

# Stripe Sets

A stripe set (RAID 0) is another way of taking unused space on various smaller disks or portions of disks and combining the sections of unused space to create a single, large entity that is recognized by the system as a drive. But combining the space is accomplished in a way that results in some additional and substantial benefit: it provides a high-performance volume. The new volume is not fault tolerant, however, which is a significant limitation.

A volume set simply appends one or more pieces of unused drive space onto another piece of unused drive space to create a single, larger piece of drive space. This means that the individual pieces can be any size, which is a handy virtue. A stripe set, on the other hand, provides a way of substantially improving the speed of access to your hard drive space. A stripe set takes two or more pieces of unused disk space on different physical drives and treats them as a single entity. But in addition, it now writes the data across the disks in sequence. This arrangement improves the speed of access to the disk space. When you save a file, for example, the first block of the file is written to the first available block on the first disk of the stripe set; the next block of the file is written to the next available disk of the stripe set, and so on, until the entire file has been saved. This is much faster than a volume set's method of writing sequentially to the same disk because the controller can handle more than one operation at a time easily. When it's time to read the data, the same advantage exists. The effective access time for the stripe set is substantially less than the time that would be required to access each drive individually.

For this to work effectively, however, the pieces of disk space in the stripe set must be similar in size and preferably on disks of similar speed. So you can't just take odd-size pieces of free space and create a useful set out of it. The total size of the stripe set will be a multiple of the smallest piece of free disk space that is included in the set.

Another limitation of stripe sets is fault tolerance. A simple stripe set is no more resistant to failure than a volume set, and it is substantially less resistant to failure than a single drive because the failure of any drive or controller involved in the stripe set will bring the entire set down. If you don't have a current backup, you will be unable to recover your data without sending the entire set of disks out to a specialized data recovery expert. These experts are neither cheap nor fast, and even they might have real problems recovering from a seriously crashed stripe set. A safer solution is a different kind of stripe set, a stripe set with parity, which we discuss later in this chapter.

## Creating a Stripe Set

To create a new stripe set, follow these steps:

1. Open Disk Administrator; click on the first area of free space that you want to include in the stripe set.

2. Hold down the Ctrl key, and click on the other pieces of free space you want to include. Remember that each piece of free space must be on a different disk. The resulting stripe set will consist of equal-size segments of free disk space that are all the size of the smallest segment of free space you have selected.

3. After you have selected all of the pieces, right-click on one of the selected free space areas. Now click Create Stripe Set on the menu (Figure 8.15).

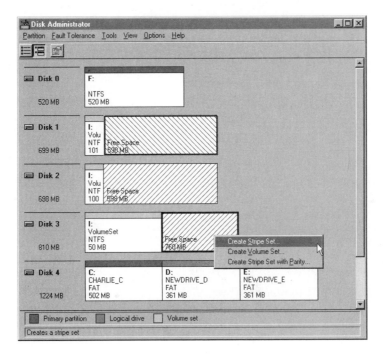

**FIGURE 8.15**

*Disk Administrator window showing a volume set and stripe set pop-up menu*

4. In the dialog box that opens (Figure 8.16 on the following page), enter the total space you want devoted to the stripe set; then click OK.

In Figure 8.15, you see that the smallest selected free space was 598 MB. Looking at the dialog box in Figure 8.16 on the following page, you can see how the size of this one space determines the total size of the stripe set. The smallest allowable stripe set is 2 MB (1 MB per disk), and the largest is 1196 MB (598 MB per disk) because all parts of a stripe set must be equal.

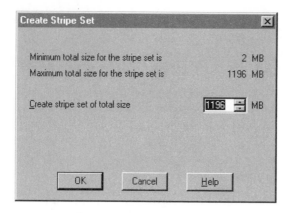

**FIGURE 8.16**

*Dialog box for creating a stripe set*

5. All of the pieces of the stripe set will be shown in the same color. Right-click in one of the pieces; choose Commit Changes Now from the pop-up menu. You'll be asked to confirm your choice. You also will be advised to update your Emergency Repair Disk (Figure 8.6 on page 124). Do take this advice.

If you're required to reboot, you'll see another dialog box telling you that. Make sure you're really in a position to shut down your server before you select Yes. Click Yes, and Windows NT Server starts the shutdown procedure.

Whether you've had to reboot or not, the next step is to format the stripe set. To format the stripe set so that you can start using it, right-click some part of the set and choose Format from the pop-up menu to open the dialog box shown in Figure 8.17. Disk Administrator will let you format a stripe set as either FAT or NTFS. Stick with NTFS.

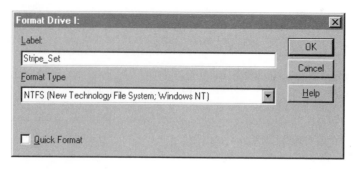

**FIGURE 8.17**

*Dialog box for formatting a stripe set*

Once you've formatted the stripe set, it will be available immediately. To your applications, it appears as just another drive, no different from any other drive. It also will be treated exactly the same as any other drive when you want to share it over the network.

Keep in mind that if any disk on which part of the stripe set is located fails or if any controller used by the stripe set fails, the entire stripe set is history. So rather than being more reliable than a standard drive, a stripe set is actually less reliable because the failure of any portion of the stripe set will cause the entire stripe set to be lost. If the failure is only a failed controller and if you replace the controller with exactly the same model, the chances are very good that you'll be back in business. But any hard drive failure is catastrophic.

### Deleting a Stripe Set

To delete an existing stripe set, open Disk Administrator. Select the stripe set by right-clicking in any portion of the set, and choose Delete from the pop-up menu. This will open a dialog box warning you that all data in the stripe set will be lost. Click Yes, and the stripe set will be deleted after you also confirm the changes.

## Stripe Sets with Parity

RAID 5 is the common name for what Disk Administrator refers to as a stripe set with parity. RAID 5 requires a minimum of three essentially similar hard drives or portions of hard drives, although Disk Administrator will support up to 32 drives in the array. Like a simple stripe set, a RAID 5 array writes data sequentially across the array. But now it creates a parity block for each block of data it writes. The parity block holds the information necessary to regenerate the data if one of the drives that make up the array should fail. Now the failure of a single drive is simply an annoyance, not a catastrophe. (Take that, Murphy!)

Of course, there's still no free lunch. The processor must calculate the parity information and write it to the disk; this means that there is substantial overhead cost for RAID 5—enough to pretty much offset the added speed of writing across multiple spindles. If your applications are primarily write-intensive, don't expect to achieve a speed increase by going to stripe sets with parity. When your "write" percentage goes above 50 percent, a simple mirror set would be a better choice than a stripe set with parity.

### NOTE

*If you must have high speed in a write-intensive application and you need redundancy, none of the Disk Administrator choices is really appropriate. Look for a hardware RAID solution that will support RAID 10 (striped, mirrored array).*

In a test of writing the same 50 MB of mixed large and small files to a stripe set, to a volume set, to a stripe set with parity, and to a mirror set, the volume set and the stripe set with parity were the slowest. The volume set required 75 seconds for the task, and the stripe set with parity required 80 seconds. The simple stripe set (using only two disks) took about 50 seconds; the mirror set took about 65 seconds. This is about what you'd expect, knowing how each array works. With more disks in the arrays, both kinds of stripe sets would be significantly faster.

However, in simple read operations, both kinds of stripe sets and the mirror set are substantially faster than a single partition set or a volume set. A RAID 5 array makes a good choice for many applications. It has a good balance of redundancy and speed and less lost capacity than a mirror set.

## Creating and Deleting a Stripe Set with Parity

The steps to creating, formatting, and deleting a RAID 5 array are exactly the same as those for creating a simple stripe set. The only difference is that you now must have a minimum of three similar areas of free space available on three separate disks; a simple stripe set requires only two. Keep in mind that with a RAID 5 array, you can't "grow it"—at least not with Disk Administrator, although we've seen hardware arrays that let you do this.

The major benefit of a stripe set with parity is that you *can* recover if one of the disks fails—and even continue to run with the failed drive present in the system. But you'll want to replace the failed drive and regenerate the parity information as soon as possible. Windows NT Server can handle only one failure in a set and still regenerate the data. A second failure would wipe you out.

## Regenerating a Damaged Stripe Set

If you have had a hard drive failure and have lost one piece of a stripe set with parity, you don't even get a warning message when the system boots up. It simply continues to work, and the data continues to be available. You can continue to read and write to it. So how will you be able to tell that something has gone *very* wrong?

The most likely source of information is the message that will appear the next time you start Disk Administrator. You'll get the message shown in Figure 8.18, which warns you that there's a disk missing.

**FIGURE 8.18**

*Warning message for a failed drive*

After you acknowledge the error message, Disk Administrator will open. Figure 8.19 shows a stripe set and a stripe set with parity, each of which is missing a piece of it-self. The stripe set is no longer available and is marked as "Unknown"; but the stripe set with parity is still perfectly usable and available, even with the missing piece. (The failed drive no longer appears on the screen because it is physically not present.)

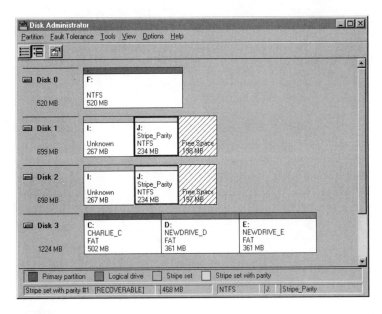

**FIGURE 8.19**

*Disk Administrator window showing a simple stripe set and a stripe set with parity after a disk failure*

To recover from the failure, shut down the system and replace the failed hard drive. Then, when the system reboots, start Disk Administrator. You'll see a Disk Adminis-trator window like the one shown in Figure 8.20 on the following page; the new disk for the RAID 5 array is displayed in red letters. The Regenerate command also is avail-able now on the Fault Tolerance menu. Disk Administrator is ready to regenerate the parity information and bring the stripe set with parity back to full functionality.

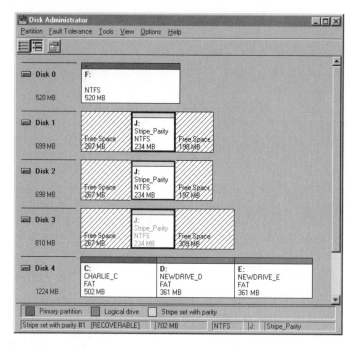

**FIGURE 8.20**

*Disk Administrator window showing a simple stripe set and a stripe set with parity after replacement of a failed disk but before regeneration of data*

## ◆ What Is Parity?

We've been bandying about the term "parity" quite a bit here, so let's take a moment to make sure we're all understanding the concept the same way. Parity is calculated by taking the Exclusive OR (XOR) of the data to be written. Everything on the computer is in binary—it's either 1 or 0. The XOR of two items is defined as "either one or the other, but not both." (If the items are both 0 or are both 1, the result of the XOR operation is 0. If the items are different, the result of the XOR operation is 1.) This is a pretty simple concept and remarkably easy for a processor to calculate, which is important because we want to keep the system overhead to a minimum.

When Disk Administrator needs to calculate parity, it has two choices. It could recalculate the data each time the data is written to disk. This would, however, require a disk access for each disk in the stripe set—not a good thing if you want to keep things moving along briskly. So, Disk Administrator takes the easy way: it simply reads the old data to be overwritten and XOR's the old data with the new data. This results in a bit map, which in turn is XOR'd with the old parity information, and a new parity is then calculated. This seems like the hard way to get there, but it actually is a much faster way because it cuts down on the number of required disk accesses.

Choose Regenerate from the Fault Tolerance menu. You'll still need to choose Commit Changes Now from the Partition menu, but once you do, Disk Administrator will start regenerating the data and bringing your array back to full functionality. In the status bar at the bottom of the Disk Administrator window, the display will show that the disk is regenerating, as shown here:

When the job's completed, the status bar will change, as shown below, displaying a message that the stripe set is "healthy" (which gives us a warm, fuzzy feeling).

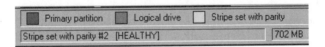

Another source of information is the event log, which is discussed in Chapter 21. When you open the Event Viewer, you'll see an error message designated by a stop sign symbol, shown in Figure 8.21. The Event Viewer will report the missing disk from a volume or stripe set.

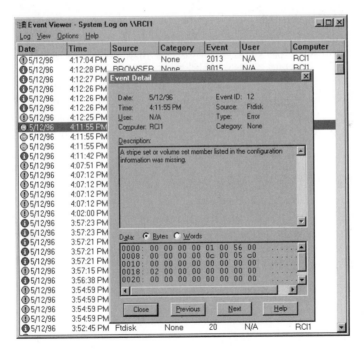

**FIGURE 8.21**

*Disk Administrator event log showing a failed drive*

**For More Information**

*Information about Event Viewer is included in Chapter 21.*

# Mirror Sets

The final type of RAID configuration that's supported by Windows NT Server and its Disk Administrator is RAID 1, which is called a mirror set. Actually, in the case of Windows NT Server, this can be either disk mirroring (two disks, with identical information written to them at the same time and running off the same controller) or disk duplexing (a separate controller for each disk, which eliminates the single point of failure in the controller). Mirroring is the most fault tolerant array supported by Windows NT Server's Disk Administrator, although, as we've mentioned before, you can do even better with some of the third-party hardware RAID controllers.

Disk mirroring, or duplexing, has a smaller initial cost than a stripe set with parity because it requires only two disks, not three. But its long-term cost is higher because it has a much higher lost-space overhead. The *worst* case loss for a RAID 5 array is a 33 percent loss of available capacity, but with RAID 1 you will always lose 50 percent of your total disk capacity.

A mirror set is slower than a stripe set with parity in read operations but faster in any write operation. It's not as fast as a simple stripe set without parity, but this is more than compensated for by its fault tolerance. If your situation limits your ability to use a hardware RAID solution and your application mix is moderately to highly write-intensive, you'll find that a mirror set is a better overall solution than a stripe set with parity. Whenever possible, opt for disk duplexing rather than simple mirroring. This will not only reduce your exposure to failure but also will be faster because two separate controllers will be doing the disk access.

## Creating a Mirror Set

To create a mirror set, click on the section of free space that will make up the primary portion of the mirror. Create a partition on the section, and format it. (If the partition already exists, you can skip this step, of course.) In the example shown in Figure 8.22, we'll create a mirror of our F: drive on disk 0 on the empty space of disk 1—that is, we're going to mirror disk 0 onto disk 1.

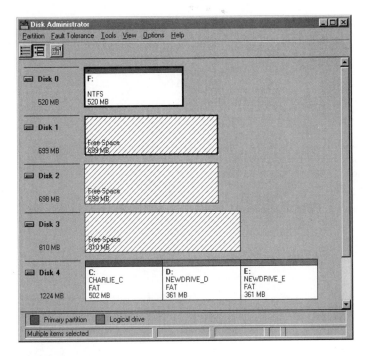

**FIGURE 8.22**

*Disk Administrator window before mirror set is created*

1. Click the partition that will be the *master* of the mirror.

2. Hold down the Ctrl key, and click on the free space that will be converted into a mirror of the original. Both the original block of space and the mirror block will be outlined in black.

3. Choose Establish Mirror from the Fault Tolerance menu. The display will immediately change to show the mirror set, as shown in Figure 8.23 on the following page. Disk Administrator will immediately identify the mirror set, although it won't start duplicating the data until you commit the changes.

4. Right-click in one of the partitions in the mirror set. Choose Commit Changes Now from the pop-up menu. Confirm your selection.

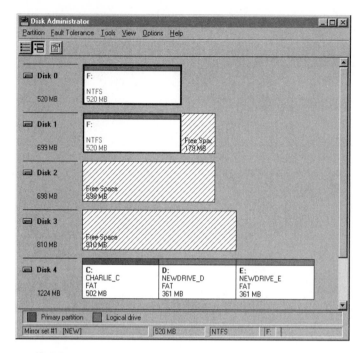

**FIGURE 8.23**

*Disk Administrator window after mirror set is created*

You'll get a warning message about updating your Emergency Repair Disk so that it shows the new information; you'll have to confirm your response to that message as well. Finally, Disk Administrator actually makes the changes, and your hard drive will start grinding away. If you tire of the constant commit, confirm, advise cycle, just remember that it's for your own protection.

The display in Disk Administrator's status bar will change to show that the new mirror is initializing, as the example below illustrates:

Your original disk will continue to be available while this goes on, which is nice; but your overall disk performance suffers a bit as the data is copied.

When the mirror set is fully initialized and the status line in Disk Administrator reads HEALTHY, the process is complete. Now when there's a change to data stored on the drive, the change will be written simultaneously to both disks. Any data that needs to be read from the drive can be read from either half of the mirror set; thus, the overall read access time will be substantially improved over a single disk partition.

## Breaking a Mirror Set

If there's a hardware failure on one portion of the mirror set, you'll continue to have access to your data. In fact, the first clue you have that there has been a failure might be when you next start Disk Administrator; you will be greeted with the error message shown in Figure 8.18 on page 139 (although Event Viewer also will have recorded the problem).

After you've acknowledged its error message, Disk Administrator will start. The half of the mirror set that remains will still be shown as a mirror set, but now the status bar description will read BROKEN, as shown below:

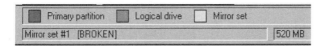

You can continue to use your disk, but you will have no redundancy until the failed hardware is replaced. When you are ready to replace the hardware, you should first break the mirror and then shut down the system. Even if the failure of the mirror set was caused by a bad controller or a loose cable on a duplexed drive or some other circumstance where the actual disk was not affected, the system still will not be able to reestablish the mirror set without breaking the mirror set first. To break the mirror set, right-click in the remaining partition and choose Break Mirror from the pop-up menu. This will bring up a confirmation request, as shown below.

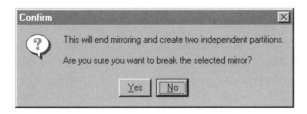

Click Yes to confirm that you do want to break the mirror set. Disk Administrator's display will change to show a single partition where the mirror was located. But the actual break won't occur until you choose Commit Changes Now from the Partition menu.

If you have chosen Yes and you see the error message shown in Figure 8.24, it means that Disk Administrator isn't able to lock the disk because another program (such as Explorer) is using some portion of the existing disk.

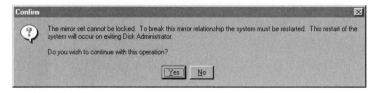

**FIGURE 8.24**

*Error message for Disk Administrator failure to lock drive*

Disk Administrator must be able to lock the mirrored drive before it will be able to break the mirror. In some cases a reboot might be required. At this point, you have two choices:

◆ You can figure out which program has an open file on the drive, shut it down, and try again; or

◆ You can simply acknowledge that Disk Administrator is the boss and let it reboot the server.

Your choice will depend on the particular situation. But let's face it; you're going to have to bring the system down soon, anyway, to replace the failed drive. So why not go ahead and do the job now? However, if you're really not ready to bring the system down yet, click No; Disk Administrator will back out of where it is. You can leave the mirrored drive alone until you're ready to break the mirror set and shut the system down.

After you have broken the mirror set, you'll see two individual partitions in the Disk Administrator window, such as the ones shown in Figure 8.25.

You then need to delete the failed partition, which creates unused space where the failed partition had been located. Now you can replace the failed hardware. When you have replaced it, reestablish the mirror set by following the steps for creating a new mirror set.

If you have postponed breaking the mirror set until after you have replaced the failed hardware, you'll see the mirror set in place when you restart the system and open Disk Administrator. But the status bar will show the mirror set as broken (Figure 8.26 on page 148). This means the partition won't actually function as a mirror set until you reestablish it—and you can't reestablish the mirror set unless you break it first. (Hey, we don't make up these rules, you know.)

**FIGURE 8.25**

*Disk Administrator window showing individual partitions after breaking the mirror set*

Before you break the mirror set, be sure to note which partition is the one with the unbroken portion of the mirror set. After you break the mirror set, you can see both of the original partitions, but they will look the same. You will need to remember which one was the unbroken portion of the set. The data probably will *not* be the same on the two partitions, even if you're dealing with a situation where the drives themselves were never damaged. You'll need to delete the failed partition and then reestablish the mirror set. If you accidentally delete the partition that was still good, you'll end up with a data loss at least back to the point where the disk failed and possibly a loss of all data in the mirror set—not at all what you want. This is why you should break the mirror set *before* you replace the failed hardware.

## NOTE

*Mirror partitions of the boot partition require special handling in the event of a system failure; these are discussed in Chapter 25. Mirror boot partitions do provide full recoverability, as you would hope and expect, but using them requires creating a special recovery boot disk and somewhat different recovery procedures, depending on whether you're running Intel x86–based or RISC-based hardware.*

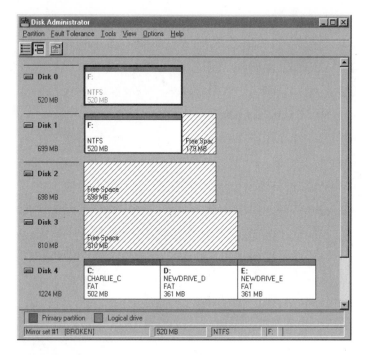

**FIGURE 8.26**

*Disk Administrator window showing a mirror set after replacement of the failed hardware*

## POINTS TO REMEMBER

♦ Disk Administrator supports RAID levels 0, 1, and 5 only. For any other levels, you'll need a hardware RAID controller.

♦ Volume sets and plain stripe sets (RAID 0) provide *no* fault tolerance and actually increase your exposure to drive failure.

♦ For general purpose fault tolerance, choose RAID 5 (stripe set with parity) unless your applications are write intensive. If they're >50% writes, choose RAID 1 (mirror) or a hardware RAID controller.

♦ If you need the ability to hot swap or have hot online spare drives, you'll need hardware RAID.

♦ The minimum number of disks for RAID 5 is three, but more would be better.

- Disk pieces for stripe sets, stripe sets with parity, and mirror sets must all be of essentially equal size and characteristics.

- You must break a failed mirror set before you can rebuild it.

**WHAT'S NEXT?**

We've covered the details of using Disk Administrator to manage your hard drive subsystem. We've shown you how to create partitions, volume sets, stripe sets (with and without parity), and mirror sets. In Chapter 9, we move from the configuration of your Windows NT Server domain to the administration of the domain, beginning with user accounts.

# Part Three

## Domain Administration

# CHAPTER 9

# CHAPTER 9

# User Accounts and the User Environment

Network administrators everywhere agree that running a network would be great fun if it were not for those pesky users. This is such a well-worn joke among administrators that it's worthwhile to take a moment and examine the truth of it. It is accurate to say that there are some users who show amazing resourcefulness in their ability to mess things up, but it is also true that many so-called "user" problems are not the fault of the users themselves. If user accounts, rights, and permissions are properly configured and tracked, many of these user problems disappear.

In this chapter we will focus on the tools that pertain to individual user accounts. We also will touch on user groups here; but we will reserve most of the discussion about tools that pertain to groups for Chapter 10, where groups are discussed in detail.

### NOTE

*If you're not experienced with Microsoft Windows NT, you should read both Chapter 9 and Chapter 10 before proceeding with setting up your user accounts. The individual user accounts on a network are important, but how the accounts are distributed in groups has a significant impact on how easy or difficult your network is to administer.*

## User Manager for Domains

The primary tool for managing user accounts, groups, and security policies for domains is User Manager for Domains. The specific User Manager for Domains functions that pertain to individual user accounts are these:

◆ Create, change, and delete user accounts in a domain.

◆ Create a user profile, which includes the user's desktop environment.

◆ Assign logon scripts to user accounts.

◆ Create home directories for users.

◆ Establish domain-wide password rules.

As an administrator, you can use all of the features of User Manager for Domains. Members of other groups will have different levels of access depending on the rights granted to them.

**For More Information**

*Managing trust relationships among domains is discussed in Chapter 16. Setting security log events is discussed in Chapter 21.*

To open User Manager for Domains, click Start. Select Programs. Follow the menus through Administrative Tools to User Manager For Domains. Your first view in User Manager for Domains will be a list of all user accounts in the domain, followed by a list of the groups in the domain. For a new Windows NT installation, there will be only two user accounts listed: Administrator and Guest. In the Groups window you will see a list of the built-in groups that come with Microsoft Windows NT Server version 4. All of the information in this view will pertain to your *home domain*. The name of the domain is in the title bar as shown in Figure 9.1

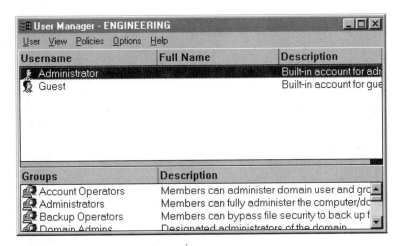

**FIGURE 9.1**

*User Manager for Domains window*

If your network is a multiple-domain network, you, as an administrator, can see the user accounts in other trusted domains as well as those in your home domain. If you are the administrator for a centrally administered network, you can see all user accounts and groups on the network. To see the user accounts and groups in other domains, choose Select Domain from the User menu. In the Select Domain dialog box that opens, select the domain you want to view. Then click OK.

**NOTE**

*If you're communicating with another computer or domain through a slow connection, select the Low Speed Connection in the Select Domain dialog box or choose Low Speed Connection from the Options menu. This will disable the View menu options, but you will still be able to manage the user accounts and groups either directly or indirectly. This option is desirable if it's taking a long time for the user and group lists to refresh.*

## Creating New User Accounts

Each user account is assigned a security identifier (SID) when it is created. The SID is an internal number generated by a Windows NT Server algorithm that identifies a specific user account on a Windows NT network, regardless of the domain in which the account resides. A SID is never reused. If a user account is deleted, the associated SID also is deleted. Even if the same user is reinstated later with the identical account information, a new SID will be generated for the account.

To add a new user account, choose New User from the User menu of User Manager for Domains. This will open the dialog box shown in Figure 9.2.

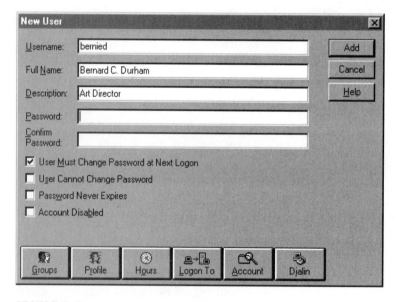

**FIGURE 9.2**

*New User dialog box in User Manager for Domains*

A user account in Windows NT Server contains a great deal of information, including the user's name and password, the groups to which this user account belongs, and the specific resources to which the user has access.

A policy for user names should be established well before you create the first user account. If there are computers running MS-DOS or Microsoft Windows 3.1 on your network, you'd do well to limit user names to eight characters. With eight characters, the user name can be the same as the name of the user's home directory on the MS-DOS and Windows 3.1 computers.

Even if you have no MS-DOS or Windows 3.1 computers on your network, you don't want to create user names that are at or close to the 20-character limit. Too much typing will be required to log on.

Here are some examples of user name conventions from which you can perhaps find a suitable one to adapt for your particular situation:

◆ First name plus last initial

Examples are MichaelG and SusanM. In the case of duplicate first names and last initials, you can add numbers, as in MichaelG1 and MichaelG2, or enough letters to provide identification, as in SusanMat and SusanMur.

◆ First name plus a number

Examples are Dave112 and Dave113. This approach is a pain for all concerned because it makes it hard to remember your *own* user name, much less identify other users.

◆ First initial plus last name

An example is Msmith. If you have both a Linda Smith and a Louise Smith, you can use LiSmith and LoSmith or Lsmith1 and Lsmith2 to distinguish between them.

◆ Last name plus an initial

An example is SmithL. This is a useful option for a large network. When you have multiple users with the same last name, you can add a few letters to the first initial, as in SmithLi and SmithLo.

No matter which user name convention you choose, you must not only be able to accommodate all of the existing users on your network but also be able to integrate future users. So even if the company's next new hire is U Ti or Chomondely Pepperell-Glossup, your user name convention will still be able to accommodate it.

# Username

The user name can have up to 20 characters and can include upper-case and lower-case letters, punctuation, and numbers. These are the only characters you can't use:

" / \ [ ] ; : | = , * ? < >

You can include blank spaces as part of the name, but it isn't recommended because their presence will require that you enclose the user name in quotes anytime you execute a command—a needless administrative time waster.

# Full Name

Although entering information in the Full Name text box is optional, you should use the field anyway, particularly if your user name convention frequently produces names that aren't easily recognizable. Lists of full names are produced by several Windows NT Server utilities. To make these lists more usable, you might want to adopt the practice of showing the full name as the last name first, followed by the first name. So instead of Bernard C. Durham, for example, the Full Name box would show Durham, Bernard C.

# Description

The Description text box is another optional field that is quite often used to identify the user's department and job title.

# Password Fields

When you add a new user, you can choose to enter a password in the Password text box and the Confirm Password text box. Passwords are case sensitive; their rules and attributes are described later in this chapter under "Managing Passwords." (See also Chapter 4, where you'll find a discussion of passwords as part of security planning.) Whether you choose to enter a password or not, the box for User Must Change Password At Next Logon should be checked; this forces the user to provide his or her own password when first logging on to the new account. The checkbox options are listed in Table 9.1.

**Table 9.1**
**Checkbox Options in the New User Dialog Box**

| Option | Default Setting | Comments |
|---|---|---|
| User Must Change Password At Next Logon | On | Requires user to enter a new password when first using the account. The check box clears automatically afterward. |
| User Cannot Change Password | Off | Makes the current password permanent. This is useful for shared accounts. |

| Option | Default Setting | Comments |
| --- | --- | --- |
| Password Never Expires | Off | Should be used with caution. Permanent passwords are a danger to system security. |
| Account Disabled | Off | Good for accounts used as templates. It's also good for temporarily suspending accounts, whatever the reason for suspension. |

## NOTE

*A grayed-out option is Account Lock Out. When an account is actually locked out because of too many failed logon attempts, this option becomes available. The settings for Account Lockout are covered in the "Managing Passwords" section later in this chapter.*

At the bottom of the New User window are six buttons: Groups, Profile, Hours, Logon To, Account, and Dialin. Each of these will open a dialog box.

## Groups

Click Groups to open the dialog box shown in Figure 9.3. This is where you specify the groups to which a new account will belong.

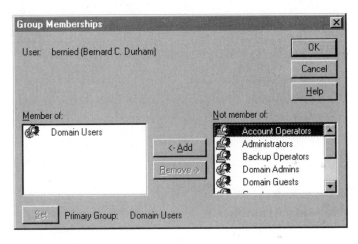

**FIGURE 9.3**

*Group Memberships dialog box*

Next to the name of each group, you'll see an icon. A globe behind the faces in the icon denotes a *global group*—a group that can be accessible to the whole network. A monitor behind the faces in the icon denotes a *local group*—a group that is confined to the domain in which it is defined. (For more information on the differences between local and global groups, see Chapter 10.)

To add new group memberships to a user's account, select the appropriate groups in the Not Member Of box; then click Add. A user must belong to at least one global group that is designated as the user's *primary group*. The existing primary group membership can't be removed from a user account without first making the account a member of another global group and designating this new global group as the account's primary group.

**NOTE**

*The primary group is actually used only by users who are running POSIX applications or by users who are logging on with Windows NT services for Macintosh; but even if there are no Macintosh or POSIX applications associated with your network, a primary group is still required for each user account.*

## Profile

The specific properties of a user's work environment on the computer are defined in the User Environment Profile dialog box.

The *user profile* contains the desktop and program settings for a user. The User Profile Path is the network path to the user's profile directory in the form \\*server*\*profiles* folder. A *logon script* is a batch file set to run when this user logs on. The *home directory* is the user's default directory for opening and saving files; it can be located either on a server or on a workstation. Information about these fields is presented in more detail under "The User Environment" on page 168 of this chapter.

**Tip**

*When you enter the location for the user profile in User Manager for Domains, be sure to use the UNC description because this will force Windows NT to connect to the correct server even if no connection exists at the time of the request. Profiles should be stored on a server that's always available so that Windows NT can find them when users log on to the system.*

The user environment does not have to be defined at the time the user account is created. If you decide you don't need profiles or logon scripts to manage your network effectively, you can leave the text box blank permanently. If you decide to use profiles or logon scripts at a later date, you can add the information at that time.

## Hours

By default, a user can log on to the system at any hour of the day or night. To improve your network's security, you might want to restrict some or all of this user's access to "normal" working hours, to weekdays only, or to some other time period. To restrict access times, click Hours to open the Logon Hours dialog box. Figure 9.4 shows the restrictions set for the user joesmith, who's allowed on the network 24-hours-a-day everyday except Sunday.

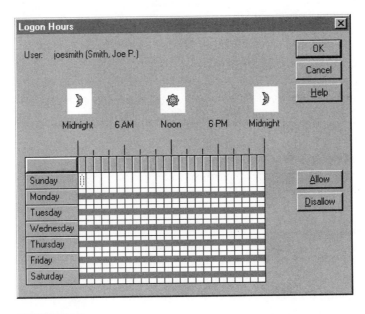

**FIGURE 9.4**

*Logon Hours dialog box showing restricted access hours*

You can disallow an entire day by clicking the button for that day of the week. To specify none-access hours, drag the mouse across the desired hours, and click Disallow. If you want to restrict the hours of all new users, you might want to use an account template. It's an excellent way to reduce the amount of mousing around you have to do. (See "Creating a Template Account" on page 165.)

You can set up the computer to forcibly disconnect a user at the end of his or her logon hours. It's drastic but not violent. (See "Account Lockout" under "Managing Passwords" later in this chapter.) If you don't forcibly disconnect a user who is already logged on, the user will be able to continue with whatever he or she is doing at the moment but will not be able to connect to additional network resources.

*A user on Windows NT Server or Microsoft Windows NT Workstation will receive a
warning message that their access is about to expire. A user on workstations running
Microsoft Windows 95, Microsoft Windows 3.x, or OS/2 will receive no such message.*

### Logon To

If you want to restrict user logon access to specific workstations, click Logon To
and type the workstation name(s) without the preceding backslashes. The default
setting allows the user to log on to all workstations.

### Account

If you want to specify an expiration date for a user account or indicate whether the
account is a global or a local account, click Account to open the Account Information dialog box shown in Figure 9.5. You can use this dialog box to configure two
user account properties:

◆ **Account Expires** Use the controls in the Account Expires area to
specify an exact date for an account to expire. This can be useful in the
case of employees who are leaving the company and for temporary
users. Otherwise, the right choice would be Never.

◆ **Account Type** Use the controls in the Account Type area to indicate
whether an account is a local account or a global account. Global is the
default setting. (See Chapter 10 for more information on local and global accounts.) Most user accounts should be global accounts because
they provide the most convenient way to control user access to system
resources, when used in conjunction with domain trust relationships.

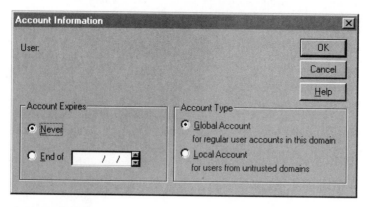

**FIGURE 9.5**

*The Account Information dialog box*

## Dialin

If you have enabled dial-up networking on your network, you can click Dialin and use the Dialin Information dialog box to grant a user permission to use dial-up networking. Use the Call Back settings to establish the level of security you require.

The Call Back settings are interesting in the types of security they offer.

◆ **No Call Back** A user calls in; the account and password are authenticated by the domain controller, and access is granted. This is the default Dialin setting.

◆ **Set By Caller** A user calls in, and the server asks the caller for the phone number from which the call is originating. The server then calls that number to make the connection. The user still has to provide his or her user name and password, but now there is a record of the number where the call originated. For users who roam about and who could be calling in from anywhere, the Set By Caller is a more secure setting than the No Call Back setting.

◆ **Preset To** A user calls in, and the server makes the connection after calling a preset phone number. This is the most secure Call Back setting. It works well for employees who always call in from the same location, such as a home office.

The dialog box in Figure 9.6 shows a user who has been granted permission to dial up the network from a remote location using a preset callback number.

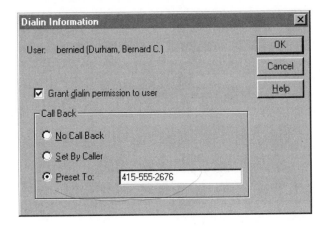

**FIGURE 9.6**

*Dialin Information dialog box showing user's preset callback number*

**NOTE**

*The Call Back feature also determines who pays for the call. If you have a technician remotely connected via a high-speed line, having the server call back the remote dial-in location means that your network pays for the calls, which is much easier (and actually cheaper) than having the technician submit regular expense reports.*

# Alternative Methods for Creating New Accounts

As you have seen, there's nothing inherently complicated about creating new user accounts. However, entering all of the required information for each user is tedious if you have a great many accounts on your network. Windows NT Server provides ways of minimizing the tedium. You can create a new account either by copying an existing account and modifying it or by making a template account that can be used to add new users in bulk to your system.

**Tip**

*If you're an experienced Windows NT administrator, the fastest way to add one or two accounts to your network is to use the Administrative Wizard designed for that purpose. Click Start; select the Programs menu. Then select the Administrative Tools menu, and choose the Administrative Wizards command.*

## Copying user accounts

If you have an existing user account that is substantially the same as the new account you want to create, copy the existing account and then modify it as necessary. The copy will have all of the information from the original, except the user name, full name, and password. To copy an existing account, follow these steps:

1. Open User Manager for Domains. Select the user account you want to copy.

2. Choose Copy from the User menu.

3. Type the new information in the Username, Full Name, Description, Password, and Confirm Password text boxes. Make any necessary modifications to the Groups, Profile, Hours, Logon To, Account, and Dialin settings; then click Add.

## Creating a template account

On a large network, template accounts can be time savers. A template account has properties that are shared by a group of users. To create a template account for a hypothetical user group called "Artists," choose New User from the User menu in User Manager for Domains. Type the required information in the New User text box; then use the buttons at the bottom of the box to specify the appropriate group memberships, profile location, logon hours, and so forth. Be sure the Account Disabled box at the bottom of the New User box is checked (as shown in Figure 9.7), to prevent anyone from logging on to the template account itself.

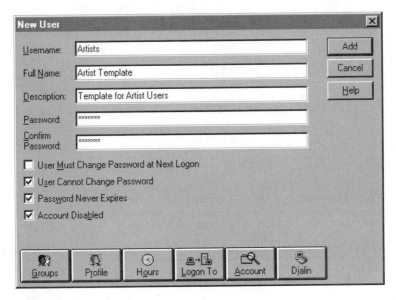

**FIGURE 9.7**

*New User template account showing Account Disabled box checked*

To create a new user account with the same account characteristics as your Artist template account, select artists in the User Manager window. (See Figure 9.8 on the following page.) Choose Copy from the User menu, and create as many Artists accounts as you want.

## NOTE

*If you want each user who is an artist to be able to log on to any computer and have his or her desktop available or if you want all artists to have the same desktop, see the section "User Profiles" later in this chapter.*

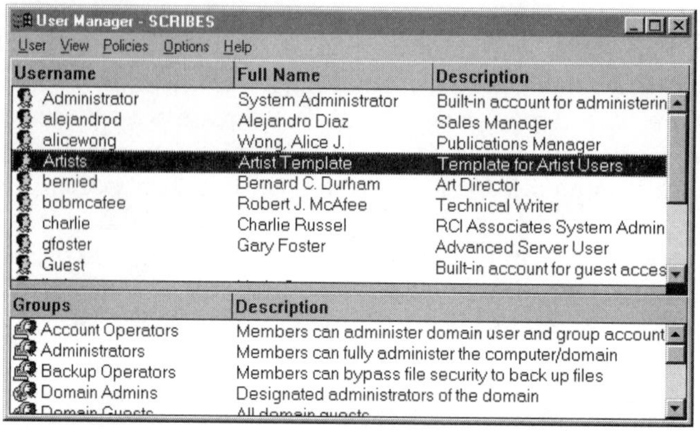

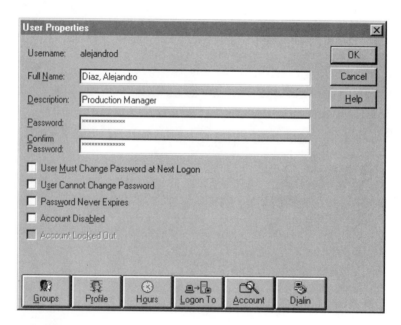

**FIGURE 9.8**

*Artist template highlighted in User Manager window*

# Changing User Accounts

You can change user account properties either individually or in groups. To modify an individual account, just double-click it in the User Manager window. The User Properties dialog box (Figure 9.9) that opens is virtually identical to the New User dialog box.

**FIGURE 9.9**

*A user account User Properties dialog box*

To change more than one account, open User Manager for Domains and, while holding down the Ctrl key, click the accounts you want to modify. Then press Enter. This will open the dialog box shown in Figure 9.10.

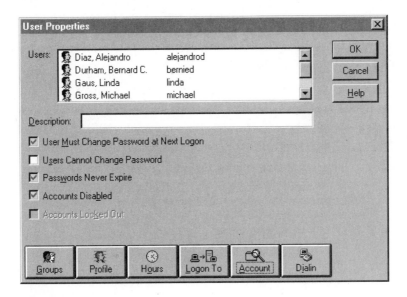

**FIGURE 9.10**

*User Properties dialog box showing changes to multiple accounts*

All of the settings in Groups, Profile, Hours, Logon To, Account, and Dialin have to be the same for all accounts. For example, only those group memberships that are common to all of the users in the group can be modified; the settings of hours also must be the same for all of the users selected.

When you change the account properties for more than one user, there are some user account fields that *can't* be changed:

◆ Full Name

◆ Description (*except* when you want to give everyone on the list the same description)

◆ Password and Confirm Password

◆ Password Never Expires

# The User Environment

Windows NT Server version 4 has a number of tools available to you for managing the user's work environment. A *user environment* includes the submenus available from the Start menu, taskbar settings, screen colors, mouse settings, printer and network connections, icons on the desktop, and so forth. Two of the most important methods for setting the environment variables are user profiles and logon scripts. User profiles work only on computers running Windows NT, which means that on a mixed network (one with machines running MS-DOS, Microsoft Windows for Workgroups, or other operating systems), you can't take full advantage of user profiles. In these circumstances, a logon script is a better choice than a user profile.

**NOTE**

*Another valuable tool for managing environments, either by user or by computer, is the System Policy Editor, which is discussed at the end of this chapter.*

## User Profiles

A *user profile*, which can be used only on a computer running Microsoft Windows NT Workstation or Windows NT Server, begins as a copy of Default User, a profile stored on every computer running Windows NT version 4.

When the user logs on to his or her workstation for the first time, Windows NT creates a user profile by recording any changes made to the profile settings during that session and storing them in that person's local user profile. The settings are specific to the workstation. If the user logs on to another workstation on the network, his or her user profile will not be available on that computer. However, the administrator can choose to set up a *roaming profile* for the user that will travel with the user when he or she logs on to another machine and will display the user's profile desktop on that machine.

Profiles offer several advantages to the user:

◆ When a user logs on to his or her computer, the settings and the desktop are the same as when he or she last logged off.

◆ Several people can use the same computer, and each one will have his or her own customized desktop.

◆ A user profile can be stored as a roaming profile on a server so that the environment is the same for that user at any Windows NT computer on the network.

Profiles offer advantages to you, the administrator, as well:

◆ You can create special user profiles that provide a consistent environment for users who are easily confused. These profiles don't include extraneous items that will add to the confusion.

◆ You can create a user profile and then assign it to a group of users.

◆ You can assign mandatory profiles so that users can't modify their desktop settings.

◆ You can make resources inaccessible to anyone assigned a particular profile to meet particular security objectives.

◆ You can make a new resource or application available to a number of users in one step, if they all share the same mandatory profile.

User profiles can be used on Windows 95 computers, although they're a great deal more trouble to set up for these machines. (See "Using Windows 95 User Profiles" under "User Profiles" later in this chapter.) User profiles cannot be assigned to computers running UNIX, MS-DOS, or OS/2.

## Settings in a user profile

A user profile is determined by the settings and choices a user makes in the environment. Table 9.2 shows the settings that are saved in a user profile.

**Table 9.2**
**Settings That Are Saved in a User Profile**

| Source | Settings Saved |
|---|---|
| Windows NT Explorer | All user-controlled settings in Explorer. |
| Control Panel | All user-controlled settings made in Control Panel. |
| Accessories | All user-controlled settings in the applets listed under Accessories. |
| Taskbar | All personal programs and groups and their settings. All taskbar settings. |
| Printers | Network printer connections. |
| Windows NT applications | Programs written for Windows NT that are designed so that the settings can be saved for each user. If such settings are available, they're saved in the user profile. |
| Online Help bookmarks | Bookmarks a user places in the Help system. |

## Profile types

Despite the potential for variation in the profile settings, there are really only three kinds of user profiles:

◆ **Local personal** This profile is available only on the user's machine. Its look and settings are determined by the user with no restrictions applied by the administrator.

◆ **Roaming personal** This profile is stored on a server and is available to the user at any Windows NT machine on the network. The settings are set by the user with no restrictions applied by the administrator.

◆ **Roaming mandatory** The profile is stored on a server and is available to the user from any Windows NT computer on the network. Some or all of the settings are determined by the administrator and cannot be changed by the user.

You may use any one or all of these types of profiles, depending on your organization's needs.

**Local personal profiles**   A local user profile is created on a single computer when a user logs on. If the computer has more than one user, there can be more than one profile on a machine. Each user's profile will be stored in the Profiles folder on that computer.

The first time the user logs on, the contents of the Default User profile (also located in the Profiles folder on the computer) and the common program groups in the All Users profile are combined to make a new user profile. When the user logs off, the changes made to the user profile are saved to a new user profile folder, which is labeled with the user name of that person. The information in the Default User profile is not changed.

When the user next logs on, the environment settings stored in the user's profile for the account are retrieved from the Profiles folder (usually in the directory C:\WINNT\PROFILES), and the desktop and other settings will be just as he or she set it up in the previous session.

### NOTE

*Someone who has more than one user account will have a different profile for each account. Changes made during a session are saved to the profile associated with the logged-on user account.*

**Roaming personal profiles**   Users also can have their own personal profiles that follow them no matter what computer they use. When you provide a user profile path in a user account, the user sets up the desktop and, when he or she logs off, a copy of this local profile is saved both locally and in the user profile path location.

The next time the user logs on, the user profile stored on the server is compared to the copy of the profile stored on the local computer; the newest version is the one that is used. If the server isn't available when the user logs on the next time, the locally stored copy of the user profile is loaded. (For a new user, a new local user profile is created.) In these circumstances, the user is asked the next time he or she logs on which profile to use, the newer copy on the local machine or the older version on the server.

To make a roaming profile that the user can configure, follow these steps:

1. Open User Manager for Domains, and double-click the user's account.

2. Click Profile.

3. Type the user profile path in the User Profile Path text box. This will create an empty folder, where the self-configured user's profile will be stored.

4. Under Home Directory, assign a path to a home directory on a server. Click OK when you've finished.

Figure 9.11 shows a path for a profile that will automatically follow the user to any workstation he or she uses. The profile will be created solely from settings chosen by the user.

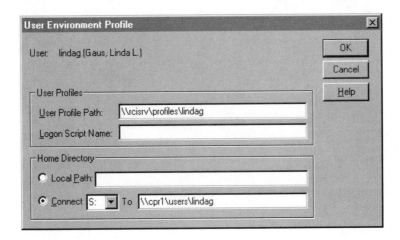

**FIGURE 9.11**

*User Environment Profile dialog box showing a roaming profile path for a user-created profile*

**Tip**

*Whenever a member of a group to which a roaming profile is assigned logs off, the personal user profile overwrites the centrally stored group user profile on the server. To retain the group profile as you originally set it up, make group user profiles mandatory. Another approach is to use System Policy Editor, described later in this chapter, to specify settings by group rather than by individual.*

**Mandatory roaming profiles**   To make a roaming profile mandatory—that is, to create a roaming profile that the user can't change—you first have to set up the profile and then assign it to the user. Mandatory profiles are seldom assigned to one user, so the easiest approach is to make a preconfigured profile for a particular group and then assign the profile to the users in the group.

Here's an example. In the Scribes domain, we want all technical writers to have the same user account specifications. The best way to create multiple user accounts with identical properties is to set up a user account template (Figure 9.12), as discussed earlier in the chapter on page 165.

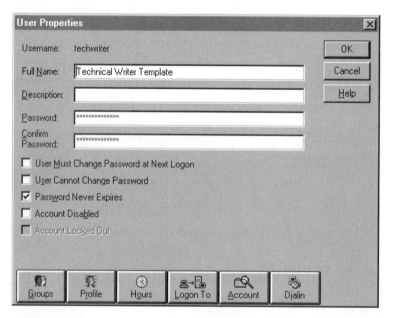

**FIGURE 9.12**

*User Properties dialog box showing example of a user profile template*

After you've created the template, follow these steps:

1. Log off; then log on again as *techwriter*.

2. Create the desktop and any other settings you want all technical writers to see when they log on.

3. Log off again; then log on using your administrator's account.

4. Use Explorer to find the newly made techwriter folder. (It's usually in C:\WINNT\PROFILES.) Open the folder; change the name of the file from NTUSER.DAT to NTUSER.MAN. (The file extension .MAN is what makes the profile mandatory.)

5. Now right-click My Computer, and choose Properties. Click the User Profiles tab, select the user profile for techwriter, and click Copy To. In the Copy To dialog box that appears, type the path to the server location for profiles in the Copy Profile To text box.

6. In the Permitted To Use area, click Change. This will open the Choose User dialog box (Figure 9.13). Here you can select a group or several individual users to be granted access to the profile. When you have made your selections, click Add. In our example, we chose everyone assigned to the Technical Writers group.

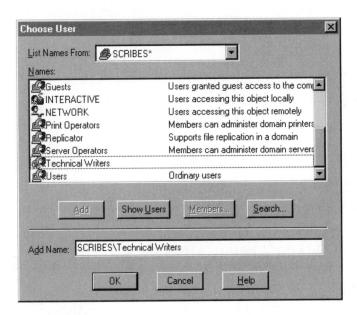

**FIGURE 9.13**

*Choose User dialog box*

Now when it's time to add a new member of the technical writing staff to the user list, the process is easy:

1. Open User Manager for Domains, and select Technical Writer Template.

2. Choose Copy from the User menu, and you'll see the dialog box shown in Figure 9.14.

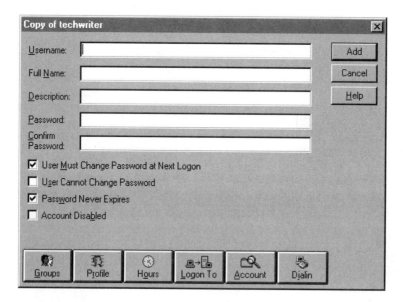

**FIGURE 9.14**

*Example of a template copy for adding a new user*

3. Fill in the text boxes for Username, Password, and so forth. Be sure the appropriate check boxes are checked so they reflect your password policies, and make sure you have *not* checked the Account Disabled box.

4. Click Profile. Verify that you have entered the appropriate profile path in the User Profile Path text box and have filled in the Connect To boxes under Home Directory correctly. Click Add when you are finished.

That's all there is to it. The profile path for the new user points to the location of the mandatory profile on the server.

## WARNING!

*When you create a profile for an individual or for a group, make sure the video hardware on the computer you're using is similar to the hardware on the computers where the profiles will be used. Incompatible hardware will result in a profile that looks peculiar or doesn't work at all.*

### Deleting a user profile

Deleting a user profile that you no longer want is simplicity itself. Click the User Profiles tab of System Option in Control Panel. (Or right-click My Computer, choose Properties, and then click the User Profiles tab of the System Properties dialog box.) Select the profile you want to remove, and click Delete.

### Using Windows 95 user profiles

Windows 95 includes provisions for user profiles, but unlike those in Windows NT Server or Windows NT Workstation, Windows 95 profiles have to be enabled on the local computer. So at each Windows 95 computer, you must enable profiles through the Passwords option in Control Panel.

Keep the following differences between Windows NT and Windows 95 in mind when using Windows 95 profiles on a Windows NT Server network:

◆ Roaming profiles can be used on a Windows NT Server network if Client For Microsoft Networks is the primary network logon client.

◆ Mandatory user profiles can be used, but they must be created separately for each user. The administrator creates a custom profile and copies this profile to the user's home directory.

◆ Windows 95 clients don't use the profile path to download roaming profiles; roaming user profiles are kept in the user's home directory.

◆ Windows 95 profiles don't copy all of the desktop, only the shortcuts (.LNK) and the program information files (.PIF).

### Upgrading Windows NT 3.5x profiles

A local profile on a system upgraded from Microsoft Windows NT 3.5*x* to Windows NT version 4 will be updated automatically to the new format at the time you install Windows NT version 4. A roaming profile remains in the same server location in its original format, but a new profile also will be created that consists of this same file updated to the Windows NT version 4 format. Users with roaming profiles can log on to both computers running Windows NT 3.5x and computers running Windows NT version 4 because the two profiles are stored and updated separately.

In Windows NT 3.5x, a user profile consisted of a single file; in Windows NT version 4, a user profile consists of a folder that contains the profile plus a folder of links to desktop items. In any case, the registry portions of the profiles are contained in the files shown in this listing:

| Windows NT Version 4 | Windows NT 3.5x | Windows 95 |
| --- | --- | --- |
| NTUSER.DAT | USERNAME.USR | USER.DAT |
| NTUSER.DAT.LOG | | USER.DAO |
| NTUSER.MAN | USERNAME.MAN | USER.MAN |

# Logon Scripts

A logon script is simply a batch file that runs automatically when a user logs on to the network. A single logon script can be assigned to one user or to many users. The name and location of a user's logon script is specified in the Profile window of the user account. By default, logon scripts are stored in the following directory:

C:\WINNT\SYSTEM32\REPL\IMPORT\SCRIPTS

It's best not to change the location of the logon scripts because the domain controller will look for a user's logon script on its local C: drive. For that reason, all logon scripts should be replicated on all of the controllers in the domain. (Chapter 14 describes the Windows NT Server Directory Replicator service.)

## Creating a logon script

Because a logon script is a batch file, it can contain any batch file commands that are in the user's operating system environment. Scripts can be as simple or as elaborate as you want to make them. For example, here's a sample logon file:

```
@echo off
net time \\rcisrv /set
net use d: \\rcisrv2\books
net use lpt1 \\rci2\hplj4
```

The net time line synchronizes the clock of the workstation to the clock of the server named rcisrv. The next line connects the D: drive to the Books folder on the computer named rcisrv2. The last line connects the LPT1 port to the shared printer named hplj4.

Both Windows 95 and Windows for Workgroups will start *before* the user logs on to the network, so logon scripts for these computers will be executed in virtual MS-DOS sessions. A Windows 95 workstation user will see a small dialog box that advises the user to wait while the script executes.

**Logon script variables**  You can use the variables in Table 9.3 if you would like to use a single logon script for many users. For example, in a script for multiple users, you can enter *%HOMEDRIVE%* in place of the user's home directory. Unfortunately, these variables work only in scripts for Windows NT workstations, not in scripts for Windows 95 workstations.

**Table 9.3**
**NT Wildcards That Are Available for Logon Scripts**

| Variable | Description |
| --- | --- |
| %HOMEDRIVE% | The user's local workstation drive letter that is associated with the user's home directory |
| %HOMEPATH% | Full path of the user's home directory |
| %HOMESHARE% | The share name that contains the user's home directory |
| %OS% | User's operating system |
| %PROCESSOR_ARCHITECTURE% | Processor type on the user's workstation |
| %PROCESSOR_LEVEL% | Processor level of the user's workstation |
| %USERDOMAIN% | Domain where the user's account is defined |
| %USERNAME% | Account user name |

**Assigning logon scripts**  To assign a logon script to a user, follow these steps:

1.  Write the batch file that will be the logon script; save it in the server's logon script path, which should be the default path:

    C:\WINNT\SYSTEM32\REPL\IMPORT\SCRIPTS

2.  Open User Manager for Domains, and double-click the user's account.

3.  In the User Properties dialog box, click Profile.

4.  In the User Environment Profile dialog box, type the name of the batch file in the Logon Script Name text box.

5.  Click OK twice, to close the dialog boxes, and then close User Manager for Domains.

You don't need to include the path in the Logon Script Name text box because when the user logs on, the server that authenticates the user's account locates the logon script by looking in the default path.

### Replicating a logon script

The logon script is always downloaded from the server that authenticates the user's logon request. Most networks have more than one domain controller (at least one primary controller and one backup controller), so you'll want to make sure that the logon scripts are on *all* of the domain controllers in case one of the controllers is out of action for some reason.

To make sure that the logon scripts always will be available, use the Directory Replicator service, which has the ability to maintain identical copies of a directory on multiple computers. The Directory Replicator service and its many uses are discussed in detail in Chapter 14.

## Home Directories

Each user on the network must have a home directory, which is usually located on a server. This directory can contain the user's personal files as well as certain user-specific files (as designated by you, the administrator). The user has control over his or her home directory.

**NOTE**

*Home directories also can be placed on a user's local hard drive. This will work as long as the user always logs on at the workstation where the home directory resides. When a user is to have access to his or her home directory from any client on the network, the home directory must be located on a server.*

To assign networked home directories for a group of users, follow these steps:

1. Open User Manager for Domains.

2. Select the account or accounts to which you want to assign home directories.

3. Choose Properties from the User menu. Click Profile to open the User Environment Profile dialog box.

4. Under Home Directory, you can select either Local Path (for a home directory on the local hard drive) or Connect.

5. For a local drive, you need only type the path in the Local Path text box. For a server, select a drive letter in the Connect combo box, and type the path in the To text box, substituting *%USERNAME%* for the actual user's name as shown in Figure 9.15. Click OK.

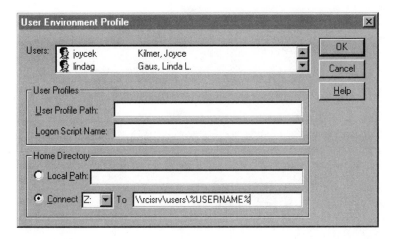

**FIGURE 9.15**

*User Environment Profile dialog box showing variable for multiple users in the path*

When the environment profile is saved, the system will replace *%USERNAME%* with the actual user's name. If the directory that you are designating as a home directory doesn't yet exist, Windows NT Server usually can create the directory and automatically make it accessible to the user.

**Tip**

*If you're using a directory that you've already created as a home directory, make sure the directory permissions allow the user access to it. For more information on setting directory permissions, see Chapter 12.*

# Managing Passwords

Passwords are often the weakest link in network security. To put it simply: users want to have an easy password, and they don't want to change it—ever. As we have previously explained in Chapter 4, from the standpoint of network security, this is a poor idea. Administrators can lecture and hector the users, but users will resist, if only to respond by doing nothing. However, an administrator can force a degree of compliance to requirements for password changes by establishing password rules for all users in a domain. To create these settings, open User Manager for Domains; choose Account from the Policy menu. This will open the Account Policy dialog box shown in Figure 9.16 on the following page.

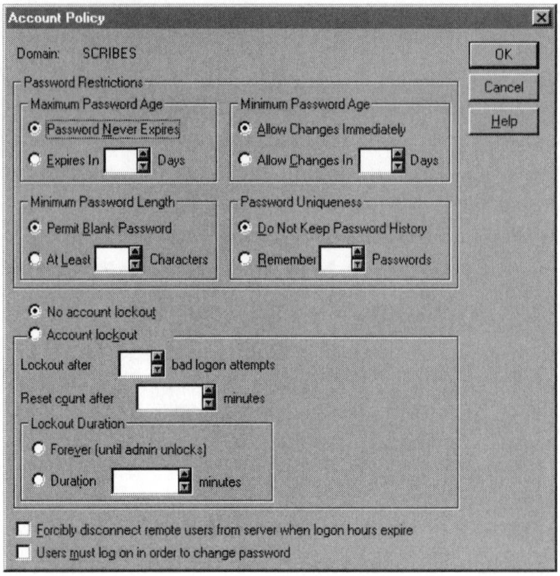

**FIGURE 9.16**

*Account Policy dialog box*

## Setting Password Rules

As you can see in the Account Policy dialog box, there are plenty of options under Password Restrictions for making sure that password rules stick:

◆ **Maximum Password Age** Specifies the maximum amount of time a password can be valid before the system requires the user to choose a new one.

◆ **Minimum Password Age** Specifies the minimum amount of time a password must be used before a new password can be chosen. This protects the system from users who, when they are required to enter new passwords, do so and then immediately switch back to the old favorites.

◆ **Minimum Password Length** Specifies the minimum number of characters a password must contain. Short passwords are easier to guess; so it's best to require a password of at least six to eight characters.

◆ **Password Uniqueness** Specifies the minimum number of new passwords that a user must choose before reusing an old favorite. If you specify a value here, you also must specify a value under Minimum Password Age.

# Account Lockout

Further down in the dialog box is a section called Account Lockout. If you fill in this section (in other words, if you select anything other than No Account Lockout), the provisions apply to all user accounts in the domain.

## NOTE

*Stricter security is called for if your network includes dial-up connections or if a user can gain access through a wide-area network. The easier it is for an outsider to get at your logon screen, the more precautions you need.*

Given enough time and opportunities for attempting to log on a system, a user can guess most passwords. To prevent this, you can limit the number of times someone can try to log on the system before being locked out.

- ◆ **Lockout After** Specifies the number of times a user can try to log on before being denied anymore opportunities to log on. We think you can probably assume that anyone who hasn't been able to log on after five tries has either forgotten the password or is an intruder.

- ◆ **Reset Count After** Specifies the number of minutes the system will wait after a set of bad logon attempts before a user can attempt to log on again. A higher value here will ensure that the user contacts the administrator about the problem—you can decide how you feel about that.

- ◆ **Lockout Duration** Specifies the length of time an account is locked after an unsuccessful logon attempt. If you're going to use Account Lockout at all, you should use the Lockout Duration Forever option. That way, no one can attempt to break in to the network without you learning of it. For example, if you specify only a limited lockout time, it can expire before the legitimate user returns to the workstation. The legitimate user then will be able to log on as usual, and neither you nor the user will know that anything untoward has happened.

At the bottom of the Account Policy window are two additional options you can choose. The first option is the forcible disconnect (discussed earlier in this chapter under "Hours" in "Creating New User Accounts"). If you have set time restrictions on access to the computer for a user, checking this box will disconnect a user who overstays his or her time. Note that this option will not regulate computers running operating systems other than Windows NT.

The second option requires a user to log on to change his or her password. If you check this box, a user with an expired password will not be able to log on. If you do not check this box, a user will be able to log on and change an expired password without having to engage the help of the administrator.

# Managing User Rights

Security is a major issue on most networks. Legitimate users must be able to log on and get to the resources they need, while unauthorized users are kept out. The challenge for the administrator is to make the network as secure as it needs to be—and no more than that.

What a user can do—or not do—depends on what rights and permissions have been granted to that user. Rights and permissions are not exactly the same thing, although they sound similar. They can be defined roughly as follows:

◆ A *right* generally applies to the system as a whole and is defined with User Manager for Domains. The ability to back up files or to log on to a server, for example, are rights the administrator giveth or taketh away. Rights can be assigned to individuals, but they are more often assigned as characteristics of a group; a user then is assigned to particular groups on the basis of the rights he or she needs.

◆ A *permission* is the access a user (or group) has to a specific object, such as a file, a directory, or a printer. For example, the question of whether a user can read a particular directory or access a network printer is a permission.

### For More Information

*See Chapter 12 for information about how to grant permissions.*

Two categories of user rights are defined in Windows NT Server—regular user rights and advanced user rights. Whole sets of user rights are included for each of the built-in groups discussed in Chapter 10. Because built-in groups are designed very cleverly, it's rarely necessary to change the assignments. However, once you've become a Windows NT Server expert, you can create new groups if you need to do so and can assign a particular combination of rights to each group.

### Tip

*Assign rights to groups of users rather than to individual users where this is possible. It is easier to administer and to keep track of rights that are assigned to groups.*

To see what rights have been assigned to a user or to a group and to change these rights, open User Manager for Domains; choose User Rights from the Policies menu. You'll see the User Rights Policy dialog box shown in Figure 9.17.

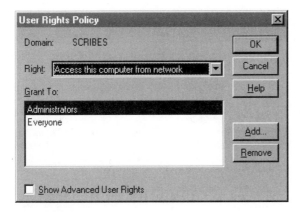

**FIGURE 9.17**

*User Rights Policy dialog box.*

## Regular Rights

At the top of the User Rights Policy dialog box is the name of the domain for which you're defining user rights. In the Grant To list box you will see the names of the individuals and groups who have the specific right displayed in the Right list box. Click Add to give a new group or individual this right. Click Remove to take away this right from the selected group or individual in the list. To see the entire list of user rights, click the arrow next to the Right list box.

Table 9.4 on the following page is a list of the regular rights that can be assigned in Windows NT Server, showing what each right actually means and which groups are assigned the right by default.

## Advanced Rights

If you check the Show Advanced User Rights check box, the list in the Right drop-down list box will become longer. Advanced rights are used mostly by programmers writing Windows NT applications, but there are two advanced rights that you, as an administrator, probably will use:

◆ **Bypass traverse checking** Allows a user to pass through directory trees (folder structures) even if the user doesn't have permission for access to these directories. The user does not have any right to change or read the directories being traversed, just the ability to pass through them.

◆ **Log on as a service** Permits a user to log on as a service. The user account that runs the Replicator service needs this right. (Replicator services are covered in Chapter 14.)

## Table 9.4
## Regular User Rights in Windows NT Server

| Regular Right | Definition | Default Assignments |
|---|---|---|
| Access this computer from network. | Permits users to log on to this computer through the network. | Administrators<br>Everyone |
| Add workstations to domain. | Allows a user to create computer accounts in this domain. | None (by default). But Administrators and Server Operators can add computers to the domain without specifically being granted this right. |
| Back up files and directories. | Grants a user the right to back up all files on this computer. | Administrators<br>Backup Operators<br>Server Operators |
| Change the system time. | Allows a user to set the computer's internal clock.* | Administrators<br>Server Operators |
| Force shutdown from a remote system. | Not implemented. | |
| Load and unload device drivers. | Permits a user to install and remove drivers for devices on the network.* | Administrators |
| Log on locally. | Allows a user to log on to a Windows NT Server.* | Account Operators<br>Administrators<br>Backup Operators<br>Print Operators<br>Server Operators |
| Manage auditing and security log. | Permits a user to manage the auditing of files, directories, and other resources.* | Administrators |
| Restore files and directories | Permits a user to restore files and directories. Supersedes any permission restrictions. | Administrators<br>Backup Operators<br>Server Operators |
| Shut down the system | Allows a user to shut down Windows NT.* | Account Operators<br>Administrators<br>Backup Operators<br>Print Operators<br>Server Operators |

| Regular Right | Definition | Default Assignments |
|---|---|---|
| Take ownership of files or other objects. | Allows a user to take ownership of files, directories, and other objects that are owned by other users.* | Administrators |

\* *In the context of domain administration, this right applies to controllers. In the context of workstation or server administration, when the server is not a controller, the right applies only to a specific computer.*

# Using System Policy Editor to Manage User Environments

In Windows NT Server the look, feel, and configuration of the user's desktop are stored as part of the user's profile in the registry. As a system administrator, you can manage user profiles either by enforcing mandatory profiles or by using System Policy Editor to manage the configuration of user accounts.

You use System Policy Editor (Figure 9.18) to change the system policy; you can create default settings for all computers and users in the domain or for individual users, specific groups of users, or specific computers in the domain, which makes it easy to customize settings for special situations. You can even use System Policy Editor to set policy for Windows 95 computers in your domain if user profiles are enabled on these machines.

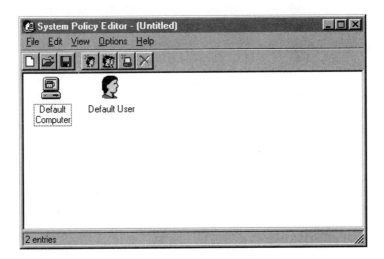

**FIGURE 9.18**

*System Policy Editor window*

System Policy Editor allows you to control what users can do from the desktop, but it won't give you the absolute control that you have with mandatory profiles. It does have the distinct advantage of allowing you to let users control some aspects of their environment without allowing them to even see the areas you don't want them to be able to change. Perhaps you want to enforce a mandatory screen saver that kicks in after two minutes of inactivity and then requires the user's password to regain access to the computer. This is a reasonable security precaution in some organizational environments and is quite easy to implement using System Policy Editor.

System Policy Editor also allows you to control logon access and network access. For example, you can decide whether to make the Shutdown button available from the logon screen or whether to allow remote access users to log on to the computer using anonymous Ftp.

## Templates

Windows NT Server includes a set of system policy templates that give you the necessary starting place to edit registry settings for Windows NT Server, Windows NT Workstation, and Windows 95 computers on your network. When System Policy Editor is installed, it copies three template files to your %SYSTEMROOT%\INF subdirectory:

◆ **COMMON.ADM** Contains template for settings common to both Windows NT and Windows 95

◆ **WINDOWS.ADM** Contains template for settings specific to Windows 95

◆ **WINNT.ADM** Contains template for settings specific to Windows NT

When you start System Policy Editor, it loads the templates for Windows NT computers automatically. You can add or remove templates from System Policy Editor.

### Adding templates to System Policy Editor

You can add a template provided by a software manufacturer to System Policy Editor by following these steps:

1. Close any policy files that are open.

2. Copy the template .ADM file to the %SYSTEMROOT%\INF subdirectory.

3. In System Policy Editor, choose Policy Template from the Options menu to bring up the Policy Template Options dialog box shown in Figure 9.19.

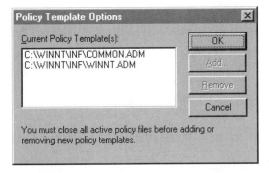

**FIGURE 9.19**

*Policy Template Options dialog box*

**4.** Click Add; select the template file you want to add.

**5.** When you've selected all of the template files you want to add, click OK; System Policy Editor will load the template files.

The templates you've added will remain loaded and available for any policies you create until you decide to remove them.

### Removing templates from System Policy Editor

To remove a template from System Policy Editor, follow these steps:

**1.** Close any policy files that are open.

**2.** Choose Policy Template from the Options menu to bring up the Policy Template Options dialog box shown in Figure 9.19.

**3.** Select all of the templates you want to remove.

**4.** Click Remove.

**5.** Click OK; System Policy Editor will unload the unwanted template files.

## Creating a New Default System Policy

You can create new default system policies that apply to either all computers or all users in a domain. After you create a new policy, you must activate it by copying it to the NETLOGON directory of the primary domain controller and giving it the name NTCONFIG.POL.

## Default computer policies

To create a new default computer policy that will be applied to all computers in the domain, follow these steps:

1. Start System Policy Editor.

2. Choose New Policy from the File menu.

3. Double-click Default Computer to bring up the Default Computer Properties dialog box shown in Figure 9.20.

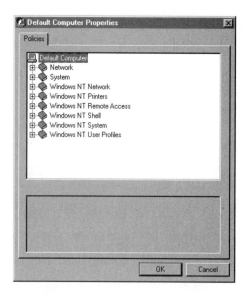

**FIGURE 9.20**

*Default Computer Properties dialog box*

4. Each book represents an area of the registry that can be changed. Double-click the icon for the registry area you want to modify. If, for example, you were going to remove the shutdown privilege from all computers in the domain, you'd double-click the icon for the Windows NT System and then open Logon, as shown in Figure 9.21. You would then clear the check box for Enable Shutdown From Authentication Dialog Box.

5. After you've made whatever changes you want to make, click OK to return to the main System Policy Editor window.

6. Proceed to the section "Saving and implementing the new system policy" on page 190.

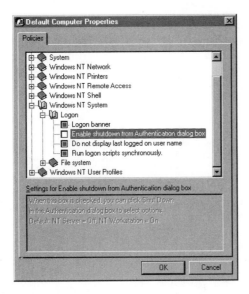

**FIGURE 9.21**

*Default Computer Properties dialog box showing change to shutdown policy for the domain*

### NOTE

*The check boxes in System Policy Editor have three states: cleared (which means disable the policy), checked (which means enable the policy), and gray (which means the option isn't available to be changed from its current state).*

## Default user policies

To create a new default user policy that will be applied to all users in the domain, follow these steps:

1. Start System Policy Editor.

2. Choose New Policy from the File menu.

3. Double-click Default User to bring up the Default User Properties dialog box shown in Figure 9.22 on the following page.

4. Make the desired changes here (such as how users will be able to configure their desktops or use Control Panel), and apply the desired restrictions to the various aspects of the user interface.

5. Click OK to return to the main System Policy Editor window.

6. Proceed to "Saving and implementing the new system policy."

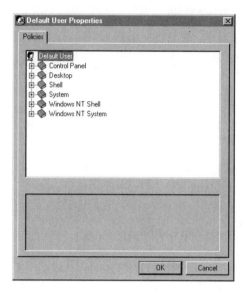

**FIGURE 9.22**

*Default User Properties dialog box*

## Saving and implementing the new system policy

The NETLOGON directory of the primary domain controller is where the default system policy profile is stored. To save the changes you've made in the system policy, follow these steps:

1. Choose Save As from the File menu.

2. When the Save As dialog box comes up (Figure 9.23), type the UNC path name of the default configuration policy in the File Name text box.

3. Click Save, and the new policy will be in effect.

**NOTE**

*We recommend that you first save the policy change to a separate folder, using a more descriptive name than NTConfig.pol, and then copy it to the default configuration file. This makes it much easier to recover to a known condition if the change you've made was not as well thought out as you might have hoped. Plus it provides you with a useful audit trail.*

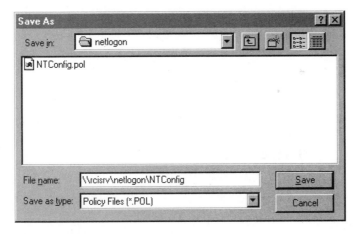

**FIGURE 9.23**

*Save As dialog box showing NETLOGON directory name*

# Editing an Existing System Policy

If you have a system policy already in place, you can easily edit it so that whatever changes you make affect only the specific areas you want to modify. The check boxes in System Policy Editor are tri-state boxes, so you change what you want to modify and leave everything else the same.

## ◆ Policy Change Management

We suggest that you always begin making changes to system policy by first making a copy of the current policy and storing it in a safe place so that you have a good fallback point if whatever you are trying to do backfires. Every good system administrator has a technique for protecting the system while making changes that could affect system stability. Ours is to keep fallback versions of things (such as the registry and system policies) in a "changes" directory and to use filenames that clearly identify the change by the date and the nature of the change. What's the point of being able to have long filenames if you can't take advantage of this capability sometimes?

Whatever method you use to protect your system as you make policy changes, be consistent and conscientious about using it. It's all too easy to make a change that doesn't work. If you make changes incrementally and document them clearly, and have known "safe" versions to fall back on, it's a *lot* easier and faster to recover when something goes wrong.

Start System Policy Editor. Then choose Open from the File menu, and open an existing policy. Remember, the current system policy always will be located in this directory:

   \\<PDCName>\NETLOGON\NTCONFIG.POL

After you've made your changes and saved the file back to the default location and name, the policy will be in effect for all users who log on to the domain in the future.

## Changing a Policy for Specific Users or Groups of Users

You've seen how to change the system policy for all users in a domain, but what if you want to make a change that affects only a subset of your users? No problem. You can change the system policy for a single user or for a whole group of users at once. Suppose we've had some problems with those pesky Technical Writers again. You spent a lot of time setting up their desktops with shortcuts that point directly to the files with which they're working for this project, but they continue to delete files accidentally or to misplace files in subfolders where they subsequently can't find them. After the fourth or fifth time you have to redo one of their desktop settings, one of the writers asks why you can't just set things up so that they can't mess them up? Makes sense. It's easy enough to do, so let's go through the steps necessary to accomplish this.

1. Open System Policy Editor; then open the current system policy for users as shown in Figure 9.24.

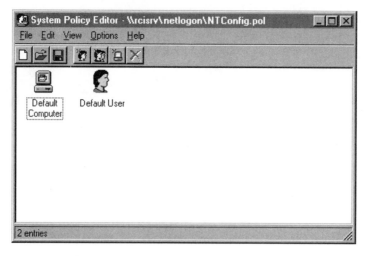

**FIGURE 9.24**

*System Policy Editor window with current user system policy*

2. Choose Add Group from the Edit menu to bring up the Add Group dialog box shown in Figure 9.25.

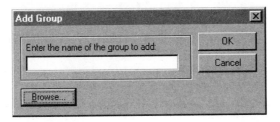

**FIGURE 9.25**

*Add Group dialog box for System Policy Editor*

3. Type the name of the group (in our example, *Technical Writers*) in the text box, or be safe and click Browse to find the group name so that you're sure you've got it right. Then click OK to create a new policy for the group.

4. Double-click the new icon for the group you've chosen (in this case Technical Writers), which opens the properties dialog box for the group as shown in Figure 9.26.

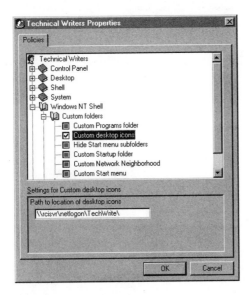

**FIGURE 9.26**

*A properties dialog box showing the Custom Desktop Icons folder for a Technical Writers group*

5. Expand the Custom Folders folder in the Windows NT Shell folder. Make sure there's a check mark in the Custom Desktop Icons check box.

6. Type the correct path name for Custom Desktop Icons in the text box, as shown in Figure 9.26.

7. Click OK to return to the main System Policy Editor window.

8. Choose Save from the File menu.

## Connecting to a Remote Computer Registry

You can use the System Policy Editor to connect to the registry of a remote computer and modify the settings for that computer and its current user. In the main System Policy Editor window, choose Connect from the File menu. Type the name of the computer, and then select a profile from the list of available user profiles. A window will open that looks like the one in Figure 9.27. Now the icons in the window are for the actual local computer and local user rather than for Default Computer and Default User.

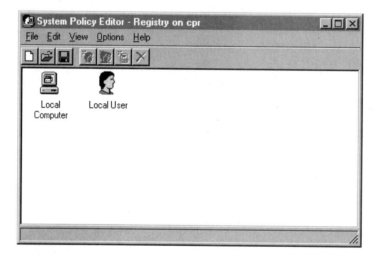

**FIGURE 9.27**

*System Policy Editor window showing icons for a remote computer and its user*

After you're connected, you can change the settings as described under "Changing a Policy for Specific Users or Groups of Users" on page 192. Note that the check boxes are now regular, binary check boxes because you're editing the value directly.

- User Manager for Domains is the Windows NT Server tool for managing user accounts, setting password rules, and managing trust relationships among domains.

- A user profile can be local to a particular computer, or it can "roam," so that a user can sign on to any computer in the domain and have his or her desktop configuration available automatically.

- MS-DOS, Windows 3.*x*, OS/2, and UNIX machines can't be assigned user profiles; use logon scripts to set up the user environment for these operating systems.

- Windows 95 user profiles can be used on a Windows NT Server version 4 network.

- Use the System Policy Editor to control particular aspects of a user's environment without imposing a mandatory profile on them.

- Use the System Policy Editor to connect to a remote registry and edit both user and computer settings.

## WHAT'S NEXT

On networks large and small—but especially on large ones—the organization of users into groups is necessary to retain any sort of administrative control. We'll now move on to the subject of groups and how to use them.

# CHAPTER 10

# CHAPTER 10

# Users and User Groups

A group, as envisioned by Microsoft Windows NT developers, is another tool for managing user accounts on a network. A Windows NT group functions as a superaccount—a collection of individual user accounts that are managed as a single unit. All individual user accounts within a particular group have identical rights on the network. Granting rights and permissions to a group automatically grants them to all users who are members of the group, which means that rights and permissions can be granted to a whole set of individuals at the same time rather than to each individual separately. Managing user accounts in groups simplifies the administrator's job of controlling and tracking users' access to resources on the network. In conjunction with trust relationships, group configurations are an integral part of the Windows NT security system.

On a large network, groups are an essential network tool; but even in a smaller organizational environment, groups are very useful for keeping track of who has access to what. In this chapter, we'll discuss the types of user groups that are built into Windows NT Server. To help you with the occasional situation that requires another type of group configuration than what is built into the system, we'll also tell you how to create a new group that fits your situation and then explain how to delete it when you don't need it anymore.

## Built-In User Accounts and Groups

When you install either Microsoft Windows NT Server version 4 or Microsoft Windows NT Workstation version 4, several groups, plus a couple of user accounts, are already provided in the system to get you started.

### Built-In User Accounts

There are two built-in user accounts provided in Windows NT: *Administrator* and *Guest*. The most important built-in user account is, of course, the Administrator account. You can use this account to create all of the other accounts, including additional administrator accounts. The Guest user account is for users who log on infrequently. You can't delete the Guest account, but it's disabled by default. If you want to permit access to a guest, you just enable the account.

You might want to consider taking the following precautions to protect your built-in Administrator account. Use the built-in Administrator account to create another account for yourself with full administrative privileges. Use this new account rather than the built-in account for all of your day-to-day work. The new account can have your name on it or be called something descriptive like Domain Administrator. Assign a special, secure password to the built-in Administrator account, and relegate it to semiretirement. Stash the password for the built-in account somewhere safe.

It's possible for an administrator to accidentally disable an administrator account, so it's wise to have a backup. That way, you'll always have an uncontaminated, known-to-be-good administrator account that you can resort to, just in case.

## Built-In Groups

Virtually all user accounts that you create on a Windows NT Server network will belong to one or more of the Windows NT built-in groups. You probably can run nearly any kind of network using no more than the Windows NT groups that have been supplied with the operating system. In any case, you should understand the built-in groups before you start creating new ones.

All individual user accounts within a particular group have identical rights on the network. A user can be added to more than one group and will have *all* of the capabilities and rights that have been granted to each group to which he or she belongs. It's important to understand that *capabilities* are part of the group identity and can't be changed. User rights can be removed or added to a group, but only for everyone in the group, not for specific individuals. If there's a capability that you don't want someone to have, don't assign his or her account to a group with that capability.

**For More Information**

*See Chapter 9 for instructions on how to change the user rights assigned to a group.*

When you create groups in Windows NT Server, they will belong to one of two general categories: global (domain) groups and local groups. A global group is one that can be assigned rights and permissions in more than one domain; it can be created and managed only from a domain controller. A local group is one that can be assigned rights and permissions only in the domain in which it was created; it can be created and managed from either a domain controller or at the local computer. If you look at the list of built-in groups in User Manager for Domains (Figure 10.1 on the following page), you'll see that the titles of all but two of the global groups start with the word "Domain" and each name is preceded by a world-globe icon.

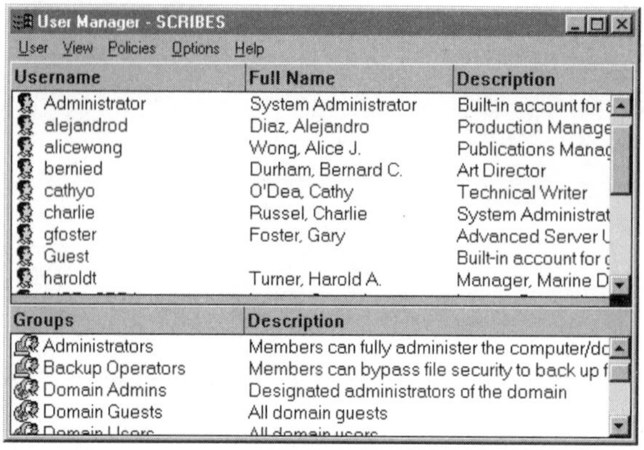

**FIGURE 10.1**

*User Manager for Domains*

## Characteristics of global groups

Global groups are very useful in a large, multidomain network because an entire group of users can be granted access to resources in other trusting domains in a single step. These are the characteristics of global groups:

♦   A global group can contain individual user accounts only from the domain in which the group was created (the *home domain*).

♦   A global group cannot contain any other groups, either local or global.

♦   A global group cannot contain local users.

♦   A global group can be assigned permissions to any resource in the domain in which the group was created (its *home domain*, if you will) and to resources in other domains that trust the home domain.

♦   A global group can be a member of a local group.

## Characteristics of local groups

Despite its name, a local group is in many ways more encompassing than a global group and more powerful. A local group can be an effective way to gather the users from domain and global groups from other trusted domains into a single package, assigning rights and permissions in the home domain to everyone in the group in a single step. These are the important characteristics of local groups:

♦   A local group can contain global groups from domains that are trusted by the home domain. It cannot contain another local group.

- A local group can be assigned permissions only in the domain in which the group was created (the home domain).

- A local group cannot be a member of any other group.

# Selecting the Right Kind of Group

Groups can be somewhat confusing so the following categories are provided to help you figure out when you should put user accounts into a local group and when you should put them into a global group.

- **A Group That Only Needs to Operate in One Domain.** A group of users that require rights and permissions within a single domain must be a local group.

- **A Group That Can Contain Users from Other Domains.** A group that contains users from more than one domain must be a local group. Although local groups can be used only in the domain in which they're created, you can get around this by manually creating the local group and defining its rights and permissions in every domain where you need it. This isn't the most elegant of solutions, but it works.

- **A Group That Can Contain Other Groups.** If you need a group that can contain both user accounts and other groups, it must be a local group.

- **A Group from One Domain That Can Be Granted Rights and Permissions in Another Domain.** If you have a bunch of users that need to use resources in another domain, the group that is created must be a global group.

- **A Group That Can Be Granted Permissions on Windows NT Workstations.** If you need a group that can be granted permissions on Windows NT workstations, it will have to be a global group. Local groups can't be granted these kinds of permissions.

# Using Built-In Groups

In the next sections, we'll cover both global and local built-in groups. Each group has specific capabilities as well as restrictions that are important to understand as you construct your user accounts.

## Built-In Global Groups

Windows NT Server has three built-in global groups: Domain Admins, Domain Users, and Domain Guests. These groups are located on the domain's primary and backup controllers; they cannot be deleted from the network. They can be removed from any local groups in which they are included as members by default.

If you're administering a multiple-domain network, you can make your job easier by following these steps when creating new groups, especially if you need to create a group that has to be in more than one domain.

1. Create *two* groups for the home domain: one local and one global. The built-in groups Administrators (local) and Domain Admins (global) are an example of this configuration.

2. Make all of the relevant user accounts in a domain members of the domain's global group. For example, all administrators in a domain would be members of the Domain Admins global group.

3. Put the global group into a local group. Domain Admins, for example, would be a member of the domain's Administrators local group. Domain Admins also could be made a member of the Administrators local group of other (trusting) domains, as appropriate.

## Domain Admins

The Administrator account for a domain is contained in the global group Domain Admins by default. Domain Admins is a member by default of both the home domain's Administrators local group and each home domain Windows NT workstation Administrators local group. A member of Domain Admins has administrator rights and permissions for the following network elements:

◆   The home domain of the user

◆   Workstations in the home domain

◆   Trusted domains

You can give other users in the domain administrative capabilities by adding them to the Domain Admins group. Only a user with an Administrator account can make changes to Domain Admins.

◆ • **Tip**

*If you don't want the global group Domain Admins to be able to administer a particular workstation or a server that's not a controller, remove Domain Admins from that workstation's or server's Administrators local group.*

## Domain Users

All of the user accounts in a domain are by default members of the global group Domain Users. When a new account is created, it is added automatically to Domain Users. Each member of Domain Users has normal access and abilities on any Windows NT workstation in the domain. Domain Users is a member of all Users local groups in the domain.

Only members of the Administrators local group or the Account Operators local group can make changes to Domain Users.

### Tip

*If you don't want members of the global group Domain Users to have access to a particular workstation or to a particular server that's not a controller, remove Domain Users from that computer's Users local group.*

## Domain Guests

All Guest user accounts are by default members of the Domain Guests global group. Initially, Domain Guests contains only the built-in Guest account. Domain Guests is by default a member of the Guests local group. Only members of the Administrators local group or the Account Operators local group can make changes to Domain Guests.

If you have a user who should have fewer rights and permissions than the typical domain user, make that person a member of Domain Guests group and remove him or her from Domain Users.

# Built-In Local Groups

It's important to note that Windows NT Server built-in local groups in a domain can exist on the domain controllers, on the individual network computers, or on both. Some computers in the domain might be running Windows NT Server but not functioning as controllers, and others might be running Windows NT Workstation. The role of a computer on the network will determine what Windows NT built-in local groups are available on that specific machine.

The following built-in local groups exist on Windows NT servers that are functioning as domain controllers:

◆ Account Operators

◆ Administrators

◆ Backup Operators

◆ Guests

- Print Operators

- Replicator

- Server Operators

- Users

The built-in local groups listed below exist on Windows NT servers that are not functioning as domain controllers and on Windows NT workstations:

- Administrators

- Backup Operators

- Guests

- Power Users

- Replicator

- Users

## Account Operators

Members of the Account Operators local group can create user accounts and groups for their home domain using User Manager for Domains. They also can modify or delete most of the domain's user accounts and groups when necessary.

### WHAT MEMBERS OF THE ACCOUNT OPERATORS GROUP CAN DO

| *Built-In Capabilities* | *Default User Rights* |
| --- | --- |
| Create and manage user accounts. | Log on locally. |
| Create and manage global groups. | Shut down the system. |
| Create and manage local groups. | |
| Add workstations to the domain. | |

### Tip

*Members of the Account Operators local group (like the members of the Administrators local group) always have the right to add workstations, even if this right isn't specifically assigned through the User Rights Policy.*

The list of what members of the Account Operators group can't do is longer than the list of what they can do. Members of the Account Operators group cannot administer security policies. They also can't change or delete either the global group Domain Admins or any of the following local groups:

- Administrators
- Backup Operators
- Print Operators
- Server Operators
- Account Operators

As you might expect, these restrictions apply as well to the user accounts in the group and to any global group that belongs to any of these local groups.

## *Administrators*

Administrators, which is the most powerful local group, has complete control over the domain and the domain's controllers. The Administrators local group is the only local group automatically granted every ability and every right in the system. When Windows NT Server is installed, the Domain Admins global group becomes a member of Administrators by default.

In the following list of the Administrators group capabilities and user rights, the word "computer" can mean domain controller, server, or Windows NT workstation.

### WHAT MEMBERS OF THE ADMINISTRATORS GROUP CAN DO

| *Built-In Capabilities* | *Default User Rights* |
|---|---|
| Create and manage user accounts. | Log on locally. |
| Create and manage local groups. | Load and unload device drivers. |
| Create and manage global groups. | Access this computer from the network. |
| Assign user rights. | Take ownership of files. |
| Lock the computer. | Change the system time. |
| Override lock of the computer. | Shut down the system. |
| Manage auditing of system events. | Force shutdown from a remote system. |
| Format computer's hard drive. | Manage auditing and the security log. |
| Create common groups. | Back up files and directories. |
| Add workstations to the domain. | Restore files and directories. |
| Control printer sharing. | |
| Control directory sharing. | |

## Backup Operators

Members of the Backup Operators local group can provide backup for two critical Administrator user account functions, but they can't perform other administrative functions. They also cannot change security settings.

### WHAT MEMBERS OF THE BACKUP OPERATORS GROUP CAN DO

| *Built-In Capabilities* | *Default User Rights* |
| --- | --- |
| None. | Log on locally. |
| | Shut down the system. |
| | Back up files and directories on servers and domain controllers. |
| | Restore files and directories on servers and domain controllers. |

## Guests

The Guests local group is for one-time or occasional network users. Guests have no rights on any of the servers, but they can log on at a workstation. A guest user can shut down the system, however, because all members of the group Everyone have that right. (See the section "Everyone" on page 208.) The global group Domain Guests is a member of the Guests local group.

## Print Operators

Members of the Print Operators group can manage every aspect of printer operations in a domain.

### WHAT MEMBERS OF THE PRINT OPERATORS GROUP CAN DO

| *Built-In Capabilities* | *Default User Rights* |
| --- | --- |
| Share and stop sharing printers. | Log on locally. |
| | Shut down the system. |

## Power Users

Power Users is a local group that exists only on Windows NT workstations and on servers that are not domain controllers. A member of the Power Users group can modify only the accounts and groups he or she has created.

### WHAT MEMBERS OF THE POWER USERS GROUP CAN DO

*Built-In Capabilities*

Create user accounts and manage these accounts.

Create local groups and manage these groups.

Lock the computer.

Create common groups.

Add and remove users from Power Users, Users, and Guests local groups.

Share and stop sharing directories.

Share and stop sharing printers.

*Default User Rights*

Log on locally.

Access this computer from the network.

Shut down the system.

Force shutdown from a remote system.

Change the system time.

## Replicator

This group is not like the other local groups—no one is automatically made a member of Replicator. In fact, no actual users should be added to this group. There probably should be only one account assigned to it. Replicator logs on to Replicator services on the domain controller and manages the replication of files and directories. (For more on Replicator services, see Chapter 14.)

## Server Operators

Every domain controller or backup controller has a Server Operators group that can administer domain servers. Members of this group can do most of the administrator's job. However, they can't manipulate security options.

### WHAT MEMBERS OF THE SERVER OPERATORS GROUP CAN DO

*Built-In Capabilities*

Lock the server.

Override lock of the server.

Format server hard drive.

Create common groups.

Share and stop sharing directories.

Share and stop sharing printers.

*Default User Rights*

Log on locally.

Change the system time.

Shut down the system.

Force shutdown from a remote system.

Back up files and directories.

Restore files and directories.

## Users

This group provides users with the rights to perform everyday end-user tasks, such as the right to:

◆ Log on to a workstation and use it to access the network.

◆ Run applications.

◆ Use local and network printers.

◆ Create and manage their own local groups.

◆ Keep a personal profile.

◆ Shut down and lock the workstation.

**NOTE**

*Although members of the Users local group have the capability to create other local groups on a server, they actually can't do this unless they also have the right to log on locally at the server or if they have access to User Manager for Domains.*

## Everyone

The Everyone local group isn't, in the strictest sense, a group, but the term does appear in a few places, such as the User Rights Policy dialog boxes. Anyone who has a user account in a domain is a member of that domain's Everyone local group by default.

### WHAT MEMBERS OF THE EVERYONE GROUP CAN DO

| *Built-In Capabilities* | *Default User Rights* |
|---|---|
| Lock the computer, if they also have the right to log on locally to the controller. | Access this computer from the network. |
| | Log on locally to workstations or servers that are not domain controllers. |
| | Shut down the system. |

Within a domain, Everyone can connect over the network to shared server directories and can print to shared printers.

## Special Built-In Groups

Windows NT Server also includes special built-in groups that are used only to show how a particular user is using the Windows NT system at any specific time. In other words, these groups have no actual members; membership in a group is implied by the means of user access to a resource. The four special built-in groups are:

- **Interactive** Any user who is logged on locally

- **Network** Any user who has gained access to a resource through the network

- **System** The operating system

- **Creator/Owner** Anyone who is creating a file, a subdirectory, or a print job

The nature of these generic groups makes it possible to assign permissions according to the type of access to resources rather than according to the locations of individual accounts, local groups, or global groups.

**NOTE**

*The Interactive group and the Network group together constitute the Everyone group, which is described in the preceding section.*

# Who Goes in What Group?

Most people on a network are going to be users. But even on a small network, you'll need at least one person assigned to the Administrators local group or Server Operators local group so that someone with backup and restore rights will be on hand during all hours of the network's operation.

Only administrators are allowed to manage the controllers, the servers, the workstations, and every other aspect of a network's operation. On a very small network, all you'll really need is one administrator to run the show and one backup administrator to take over in case the first administrator is suddenly rendered non compos mentis. (It's rare, true, but it should never be completely unexpected.)

At least one person who is not a member of the Administrators local group should be assigned to the Server Operators local group. This person won't have all the powers of an administrator, but he or she can keep the domain servers going.

If your operation frequently hires new employees or uses temporary employees, a member of the Account Operators group can be the one who creates new user accounts, assigns users to the correct groups, and adds workstations to the domain.

What groups you will want to use and how many people you want to have in each group will depend a great deal on the size and the specific needs of your network. If backups are automated and relatively simple, one administrator can take care of them. But in organizations where backups are frequent, complicated, and are done religiously, you might want to give this task to someone in the Backup Operators group—without giving him or her any other administrative rights.

These are four things you will need to remember about how global and local groups are used:

- If user accounts in one domain (let's call this Domain A) need to be used on the servers and workstations of both Domain A and other domains, they must be put in a global group.

- If user accounts in both Domain A and other domains are to be used on the servers of Domain A, they must be put in a local group.

- If a global group in Domain A or a global group in another domain needs to be used on the servers of Domain A, this global group must be added as a member to the relevant local group.

- If a user group needs permissions on computers running Windows NT Workstation or on Windows NT servers that are not domain controllers, the group must be a global group.

# Adding and Removing Users from Groups

One of the reasons you will want to assign rights and permissions by group is that it's so easy to move individuals in and out of groups.

## Adding Users to a Local Group or a Global Group

The procedures for adding members to a group are essentially the same, whether it's a local group or a global group.

1. Open User Manager for Domains.

2. In the lower pane, double-click the group name. The Properties dialog box for the type of group you chose—local or global—appears.

3. For a local group, click Add to open the Add Users And Groups dialog box. Select the users. Click Add, and then click OK. Click OK to close the Properties dialog box.

4. For a global group in the Not Members box, select the users to be added. Click Add, and then click OK.

## Removing Users from a Local Group or a Global Group

To remove users from either a local group or a global group, follow these steps:

1. Open User Manager for Domains.

2. Double-click the group name.

3. Select the name (or group) you want to remove; then click Remove. Click OK when you're done.

# Creating New Groups

Creating groups is a very simple process. The ways in which local and global groups are created are similar, but the steps are slightly different because local groups can contain global groups.

In general, new local groups are created to grant permissions for access to different resources, and global groups are created to organize users according to the work they do or according to some other role they play in the organization. Here's an example. Suppose you have a new high-speed printer on the network. The printer is to be used by certain members of the production department; you want to prevent other users from tying it up. To make this happen, you would:

1. Create a local group, and give it permission to use the new printer.

2. Create a global group that consists of all individuals on the network who have permission to use the new printer.

3. Add the global group to the local group.

You can give individual users access to the printer (or remove their access) just by adding or removing them from the global group. If you want the global group to have access to a printer that's connected to a workstation, add this group to the local group at the workstation that has permission to use the workstation printer.

> **For More Information**
>
> *The granting and managing of permissions is covered in Chapter 12.*

## Creating a New Global Group

To create a new global group, assign a name to the group and then add users to it, following these steps:

1. Open User Manager for Domains.

2. Choose New Global Group from the User menu. A dialog box like the one in Figure 10.2 on the following page will open.

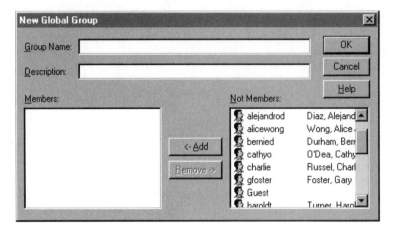

**FIGURE 10.2**

*Dialog box for creating a new global group*

3. Type the name of the group in the Group Name box.

4. Type a description of the group in the Description box (optional, but highly recommended).

5. Add members by highlighting their names in the Not Members window; click Add.

6. Click OK to close the dialog box.

## Creating a New Local Group

To create a new local group, assign a name to the new group; then add individual members or global groups from the local domain or from a trusted domain.

1. Start User Manager for Domains.

2. Choose New Local Group from the User menu. A dialog box will open like the one shown in Figure 10.3.

3. Type the name of the group in the Group Name box.

4. Type a description of the group in the Description box (optional, but highly recommended).

5. Click Add to open the dialog box shown in Figure 10.4.

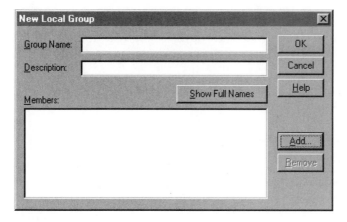

**FIGURE 10.3**

*Dialog box for creating a new local group*

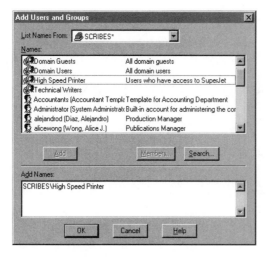

**FIGURE 10.4**

*Dialog box for adding users and groups to a new local group*

**6.** Click the names of the individuals or global groups that you want as members of the new local group; then click Add.

**7.** When you're done selecting members for the new group, click OK.

## Copying a Group

If you need to create a new group and you already have a group that closely matches the one you need, use the Copy function in User Manager for Domains to do the job.

1. Start User Manager for Domains.

2. Select the group you want to copy. Choose Copy from the User menu and the New Local Group dialog box appears.

3. In the Group Name box, type the new name for the copy. Changing the description of the group is optional but very advisable.

4. To add users, click Add. In the Add Users and Groups dialog box, add users you want in the group who weren't in the original group that you copied. Click OK.

5. To remove users from the original group that you don't want in the new group, select the users and click Remove.

6. Click OK when you're done.

## Deleting a Group

You can delete only the groups that you created with User Manager for Domains. You can't delete any of the built-in groups. Once you delete a group, you can't recover it because the SID for the group is deleted when the group is deleted and is never reused. You'll see the following warning message that reminds you of this fact.

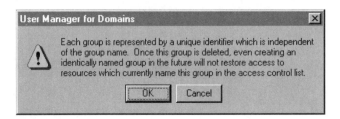

If you decide you do want a group that you have deleted already, you will have to recreate it from scratch, including all of the permissions associated with it.

To delete a group, follow these steps:

1. Start User Manager for Domains.

2. Select the group you want to delete.

3. Press Del, or choose Delete from the User menu.

4. Confirm the deletion by clicking OK, and then click Yes.

*Deleting a group removes the group from Windows NT Server but not the user accounts (or global groups, in the case of a deleted local group) that were members of this group.*

## POINTS TO REMEMBER

♦ User rights can be assigned to individuals or to groups.

♦ Capabilities are assigned to groups. To grant a user a specific capability, you must assign the user to a group that has that capability.

♦ A global group can be assigned rights and permissions in more than one domain.

♦ A local group can be assigned rights and permissions only in the domain in which it was created.

♦ A global group can contain only user accounts from the domain in which it is created. A global group can't contain other groups.

♦ A local group can contain user accounts and global groups from multiple domains.

♦ Create new local groups to grant permissions to resources.

♦ Create new global groups to organize users.

## WHAT'S NEXT?

In this chapter we've covered a lot of ground very quickly. Groups are not a simple concept, so don't be surprised if you find yourself back in this chapter for a refresher—more than once. In Chapter 11, we'll talk about setting up printers and configuring how they're used.

# CHAPTER 11

# CHAPTER 11

# Printers and Other Resources

Hardware is expensive and companies don't like to invest in it until they absolutely have to. And as hard as it is to get permission to buy new equipment, it's even harder to get permission to buy equipment that is used only infrequently. From an economics point of view, the investment in equipment pays off only to the extent that the equipment is used. One of the great advantages of a network—although far from being the only one—is the ability to share equipment that otherwise would stand idle much of the time. Printers are a perfect example of this, and they are an obvious item to share. One could, certainly, consider providing an inexpensive dot matrix or ink jet printer for most users, but it's unlikely that many people would consider putting an expensive, high-end color printer or even a good, fast laser printer on everyone's desk. And you don't really need to. By putting one high-end printer on the network, you spread the cost and machine use across all of your users, which makes the investment in the equipment much easier to justify.

**NOTE**

*Microsoft Windows NT version 4 uses some special and sometimes confusing terms when referring to printers. First it's important to differentiate between a* print device, *which is the actual machine that does the printing, and a* printer, *which in Microsoft terminology is the software interface between the application and the actual print device. Therefore, a printer in Microsoft terminology is actually a* logical *entity.*

## Printer Setup Options

To keep confusion to a minimum, we will refer to the print device simply as the "printer." We will refer to the software interface as the "logical printer." You should be aware, however, that the Windows NT documentation either doesn't use these terms or doesn't use them in this way. In a Novell NetWare or OS/2 networking environment, the term *print queue* is used instead of printer (meaning the logical printer), but the net effect is the same. Windows NT Server supports a broad range of printers. Figure 11.1 shows the simplest possible arrangement—a print job in Windows NT going to a logical printer, from which the job is spooled to a printer.

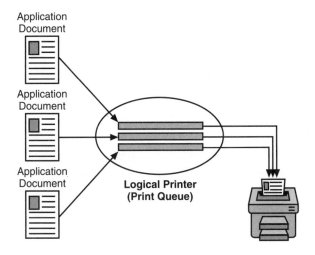

**FIGURE 11.1**

*Example of jobs routing through a logical printer to a printer*

You can have one logical printer associated with a single printer, which is the arrangement shown in Figure 11.1. Or you can have several logical printers associated with a single printer. In this arrangement, logical printers can be configured at different priority levels, so that one is for normal printing and the others are for jobs that can wait to be printed later. For a printer that uses both Postscript and PCL, having two logical printers allows users to choose either type of printing.

You also can have a single logical printer associated with multiple printers. If all of the printers use the same printer driver—an arrangement called a *printer pool*—a single logical printer will send jobs to the first available printer. The advantage of a printer pool is that the administrator can add or remove printers without affecting user configurations because the printers are interchangeable. The disadvantage of a printer pool is that there's no way to predict which printer will receive which job. So don't pool printers when they are physically far apart!

# Planning Network Printing

As for everything you do on a network, you need to actually *plan* where and how your printers will be set up, configured, shared, and managed—a nuisance, but a necessary nuisance if you want to keep your trouble and your support calls down. You need to think about how your users really use printers, where the heaviest users are physically located, where to physically locate highly specialized printers such as plotters and color laser printers, and how you're going to physically connect all of the printers to the network.

Let's look at the last of these questions for a moment. To the average PC user, printers are always attached to a parallel port. But that doesn't work well for a network or for a server. Parallel ports require a fair amount of CPU attention to do their thing, which is the last thing you want on a server. You're also usually limited to three parallel ports. The other two choices are a serial connection (preferably using a "smart," multiport serial card) or a network connection. Either works well, but, in most cases these days, your best bet is a direct network connection.

How you choose to connect your printers will be influenced by several factors. You'll need to consider your physical layout. Are your users all in central physical locations? If so, you might find it easiest to simply recycle an older PC as a print server by installing a multiport serial card in it and using it to drive the printers. Or are your users (and their associated print needs) located in separate offices spread over several floors? If so, you'll probably want to use network connections, either external connections or connections built into the printers, to connect printers that are conveniently located for each group of offices.

There are two basic methods for connecting your printers directly to the network. You can use a high-end printer that comes with a network card that is either built in or available as an option. Or you can use a stand-alone network print server—the Hewlett-Packard JetDirect EX is a good example—that supports a variety of protocols and usually comes with drivers to support many network operating systems, including Windows NT Server. This is useful in a typical organizational environment, where your network might well consist of multiple operating systems—all of which require access to that expensive color laser printer.

In any case, once you've decided where and how to physically locate and connect the printers, you'll need to create and manage the logical printers that your users will actually see.

# Managing Printers

Managing printers is not about the printers themselves but about how they are connected to and managed as part of your overall Windows NT Server network. You'll have to choose which networking protocol to use if the printers are network printers, decide which server you will use to manage them, and decide what functions you will allow your users to have access to.

## Installing the DLC Protocol

If you have a Hewlett-Packard (HP) network printer, you have several options for controlling it; the simplest option is probably to use the DLC protocol. Another option is to use TCP/IP, which is probably the better option in the long run; but we'll save the discussion of TCP/IP printing installation for Chapter 17, where we discuss the TCP/IP protocol in detail. For the moment, let's stick with DLC. It has the advantage of being simple and straightforward, so we can focus on the printer side of what we're doing and not get bogged down in the intricacies of TCP/IP. If you will be managing HP printers and if you haven't already installed DLC, now is a good time to install it. Remember, installing any protocol will require a reboot of the server, so plan the installation for a time when there will be minimal disruption to your users. To install the DLC protocol, follow these steps:

1. Open Control Panel, and double-click the Network icon to bring up the Network dialog box.

2. Click the Protocols tab (shown in Figure 11.2).

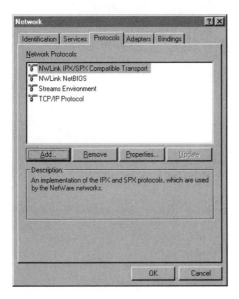

**FIGURE 11.2**

*The Protocols page in the Network dialog box*

3. Click Add, and select the DLC protocol from the list, as shown on the following page in Figure 11.3.

4. The system will prompt you for your Windows NT Server version 4 CD-ROM, of course, so that the necessary files can be loaded. If Windows NT Server is looking in the wrong place, you can browse for the correct location.

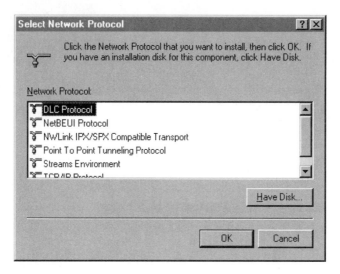

**FIGURE 11.3**

*The Select Network Protocol dialog box showing the selected protocol*

5. After the necessary files are loaded, go ahead and close the Network properties dialog box; Windows NT Server will make the necessary changes to network bindings. When it's finished, it will prompt you to reboot your server, as shown in Figure 11.4. Click Yes. When the rebooting is complete, the new protocol will be in place.

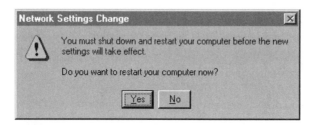

**FIGURE 11.4**

*Network Settings Change confirmation message*

Now that you have the DLC protocol installed, you will be able to manipulate the HP network printers and JetDirect print servers directly, just as if they were physically attached to the server.

# Adding a New Printer

Before you can make a printer available to the rest of your network, you must add it to the server that will control it. Try to centralize the control of your printers to make managing them simpler. But whenever possible, you also should have at least two different servers sharing the same network printer. This allows the users access to a printer pool that consists of two logical printers that point to the same printer. Now if you need to take down one of the servers for some reason, users will still have access to the printer.

Adding a new printer to the network involves several actions:

◆ Adding the printer port, if it doesn't already exist

◆ Logically connecting the printer to the port

◆ Setting the device-specific options for the printer

◆ Loading the necessary drivers for Windows clients who will be using the printer

◆ Sharing the printer to the rest of the network, and then setting permissions for who can control the printer and manage the documents that are printed on it

◆ Testing the new logical printer

◆ Adding the printer to the network clients and testing the connections

The Add Printer Wizard will take you through the process of adding a new logical printer to a server—creating the logical printer, connecting it to the print device, and testing the result. To add a printer to the server, follow these steps:

1. Click Start. Choose Settings and then Printers from the submenus that open from the Start menu.

2. Double-click Add Printer to start the Add Printer Wizard (Figure 11.5 on the following page).

3. Click the My Computer option button, even if the printer you are adding is physically connected to the network and not to the server. Then click Next.

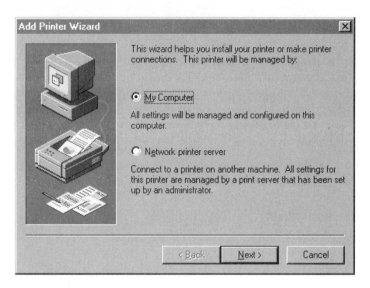

**FIGURE 11.5**

*Add Printer Wizard opening window*

4. If the port to which the printer is physically attached is present on the list that is displayed, check that box and jump to step 7. Otherwise, click Add Port to bring up the Printer Ports dialog box shown in Figure 11.6.

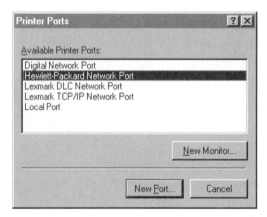

**FIGURE 11.6**

*Printer Ports dialog box*

5. Select the kind of port you want to add, and click New Port. If the necessary files are not yet on the server, the Add Printer Wizard will prompt for your Windows NT Server version 4 CD-ROM to install them. Then it will prompt you to specify the name and network card address for the type of port you are adding. To add an HP DLC printer, for example, select Hewlett-Packard Network Port and click New Port. You'll see the dialog box shown in Figure 11.7.

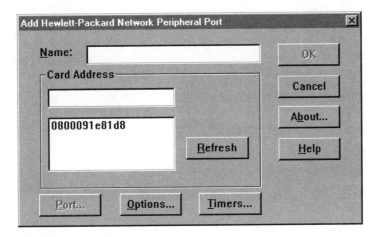

**FIGURE 11.7**

*Example of an Add Network Peripheral Port dialog box*

6. Select the hardware address of the printer or print server network card you want to add, and then double-click it. If you are adding an HP network printer, you must know the hardware MAC address for the printer or print server's network card.

7. Choose a name for the new port. Be sure to choose a name that describes the printer or printer port clearly because you won't be able to change it later. Type the name in the Name text box. Click OK. The main Add Printer Wizard screen will return with the new port checked, as shown in Figure 11.8 on the following page.

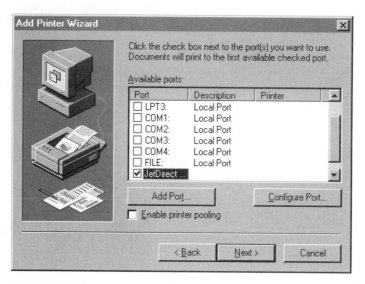

**FIGURE 11.8**

*Example of Add Printer Wizard dialog box showing a new port*

8. Click Next to choose the type of printer you are attaching to the port, as shown in the example in Figure 11.9. Select the printer manufacturer in the left-hand pane of the window, and then select the model of printer from the list in the right-hand pane.

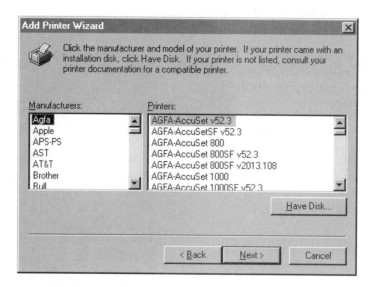

**FIGURE 11.9**

*Add Printer Wizard showing list of printers and manufacturers*

**9.** If your printer manufacturer has provided a special driver disk for Windows NT version 4, click Have Disk to manually add this driver.

**10.** After you've chosen the type of printer you are adding, click Next. If there is already a driver for this type of printer loaded, you'll get a message like the one shown in Figure 11.10. You can use that driver or replace it with a new driver. Click the appropriate option button, and then click Next.

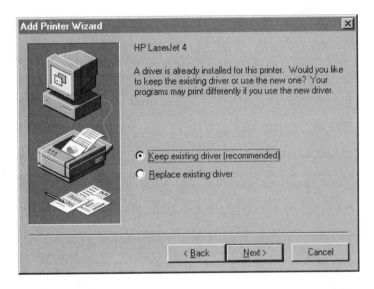

**FIGURE 11.10**

*Add Printer Wizard showing existing driver message*

**11.** Give the new printer a name that describes its function or its location clearly. Type the name in the Printer Name text box, as shown on the following page in Figure 11.11. Click the Yes or the No option button to specify whether this printer will be the default Windows NT Server printer. Then click Next.

**12.** If you're sharing this printer on the network, click the Shared option button. Choose a share name for the printer, and type the name in the Share Name text box, as shown on the following page in Figure 11.12. If the printer will be shared with MS-DOS or Microsoft Windows 3.*x* clients, make sure you stick to a maximum of eight characters for the name and don't use spaces or weird characters in the name.

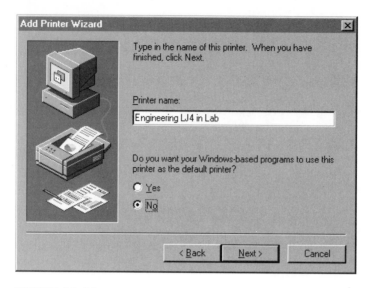

**FIGURE 11.11**

*Add Printer Wizard showing Printer Name text box*

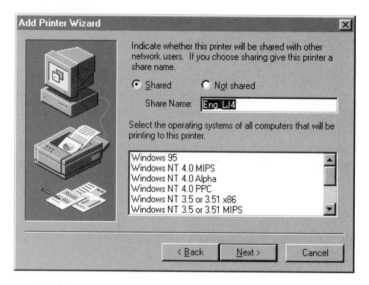

**FIGURE 11.12**

*Add Printer Wizard showing shared printer dialog box*

**13.** Windows NT Server can load printer drivers for other 32-bit Microsoft operating systems in addition to the current version of Windows NT, including drivers for previous versions of Windows NT and Microsoft Windows 95. Select all operating systems on the network that will be using this printer, and click Next.

**14.** The Add Printer Wizard will now prompt you for a variety of disks, CD-ROMs, and source directories for the various operating systems you selected. Just browse to the proper places in the dialog boxes, and you'll eventually get to the last screen in this process, which is shown in Figure 11.13.

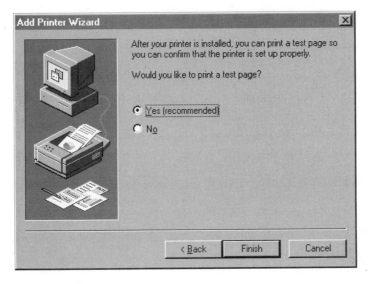

**FIGURE 11.13**

*Add Printer Wizard showing print test message*

**15.** Always choose to print a test page to make sure everything works as it should from the server. You'll also want to test each client machine as you add this printer to them, but first things first. The printer should work from the server before it's added to the network clients. Click Finish, and you're almost done.

**16.** When it has finished printing the test page, Windows NT Server will give you a chance to confirm that all went as expected. (See Figure 11.14 on the following page.)

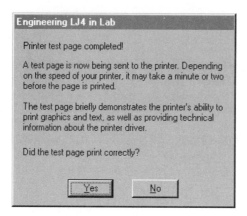

**FIGURE 11.14**

*Add Printer Wizard test page confirmation message*

**17.** If the test page printed correctly, you're done. If it did not print correctly, click No to start up the Windows NT Help system (Figure 11.15). The Windows NT Help application will walk you through the steps to troubleshoot and fix your printer.

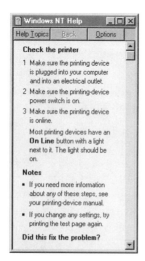

**FIGURE 11.15**

*Windows NT Help window*

Whew! We've now added a new printer to the system and shared it to the network. You'll use an essentially similar series of steps to add a printer to the system no matter what kind of connection you have to the printer, although the particular options obviously will differ for each type of connection.

# Sharing a Printer

Sharing a printer in Windows NT Server is easy. As you have seen in the preceding section, the normal printer installation process allows you to share the printer during installation. But you also can choose to share a printer on the network later, after installation, as a separate step. Perhaps you're experimenting with the printer locally before making it available to the network. Or perhaps something about the printer has changed, and you want to change the share name. Or maybe you have a printer with multiple personalities, and you want to share it with a different name for each personality. Whatever the reason, the steps to share a printer are the same.

1. Choose Settings and then Printers from the submenus that open from the Start menu.

2. Right-click the printer you want to share. Choose Sharing from the menu that appears, which brings up the Properties dialog box for the printer with the Sharing page in front, as shown in Figure 11.16. Now click the Shared option button.

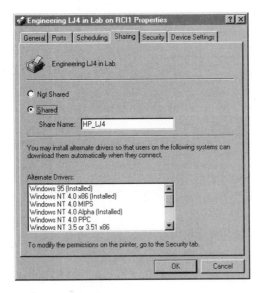

**FIGURE 11.16**

*Printer Properties dialog box showing Sharing page*

3. If your printer will be used by other operating systems, such as earlier versions of Windows NT or Windows 95, you can choose to have the printer drivers for these operating systems loaded on the server, which further reduces the overhead to the clients. Select the drivers you want to support in the Alternate Drivers list box.

4. Click the Security tab to establish the permissions for the printer. From here you can control who has access to a printer and who manages the printer queue. The default settings are shown in Figure 11.17, but you can change them easily to, for example, allow only a special group to use the printer. See "Configuring Printer Security" on page 240 for instructions on printer security specifications.

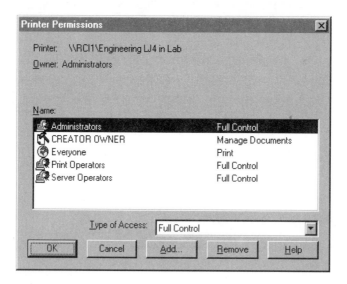

**FIGURE 11.17**

*Printer Permissions dialog box*

5. After you've made your changes (if any) to the security settings for the printer, click OK and the printer will be shared to the network.

That's it. Pretty straightforward. You should now add the printer to at least one client of each operating system type that you expect to support and print a test page, just to make sure that everything works as you expect.

## Deleting a Printer

If you change your network's printer configuration, you might have to delete a printer from the list of currently available printers stored in the system. This is one procedure that is a bit awkward in Windows NT Server. There is no simple way to remove a printer and change all of the workstation references to it.

You can remove the printer easily enough, of course. That's not hard. Simply select the printer in the Printers folder, and press Delete. ZAP! It's gone. But this does nothing to remove the printer reference from workstations that may have been using the printer. They're going to end up with a reference that points to a non-existent printer. This isn't generally a polite way to run your network. Now you could, and obviously *should*, send around an E-mail message to all users on your system who might be using the printer and let them know the printer is going to be removed—preferably with a bit of advance notice, although one doesn't always have a lot of choice in this matter.

However, there's a better choice than simply removing the printer—replace it. In most cases, there will be a functionally equivalent printer available somewhere in your system, maybe one in the same geographical area as the printer you are removing. Perhaps it's the printer you bought to replace that aged and infirm printer you now want to remove. Or maybe it's another printer in the same general vicinity as the one you want to remove. Whatever it is, you'll do your users a favor by sharing the replacement printer with the same name as the name of the printer you're removing. Or create a second name for an existing printer that matches the name of the one you're removing. But however you make the change, notify your users. It cuts down on the noise level substantially.

## Changing a Printer

Changing a printer—that is, replacing one printer with another—requires little if any change to your user configurations if the printers are close relatives. Just swap the two printers and keep the printers' shared name the same, even if some of the underlying configuration has changed. As long as there is no real difference in the overall capabilities of the two printers, this will work. This is one advantage in the way Windows NT Server version 4 handles printers. Because printer drivers are maintained at the server level instead of at the workstation level, even fairly significant changes in the printer will be transparent to the user. When you physically change the printer out, however, don't forget to change the printer driver that is associated with the printer.

### Changing the printer driver

One of the tasks you inevitably will have to do is change a printer driver. The reason—whether it's because you've physically changed a printer or because the manufacturer of the printer has provided an updated driver—doesn't really matter. This is a nuisance, but at least now you only have to do it in one place, although you will need drivers for all of the operating systems you're supporting. Be aware that changing a printer driver can change the available features of the printer.

To change the printer driver for a printer, follow these steps:

1. Choose Settings and then Printers from the submenus that open from the Start menu.

2. Right-click the printer for which you are changing the driver, and choose Properties to bring up the Properties dialog box for the printer.

3. Click New Driver. You'll get a warning message like the one shown in Figure 11.18. Click Yes to continue.

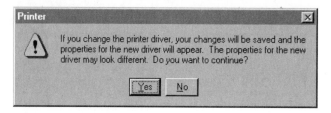

**FIGURE 11.18**

*Printer change driver warning message*

4. A list of printers like the one shown in Figure 11.19 will appear. Select your printer from this list of available printer drivers; click OK. Or select Have Disk to use an updated driver from the manufacturer.

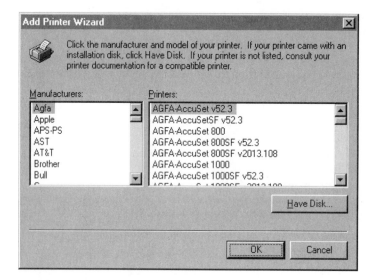

**FIGURE 11.19**

*Add Printer Wizard showing available printer drivers*

5. If you select Have Disk, browse to the location of the new driver's .INF file. Or select the correct printer manufacturer and correct model of your printer from the list. Click OK.

6. If you already have a driver for the selected printer on the system, you will see a warning message like the one in Figure 11.20. If you're updat-

ing the printer driver, you'll generally want to overwrite the existing driver. Otherwise, you can keep the existing driver. Click the appropriate option button, and then click OK.

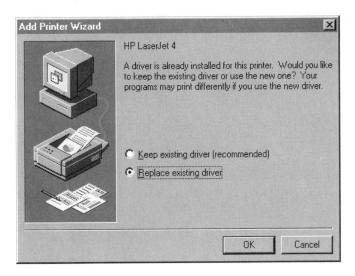

**FIGURE 11.20**

*Existing driver warning message*

7. After you've updated the driver, also update all versions of the driver that you have on the system to support other operating systems. Click the Sharing tab of the Properties dialog box for the printer. In the Alternate Drivers list box, click the operating systems you'll be updating, and then click OK. You might have to browse to the correct location for the necessary files.

8. When the files have been updated, the new drivers are in place.

## Modifying printer properties

Each printer has its own unique set of device-specific settings, which you can modify to match your needs. We won't attempt to tell you what all the possibilities are but will point you in the direction of where to go to change them.

The printer's device-specific properties are a tab in the printer's Properties dialog box that we've been working with in the preceding sections. Right-click the printer icon, and choose Properties. Now click the Device Settings tab. You'll see a long list of device-specific settings that you can change, assuming you have the permission to do so. A typical example is the list of settings for an HP LaserJet 4 printer shown in Figure 11.21 on the following page.

**FIGURE 11.21**

*A Device Settings dialog box showing the settings for a specific printer*

If you have anything other than the default amount of memory installed on the printer, the value for Installed Memory is often incorrect. Change this if you've added extra memory. If you have added print cartridges to the printer since the device settings were last updated, also add them here.

# Logical Printer or Print Queue

In addition to managing your printer and the drivers that are associated with it, you'll also need to manage the print jobs that are sent to the logical printer (print queue). Generally, you can do the following things:

◆ Attach a device name to a logical printer (necessary for many legacy MS-DOS programs).

◆ Change the times when a printer is available.

◆ Pause a printer. (Jobs can continue to be sent to the printer, but nothing comes out.)

◆ Pause a specific document in the queue.

◆ Resume printing a paused document.

◆ Restart a specific document in the queue.

◆ Change the priority of the documents in the queue.

- Cancel (delete) a print job from the queue.

- Schedule a specific time to print a particular job in the queue.

- Change which user gets notified when a job is done printing.

The way you do the things in the bulleted list is pretty straightforward and can be performed from the printer's window. However, redirecting a logical printer to a print device is specific to each workstation and is done at the workstation. It's not something that is done at the server. But because Windows NT Server can do this for legacy MS-DOS applications only by using a command line, we'll show you the specifics of how to do that.

## Attaching a Device Name to a Logical Printer

Many legacy MS-DOS programs don't really "understand" network logical printers. They understand good old-fashioned device names such as LPT1 and LPT2. So you have to fool them into thinking they're printing to one of those devices, even though you are actually redirecting their output to one of the logical printers. You have to do it at each workstation or server that will have programs printing to the specific device in question. Unfortunately, there's no cute GUI way to do this in Windows NT Server. The only way you can do it is to use a command line that reassigns a device name to the logical printer. For example, you might want to assign the device name LPT1 to a network printer. The command line to accomplish this task is this:

```
net use lpt1 \\<servername>\<sharename>
```

You can add this command easily to the users' logon script to make this happen automatically. Or you can let your users know about the command, and they can run the command manually as needed. Normally, the connection will not be remembered between logon sessions, but you can change that by changing the command line to read:

```
net use lpt1 \\<servername>\<sharename> /persistent:yes
```

## Changing the Times a Printer Is Available

By default, printers are available on the network at all times of the day. But if you have an expensive printer, you might want to restrict access to the printer to a particular time of the day. You can change the schedule for the printer. Right-click the printer icon, and choose Properties. Then click the Scheduling tab in the dialog box that appears (Figure 11.22 on the following page). Click the option button next to From, and choose the begin and end times from the From and To list boxes.

You also can change a number of other options on this page, but, in general, you'll find that the default settings for these other options are perfectly adequate.

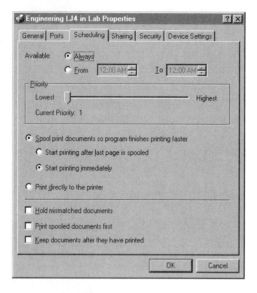

**FIGURE 11.22**

*Printer Properties dialog box showing Scheduling tab*

## Managing Documents in a Logical Printer

You can manipulate the documents in a logical printer by opening the printer window on your screen and then selecting which document you want to manipulate. Open the printer by double-clicking its icon. A window will open, the one shown in Figure 11.23, which shows a printer that has been directed to pause with three documents waiting in the queue to print.

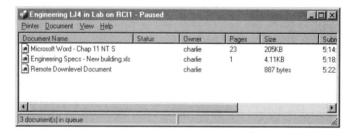

**FIGURE 11.23**

*Printer Properties dialog box showing documents paused in print queue*

Right-click a document to bring up the menu shown here:

From this menu, you can pause the printing of a document in the queue, resume printing a document that is paused in the queue, restart a document from the beginning, or select Cancel to delete it from the queue entirely. Pause is a useful option when you have a problem with a printer and you need to stop any jobs that are being sent to it while you fix the problem.

You also can use this menu to change the properties of a print job on the fly. Perhaps you realize that your 400-page document is going to tie up the printer for a while and your boss really needs that shopping list printed out before he goes home. Or you want to notify the administrative assistant that you've printed out a stack of new hardware requisitions, which now need to be entered into the system. No problem. Right-click the document, and choose Properties. You'll get the dialog box shown in Figure 11.24.

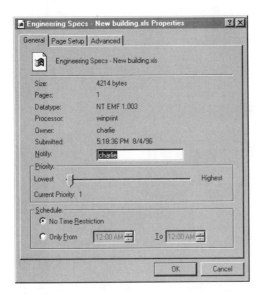

**FIGURE 11.24**

*Example of a document Properties dialog box*

In the document Properties dialog box, you can change or view the properties of the documents in the queue for printing. You can change the document's priority in the queue—making sure that a specific document is the next one printed, for example, by giving it the highest priority of any of the documents currently in the queue. You also can change the time when the document is scheduled to print and who will be notified when the document is finished printing. So you can take that 400-page document and schedule it to print after everyone else has gone home; you then can change the Notify field so that the system notifies your administrative assistant when the requisitions are finished. All you have left to do is crank up the priority on your boss's shopping list. You look like a genius. We wish administrative tasks were all that easy.

## Configuring Printer Security

When a printer is to be shared on the network, one of the decisions you will have to make is which users will be allowed access to the printer. As for all security features of Windows NT Server, you, as the system administrator, have a great deal of control over who can use the printer and what level of control each individual can have over the printer and the print jobs on it. Windows NT Server is definite about defining levels of individual access to a printer.

There are four basic levels of user access to a printer:

◆ **No Access**

The printer is not available to users who have this level of access. They can see the printer when browsing, but if they attempt to add the printer, the result is the rather rude message shown in Figure 11.25.

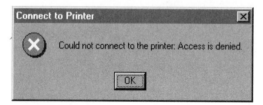

**FIGURE 11.25**

*No-access-to-printer message*

◆ **Print**

The user can print to the printer but has no control over the printer queue or the documents in it unless he or she created the print job.

◆ **Manage Documents**

The user can pause print jobs that are scheduled to print on the printer, change their priority, or even delete them.

◆ **Full Control**

The user can make all changes to the printer, including taking ownership of the printer.

# Viewing or Changing Printer Permissions

The default printer security settings for Windows NT Server are designed to give everyone the ability to print, to give the owner of a print job the ability to manage that specific print job, and to allow Administrators, Print Operators, and Server Operators to set or change security settings for a printer. To set or change the printer security settings, follow these steps:

**1.** Choose Settings and then Printers from the submenus that open from the Start menu.

**2.** Right-click the printer for which you want to change the security settings. Choose Properties from the menu to bring up the printer's Properties dialog box. Click the Security tab to bring the Security page to the top, as shown in Figure 11.26.

**FIGURE 11.26**

*Printer Properties dialog box showing Security page*

3. Click Permissions to view or to modify user permissions. You'll see a dialog box like the one shown in Figure 11.17 on page 232.

4. To change printer access permission for one of the users or groups listed, select the user or group. Then select the type of access from the Type Of Access drop-down list box. Click OK, and the user or group access is changed.

5. To add a new user or group to the set of permissions, click Add. The familiar Add Users And Groups dialog box will appear (Figure 11.27). The dialog box lets you assign specific users and groups a permission level to an object. Select the user or group you want to add. (Click Show Users to include individual users in the list.) Select the type of access you want to grant to the user or group, and then click Add. When you are finished adding the users or groups you want for that permission level, click OK.

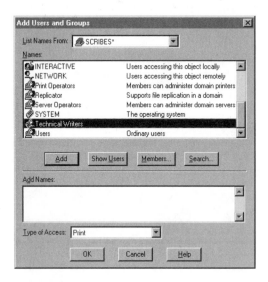

**FIGURE 11.27**

*Add Users And Groups dialog box*

## NOTE

*You can only add one type of permission at a time from the Add Users And Groups dialog box. You'll have to make repeated trips here if you want to set more than one type of permission.*

6. If you want to delete the permissions setting for a particular user or group, select the user or group and click Remove in the Printer Permissions dialog box.

7. When you are finished viewing or modifying the permissions for the printer, click OK in the Printer Permissions dialog box.

## Auditing Printer Operations

Another important aspect of printer security and administration is being able to see who has been using and, more to the point, abusing the system. Printer auditing allows you to keep track of whether a user or a group is successfully using a particular printer option.

Do you want to make sure you always know if your boss is having any difficulty using the printer? No problem; set up an audit log to record any failures from his account. Do you have a hunch that some of your users are abusing their privileges to jump their printing jobs ahead of others? Set up an audit log for the event.

What events can you audit? Pretty much what you'd expect. You can keep track of either the success or failure (or both) of the following events:

◆ **Print** Monitors the changes to print status, priority, and so forth

◆ **Full Control** Monitors the changes to the print spooler status, priority, and so forth

◆ **Delete** Monitors the deletions of print jobs

◆ **Change Permissions** Monitors the changes to permissions

◆ **Take Ownership** Monitors the changes to ownership of the printer

### WARNING!

*Event logs can get very large, very quickly, on a busy system. Use printer auditing sparingly. It increases the overhead on any actions being audited because it requires the events to be written to the event log—and the logs can grow very rapidly. For more on auditing and security, see Chapter 21.*

**NOTE**

*To enable logging of the events for a particular printer, you must enable auditing for the domain as a whole. You can set up the log, but nothing will actually get written to the log unless you have the auditing function enabled. See Chapter 21 for more on auditing.*

To view or change the auditing on a print queue, follow these steps:

1. Choose Settings and then Printers from the submenus that open from the Start menu.

2. Right-click the printer you want to audit or for the audit record to view. Choose Properties from the menu to bring up the printer's Properties dialog box. Click the Security tab.

3. Click Auditing to view the current auditing status of the printer. If the audit function is enabled on this printer, the window will look like the one in Figure 11.28. The default setting for printer auditing is disabled.

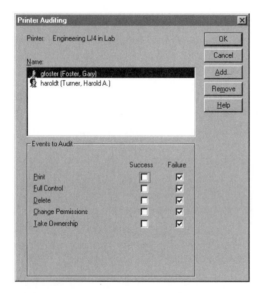

**FIGURE 11.28**

*Printer Auditing dialog box showing auditing enabled*

4. To audit an event for a user or group, click Add to bring up the standard Add Users And Groups dialog box used throughout Windows NT (Figure 11.29).

Type the name of the individual users or groups whose use of the printer you want to monitor in the Add Names text box. Click OK to return to the Printer Auditing dialog box.

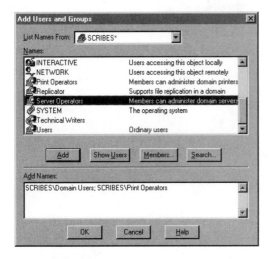

**FIGURE 11.29**

*Add Users And Groups dialog box showing group to be added to audit list*

5. The Printer Auditing dialog box will display the users or groups you have chosen to audit and also the kinds of printing events you can audit as shown in Figure 11.30 on the following page.

6. Select the user or group name, and then click the check boxes for the events you want to audit for that user or group of users. You can choose to audit both the success and the failure of any event.

7. If you decide to stop auditing a particular user or group, select the user or group name and click Remove.

8. When you're done viewing or modifying the events being audited for this printer, click OK. Then click OK again to exit the printer's Properties dialog box.

Auditing print operations can be an effective and useful tool for troubleshooting, but we find that it's a management tool best used judiciously. It's easy to get buried in so much detail that it's hard to find the root problem.

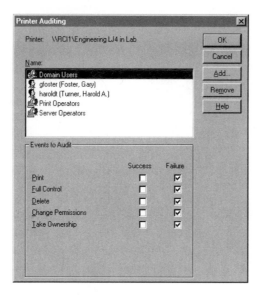

**FIGURE 11.30**

*Printer Auditing dialog box showing users and groups added to audit log*

## POINTS TO REMEMBER

◆ Choose your printer locations on the basis of the projected use (and users) of the printer.

◆ Use network or serial connections rather than parallel connections to the printer; it reduces the load on the server and increases your flexibility in being able to move printers from one location to another.

◆ The *physical* printer and the *logical* printer are managed separately.

◆ Use auditing as a troubleshooting tool, but use it sparingly.

## WHAT'S NEXT?

In Chapter 12, we'll talk about managing your disk resources—the files, the folders, and the sharing of these resources on the network.

# CHAPTER 12

# CHAPTER 12

## Sharing Disk Resources

The whole point of a network is sharing resources among users. However, sharing of network resources requires an extension of the security features that begin with user accounts and passwords. In other words, you, as a system administrator, must make sure that everyone can use the resources they need without the security of files and other resources being compromised.

Microsoft Windows NT version 4 network security rests on four types of capabilities that can be granted to users:

◆ **Abilities** File system capabilities granted to built-in groups and, hence, to users by virtue of their being assigned to these groups

◆ **Rights** Authorization to perform specific actions on the system; assigned to built-in groups but can be extended to specific groups or individuals by the administrator

◆ **Shares** Directories (folders) that are made available to users over the network

◆ **Permissions** File system capabilities that can be granted both to individuals and to groups

In the normal course of events, you'll deal only rarely with rights and abilities. Shares and permissions, however, are the bread and butter of an administrator's job and are the subject of this chapter.

## Shares vs. Permissions

Shares and permissions, which sound very much alike, are not at all the same. Shares apply to directories only. Until a directory (folder) is shared, no one on the network can see it or gain access to it. Once a directory is shared, everyone on the network, by default, has access to the directory, to all files in the directory, and to all subdirectories and their files.

On a FAT volume, a directory can be shared and then additional restrictions added in the form of *share permissions*. However, the restrictions are only at the directory level (not at the file level) and are limited to Full Control, Read, Change, or No Access. (See "Share Permissions" later in this chapter for more information.)

*Shares act to control user access only over the network. If a user can log on locally to a computer, any directory on that computer (shared or unshared) will be available to that user (unless additional restrictions have been assigned).*

On NTFS volumes, directories have the same share permissions as those on a FAT volume, but another layer of permission is available beyond that. Each directory has a Security property sheet that allows more precise restrictions. Each file also has this Security properties sheet, so access also can be restricted or granted for individual files. These *directory permissions* and *file permissions* can further restrict access across the network *and* locally. For example, you can share a directory granting Full Control Everyone at the share permissions level; then you can use the Security properties sheets to set more restrictive permissions by group or by individual— either for the directory as a whole or file-by-file within the directory.

Share permissions determine the maximum access over the network to resources. This means that if you set share permissions to Read, that's the maximum access any user or group will be able to make over the network. However, you can grant a user more extensive access to the directory (such as Change) and this expanded access will be available to the user if he or she logs on *locally*.

As a rule, it's best to leave share permissions at their default settings, giving Full Control to Everyone. Then, if need be, you can use the directory and file permissions for security control. Experiment with various combinations of permissions only on computers and files that won't affect any real users. The ability to apply restrictions to practically the microscopic level in Windows NT Server can quickly produce complexities you do not want to deal with on "live" files. Start with the very least amount of restrictions on your users, and add to them only as necessary. Keep it simple.

# Sharing Directories

How and where you're logged on determines how you can share directories:

◆ Log on to a domain controller as a member of the Administrators group or Server Operators group to share directories on the domain.

◆ Log on to a member server or a computer running Microsoft Windows NT Workstation as a member of the Administrators or Power Users group to share directories on the local computer.

◆ Log on to a domain account as a member of the Administrators local group to share directories remotely using Server Manager.

The steps to sharing a directory are very simple:

1. Open Explorer, and right-click the directory that you want to share.

2. Choose Sharing from the pop-up menu; then click Sharing on the properties sheet that opens.

3. Click the Shared As option button. A *share name* will appear, as shown in Figure 12.1. You can use this name or create another name. (If you have MS-DOS–based computers on your network, see the "Share Names and Filenames in MS-DOS" sidebar on the next page.)

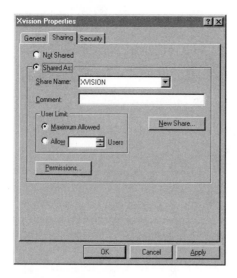

**FIGURE 12.1**

*Directory Properties sheet showing assigned share name*

4. Enter the maximum number of users only if there's a licensing restriction or some other reason to limit access. Remember that users must explicitly stop a share to free a share account for other users, and they usually will forget to do so.

5. By default, the share grants full control to the Everyone group. To restrict access, click Permissions. Assigning share permissions is covered under "Share Permissions" in this chapter.

6. Click OK when you're finished.

If you have MS-DOS–based (which includes Microsoft Windows through version 3.11) computers on your network that will have access to a shared directory, you must follow the 8.3 naming convention for the share name. A share name that doesn't conform to this naming convention will not be visible to users with MS-DOS or Windows 3.*x* machines.

Although the names of Windows NT files or directories can have up to 255 characters, MS-DOS users connecting to the file or directory over the network will see the name in the 8.3 naming format. Windows NT will truncate long filenames and directory names to a size that an MS-DOS computer can recognize, but it will not do this for share names. Yes, it's odd.

Windows NT Server converts the long filenames and directory names to short names according to the following conventions:

- ◆ Spaces are removed.

- ◆ A character that is not allowed in MS-DOS names is replaced by an underscore ( _ ).

- ◆ The name is shortened to the first six remaining characters, and a tilde and a digit are added to it. For the first file, the digit will be 1. For a second file using the same six characters, the digit will be 2. For example, your file named Budget Figures For March.XLS will be shortened to BUDGET~1.XLS. A second Budget file called Budget Figures For June will be shortened to BUDGET~2.XLS.

- ◆ If a long name contains more than one period followed by other characters, the last period and the three characters following that period are used as the file extension for the short version of the filename. For example, a file called December.Sales.Presentation will be shortened to DECEMB~1.PRE.

As you can see, long filenames, when truncated, can be a mystery. If your network includes MS-DOS computers, you might want to continue using MS-DOS naming conventions for the first six characters. In our previous example, the files would become MARBUD~Budget Figures For March.XLS and JUNBUD~Budget Figures For June.XLS. To an MS-DOS computer, the files would appear as MARBUD~1.XLS and JUNBUD~1.XLS.

## Adding a New Share to a Shared Directory

A single directory can be shared on more than one level (that is, it would have more than one share assigned to it). For example, one share might include full control for Administrators, and another share might be more restricted for other users. Each share must have a unique name.

To add a new share for a directory, find the directory in Explorer and right-click it. Choose Sharing from the pop-up menu. In the dialog box that opens, click New Share. In the New Share dialog box (Figure 12.2), enter the new share name in the Share Name text box. Set a user limit, if necessary. Click Permissions to restrict access. Remember that by default, the shared directory grants full control to the Everyone group.

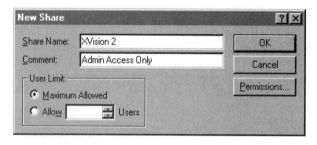

**FIGURE 12.2**

*New Share dialog box*

## Terminating a Directory Share

To terminate a directory's shared status, open Server Manager and select the computer on which the directory resides. Choose Shared Directories from the Computer menu. Select the directory, and click Stop Sharing.

If a user currently is connected to the directory you want to stop sharing, a dialog box like the one in Figure 12.3 will appear. To prevent a possible loss of data, click Cancel and wait until the directory is not being used before attempting to terminate its share status.

However, if you're in a hurry or if there are lots of people who are connecting to this directory often, go to the Server Manager window, select the computer in question, and choose Send Message from the Computer menu. From here you can send a message to everyone connected to the computer and tell them to save their work and disconnect—the reason you give for the disconnect is up to you.

When no one is connected to the computer any longer, go back to the directory in the Shared Directories dialog box and click Stop Sharing again. This time, you should be able to proceed without bringing up the dialog box.

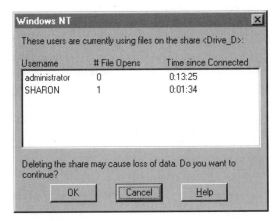

**FIGURE 12.3**

*Shared-directory-in-use message*

## ◆ What Are Administrative Shares?

In the list of shares on a computer, you'll see some shares that each have a dollar sign ($) in the share name and that you can't recall creating. These are called *administrative shares*, and they are part of the installed operating system. Depending on the computer's configuration, some or all of these administrative shares may be present on the computer. Do not modify or delete any of them. Here's what the different ones mean:

◆ **ADMIN$** Used during the remote administration of the computer. The path is always the location of the directory in which Windows NT was installed (that is, the system root). Only Administrators, Backup Operators, and Server Operators can connect to this share.

◆ **driveletter$** Used as the root directory of the named drive. Only Administrators, Backup Operators, and Server Operators can connect to this share.

◆ **IPC$** Used during remote administration of the computer and when viewing shared resources. It's essential to network communication.

◆ **NETLOGON** Used by the Net Logon service of a server running Windows NT Server as it processes domain logon scripts. This resource is provided only for servers, not for Windows NT workstations.

◆ **PRINT$** Used to support shared printers.

◆ **REPL$** Created when a server is used as a replication export server.

# Share Permissions

A share permission establishes the maximum level of access for the directory being shared. The permissions assigned on the Security properties pages for shared directories (or for the files within shared directories) can be more restrictive than the share permissions but can't expand permission. Share permissions can be assigned to individual users, to groups, and to the special categories Everyone, System, Interactive, Network, and Creator Owner; these share permissions, from most restrictive to least restrictive, are described in Table 12.1.

**Table 12.1**
**Share Permissions**

| Type of Share Permission | Type of Access Allowed |
|---|---|
| No Access | Prevents all access to the directory and its files and subdirectories. The owner always retains access. (See "Ownership and How It Works" later in this chapter.) |
| Read | Allows viewing of the file and subdirectory names, viewing of the data in files, and running applications. |
| Change | Allows Read access and, in addition, allows adding files and subdirectories to the shared directory, changing data in the files, and deleting files and subdirectories. |
| Full Control | Allows Change access and, in addition, allows changing permissions (NTFS volumes only) and taking ownership (NTFS volumes only). |

## NOTE

*Remember that the rules change depending on whether a user is logging on locally or over the network. For a local logon, a file permission can indeed expand a particular user's or group's permissions. But over the network, the share permission represents the maximum access available.*

## Assigning Share Permissions Locally

To assign the share permission, right-click the directory and choose Sharing from the pop-up menu. Click the Security tab, and then click Permissions to open the dialog box shown in Figure 12.4. Choose the type of access you want to assign from the drop-down list at the bottom of the dialog box. Use the Add button and the Remove button to add and remove individuals or groups from the list of users who have this type of access.

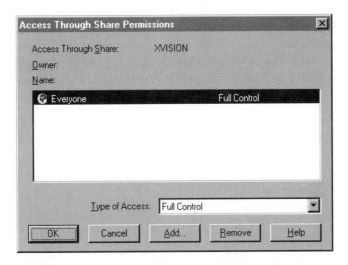

**FIGURE 12.4**

*Access Through Share Permissions dialog box showing share permissions*

## Assigning Share Permissions from a Remote Location

You also can assign share permissions from a domain controller using Server Manager. Choose Programs from the Start menu. Then choose Administrative Tools and Server Manager from the submenus that open from Programs. Select the computer, and then choose Shared Directories from the Computer menu.

In the Shared Directories window (Figure 12.5), you can add shares, terminate sharing, and, with the Properties button, assign share permissions directly.

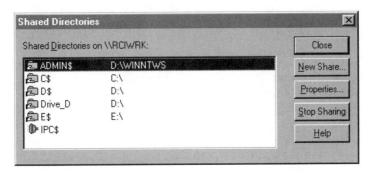

**FIGURE 12.5**

*Example of a Shared Directories dialog box*

# Mapping Shared Directories and Drives

After traipsing through Network Neighborhood's various windows to find a particular shared directory, users can double-click the folder to open it and gain access to its contents. For easier access, right-click the directory, and drag it to the desktop. Choose Create Shortcut Here from the pop-up menu after releasing the mouse button.

However, for frequent use, it's simple to map a directory or drive so that it appears in Explorer (or My Computer) as simply another local drive.

### NOTE

*A mapped drive is even better than a shortcut in one important respect. Your older 16-bit programs will not recognize Network Neighborhood and will not open or save files anywhere other than your own computer. But when you map a drive, the program co-operates because now the drive on the other computer appears (to the program at least) to be local.*

You can set up these connections for users or they can do it for themselves. Here's how it's done:

1. Double-click Network Neighborhood, and find the shared resource you want.

2. Right-click the object, and choose Map Network Drive from the pop-up menu. The next dialog box that appears (Figure 12.6 ) has three options:

   ◆ **Drive** This is the letter that will be assigned to the new directory or drive on the local computer.

   ◆ **Connect As** Specify the user account that you are mapping. If it's the account of the current user on this computer, leave this field blank.

   ◆ **Reconnect at Logon** Click this box to have the connection made automatically when the user logs on to the computer where this resource physically resides.

**FIGURE 12.6**

*Map Network Drive dialog box*

3. Enter the appropriate information and, click OK when you're finished. Open either Explorer or My Computer and take a look. Figure 12.7 shows how the drive looks after it has been mapped.

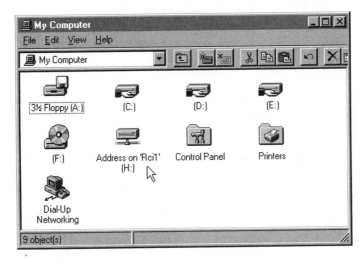

**FIGURE 12.7**

*My Computer window showing a mapped drive*

# Disconnecting from Mapped Resources

To remove a mapped drive or directory, you can right-click the drive's icon and choose Disconnect from the pop-up menu (Figure 12.8 on the following page).

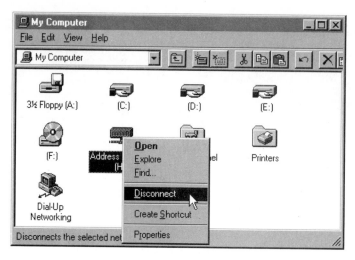

**FIGURE 12.8**

*Mapped resource pop-up menu with Disconnect selected*

If you're working in Explorer, click the Disconnect Net Drive icon on the toolbar.

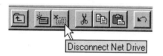

From the list that appears, select the mapped drive you want to disconnect and click OK.

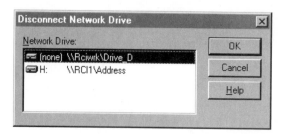

# Directory and File Permissions

On an NTFS volume, you can set permissions down to the file level, which means that you can give one user read-only access, another user full control, and everyone else no access to the same file. We repeat, you *can* do this—but in this direction lies madness for all but the most meticulous of control freaks (who are, arguably, already mad).

Always try to operate your system with the simplest possible set of permissions. Assign as few restrictions as possible and assign them to groups, not to individuals. Don't assign file-by-file permissions unless it is truly unavoidable. Managing the minutiae of permissions can easily and quickly soak up all of your time—and much of your life's blood as well—unless you guard against it.

## Available Permissions

Windows NT Server has a set of standard permissions that are combinations of specific kinds of access. The permissions and their abbreviations are these:

| | |
|---|---|
| Read (R) | Execute (X) |
| Write (W) | Change Permissions (P) |
| Delete (D) | Take Ownership (O) |

You can assign these as individual permissions, or you can assign combinations of these permissions. Each level of access builds on the previous level of access, adding new permissions to the permissions granted previously. Table 12.2 shows the permissions that can be assigned for directories and what each of them means. Table 12.3, on the following page, shows the permissions that can be assigned for individual files.

**Table 12.2**
**Directory Permissions**

| Type of Permission | Abbreviated Name of Permission | User Action Allowed |
|---|---|---|
| No Access | None | User has no access to the directory. |
| List | (RX) | User can view the directory and filenames in the directory and can change to a subdirectory in the directory to view other filenames. |
| Read | (RX) | User can read files in the directory and can run applications. |
| Add | (WX) | User can add files to the directory but can't read or change the contents of the files in the directory. |
| Add & Read | (RWX) | User has Read and Add permissions for the directory. |
| Change | (RWXD) | User has Read and Add permissions and, in addition, can change the contents of the files and delete files. |
| Full Control | All | User has Read, Add, and Change permissions and, in addition, can change permissions and take ownership of files. |

**Table 12.3**
**File Permissions**

| Type of Permission* | Abbreviated Name of Permission | User Action Allowed |
|---|---|---|
| No Access | None | User has no access to the file. |
| Read | RX | User can read the file and can execute the file if it's an application. |
| Change | RWXD | User can read the file, change it, or delete it. |
| Full Control | All | User can read the file, change it, delete it, assign permissions for it, and change its ownership. |

\* *A category called Special Access permissions, described on page 264, is also available under directory and file permissions.*

# How Permissions Work

If you take no action at all, the files and subdirectories within a shared directory have the same permissions as the share. Permissions for both directories and files can be assigned to these entities:

◆ Local groups, global groups, and individual users

◆ Global groups and individual users from trusted domains

◆ Special groups, such as Everyone, Creator Owner, and Interactive

The important characteristics of permissions can be summarized as follows:

◆ By default, subdirectories inherit their permissions from their parent directories. Files inherit their permissions from the directory in which they reside. However, neither files nor subdirectories can inherit *share* permissions.

◆ Users can gain access to a directory or to a file only if they've been granted permission to do so as individuals or if they belong to a group that has been granted such permission.

◆ Permissions are cumulative, but No Access trumps all others. For example, if the Technical Writers group has Read access to a folder, the Project group has Change permission for this folder, and Alex is a member of both groups, Alex will have the higher level of permission, which is Change. However, if the permission for the Technical Writers group is changed to No Access, Alex will be unable to use the folder, despite his higher level of access as a member of the Project group.

- The user who creates a file or directory owns that file or directory and can set permissions to control access to it.

- An administrator can take ownership of any file or directory, but he or she cannot transfer this ownership to anyone else.

# Assigning Permissions for Directories

Before you share a directory on an NTFS volume on the network, assign all of the permissions for the directory. Remember that when you assign directory permissions, you are also assigning permissions for all of the files and subdirectories in the directory.

1. Right-click the directory in Explorer, and choose Properties from the pop-up menu that appears.

2. Click the Security tab, and click Permissions. Figure 12.9, on the following page, shows a directory with the permissions that were assigned by default.

3. To remove an individual or group from the list of users and groups with directory permission, select the name and click Remove.

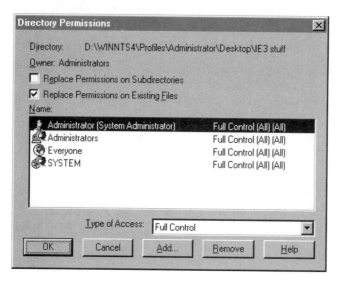

**FIGURE 12.9**

*The Directory Permissions dialog box showing default permissions for the directory*

4. To add an individual or group to the list of those with directory permissions, click Add. This will open the Add Users and Groups dialog box (Figure 12.10).

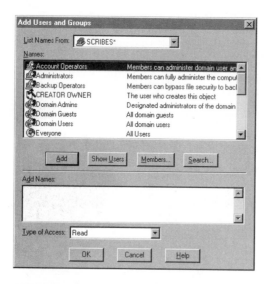

**FIGURE 12.10**

*Example of Add Users and Groups dialog box*

Here's the breakdown of options in this dialog box:

- **List Names From** You can choose from multiple domains or, in the case of a local workstation, from the local users for that computer.

- **Names** The initial list of names consists of all of the groups and special system entities available in Windows NT Server. Select all of the ones you want to add and then click Add.

- **Show Users** To see the individual users' names, click Show Users. You'll have to scroll down to see these names because they're at the bottom of the list.

- **Members** To see the members of a group, select the group and click Members.

- **Search** Can't see a particular user or group? Click Search to open the Find Account dialog box, where you can search for an individual or a group.

- **Add Names** As you select the groups and individuals you want to add to the directory permissions list and click Add, these names will appear in the Add Names box.

- **Type of Access** If all of the individuals, groups, or system entities you are adding to the directory permissions list are to have the same level of permission, select that permission in the Type Of Access drop-down list box.

5. Click OK when you're finished, and the Directory Permissions dialog box will open, showing the new names you've added to the directory permissions list. By each name, two sets of user or group permissions are displayed next to each standard share permission assigned to the share. The first set is directory permissions; the second is file permissions for the directory.

6. To change the permissions assigned to an individual or group, select the name of the individual or group, choose the type of access you want for that person or group from the drop-down list that appears, and then click OK.

# Assigning Permissions for Files

File permissions are assigned the same way as directory permissions. But there are two guidelines to keep in mind while assigning file permissions:

◆ Grant permissions to groups, not to individuals.

◆ Create local groups and assign file permissions to these groups rather than assigning permissions directly to individual users.

Table 12.4 shows the permissions that can be assigned for files and the actions that are available with each permission.

**Table 12.4**
**File Permissions and What They Mean**

| Action | Permission | | | |
|---|---|---|---|---|
| | No Access | Read | Change | Full Control |
| Display the file's data. | | x* | x | x |
| Display the file attributes. | | x | x | x |
| Execute the file if it's a program. | | x | x | x |
| Display the file's permissions and owner. | | x | x | x |
| Change file attributes. | | | x | x |
| Change data in the file. | | | x | x |
| Delete the file. | | | x | x |
| Change the file's permissions and owner. | | | | x |

\*   *x=Use allowed*

# Special Access Permissions

Just in case the many permutations of permissions we've discussed so far aren't enough, you also can assign special access permissions for either files or directories. (Special access permissions for a directory apply only to the directory.) In the Directory Permissions dialog box or in the File Permissions dialog box, select the name of a group or an individual and then select Special Access from the Type Of Access drop-down list. This opens the Special Directory Access dialog box shown in Figure 12.11.

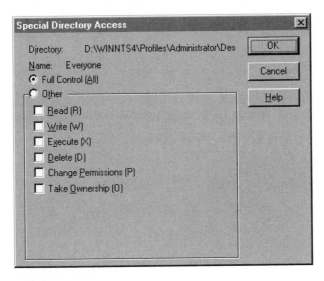

**FIGURE 12.11**

*Special Directory Access dialog box*

Table 12.5 shows the effect of special access permissions on directories. Table 12.6, on the following page, shows the effect of special access permissions on files.

**Table 12.5**
**Special Access Permissions for Directories**

| Permitted Action on the Directory | (R) | (W) | (X) | (D) | (P) | (O) | (All) |
|---|---|---|---|---|---|---|---|
| Display file names in the directory. | x* | | | | | | x |
| Display directory attributes. | x | | x | | | | x |
| Add files and subdirectories. | | x | | | | | x |
| Change attributes. | | x | | | | | x |
| Go to subdirectories. | | | x | | | | x |
| View directory owner and permissions. | x | x | x | | | | x |
| Delete directory. | | | | x | | | x |
| Change permissions. | | | | | x | | x |
| Take ownership. | | | | | | x | x |

\* x=Use allowed

**Table 12.6**
**Special Access Permissions for Files**

| Permitted Action on the File | (R) | (W) | (X) | (D) | (P) | (0) | (All) |
|---|---|---|---|---|---|---|---|
| Display file data. | x* | | | | | | x |
| Display attributes. | x | | x | | | | x |
| Display the file's data. | x | | | | | | x |
| Change attributes. | | x | | | | | x |
| Change data and append data in file. | | x | | | | | x |
| Run file if it's a program. | | | x | | | | x |
| Delete file. | | | | x | | | x |
| Change permissions. | | | | | x | | x |
| Take ownership. | | | | | | x | x |

\*   *x=Use allowed*

# Ownership and How It Works

As you've seen, only Administrators and the members of a few other select groups can grant and change permissions—*except* when the user is the *owner* of the directory or file in question. Every object on an NTFS partition has an owner, and the owner is the person who created the file or directory. The owner controls access to the file or directory and can keep anyone out that he or she chooses to keep out. Figure 12.12 shows an example of a folder named Harold's Private Stuff created by the user haroldt.

To see who has access to his folder, Harold right-clicks the folder, chooses Properties, and then clicks the Security tab. When he clicks Permissions, the dialog box shown in Figure 12.13 opens. Yikes! It looks like everyone on the network has rights to his private files. But because Harold is the owner of the folder, he can remove everyone from the list except Creator Owner and, thus, have his folder all to himself. Even the administrator will see an Access Denied message if he or she tries to open the folder.

Of course, nothing on the network is completely beyond the reach of the administrator. No matter what the status of the folder, the administrator can take ownership by right-clicking the folder, choosing Properties from the pop-up menu, and then clicking Ownership on the Security page of the Properties dialog box that appears. When Harold logs on the next time, he'll discover that he no longer has access to Harold's Private Stuff. Once the administrator takes ownership of the folder, it cannot be given back to the original owner. So, even though an administrator can go into areas without an invitation, he will leave an unmistakable sign of his having been there.

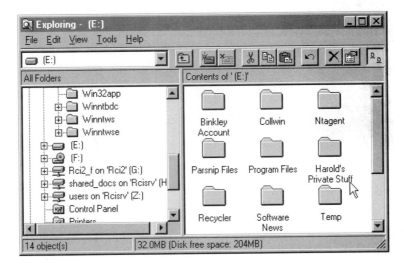

**FIGURE 12.12**

*Example of user's folder*

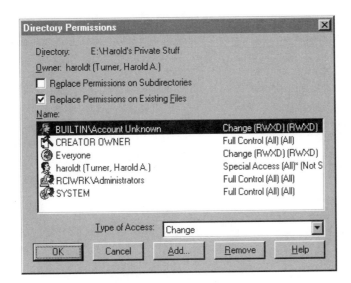

**FIGURE 12.13**

*Example of the default permissions for a directory*

- Until a directory is shared, no one has access to it over the network.

- Share permissions are the only restrictions available for directories on FAT partitions, and these restrictions work only over the network—they do not apply to or regulate a user who logs on locally.

- Share permissions establish the maximum level of access available to resources shared on the network. Other permissions assigned to a directory or file (on an NTFS volume) can be more restrictive, but they can't be less restrictive than the share permissions.

- Permissions are additive, except for the No Access permission, which can override all other permissions.

- Keep share and permission assignments as simple as possible. It's very, very easy to weave a tangled web—and very, very hard to extricate yourself from it later.

## WHAT'S NEXT?

Chapter 13 guides you through the process of setting up the Messaging Services in Windows NT Server version 4, including Internet mail and Microsoft Mail.

# CHAPTER 13

**Messaging Services**

# CHAPTER 13

## Messaging Services

One of the most basic services that users on a network expect and need is electronic mail, or, as it is more commonly known, E-mail. This is, if you think about it, really a revolutionary change from the earlier days of desktop PCs, when the primary form of communication was "sneaker net," and when "electronic mail" meant writing your memo on the computer, printing it, and then putting the printed memo in an envelope to send in the interoffice mail.

Today, users expect to be able to handle the vast majority of their office correspondence electronically. And they expect to be able to use the E-mail system 100 percent of the time—not 90 percent or even 98.7 percent of the time, but 100 percent of the time. They use it to work collectively on projects and to connect to the outside world. If you really want to increase your user noise level, mess up the E-mail.

As the role of electronic mail has changed, the programs to use and manage it also have changed. Microsoft has kept up with the changes by providing a full-feature, client/server, groupware application and not just another mail program. A full discussion of Microsoft Exchange Server is a book in and of itself, so we won't attempt to cover everything here. We summarize the important features here and point you in the direction of the recent books from Microsoft Press—*Microsoft Exchange Connectivity Guide; Microsoft Exchange in Business; Microsoft BackOffice Resource Kit, Part One*—for more information.

One of the great strengths of Exchange is its ability to work with a variety of E-mail systems. At present, we know of clients for handling Internet mail, Lotus Notes Mail, CompuServe Mail, Microsoft Mail, and native Exchange documents, and there might well be others. Exchange lets you integrate this wide variety of E-mail addresses and services in one easily managed location. If you're running in an environment with Exchange Server, you also can create a whole series of rules that permit intelligent and automatic management of your E-mail. However, the most advanced Exchange capabilities are available only for messages processed through Exchange Server. Not all of the slick, rules-based, message handling capability is available for messages received through other mail systems, even when they are included with Microsoft Windows NT Server version 4. But if you are using Exchange Server and its available connectors for the majority of your mail, you'll be able to realize the full potential of these extra capabilities.

# Installing and Configuring Windows Messaging

Windows NT Server includes a limited version of Exchange in the box. This limited version of Exchange is known as Windows Messaging, to distinguish it from the full-capability Exchange product. When you install Windows NT Server, Windows Messaging is installed automatically but not configured. You'll be asked to configure it the first time you double-click the Inbox icon (shown below).

Inbox

Just in case you didn't install Windows Messaging as part of the original Windows NT Server installation, let's take care of that little detail now.

**NOTE**

*You can always add the portions of Windows NT Server that you left off during the initial installation of the system.*

## Installing Windows Messaging

To install Windows Messaging (we think of it as "Exchange Lite"), you have to open Control Panel and then double-click the Add/Remove Programs icon you see here:

Add/Remove
Programs

This will bring up the Add/Remove Programs Properties dialog box shown in Figure 13.1 on the following page.

From there, you'll do the following:

1. Click the Windows NT Setup tab on the properties sheet to bring up the page shown in Figure 13.2 on the following page.

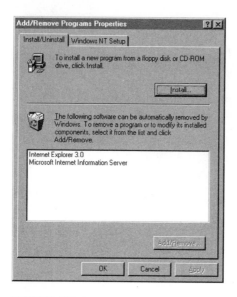

**FIGURE 13.1**

*Add/Remove Programs Properties dialog box*

**FIGURE 13.2**

*Windows NT Setup dialog box showing the checked
Microsoft Exchange option*

2. Click the check box for Microsoft Exchange, and then click OK. Windows NT Server will start loading the necessary files. If Windows NT Server can't find the installation files it needs, you have to point it in the right direction. It will prompt you for the location of the original installation CD-ROM, as shown in Figure 13.3.

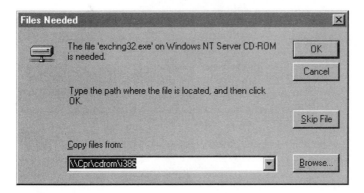

**FIGURE 13.3**

*Files Needed message for missing Windows NT Server installation disc*

3. That's it. Windows NT Server will load all of the necessary files. It will prompt you to provide configuration information the first time you double-click the Inbox icon.

## Configuring Windows Messaging

Before you start Windows Messaging for the first time, use the checklist in Table 13.1 to make sure that you have all of the information you will need to configure the service before you start, or you will end up scrambling around trying to find the information in the middle of the configuration process.

For the purpose of this discussion, we'll assume that you chose to install all of the available options when you installed Microsoft Exchange; we'll take you through the configuration process for each of them. We'll also assume that you'll be using both of the default mail services, and we'll go through each of them step by step. To start Windows Messaging, double-click the Inbox icon. The Exchange Setup Wizard will prompt you to set up your information services as shown in Figure 13.4 on page 275.

**Table 13.1**
**Checklist for Setting Up Microsoft Messaging (Exchange)**

| Mail System | Option | Value |
|---|---|---|
| Microsoft Mail | post office location<br>user name<br>mailbox<br>password | |
| Internet Mail (Modem) | connection information (phone book entry)<br>mail server name or IP address<br>Internet mail address *(name@company.com)*<br>account name<br>account password | |
| Internet Mail (Network) | mail server name or IP address<br>Internet mail address *(name@company.com)*<br>account name<br>account password | |

1. Click the check box for both Microsoft Mail and Internet Mail, and then click Next.

2. The Exchange Setup Wizard will prompt you for your Microsoft Mail post office location, as shown in Figure 13.5. You need to know your Microsoft Mail post office box location to complete the Windows Messaging installation. Type the path in the text box, or click Browse to find and point to the root directory of your "postoffice." Click Next when you're finished.

**NOTE**

*If a Microsoft Mail post office hasn't yet been set up on your network, you might want to skip installing Microsoft Mail and go only with Exchange. For new installations, this would make sense. Click Cancel to exit Exchange Setup Wizard and start over again; but this time remove the check mark for the Microsoft Mail in the check box of the Exchange Setup Wizard dialog box.*

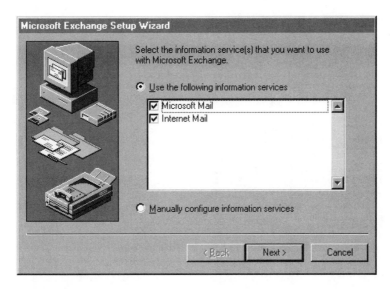

**FIGURE 13.4**

*Microsoft Exchange Setup Wizard dialog box showing mail service options*

**FIGURE 13.5**

*Microsoft Mail post office location dialog box in Exchange Setup Wizard*

3. Select your name from the list of users who are authorized to use Microsoft Mail and are displayed in the list box, as shown in Figure 13.6. If you're not on this list, you'll have to contact your mail administrator to get yourself added to the list of users for Microsoft Mail.

**FIGURE 13.6**

*Example of authorized Microsoft Mail users list in Exchange Setup Wizard*

4. Click Next; you'll see your Microsoft Mail user name and your mailbox name as shown in Figure 13.7. Your Microsoft Mail user name might be different from your Windows NT Server user name. Type your password for Microsoft Mail in the Password text box. This can be a completely different password than the password you use for Windows NT Server. Click Next to move on to setting up your Internet mail connection.

5. When you set up your Internet mail configuration, you will have to decide how you want to connect to the Internet to collect your mail— through a modem or via the network—as shown in Figure 13.8. If you have more than one Internet mail account, you'll have to create a separate profile for each account.

**FIGURE 13.7**

*Example of Microsoft Mail password dialog box in Exchange Setup Wizard*

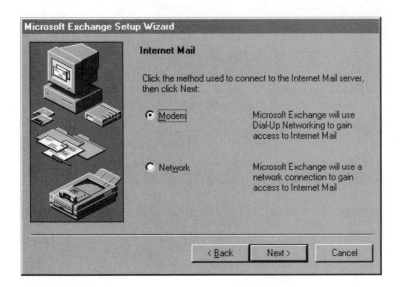

**FIGURE 13.8**

*Example of selecting an Internet mail connection in Exchange Setup Wizard*

6. If you will be using a direct network connection to pick up your Internet mail, click the Network option button and jump ahead to step 11.

7. If your connection to the Internet mail server will be via modem, ISDN modem, or other RAS device, click the Modem option button, and then click Next. This brings up the New Phonebook Entry Wizard shown in Figure 13.9.

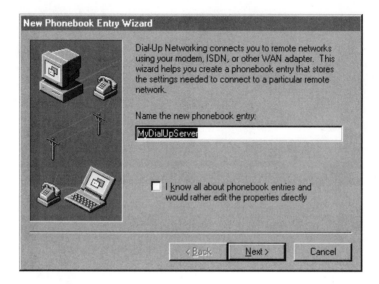

**FIGURE 13.9**

*New Phonebook Entry Wizard dialog box in Exchange Setup Wizard*

Type the name of the phonebook in the Name The New Phonebook Entry text box. If you think you know all you need to know about setting up a modem connection, you can bypass several steps by clicking the "I know all about the phonebook entries…" check box (otherwise known as the "I'm Smart" box). Here, however, we won't assume previous knowledge and will cover all of the steps. Click Next.

8. If you already have a dial-up connection to this server, select this dial-up connection from the list and jump ahead to step 11. If you want to create a new dial-up connection, click New.

9. Give the connection a name. Click Next to bring up the Server dialog box shown in Figure 13.10.

**NOTE**

*If you use a modem to connect to your mail, Windows Messaging works with RAS to connect you to your Internet mail server. You must already have RAS set up before you can add a modem connection for Internet mail.*

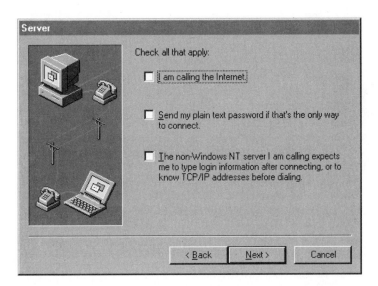

**FIGURE 13.10**

*Server dialog box for setting the Internet Mail server options*

If you will be connecting to a Windows NT Server to collect your Internet mail, leave all of these boxes clear. If you will have to interact with your Internet connection directly to handle logging on, you'll have to click the appropriate check boxes here. Click Next to get to the Phone Number dialog box. (See Figure 13.11 on the following page.)

**10.** Enter the phone number of your Internet service provider, RAS, or other dial-up connection to your Internet mail server. If you'll be taking advantage of TAPI to control some of the dialing properties and make your dial-up connection smarter, click the Use Telephony Dialing Properties check box. This brings up the dialog box shown in Figure 13.12 on the following page.

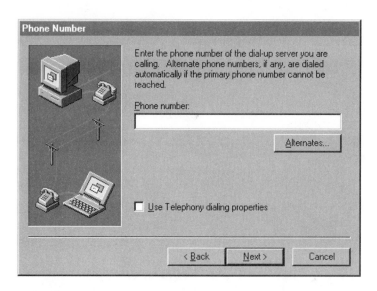

**FIGURE 13.11**

*Phone Number dialog box for your Internet Mail server*

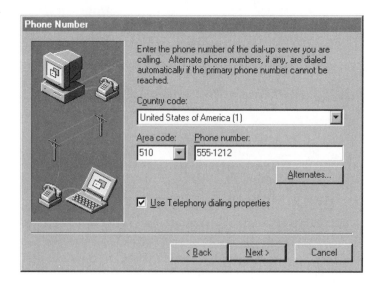

**FIGURE 13.12**

*Example of Phone Number dialog box with number and TAPI option*

Enter the required information in the text boxes. Click Alternates if you have more than one phone number you will use to connect to your Internet mail server. Now that you've set up the connection information, click Next to get back to the Internet Mail Wizard.

11. Click Next to bring up the dialog box shown in Figure 13.13. Select either Specify the Name or Specify The IP Address for your POP3 server.

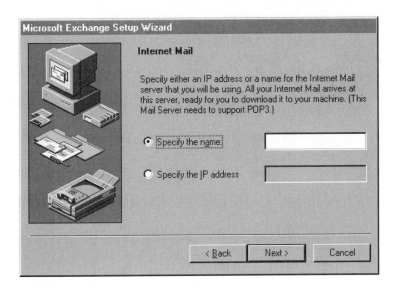

**FIGURE 13.13**

*Internet Mail dialog box in Exchange Setup Wizard for the name or IP address of your POP3 server*

12. Type the name or the IP address of your POP3 server in the appropriate text box. Click Next to choose your mail retrieval method. The default is Off-line for modem connections (choosing which messages to download before you actually download them). The default is Automatic for Network connections. Don't worry too much about which default setting to choose; you can change it easily later. Click either Off-line or Automatic. Then click Next to bring up the dialog box shown in Figure 13.14 on the following page.

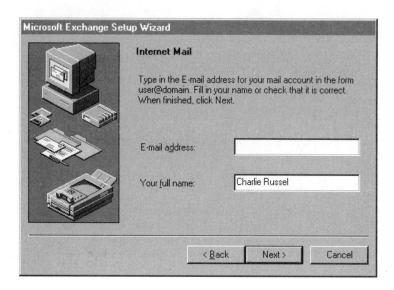

**FIGURE 13.14**

*Internet Mail dialog box in Exchange Setup Wizard for your name and
E-mail address*

1 3. Type your Internet E-mail address in the E-Mail Address text box. This
will be in the form *username@company.com* or something similar. Your
E-mail address is the mail address that other users on the Internet will
use to send mail to you. Type your full name in the Your Full Name text
box. This is the name that appears in the header of all messages that
you send. When you're finished, click Next.

1 4. In the dialog box that appears (Figure 13.15), type the mailbox name on
the server and the password for that mailbox in the respective text boxes.
The mailbox name frequently is referred to as the account name, and it
is often quite different from your E-mail address, depending on the system to which you're connecting.

1 5. After you've entered the mailbox name and password, click Next to
bring up the Personal Address Book dialog box (Figure 13.16). The default location for the personal address book is the main directory of Exchange—not really appropriate for a server and probably not the best
choice of locations if you're going to have more than one user logging
on to the server and using Internet mail from it. We suggest that you
put the personal address book in your home directory. Type the new
path for the address book in the text box or browse to the new location.

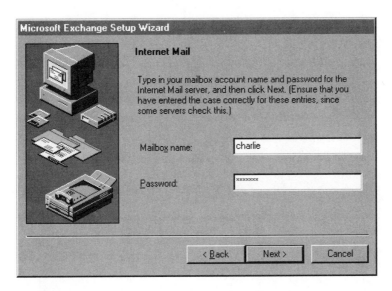

**FIGURE 13.15**

*Internet Mail dialog box in Exchange Setup Wizard for mailbox name and password*

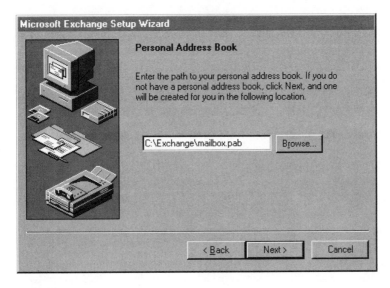

**FIGURE 13.16**

*Dialog box in Exchange Wizard Setup for choosing personal address book file location*

16. Click Next to bring up the dialog box for creating a set of default personal folders (Figure 13.17). The default location for these folders is the main directory of Exchange—this is a bad idea as a place to store personal files. Put the personal folders where you put your personal address book, and it will be easy to keep track of both of them. After you've chosen the location for your file, click Next. You're almost finished with the Windows Messaging setup.

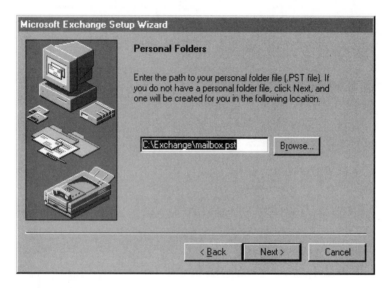

**FIGURE 13.17**

*Dialog box in Exchange Setup Wizard for choosing personal folders file location*

17. Decide whether or not you want to have Exchange start up automatically when you log on to the server, and click the appropriate option button. Then click Next, and you're done. You'll see a final message that tells you what services and folders have been set up and that you're actually ready to start Windows Messaging. Click Finish.

## Main Features of Windows Messaging

Once you have Exchange up and running, you'll have access to a wide variety of E-mail systems. Each one of them will add a slightly different flavor to the mix, but let's take a look at some of the features they will have in common.

The main screen of Windows Messaging will look like the window in Figure 13.18 when you first install it. There's not much there—no messages—and it doesn't look particularly exciting.

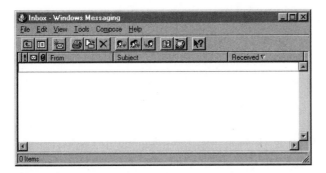

**FIGURE 13.18**

*Default screen configuration of Windows Messaging window*

Well, let's spruce it up a little bit, and make it a bit easier to see what's going on. Click the Show/Hide Folder List button (the second button from the left edge of the toolbar, as you see here), which will give you a view that allows you to see the folders in your personal folder file.

Another way to get this view is to choose Folders from the View menu. Now you should have something that looks like the view in Figure 13.19. It's still not terribly exciting because you don't have any interesting mail in it, but at least you can see where your mail would go and what some of the other default folders are.

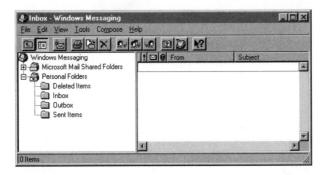

**FIGURE 13.19**

*View of folders in Windows Messaging*

# Working with Folders

You can add, delete, or change the name of any folder in Windows Messaging. Folders can have subfolders. They can be shared with other users if they are part of Microsoft Mail Shared Folders. You can move the folders you own from your personal folders area to the shared area and from the shared area to your personal folders area.

One of the things we find useful to do is to set up special folders for saving important messages. You can create new folders under your personal folder, and no one else will have access to them. You could have one folder just for messages about hot scuba diving sites in French Polynesia, for example, as you prepare for your vacation. You wouldn't want to mix up those messages with messages from your boss about the new project you're supposed to be working on while you're surfing the net looking for more information about Tahiti.

To create a new folder, you might expect that you would be able to right-click on the area in which you wanted to locate the folder, and then choose New Folder from a pop-up menu. Sorry, the right mouse button seems to have suffered a setback in its functionality. You have to select the folder that you want to have as a parent folder for the new folder, from the left pane of the window, and then choose New Folder from the File menu to create the folder. Windows Messaging will prompt you to provide a name for the folder. Type *Tahiti Dive Sites*, for example, for the new vacation folder—and you'll have a folder for storing vacation information, as shown in Figure 13.20.

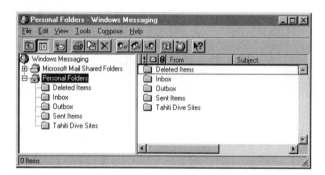

**FIGURE 13.20**

*Example of special archive folder for important messages in Windows Messaging*

Another useful capability in Windows Messaging is the ability to share folders and documents with other users. For this, you use Microsoft Mail. You'll notice a folder called Microsoft Mail Shared Folders under the Windows Messaging icon in the left pane of the window; folders here are shared among all users of your Microsoft Mail post office. For example, you are assigned to a project that involves integrating a new technology recently developed by Engineering into your widget manufacturing process. One of your first tasks is to create a set of folders where the project team can share information. As an example, we created a folder called Update Project that contains several subfolders (Figure 13.21).

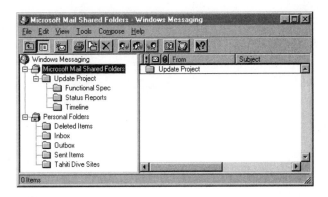

**FIGURE 13.21**

*Example of shared project folders created in Microsoft Mail*

These shared folders and all of the documents contained in them are seen automatically by all users who share the same Microsoft Mail Postoffice, which makes this an ideal way to share documents. The user who creates the shared folder controls the permissions for that folder. You can see the permissions of a folder by right-clicking the folder, choosing Properties from the pop-up menu that appears, and then clicking the Permissions tab on the properties sheet. A page like the one shown in Figure 13.22 on the following page will appear on the screen.

Do you want to add a document to a shared folder? You can click the document in Explorer or on your desktop and drag it to the shared folder. Or you can mail the document to a user by right-clicking it, choosing Send To from the pop-up menu, and then choosing Mail Recipient from the menu that opens from Send To. This opens Windows Messaging and allows you to send the document or file directly to anyone whose E-mail address you know.

You also can do the usual things with a Windows Messaging folder that you'd expect to be able to do with a folder—change its name, move it around, delete it, change its properties if you have the rights to do so, and so forth.

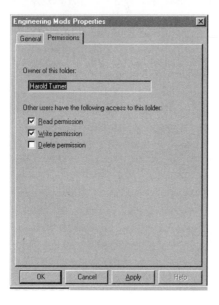

**FIGURE 13.22**

*Example of a permissions page for a shared folder in Microsoft Mail*

## Working with the Address Book

In order to mail something to someone, you first need to know his or her address. This is true whether you are using snail mail or E-mail. So how do you find a person's address? And once you have the address, where do you keep it so that you don't have to memorize it?

There are lots of ways to find out a person's E-mail address. The simplest, of course, is to ask him or her! If the person is using the same Microsoft Mail Postoffice that you are, his or her address will be part of the Postoffice Address List and available to all users of that post office, as shown in the example in Figure 13.23. Users who share a Microsoft Mail post office are added automatically to the main address book for that post office.

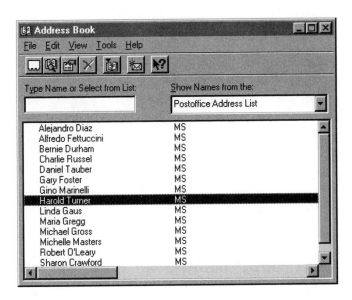

**FIGURE 13.23**

*Example of an Address Book dialog box showing a post office address list*

Another way to get someone's E-mail address is to capture it from a message that was sent to you. This is easy and foolproof; you don't have to worry about typing the address incorrectly or any other such problem. To capture a person's E-mail address from a message to you, open the message and, while it's open, double-click the name in whatever field it appears in the header. This opens up a property page for the person; you click Personal Address Book, and the address is added to your personal address book. Figures 13.24 and 13.25 on the following page show this.

After you have the person's address in your address book, it's easy to use it. Start a new message either by clicking the New Message icon on the toolbar (shown here),

or by choosing New Message from the Compose menu. This will get you a blank message form like the one shown in Figure 13.26.

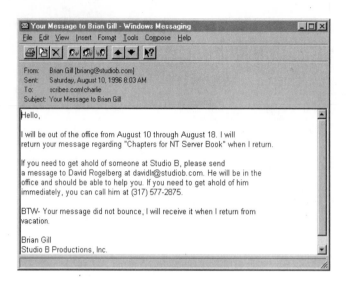

**FIGURE 13.24**

*Example of a message with a user's E-mail address in the header*

**FIGURE 13.25**

*Example of a user property sheet showing E-mail address*

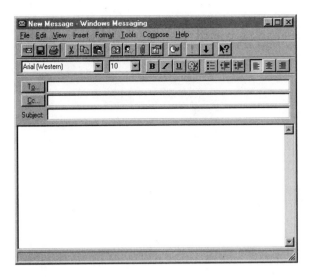

**FIGURE 13.26**

*A blank New Message form in Windows Messaging*

If you know the E-mail address of the message recipient, you can type the address into the To: or Cc: address fields directly. You don't have to have the address in your address book, just type it in the field. Windows Messaging is smart enough to parse the address and send it on its merry way.

To add a recipient for the message when you don't know the E-mail address, click either the To: or the Cc: address field. Either option will get you to the Address Book dialog box. (See Figure 13.27 on the following page.) From this Address Book dialog box, you can add one or more recipients to any of the recipient fields.

You also can choose addresses of different types from this same screen. You can add a Microsoft Mail address, an Internet Mail address, and a CompuServe Mail address, all in the same message, by choosing the respective types of addresses in the Show Names From The drop-down list box and then selecting an address from the list of each type of address. When it's time to do the delivery, Windows Messaging will handle the differences without a burp.

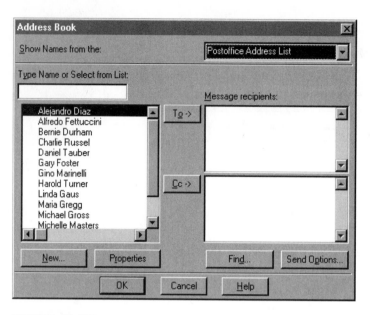

**FIGURE 13.27**

*Example of Address Book dialog box for adding names to address fields in a message header*

All of the people who are listed in the To: and Cc: fields will see the entire message and the names of all of the people listed in the address fields. But one thing you won't see, by default, is what's called a "blind copy." Sometimes you might want to copy a message to someone without everyone else knowing that you're copying that person. Without going into the ethics of the practice, there's a way to do this in Windows Messaging. You can "drop a dime" in E-mail by using the Blind Copy option. Choose Bcc Box from the View menu of the blank message form, and suddenly the message form looks different. As you can see in Figure 13.28, a new address field named Bcc has been added to the message header. You can enter multiple names in this field, just as you can in the other address fields.

# Microsoft Exchange Client

If you're running in an environment with Exchange Server, you'll definitely want to be using the vastly enhanced Microsoft Exchange Client that is included with

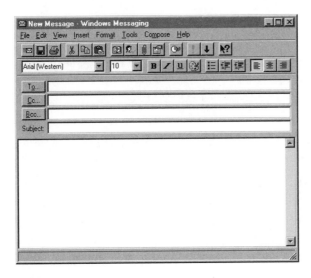

**FIGURE 13.28**

*New Message form with Blind Copy address field added*

Exchange Server. It's lots cuter, and it adds a whole raft of new capabilities and features that aren't available with the limited Exchange application that is included with Windows NT Server.

You can create a whole set of rules that will allow Exchange Client to handle your mail automatically—dumping some of it straight into the bit bucket if it's junk mail, moving other mail into a special folder for the project you're working on, or treating mail on a particular subject, with a particular text, or from a particular user as extremely high priority mail. You can have a high priority message sent to your screen immediately upon its arrival; add sounds to this notification of incoming priority mail, and you won't be likely to miss that important message from your boss.

## Connecting with Other Mail Systems

One of the important innovations in Exchange is the integration of a wide variety of E-mail systems in a single, easily managed application. It doesn't matter whether your E-mail is from the Internet, Lotus Notes Mail, CompuServe, or some other variety of mail system—there's an Exchange Mail Transport Agent that is either already written or being written for it, and you can integrate this transport agent directly into your Inbox.

## POINTS TO REMEMBER

- Microsoft's Windows Messaging comes with Internet Mail and Microsoft Mail clients.

- You can easily add more Mail Transport Agents to handle other types of E-mail.

- Microsoft Exchange Server adds significant additional capabilities to the basic version of Exchange that is included in Windows NT Server.

- You can use Microsoft Mail Shared Folders to share documents with other users.

- E-mail in Microsoft Exchange is "transport independent." All mail, both incoming mail and outgoing mail, gets handled by the same interface regardless of its point of origin or its destination.

## WHAT'S NEXT?

In this chapter, we've covered how to use the built-in Windows Messaging system—the "Exchange Lite" version of Microsoft Exchange. In Chapter 14 we'll discuss Windows NT Server as an application server, which takes your network operating system beyond simple file sharing and print sharing.

# CHAPTER 14

Applications Software

# CHAPTER 14

## Applications Software

One of the most confusing areas when dealing with the design of an enterprise network is the use of software applications over the network. Often even more confusing is the issue of software licenses. In this chapter, we will provide you with some guidelines to ease you through these murky waters and to help you prevent the errors often associated with using software applications over the network.

## Windows NT Server as an Application Server

Microsoft Windows NT Server version 4 is a flexible network operating system that can be used in different ways:

◆ As a simple data file server, with clients storing their data in a central location.

◆ As the underlying operating system for a database server, such as Microsoft SQL Server 6.5, which runs as a service on Windows NT Server, storing the database and processing queries from clients.

◆ As an application server, providing the ability to run applications from the server either in a simple file serving mode, as older networked operating systems have run them, or in an actual client/server mode, where processing is shared between the client and the server, each taking responsibility for a portion of the application.

A key difference between Windows NT Server version 4 and other network operating systems is the ability of Windows NT Server to provide a stable, dependable server platform for client/server applications. The use of Windows NT Server as a full client/server applications server is what permits other tools, such as the remote administration tools, to do their jobs. In the case of remote administration tools, the applications and services that actually are being administered reside on the server; but the local applications that communicate with and control these services are run from a client machine, just as if they were being run locally off the console. With the addition of the Distributed Component Object Model (DCOM)—sometimes referred to as Network OLE—to Windows NT Server version 4, we expect to see many more applications take advantage of the Windows NT ability to run distributed applications.

# Running Applications from the Server

The most common use and configuration of a Windows NT Server is that of a simple file server architecture, where the server is used to run applications and provide basic networking services. (See Figure 14.1.) Shared applications are stored on the central file server, and any client on the network can have access to them, even remote clients—via RAS.

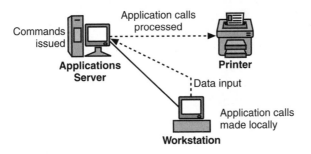

**FIGURE 14.1**

*Process diagram for applications stored and run from the file server*

The applications on the file server can be one of two types: a network version of the application or a stand-alone version of the application. Network versions of most applications, while often still functioning as straightforward file-shared applications, are moving more and more in the direction of running in full client/server mode, with the majority of the processing occurring on the server. Existing stand-alone applications might be stored on the server with client access through the server, but the actual processing is done on the client itself. (See Figure 14.2.)

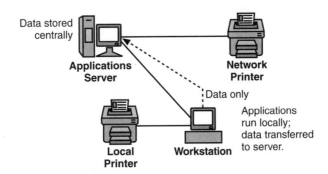

**FIGURE 14.2**

*Process diagram for applications stored on the server and run on the workstation*

Both network and stand-alone applications have their advantages and disadvantages. Network versions are easy to monitor for access by the licensed users of the application. Applications run from a server might run more slowly because they are sent over the network, but this overhead can be more than offset by the potentially increased power of the server hardware and the more powerful database or application engine running there. It also might mean that you wouldn't need as powerful a workstation computer. With a single-user version of an application, you are likely to need more power at the workstation because all of the processing will be done there. The biggest problem for stand-alone versions of applications is in the area of license issues. If you own only 10 licenses of an application, that means that you can allow only ten users legal access to that application at any given time. Some applications leave this to the honor system by not restricting access to anyone. Other applications, however, do restrict access by checking users that log on against a license file associated with the application.

Either method for running applications from the file server will require that hard drive space be used for cache files and that RAM be used in the processing of the program. Running the application on the workstation rather than on the server will reduce the burden on the RAM requirements of the server, but it usually increases disk traffic.

## Running Applications as a Service

The server components and routines that are a key part of the network operating system can use a great portion of the network server's memory and system resources. As Windows applications in general, and network server applications specifically, grow in size and resource requirements, it is essential that basic networking functions be provided in a way that utilizes memory and space efficiently.

In Windows NT Server version 4, most of the underlying network applications and functions run as a service. (See Figure 14.3.) As a service, the application runs in the background and in a minimized mode that makes calls for more RAM and resources only when it is called upon to perform its functions.

# Windows NT Server as a Replication Server

It can be a complicated matter to keep versions of files straight on a network. Windows NT Server includes a replication service that ensures everyone is working with the same information. Directory replication also can help balance a server workload. When you have too many people who need access to a particular directory, you can export the directory to another server and point some of the workstations there. Directories are *exported* by the replication service on the server and dynamically updated when the master copy on the exporting machine is changed.

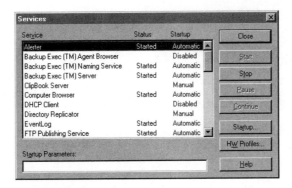

**FIGURE 14.3**

*Example of a Services dialog box showing the services run on a Windows NT server*

It's a fairly simple process once it's set up. A Windows NT server exports directories to import servers. At regular intervals, the import servers connect to the export server, and the files in their directories are synchronized with the master directories on the export server. Only a Windows NT server can be an export server. Only computers running either Windows NT Server or Windows NT Workstation can be import servers.

Replication is possible between computers both within a single domain and also across domains. When you set up to export within a single domain, all import servers in the domain receive the export data. Replication between computers in different domains is possible only if the domains have the proper trust relationships set up between them.

Setting up replication between computers requires several steps. First you create a user account to run the directory replication services and set it up so the services run automatically; then you configure the export server and the import server.

## Setting Up a Replicator Account

A user account must be configured with very specific settings for you to run replication services. Open User Manager for Domains, and create a new account with these properties:

◆ Assign a recognizable user name such as Replication or ReplicatorAcct.

◆ Set the password to Password Never Expires.

◆ Make the account a member of the following groups: Backup Operators, Domain Users, and Replicator.

◆ Hours of permitted access should be 24 hours a day, seven days a week.

Distributed Component Object Model (Distributed COM, or DCOM) is a new technology with deep roots in the Windows environment. It is the network-distributed version of COM, the object model of OLE. It extends the functionality of OLE across the network—that is, it permits the distribution of the workload across nodes in much the same way that we've been able to distribute resources across nodes with sharing.

DCOM allows two or more COM objects on different systems to communicate easily with each other. It is DCOM that handles all of the network communications and security checks to dispatch programming calls.

DCOM is now in its infancy and its usefulness in the development of applications has barely been scratched, but it offers the Windows networking world some of the same functionality that XWindows offers the UNIX world for remotely displaying an application—but with the added capability of running applications distributed across multiple computers transparently. Its current capabilities allow smoother interaction between OLE-enabled applications. The benefits of OLE providing connectivity and interaction between programs on a single computer are magnified in DCOM for communicating across a network.

A list of DCOM features and capabilities is provided below.

◆ DCOM can work over a LAN or a WAN, including the Internet. With its capability for being used over the Internet, DCOM might become the basis for clients to execute processes on server systems. Microsoft's active components are COM objects and can operate remotely under DCOM.

◆ DCOM's modular approach allows the processing of complex applications that are to be distributed to multiple computers. This could allow a seamless transferal of processing when one server fails so that a duplicate computer continues to process the application calls.

◆ DCOM provides network transparency and communication automation, which allows communications to take place between objects without one object needing to be aware of the location of the other. The objects thus could be in different processes on the same machine, or they could be in separate processes on different machines located anywhere in the world.

◆ DCOM provides the connectivity of OLE-enabled applications running on different machines, using a standards-based Remote Procedure Call (RPC) mechanism.

◆ DCOM allows developers to split an application into component modules that can each execute transparently on different computers. Because DCOM provides network transparency, the component modules appear to users and to programmers as if they were located on a single machine.

*(continued)*

♦ DCOM technology also can be used to make global networks and information resources appear to be local, making it easier and faster for users to gain access to critical business information. Through DCOM, users can locate and execute components across global networks, without even knowing that the information is actually found on a computer that could be halfway around the world.

## Setting Up Automatic Startup

After the account is configured correctly, the Directory Replicator service then must be configured to start automatically for this new user account. On the export server follow these steps:

1. Open Server Manager, and select the name of the export server.

2. Choose Services from the Computer menu.

3. In the dialog box that opens, select Directory Replicator; then click Startup.

4. This will open the dialog box shown in Figure 14.4. Change the Startup type to Automatic. In the Log On As section, click This Account.

**FIGURE 14.4**

*Starting Directory Replicator service*

5. Next, click the button on the right side of the This Account text box to open the Add User dialog box. Select the Replicator Account to add it to the Add Name text box (Figure 14.5), and then click OK.

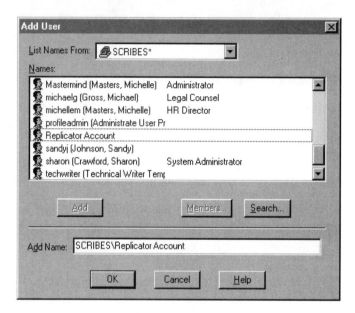

**FIGURE 14.5**

*Adding Replicator Account*

6. Enter the password for the user account, and click OK. You'll see the dialog box shown in Figure 14.6, which confirms that the account is configured correctly.

**FIGURE F14.6**

*Setup confirmation message*

## Configuring the Export Server

After the replication account is set up and the replication service is configured to start automatically for that account, your task is to identify both the directory tree that will export data and the destination for the exported data.

1. Start Server Manager; then double-click the name of the export server.

2. In the Properties window, click Replication.

3. Click the Export Directories option box. The default From Path is winnt\system32\repl\export. Any directories created in the export path are automatically exported.

## NOTE

*If the To List list box is left blank, the export server will export to the local domain. If you add entries in this box, the local domain will no longer be an export destination unless you explicitly specify the domain name here also.*

4. Click Add to add domains or individual import computers.

5. If you need to export specific subdirectories, click Manage to open the dialog box shown in Figure 14.7.

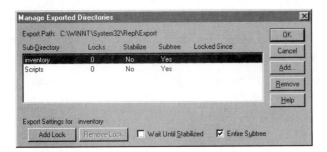

**FIGURE 14.7**

*Managing directories for export*

Here's what the entries in this dialog box mean:

◆ **Export Path**  The path to the directory from which files and folders are exported.

◆ **Subdirectory**  The subdirectories that are exported.

◆ **Locks**  The number of locks applied to the subdirectory. A lock prevents a directory from being replicated. You might want to add a lock while doing maintenance on a directory and then remove the lock when you're done.

◆ **Stabilize** Indicates whether files and folders in that sub-directory must be stable for at least two minutes before replication takes place. The default is No, which means that any change triggers a replication at once. This field is controlled by the Wait Until Stabilized check box at the bottom of the dialog box.

◆ **Entire Subtree** Indicates whether the entire subdirectory will be exported. If the setting is No, only the first-level subdirectory will be exported. This field is controlled by the Entire Subtree check box at the bottom of the dialog box.

◆ **Locked Since** The date and time of the oldest lock on this directory.

## Configuring the Import Server

To set up the importing computer, you need to identify both the directory tree that will receive the imported data and also the computer names or domain names from which the data will be exported. Here are the steps for setting up the import server:

1. On the import computer, double-click Server in Control Panel; then click Replication.

2. Click the Import Directories option button. The default path is winnt\system32\repl\imports.

   The From List list box shows the computers and domains from which the data will be imported. If the list box is blank, it means that data is imported only from the local domain.

### NOTE

*If the From List list box is left blank, the import server will import data only from the local domain. If you add entries in this box, directories will no longer be imported from the local domain unless you explicitly specify the domain name here also.*

3. Click Add to add export computers or domains. The Select Domain dialog box shown in Figure 14.8 will open. Double-click a domain name to see a list of the computers in the domain.

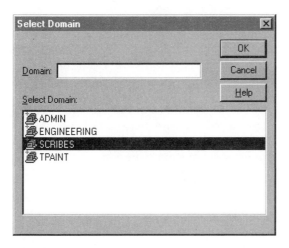

**FIGURE 14.8**

*Selecting the computer or domain from which to import*

4. To import specific subdirectories in the export path, click Manage. The window that opens is similar to the one for the export server, but with fewer options. You can add or remove locks and add or remove directories in the list.

#### ◆ Manage Imported Directories Terms

| Status Column Term | Definition |
| --- | --- |
| OK | The subdirectory is getting regular updates from the export server. |
| No Synch | The subdirectory has received updates but the data isn't synchronized with the master list. The cause could be open files, a communications failure, or incorrect permissions. |
| No Master | The import computer isn't receiving updates. This is probably because the export server isn't running or has stopped sending updates. |
| Blank entry | No replication has happened in that subdirectory, so there's undoubtedly something wrong with the setup of either the export server or the import computer. |

# Systems Management Server

Microsoft Systems Management Server (SMS) is part of the Microsoft BackOffice suite of products that can help you manage your network more easily and more efficiently. It gives you the ability to monitor and manage your networked hardware and software from a central location, and it allows you to see the entire organization, including your inventory of hardware and software, from this central site. The major advantages of using System Management Server are these:

♦ You can identify which PCs and printers are due for hardware or driver upgrades and what software packages are being used. You can not only see what version of a software package is running but also actually upgrade everyone to the latest version from your console.

♦ You can monitor network traffic so you can tune your network's performance. You can identify bottlenecks easily and compare installed hardware against the hardware inventory to identify network components that need upgrading. You can even use SMS to take direct control of remote PCs to aid troubleshooting and Help desk functions.

♦ You can maintain uniform software applications standards across your network easily, ensuring that licenses are up to date and enforced, that the software versions are the same for all clients, and that software updates are propagated quickly as they are needed.

♦ You can manage a software upgrade by first testing the software in a controlled environment and then implementing it across the enterprise when you're sure you're ready.

♦ You can use both local and wide area networking protocols and connections, including TCP/IP, IPX/SPX, NetBEUI, and AppleTalk over most network connections, including asynchronous, ISDN, and X.25.

### ♦ Why Uniform Software Standards on the Network?

Recent studies have shown that technical support and the administration of existing software and hardware can easily account for 25 percent to 50 percent of the actual cost of running a network. These costs are much more manageable if you are able to set up your network with a central point of administration and if you support one suite of applications and hardware across the network. The cost of training also is reduced, because both support staff and users have less to learn. And maintaining uniform network software applications allows you to thoroughly test new software and make sure that it won't interact adversely with existing applications when it is deployed to the network. This cuts down greatly on problems. Some other obvious and not so obvious advantages to enforcing common standards on the network include the following:

*(continued)*

# Licensing

In the bad old days, most software was copy protected and a whole industry grew up around developing ways to either improve copy protection or find a way around it. Eventually, however, most software companies realized that the overall cost of copy protection was greater than its benefits, and copy protection was removed from all except the most expensive software packages.

This was and is a "good thing"; it makes it easier to support and manage software for both individuals and corporations. But if we are going to continue to enjoy this good thing, we need to ensure that software licenses are enforced on our networks. The costs of allowing, much less encouraging, software piracy are not trivial, with judgments in the hundreds of thousands of dollars handed down in recent years.

As we discussed in Chapter 6, Windows NT Server provides two very different licensing options in version 4—Per Server and Per Seat. At the time you installed Windows NT Server, you had to choose one of these models. In most cases, if you weren't sure how your network traffic would look, you'll have chosen to leave the default licensing in place and, consequently, will be using Per Server licensing. As we said in Chapter 6, this is a safe way to start because you have a one-time, one-way option to convert your existing Per Server licenses to Per Seat client access licenses if you decide that makes sense.

## Choosing a Licensing Model

Choosing the best licensing model is a simple matter of mathematics. Well, actually, the mathematics are simple; gathering the actual data you will need before you can do the calculations is a lot trickier. System Management Server can help with that, of course; you don't really need to buy any additional software to do the numbers.

When you choose the Per Server option for your licensing, Windows NT Server starts tracking who connects to the server and the total number of connections. If you exceed the number of licensed connections for the server, it will write an event to the application event log. You can view this event log using the Event Viewer application.

You can use the event log and the License Manager application to keep track of how many clients connect to each of your servers and whether you have exceeded your licenses on any of the servers.

**For More Information**

*For additional information about Event Viewer, see Chapter 15 and Chapter 21.*

## Doing the Math for Licensing

The math calculations are quite simple. Multiply the maximum number of licenses connected to each server at any one time by the total number of servers. The result is the number of Per Server licenses you need.

For the Per Client licensing, it's even easier. Just count the total number of computers that are connected to the domain. Or, if you're using an enterprise model, the total number of computers connected to the whole network. That's the number of client access licenses you need for Per Client licensing. Note that you *don't* need an additional license for Windows NT Server computers that are also functioning as workstations. And you don't need to count the computers that are connected only to a workgroup and do not use any resources on any of the Windows NT server machines.

Take the two numbers—for Per Server and for Per Client—and whichever one is smaller, that's your choice. If you're right on the edge, we'd suggest you stick to Per Server, if only because, once you make the transition, you'll have to stay with it. Also, you can easily mix and match your licenses, although we find it a pain to keep track of mixed licensing on a network. If you have a particular group of clients that connects only to one specific server and if most of these clients are connected only intermittently and never all at once, you might want to consider keeping that server in a Per Server license mode, even if you change the rest of the network to Per Client licensing. An example of where you might do this is a remote access server used only to provide mail services to the connecting computers.

# Using License Manager Applications

Network administrators have two tools for managing licenses across the network available to them as part of Windows NT Server: the Control Panel Licensing applet and License Manager, which is found in the Administrative Tools group.

The Control Panel's Licensing applet is a simple tool that allows you to choose between Per Server and Per Seat licensing options. Figure 14.9 shows the Licensing applet set up to select a Per Server licensing option.

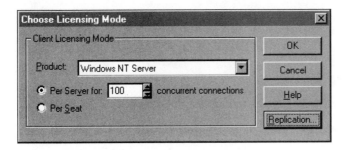

**FIGURE 14.9**

*The Licensing applet from Control Panel*

License Manager provides a graphical representation of the licenses across the network. Figure 14.10 on the following page shows License Manager's Server Browser window, where all of the server installations can be viewed. With License Manager, you can carry out the following tasks:

◆ Manage the purchase of licenses for products on the network.

◆ Remove unnecessary licenses from the network.

◆ Balance the replication load across the whole network.

◆ View usage statistics of licenses based upon per user.

◆ Ensure compliance to license agreements.

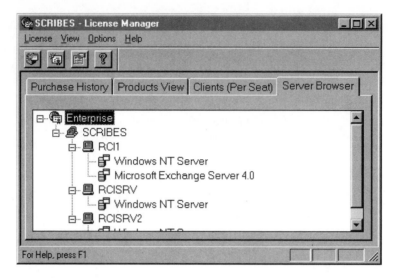

**FIGURE 14.10**

*License Manager dialog box showing the Server Browser page*

## Purchase history

The Purchase History option in License Manager keeps track of all licenses for a domain or for an entire enterprise. For License Manager to do its job, you'll need to enter the following information:

◆  Quantity of licenses purchased

◆  Quantity of licenses deleted

◆  Name of the administrator responsible for recording the purchase history

◆  Name of licensed product

◆  Date of installation

◆  Additional comments

This information is critical when it comes to planning for future acquisitions and product introductions. With a quick glance at the purchase history, you can respond to any question regarding the availability of licenses for new employees or the transition from an older or competitive product.

## Products view

The information reported in this view of License Manager depends on which model of licensing you have selected to use. If you have selected Per Seat licensing, it shows how many licenses have been purchased and how many have been assigned to users' computers for all the products registered in License Manager. If you have chosen Per Server licensing, it shows the total number of licenses that have been purchased (shown in Figure 14.11). It also provides information about the number of concurrent licenses that have been used.

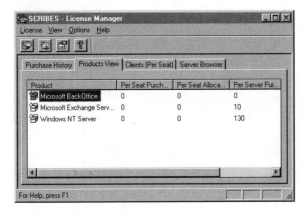

**FIGURE 14.11**

*View of license purchase history in License Manager*

Numerical and graphical information is provided in this module that will allow you to determine which of your products do the following:

◆ Meet the legal licensing requirements.

◆ Do not comply with licensing requirements.

◆ Have reached their license limit.

## Clients (Per Seat)

This page of License Manager shows information about Per Seat licenses only. It displays, by product, who is using products legally and who is not—a useful management tool, if the cost of the licenses is spread over several departments.

## Browsing servers

The fourth tab in License Manager is Server Browser. In Server Browser, you can see and edit server and server product licensing information in any domain in which you have administrative rights.

## Adding and Removing Licenses

To keep your database of licenses current, you have to remember to record all new licenses that have been acquired and to remove licenses that are no longer useful. (See Figure 14.12.) This tool, together with System Management Server, will permit you to maintain an accurate accounting of all your products and licenses.

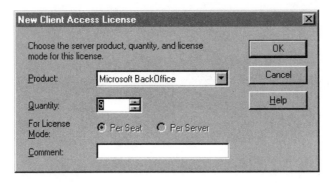

**FIGURE 14.12**

*Dialog box for adding licenses to your server*

### POINTS TO REMEMBER

♦ DCOM-enabled applications help distribute the computing load across the network.

♦ You have only one opportunity to convert from Per Server licensing to Per Seat licensing.

♦ You can mix and match Per Server and Per Seat licenses on the network to accommodate varying network needs.

♦ Systems Management Server can make your Help desk and trouble-shooting operations more efficient.

### WHAT'S NEXT?

In most circumstances, the computer you use on a daily basis as an administrator will *not* be a domain controller. Nonetheless, you will need to be able to perform administrative tasks from the computer you use every day. Chapter 15 discusses the server tools that can be installed on a Microsoft Windows 95 client so that you can do just that.

# CHAPTER 15

Remote Administration Tools

# CHAPTER 15

# Remote Administration Tools

A wise administrator does not use a server as an everyday work machine. Too many things can go wrong, including the accidental deletion of critical files or an untimely reboot. However, you also don't want to be running off to find a server whenever a share permission or user account must be changed. Microsoft Windows NT Server version 4 comes with a package of tools that can be installed under Microsoft Windows 95 so that you—or any other authorized person—can remotely administer servers running Microsoft File and Print Services for NetWare (FPNW) and Windows NT Server.

The server tools supplied are the crucial ones: Event Viewer, Server Manager, and User Manager for Domains. Probably 90 percent of your administrative chores are done with these three applications. The server tools also include extensions to the Windows 95 Explorer, which enables Explorer to edit the security properties of printers and NTFS file objects on computers running Microsoft Windows NT and to administer File and Print Services for NetWare and Novell NetWare-enabled users.

When you install the Windows NT server tools, the installation program will copy the tool files to C:\SRVTOOLS (assuming that C: is the boot drive) and add extensions to Explorer that allow you to change security settings when viewing an NTFS drive or a print queue on a computer running Windows NT.

## Installing the Server Tools

To install the Windows NT server tools on a computer running Windows 95, you must have at least 3 MB of free space on your boot drive. Open Control Panel and follow these steps:

1. Double-click Add/Remove Programs.

2. Click the Windows Setup tab, and then click Have Disk.

3. In the Copy Manufacturer's Files From combo box, enter the location for the client-based Network Administration Tools files. You also can click Browse to browse for the files. (There will be a SRVTOOLS.INF file in this directory as shown in Figure 15.1. On the Windows NT Server CD-ROM, these files are in \CLIENTS\SRVTOOLS\WIN95.) Click OK.

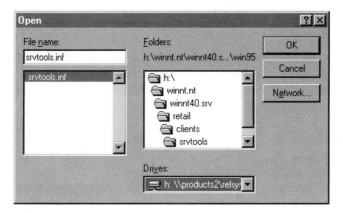

**FIGURE 15.1**

*The Open dialog box showing Windows NT Server Tools*

**4.** In the Have Disk dialog box that opens, be sure you select Windows NT Server Tools, as shown in Figure 15.2. Then click Install. The Windows NT server tools are installed in a \SRVTOOLS folder on the computer's boot drive.

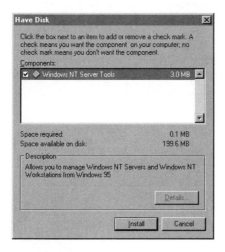

**FIGURE 15.2**

*Have Disk dialog box showing the Windows NT Server Tools option selected*

**5.** Manually adjust the AUTOEXEC.BAT file to include \SRVTOOLS in the path. For the new path to take effect, you must restart the computer.

# Establishing Trust Relationships

User Manager for Domains in Windows NT Server Tools can be used to create or to dismantle trust relationships between domains, but you can't verify these changes until you log on to a domain controller. Be careful to enter the correct passwords for the trust relationships.

## NOTE

*If you start any of the Windows NT server tools when you are not yet logged on, you will get a message that says the computer is not logged on to the network. First log on to the network; then run any of the Windows NT server tools.*

# Using Event Viewer

When computers on the network run into trouble, you need to find out just what occurred. Not to put too fine a point on it—but users are not the most reliable source of this information. In addition, many of the things that can go wrong aren't visible to users anyway.

Computers running Windows NT Server and Microsoft Windows NT Workstation all maintain System, Security, and Application logs, tracking both successful and unsuccessful events. Event Viewer is a useful tool for viewing these logs. To start Event Viewer, follow these steps:

1. Choose Windows NT Server Tools from the Programs menu on the Start menu. Click Event Viewer. This will open a dialog box that displays a list of the available computers (Figure 15.3).

2. Double-click the computer in the Select Computer list, or type the name of the computer running Windows NT Server or Windows NT Workstation in the Computer text box, and click OK.

3. Choose System, Security, or Applications from the Log menu to view the available logs.

4. To view the content of an entry, select it and press Enter or double-click the entry. The dialog box shown in Figure 15.4 will open.

### For More Information

*Chapter 21 has more on reading and deciphering Event Viewer.*

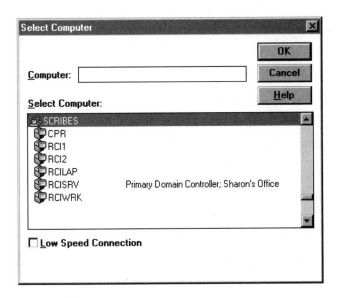

**FIGURE 15.3**

*Example of a Select Computer dialog box in Event Viewer*

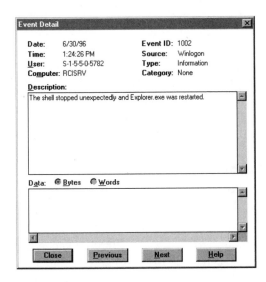

**FIGURE 15.4**

*Example of an Event Detail dialog box in Event Viewer*

# Using Server Manager

Server Manager is the Windows NT tool for sharing directories, administering services, and adding and removing computers from the domain. To use Server Manager, follow these steps:

1. Choose Windows NT Server Tools from the Programs menu on the Start menu. Click Server Manager.

2. Select the computer you want to administer. To see computers in another domain, choose Select Domain from the Computer menu.

3. After you have selected a computer, you can choose the desired action from the menus.

   For example, choose Properties from the Computer menu, and a dialog box will open like the one in Figure 15.5.

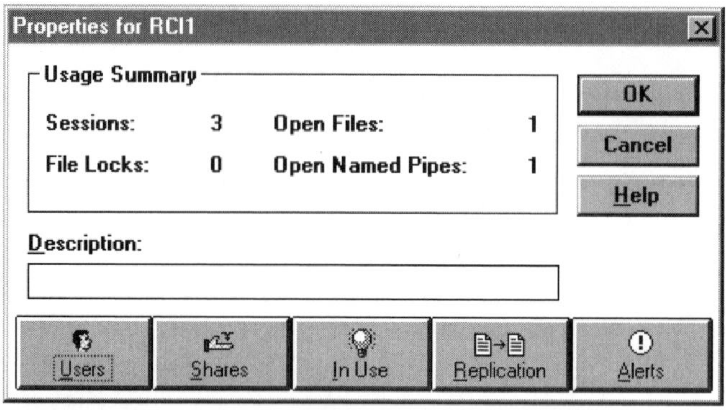

**FIGURE 15.5**

*Example of a Properties dialog box for a computer in Server Manager*

From there, you can click buttons at the bottom of the window to view information about the selected computer. For example, if you click Users, a User Sessions dialog box will open that shows you all of the users currently connected to that computer, as shown in Figure 15.6.

In addition, you can view a list of the resources that have been opened by a particular user. You also can disconnect any or all of the users who are currently connected to the computer.

Other actions that can be taken from Server Manager include viewing and changing services and viewing and changing shared directories.

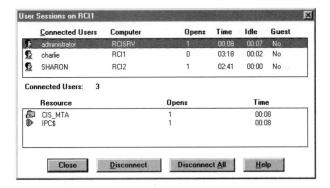

**FIGURE 15.6**

*Example of a User Sessions dialog box in Server Manager*

For More Information

*For more on sharing directories, see Chapter 12.*

# Using User Manager for Domains

User Manager for Domains lets you set up and modify user accounts, create and administer groups, and set account policies for passwords. To open User Manager for Domains, follow these steps:

1. Choose Windows NT Server Tools from the Programs menu on the Start menu. Click User Manager for Domains. This will open the window shown in Figure 15.7 on the following page.

2. Select the user account or group you want to administer.

3. If you want to see accounts in another domain, choose Select Domain from the User menu.

Account, User Rights, and Audit policies can be set from the Policies menu. You also can establish or remove trust relationships from this menu, although you won't get back any verification.

For More Information

*The details on User Manager for Domains can be found in Chapter 9 and Chapter 10.*

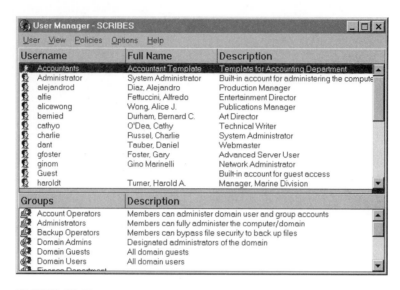

**FIGURE 15.7**

*Example of a User Manager for Domains window*

# Editing Security Properties

Windows NT server tools let you edit permissions and other security properties of the files on NTFS partitions as well as on printers. To edit the security properties of NTFS-file objects or printers, just follow these steps:

1. Double-click Network Neighborhood, and then double-click the name of the computer to be administered.

2. Click the printer or Windows file object you want to administer; then click Properties.

3. Click the Security tab to open the dialog box shown in Figure 15.8.

4. Make the changes you want to make to the Permissions, Auditing, and object Ownership settings. Click OK when you're finished.

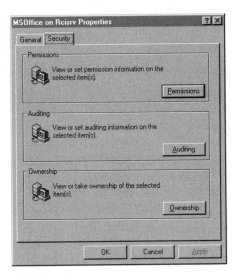

**FIGURE 15.8**

*Security page on a remote directory*

Some administrative tasks can't be done using Windows NT server tools. A few examples of such tasks include the following:

◆ Administering print queues through the Printers list in My Computer. The printer objects represent print queues local to a Windows 95 computer, even if the queue is redirected to a Windows NT server or Windows NT workstation print queue.

◆ Printing a file using the Windows 3.*x* Print Manager, which no longer exists in Windows 95. If, for some reason, you're using Program Manager in Windows 95 (which can be done), the Printers icon in the Main group of Program Manager is just a shortcut to the Printers list in My Computer.

◆ Using File Manager. A Security menu is not added to Explorer when you install the Windows NT server tools on a Windows 95 computer as it was added to File Manager when previous versions of the Windows NT server tools were installed for Windows 3.*x*.

# Sharing File and Print Services for Novell NetWare

To share File and Print Services for NetWare (FPNW) volumes and manage shared volumes, follow these steps:

1. Connect to the server running File and Print Services for NetWare. For example, to connect from the command line, type:

```
net use z: \\servername\c$
```

2. In Explorer, right-click the drive for the server running File and Print Services for NetWare. Then choose Properties from the pop-up menu that appears.

3. Click the FPNW tab. A dialog box will appear, containing options that allow you to manage shared volumes and to share directories as File and Print Services for NetWare volumes.

**NOTE**

*For other administrative tasks, use Server Manager and User Manager, which include options for administering File and Print Services for NetWare and NetWare-enabled users. These are the same Server Manager and User Manager options that are available on computers running Windows NT Server with File and Print Services for NetWare.*

# Removing the Windows NT Server Tools

To remove the Windows NT server tools from a computer running Windows 95, follow these steps:

1. Choose Settings from the Start menu. Click Control Panel.

2. Double-click Add/Remove Programs.

3. Click the Install/Uninstall tab.

4. Select Windows NT Server Tools, as shown in Figure 15.9, and then click Add/Remove.

**NOTE**

*If you want to remove the directory for Windows NT server tools, you must do it manually. The directory is usually C:\SRVTOOLS.*

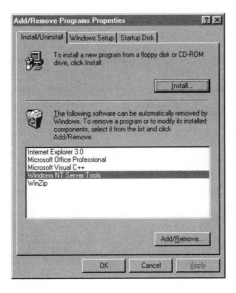

**FIGURE 15.9**

*Install/Uninstall dialog box for removing Windows NT Server Tools*

## POINTS TO REMEMBER

◆ If you want to administer a Windows NT computer from a Windows 95 computer using Windows NT server tools, you must have administrative rights on that computer.

◆ You must be logged on to the network before you can use the Windows NT server tools.

◆ The Windows NT server tools also can be used to administer and share File and Print Services for NetWare volumes.

◆ The server tools will help you on many minor chores, but some tasks must still be performed on a domain controller.

## WHAT'S NEXT?

This chapter winds up the section on administering a single Windows NT domain. Part Four of this book deals with issues that arise when your network must encompass many different types of communication and information sharing needs in a larger or more complex organization than can be served by a single domain or by simple trust relationships. In Chapter 16, we begin with the management of multiple domains and then move on to TCP/IP remote access, and integration of non-Windows NT networks into the enterprise.

# Part Four

## Enterprise NT

# CHAPTER 16

**Managing Multiple Domains**

# CHAPTER 16

# Managing Multiple Domains

Most of our discussion thus far has assumed a network that consists of a single domain. But in the real world, a Windows NT domain is often part of a larger organizational network—one that can include other Windows NT domains, mobile employees who need access to the network from remote locations, a Novell NetWare server or two, and a corporate intranet or a connection to the Internet. These things—multiple domains, Internet support, remote access services, using the Internet Information Explorer, and coexistence with NetWare—are the focus of Part Four of this book: "Enterprise NT."

What separates Windows NT from many other network systems, including earlier Microsoft offerings, is its enterprise-wide structure. By using global groups and a good knowledge of cross-domain techniques, you can build a network that is easy to administer, even from miles away.

## Multiple-Domain Management Tasks

How does managing a multiple-domain network differ from running a single-domain network? The tools you use to manage a single-domain network (User Manager, Server Manager, and Windows Explorer, for example) are the tools you also use for a multiple-domain network, but with a few twists. There are a number of new activities involved in multiple-domain systems:

◆ One domain communicating with another, a relationship that is called a *trust relationship*

◆ Users from one domain logging on at computers in another domain

◆ Users in one domain accessing directories and files on computers in another domain

◆ Users in one domain printing on printers in another domain

◆ Users in one domain becoming users in another domain

Cross-domain stuff probably sounds a good deal more complicated and tricky than it is in actual practice. To make this chapter easier to follow, we've structured it around two actual domains on our own network: Scribes, which is the writing side of our business, and Engineering, which is the software development side of our business.

# Trust Relationships—Getting Acquainted

Because a superior security system is an essential part of Windows NT Server, communication between domains is tightly restricted. Domains can't even *recognize* each other until they have been properly introduced, so to speak. Furthermore, someone from domain A can't log on at a computer that is a member of domain B unless domain B trusts domain A. *That's* how strict Windows NT security is—it doesn't even want you to be working at a workstation unless the workstation is in your home domain. Trust relationships between domains are controlled with User Manager for Domains.

**NOTE**

*We're referring to Windows NT workstations and servers here; you don't have to be a member of a given domain to log on locally at a computer running Microsoft Windows 95, Microsoft Windows 3.x, or Microsoft Windows for Workgroups.*

As you know from Chapter 2, a domain is the basic unit of a Windows NT Server network structure. But when there is more than one domain on a network, these domains, by default, cannot communicate with one another; it takes a deliberate act to make communication between two domains possible. The "introduction" of one domain to another is accomplished through trust relationships. (See Chapter 2 for a detailed explanation of trust relationships.) So the first step in domain-to-domain communication is to establish a *trust relationship* between them. But this step is just that—a starting point—with lots more steps to follow. For example, here's how things are *before* the domain called Engineering trusts the domain called Scribes on the authors' network:

◆ An Engineering administrator can't extend permissions for shares, files, directories, or printers to a Scribes user.

◆ A Scribes user can't log on at a Windows NT workstation that's a member of Engineering, even if all that the Scribes user wants to do is connect to some resource on the Scribes domain.

After a trust relationship has been established, the picture looks like this:

◆ Scribes members can sit down and log on to Windows NT workstations, although they won't have access to Engineering resources unless they have been given permission to do so by an Engineering administrator.

◆ The definition of the Everyone group in Engineering is now "all of the Engineering users and guests and all of the Scribes users and guests."

It doesn't sound like a whole heck of a lot, does it? But a trust relationship opens the lines of communication between domains, which makes it possible for an administrator in the *trusting* domain to extend permissions and rights to users in the *trusted* domain. In some respects, it's rather like a trade agreement between two countries: the agreement itself involves no action, and no money changes hands—but the agreement makes it possible for businesses on either side of the border to do business with one another. Without the agreement, these trade relationships couldn't exist. Not surprisingly, like a trade agreement that involves approvals by lofty governmental officials, trust relationships can be approved only by an administrator from each domain.

A trust relationship allows one domain (B, the trust*ing* domain) to recognize all global user accounts and global user groups from another domain (A, the trust*ed* domain). And just what is domain B (the trusting domain) actually trusting domain A (the trusted domain) to do? It is trusting domain A to authenticate domain A's users when they log on to domain B so that domain B can accept these users as legitimate and authorized.

A trust relationship makes it possible to have only one user account on the network for each user (defined in the user's home domain) and yet allow the user access to network resources in other trusted domains. For example, Figure 16.1 shows a network containing two domains whose names are Engineering and Scribes. If Engineering establishes a trust relationship with Scribes, all users who have accounts in Scribes (the trusted domain) can have access to resources in the Engineering domain.

As we discussed in Chapter 2, a trust relationship can be a one-way or a two-way relationship. But a two-way trust relationship is actually a pair of one-way trust relationships and must be set up that way.

## Adding a Trust Relationship

Establishing a trust relationship between domains requires at least two steps: first one domain must *allow* the second domain to trust it; then the second domain can be set up to trust the first domain. After these two steps have been completed successfully, the users in the first domain can be granted access to the resources of the second domain.

These two steps—domain A allowing domain B to trust it, and domain B actually trusting domain A—can be performed in any order; but if you follow the sequence "permit the trust, then trust," the new trust relationship takes effect immediately.

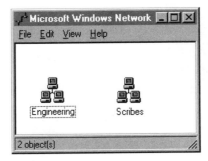

**FIGURE 16.1**

*The Microsoft Windows Network dialog box showing the Engineering and Scribes domains*

## NOTE

*If you reverse the order of the steps when you add a trust relationship, the trust relationship will be established, but you won't receive any confirmation of this fact. The process of establishing the trust relationship might be delayed for up to fifteen minutes.*

To see how this works, let's set up domain B (Engineering) to trust domain A (Scribes).

You, as the administrator, begin at the workstation of the domain that is to be the trusted domain (in this example, domain A, the Scribes domain).

1. Log on to domain A (Scribes) as the Scribes administrator.

2. Open User Manager For Domains.

3. Choose Trust Relationships from the Policies menu. You'll see the Trust Relationships dialog box shown in Figure 16.2 on the following page. The dialog box shows the domains that domain A (Scribes) is permitted to trust, as well as those that are already trusted—in this case, none.

4. Click Add next to the Trusting Domains list box. This will open the dialog box shown in Figure 16.3 on the following page.

5. Type the name of the domain that you want to permit to trust (in our example, domain B, Engineering) in the Trusting Domain text box.

6. Type a password in both the Initial Password and Confirm Password text boxes. The use of a password during the process of adding a trusting domain is optional and only applies during the brief period between

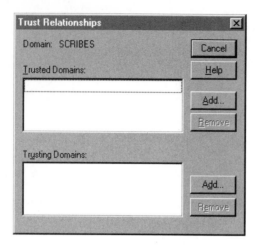

**FIGURE 16.2**

*Trust relationships dialog box for the Scribes domain*

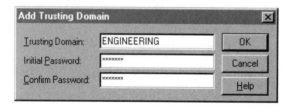

**FIGURE 16.3**

*Add Trusting Domain dialog box for the Scribes domain*

the time Scribes permits Engineering to trust it and the time Engineering actually gets around to trusting Scribes. Passwords are case-sensitive.

7. Click OK. Engineering, the added domain, will now appear in the Trusting Domains section in the Trust Relationships dialog box.

8. Close the Trust Relationships dialog box by clicking the button in the top right corner of the window.

You've now given domain B (Engineering) permission to trust domain A (Scribes), but the trust relationship isn't complete until domain B is actually set up to trust domain A.

After domain A (Scribes) is set up to allow domain B (Engineering) to trust it, domain B must be set up to trust domain A. As the administrator of domain A, you must pass on the password you entered in the Add Trusting Domain dialog box to the administrator of domain B (Engineering). The administrator for domain B must then do the following:

1. Log on to domain B (Engineering) as the administrator.

2. Open User Manager for Domains.

3. Choose Trust Relationships from the Policies menu.

4. Click Add next to the Trusted Domains list box.

5. In the Domain and Password boxes, the Engineering domain administrator would type *Scribes* and the password that you provided and then click OK. (If you didn't use a password, the Engineering administrator wouldn't put anything in the password field.)

   The added domain name, Scribes, should now appear in the Trusted Domains list of the Trust Relationships dialog box—Engineering now trusts Scribes. And you'll see a dialog box informing you that the trust relationship has been successfully established (Figure 16.4). Click OK.

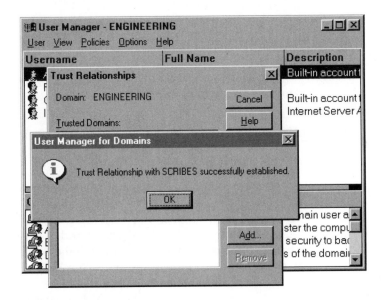

**FIGURE 16.4**

*Example of a Trust Relationship Established confirmation message*

6. Close the Trust Relationships dialog box by clicking the button in the top right corner of the window.

At the end of this process, the users in domain A (Scribes) are trusted by domain B (Engineering). So what does this mean? It means that the Engineering security database is going to rely on the accuracy of the user logon process in Scribes. If you also want the domain Scribes to accept the reliability of the logons from the domain Engineering, a second trust relationship will have to be established, this time in reverse so that domain A (Scribes) will trust the logon verifications performed by domain B (Engineering).

## NOTE

*Trust relationships are one of the most difficult Windows NT concepts to wrap your head around. Before starting to set them up, work out on paper what you want to have happen. Most important, use the simplest multiple-domain setup possible.*

The specific manifestations of a trust relationship include these:

◆ The trusted domain shows up as an option in the logon box on a Windows NT workstation, which means that users from the trusted domain can log on at workstations in the domain that trusts it.

◆ When a user logs on to a Windows NT machine and tries to browse an untrusted domain, he or she *can* see the list of servers on that domain. But if the user tries to view the shares on one of the domain's servers, he or she will be refused. Even if there *is* a trust relationship, the user has to have an account on the domain being browsed to view the list of shares on one of the domain's servers.

◆ Network connections can be made to shared directories on the trusting domain's servers.

When domain A is trusted, its users have access to domain B, which is trusting. In our example, this means that users in domain A, Scribes, have access to domain B, Engineering. Scribes users can log on at Engineering's workstations; user accounts created in Scribes can be placed in Engineering's local groups and be given permissions and rights within the Engineering domain, even though they don't have accounts there. This does *not* mean that Engineering users can log on at Scribes workstations or that they can use Scribes servers or printers. Unless domain A, Scribes, also establishes a trust relationship with domain B, Engineering (domain A *trusts* Engineering, and domain B allows domain A, Scribes, to trust it), accounts in the Engineering domain can't be used in Scribes. In other words, Engineering might trust Scribes, but that doesn't mean that Scribes trusts Engineering.

As you saw in Chapter 2, trust between domains is not transferable. For example, if the Engineering domain trusts the Scribes domain, and the Scribes domain trusts a domain named Admin, the Engineering domain does not automatically trust the

Admin domain. If the Engineering domain network administrator wants to be able to use Admin accounts in the Engineering domain, he or she would have to set up the Engineering domain to trust the Admin domain.

**NOTE**

*Trust relationships can be established only between Windows NT Server domains. The Trust Relationships command isn't available when you are administering a Microsoft LAN Manager 2.x domain or a Windows NT workstation.*

## Terminating a Trust Relationship

Just as establishing a trust relationship is a two-part process, so is dissolving that relationship. First one domain has to stop trusting another domain; then the other domain has to take away the permission for the first domain to trust it. To stop trusting another domain, follow these steps:

1. Open User Manager for Domains.

2. Choose Trust Relationships from the Policies menu.

3. In the Trusted Domains box, select the name of the domain that will no longer trust your domain, and then click Remove. You'll see a message to remind you about the two-part process.

4. Click Yes; then close the Trust Relationships dialog box.

Now, still following our "Engineering trusts Scribes" example, the administrator in Scribes has to stop permitting the Engineering domain to trust it.

1. Open User Manager For Domains in Scribes.

2. Choose Trust Relationships from the Policies menu.

3. Select Engineering in the Trusting Domains dialog box. Click Remove.

4. When you are finished, click Yes and close the Trust Relationships dialog box.

## Troubleshooting Trusts

Understanding the subtleties of trusts may not be easy, but the process of setting up and maintaining trust relationships is fairly straightforward. Of course, problems can arise. Here are the more common problems and their solutions:

◆ **Cannot establish a trust relationship** You'll get this message if the primary domain controller on either domain isn't available on the network or if you're not using the correct password.

- **Cannot verify the trust** This message means that you didn't permit the trust before trusting, which is usually not a problem. However, the trust relationship won't be usable for some period of time—up to fifteen minutes on some networks.

- **Cannot reestablish a broken trust** If you've terminated one part of the trust relationship between two domains and then want to reestablish it, you won't be able to do so until you dissolve the *entire* trust relationship. Remove all trust between the two domains, and start over.

- **Cannot use trusted accounts** This message means that you've established the trust in the wrong direction. Terminate the trust, and set it up in the correct direction.

# Extending File Permissions Across Domains

When domains have a trust relationship, you can make use of it. To continue with our example of the two domains, Engineering and Scribes, how does a member of Scribes get access to files that are on computers in the Engineering domain? For example, suppose there's a shared folder on one of the Engineering servers named TOP SECRET—how can a Scribes user get to it? We'll employ the energetic and ubiquitous user, haroldt, for this task.

## Is Everyone Really *Everyone*?

Well, first of all, haroldt might have access to TOP SECRET already. As you've seen, when you create a directory share, that share automatically assigns Full Control to Everyone. So unless the Engineering administrator has customized the share permissions in some way, members of the Everyone group can get to the share—and the Everyone group includes all users *from all trusted domains*. Because Engineering trusts Scribes, all Scribes users are part of Engineering's Everyone group. This means that haroldt's account from Scribes can get to the TOP SECRET share.

## Adding a User from Another Domain to Share Permissions

But suppose share permission has not been granted to Everyone. The administrator of domain B (Engineering) has assigned TOP SECRET a different set of share level permissions, perhaps to Engineering's group of regular users called Domain Users. The Engineering administrator can grant access to haroldt (or to any other individual or global group in domain A, Scribes) also by using share permissions, as described in Chapter 12; but now there's an extra step to the process, the step of asking for the list of users and groups from Scribes.

The domain B (Engineering) administrator would follow these steps to extend file permissions for a share named TOP SECRET to the domain A (Scribes) user named haroldt.

1. Start off by displaying the permissions dialog box for the TOP SECRET share, as shown in Figure 16.5.

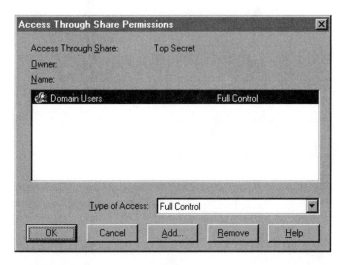

**FIGURE 16.5**

*Access Through Share Permissions dialog box for the share TOP SECRET*

2. To add an individual to the share list, click Add to open the dialog box shown in Figure 16.6 on the following page.

3. In the Add Users and Groups dialog box, select the domain in which the user resides (in this case, Scribes) from the List Names From drop-down list. After you select that option and wait a few seconds, the Add Users and Groups dialog box will display the domain you have chosen, as shown in Figure 16.7 on the following page.

   This dialog box is the same as the previous dialog box, but now we're looking at the users in the Scribes domain. Notice that the Scribes domain, like the Engineering domain, has a group called Domain Users. You could add the Scribes\Domain Users group to the share permission list for TOP SECRET, and then every user from Scribes would have access to the TOP SECRET share in Engineering. But for now, we just want to add one of the Scribes users, haroldt.

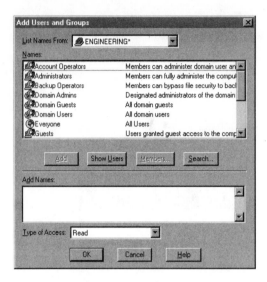

**FIGURE 16.6**

*Add Users and Groups dialog box showing the users and groups in the Engineering domain*

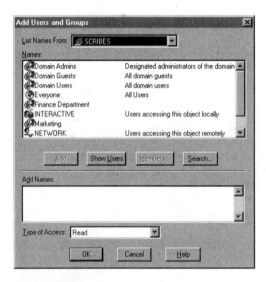

**FIGURE 16.7**

*Add Users and Groups dialog box showing users and groups in the Scribes domain*

**4.** Click Show Users. Select the user haroldt. Click Add, and give the user (in this case haroldt) Full Control. The Access Through Share Permissions dialog box now looks like the one in Figure 16.8.

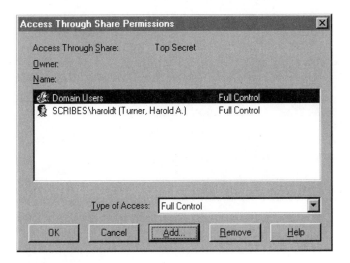

**FIGURE 16.8**

*Access Through Share Permissions dialog box showing changes in share permissions for the user haroldt*

Notice the notation describing the haroldt account (Scribes\haroldt). This notation prevents Engineering from confusing this account with a possible identical account in the Engineering domain.

If the volume on which the TOP SECRET directory resides is an NTFS volume, you also might have to set file and directory permissions for the new account. You set file and directory permissions across domains the same way that you do for a single domain (Chapter 12), except that you'll have to take the extra step of clicking List Names From and selecting the foreign domain.

## Cross-Domain Groups

Clearly, it's a bit of a chore just to get a single user access to one shared directory on another domain. If haroldt, as an individual, needs as much access to Engineering as a regular Engineering user, there's no easy way to go about it. If there are 5 servers in Engineering, each with 10 shares, and if we want haroldt from Scribes to have access to all 50 shares, he has to be added to each share one by one.

If haroldt were added to a group that had access to the entire domain, however, he also would have this access. The group in the Engineering domain that has this kind of access is called Domain Users. Can haroldt from Scribes be added to Engineering's Domain Users group? You remember that adding users is done through User Manager for Domains. So you open User Manager and double-click Domain Users. You see a dialog box similar to the one shown in Figure 16.9.

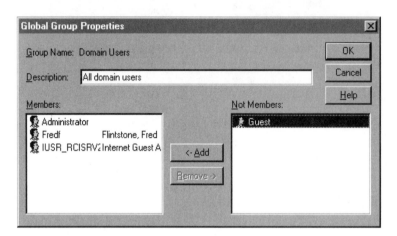

**FIGURE 16.9**

*Global Group Properties dialog box showing members of Domain Users group*

If you think back to earlier discussions of local and global groups (Chapter 10), you will recall that global groups (such as Domain Users) can't contain users from other domains. If Domain Users were a *local* group, it could contain the Scribes\haroldt account, but even that wouldn't help; most servers in the Engineering domain are not able to see a specific local group.

Just as a reminder, these are the types of groups that you have available to work with:

◆ Local groups, which can contain not only user accounts from the home domain or from other trusted domains, but also global groups from the home domain or other trusted domains.

◆ Global groups, which can contain user accounts from the home domain, and that's it. They cannot contain users from other domains or from other groups.

This is a tough concept to remember because the names "local" and "global" sound like the opposite of what they are. If it helps, call local groups "Group A" and global groups "Group B": A's can contain B's, but A's can't contain A's; B's can't contain B's, and B's can't contain A's. Or make it into a mantra—"Globals go into locals, globals go into locals, globals go into locals..." Use whatever trick it takes to get yourself to remember the concept.

By creating two types of groups, Microsoft developers guaranteed that you couldn't go further than putting one group inside another group. Put a global group inside a local group, and you have one level of nesting in groups. But you can't go any further because you can't put a local group into another group or a global group into another global group.

### Using local and global groups inside a domain

Every Windows NT computer has a Users group that is a local group. Every domain has a Domain Users group that is a global group. Because globals go into locals, the domain's Domain Users group can be put into each computer's (local) Users group.

The concepts to remember, then, are these:

◆   To create a group that can be seen and exported all over your domain, you have to make it a global group and place that global group in whatever local groups you require.

◆   The domain's Administrators group has administrative powers only over domain controller computers.

◆   The domain's Domain Admins group has administrative powers over *all* computers in the domain.

### Using global groups across domains

A global group is not only "global" in the sense that it can be placed in any local group of a Windows NT computer in its home domain; it also can be placed in a local group of any Windows NT computer—whether a workstation, a server, or a domain controller—in a *trusted* domain.

Let's use this information to answer our earlier question (page 336): How can we give users in the Scribes domain (such as haroldt) access to accounts in the Engineering domain that is equivalent to the access available to users whose accounts reside in the Engineering domain?

First, recall that the simple action of having Engineering trust Scribes put all Scribes users into Engineering's Everyone group, which means they are automatically granted Engineering-like access to anything that is shared to Everyone in the Engineering domain.

Second, if you've set restrictions on a share's permissions, you've had to add permitted users or groups one by one. Most commonly, you'll add the Domain Users group from your domain to the share-level permission list of any share on a Windows NT server or workstation in your domain. It would be great if you could say,

"Well, because the Engineering\Domain Users group has access to a whole bunch of shares and I want the Scribes folks to get to that too, I'll just put the Scribes-\Domain Users group into the Engineering\Domain Users group." But you know you can't do that because a global group can't be put into another global group. Unfortunately, there's no shortcut; you just have to go to each share and add the Scribes\Domain Users group manually.

But here's a way to save yourself much of that grief. Recall that a directory share on an NTFS volume has two levels of security—the share-level permissions and the directory-level and file-level permissions. In Chapter 12, we advised you to leave all directory share permissions at their default setting (Full Control to the Everyone group) and to use directory and file permissions for the places where you set the "real" permissions. If you've done that, you can use the command line utility CACLS (in your WINNT\SYSTEM32 directory) in a batch file to set file and directory permissions. For the syntax of CACLS, open a command prompt window and type the following:

    CACLS /?

## Logging on from other domains

Many companies adopt a model with user departments organized into domains and the IS group in its own domain, from which all other domains are managed. In this model, the trust relationships look like the illustration in Figure 16.10. (See also Chapter 4, page 47.)

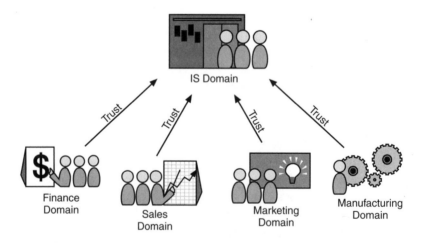

**FIGURE 16.10**

*Example of a central administration model*

All of the user departments trust the IS domain. But the trust relationship is only a one-way relationship, and the IS domain does not trust any of the user domains. So if an administrator, a member of the IS domain, wants to be able to log onto a server in *any* domain to perform maintenance, how can this be done? It doesn't make sense to give this administrator an account on every domain—aside from the amount of work involved, it's an untidy solution and a violation of our basic rule to Keep It Simple.

All you need to do is make the Domain Admins group in the IS domain a member of the Administrators group in every user department domain. This grants all IS administrators the right to log on to any domain controller and have the status of Administrator.

### Getting domain resources when you're not a domain member

Odd things can happen on networks, and here's one of the oddest. Let's imagine a regular user in the IS domain (not an administrator) sits down at a Windows for Workgroups computer in the Finance department and logs on to the IS domain. Everything proceeds smoothly; the user's access to IS appears quite normal. Then the user notices some connections to resources in Finance that *shouldn't be there*. And yet, there they are. Will this hypothetical user be able to resist checking the salary figures for everyone in IS?

The culprit in this situation is the Guest account. If the Guest account doesn't have a password and if you haven't restricted the account's access to domain resources, a user gets logged onto the local domain's resources as a guest when he or she logs on and the domain doesn't recognize the account. This is true even if the user is from a trusted domain. If the Guest account has been disabled, you are prompted for a password before you can go any further because the Windows for Workgroups computer wants to finish establishing persistent connections.

## Do You Need Multiple Domains at All?

It's clear that setting up an enterprise with multiple domains is a lot of work and requires a *lot* of administration. So why not save some grief and just have one big domain? Lots of times that's a good answer, but not always. Here are some of the advantages of a single-domain network vs. a multiple-domain network.

### The fewer domains, the better

Domains are the basic building blocks of Windows NT and the foundation of its security system, but if your goal is to keep administrative work to a minimum, you also had better plan on keeping the number of domains to a minimum. The complexities of managing a network increase geometrically as the number of domains increases arithmetically; each additional domain creates new problems and layers of difficulty. Of course, if impregnable security is your number one priority, by all means separate functional units into domains, arm the barricades, and put on 24-hour guards.

## Domains that follow organizational lines

Sometimes multiple domains serve to keep separate divisions happy. Perhaps the manufacturing people already have their own network and their own support people, and they really don't share much with the sales division, which also has its own network and support people. In a case like this, the IS department serves mainly in an advisory capacity, making recommendations about hardware and software. Eventually, however, user departments will encounter situations where the exchange of data and the sharing of resources really could be useful, and then they'll come to you for assistance in making that possible. That's when an understanding of the concepts in this chapter will come in handy.

## Domains that follow geographic lines

Domains and workgroups do a lot of chatting among themselves. The server must announce its presence every 12 minutes to maintain the browser. Periodically, each side of a session says "I'm still here" to the other side. These messages are called "keepalive" messages, and they occur as often as every 30 seconds or as infrequently as once an hour, as shown in Table 16.1.

**Table 16.1**
**Regular Communications on Windows NT Networks**

| Type of Message | Protocol/Transport | Default Interval |
|---|---|---|
| PDC-BDC message replication | Any | Every 5 minutes |
| Master browser to backup browser replication | Any | Every 15 minutes |
| Server announcement to master browser | Any | Once each minute, then every 2 minutes, then every 4 minutes, then every 8 minutes, then every 12 minutes, and every 12 minutes thereafter |
| NetBIOS keepalive message | TCP/IP | Every 60 minutes |
| NetBIOS keepalive message | IPX, NetBEUI | Every 30 seconds |

Some of this chatter goes on quite frequently, as you can see. You might decide that this overhead takes up too much of your connections' bandwidth and slows down the entire network. If that's the case, it would make sense to bite the bullet and draw up domain boundaries that match geographical ones.

## Too many accounts for one domain?

The most compelling reason for building more than one domain is simply that a domain gets too large; there are too many accounts in the domain for users to find their resources easily.

The cutoff point comes when your Security Accounts Manager (SAM) database is too large. A SAM contains roughly 1 KB per user plus 0.5 KB per machine account. You don't need a machine account for each computer, only a machine account for each Windows NT workstation and server that's a member of the domain.

The size of the SAM database is important because the entire database is resident in the memory of your domain controllers at all times, so the bigger the SAM database, the more RAM *every* domain controller must have. For example, let's say a company with 100,000 Windows NT machines doesn't want to bother with all that multiple-domain stuff and wants just one really large domain. They would have a SAM database that would require at least 150 MB of physical RAM on every domain controller—clearly not something you could sneak through the budget process without attracting attention from upper management. In addition, every controller must read and parse that huge database at boot up, adding substantial time to the process.

To get the best answer to the question of how large a SAM database your patience and budget can tolerate, try this test on a machine that represents your typical domain controller. Load the machine with 500 user accounts. Time how long the machine takes to boot and how long it takes for a single user to log on. Now add another 500 accounts and note the boot and user logon times again. Then add still another 500 accounts and note the boot and user logon times a third time. Use the data points from these tests to give you a rough idea of how large your SAM database can be and, therefore, how many domains are workable in your organization.

Here's an example. Let's say your company has 12,000 employees and 1,000 Windows NT computers. Your experiments with SAM have convinced you that 10 MB is the most physical RAM you can allot to your SAM database. Figure the 12,000 employees with 1000 Windows NT computers create a SAM database that's 12 MB (plus 4 MB to equal 16 MB). Divide 16 by 10 (the maximum acceptable size for your SAM) to get 1.6. If you want to give your domains room to grow, round up and plan for two domains. If you prefer fewer domains and less administrative work and if you don't mind taking a hit in terms of slower network response time, plan for one overgrown domain.

# Managing Domain Controllers

Each primary domain controller holds the master copy of the SAM database for its domain, and each backup domain controller in the domain has a backup copy of the database. The purpose of having backup copies is to avoid having a single point of failure in the SAM database. If the primary domain controller fails, a backup domain controller can be promoted to primary domain controller using Server Manager.

You can make changes to the SAM database only on the primary domain controller. This doesn't mean that you, the administrator, have to physically be sitting at the primary domain controller, but the changes are made at the primary domain controller. Backup domain controllers can be used for authentication because they each maintain a read-only *copy* of the database, but changes cannot be made to the copies except from the primary domain controller's original.

## ◆ Important Domain Controller Issues

◆ Domain controllers are created at the time of installation. When you install Windows NT Server, you're given an opportunity to choose whether the computer will be a domain controller—either a primary controller or a backup controller—or a server. (See Chapter 6 for specific information about creating a domain controller, and see Chapter 2 for more theoretical information about domain controllers.)

◆ A primary domain controller can't be added to an existing domain (one primary domain controller to a customer, please).

◆ A backup domain controller can't be added to an unavailable domain.

◆ Each domain must have a unique name. (See Chapter 7 for the specifics on choosing a domain name.)

◆ Never forget that Windows NT keeps track of domain controllers by means of their SIDs. When you create a primary domain controller, the operating system knows that computer by its SID, a number that is unique in time and space. The backup domain controllers in the domain also are assigned SIDs that are unique, but they have the primary domain controller's SID as a prefix to their own number. So all questions of identity come down to the SID number of the primary domain controller. This means you must never make a new installation of Windows NT Server on a primary domain controller. Even if you use the same name for the computer, a new SID will be assigned to it, and the other

*(continued)*

computers on the domain will not be able to find it. They will be looking for the old SID. This is a very undesirable situation, as you might imagine.

◆ Never install a backup domain controller when the existing primary domain controller for that domain is not operating. If Setup cannot find a primary domain controller, it will make the new computer a primary domain controller. When the old primary domain controller wakes up, there will be hell to pay. Instead, install the new backup domain controller while the primary domain controller is running.

◆ If you want to promote a backup domain controller to a primary domain controller, do so while both machines are running.

◆ If you want to create a new primary domain controller while the existing primary domain controller is down, you can do so; but you'll have to reinstall Windows NT Server on the original primary domain controller and configure it as a backup domain controller.

◆ If you create a primary domain controller and lose your administrator account password before you've created your other administrative accounts, you'll have to reinstall Windows NT Server and start over.

## Promoting a Backup Domain Controller to Primary Domain Controller

If your primary domain controller is out of action and if there's a reasonable expectation it will be back at work shortly, there's no need to promote a backup domain controller to primary domain controller right away. You can't make any changes to the domain without a primary domain controller, however, so you wouldn't want to try to run your network for very long without it.

If you promote a backup domain controller to a primary domain controller while the existing primary domain controller is online, the existing primary domain controller is demoted automatically to a backup domain controller. Although Server Manager has a Promote to Primary Domain Controller command on the Computer menu, there's no command for demoting to backup domain controller, as you can see in Figure 16.11 on the following page. The only way to demote a primary domain controller is to do it indirectly, by promoting a backup domain controller. This has the advantage of preventing you from inadvertently demoting your only primary domain controller.

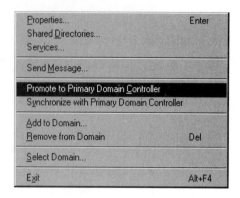

**FIGURE 16.11**

*Server Manager's Computer menu*

## Synchronizing a Domain

Normally, domains are synchronized automatically and in the background. But if you've made a change or two in the SAM database and want to get the news out to all of the backup domain controllers in the domain, you can do the synchronization manually by following these steps:

1. Open Server Manager, and choose Servers from the View menu.

2. Select the primary domain controller in the Server Manager list.

3. Choose Synchronize Entire Domain from the Computer menu.

4. In the dialog box that appears (Figure 16.12), you will be asked to confirm that you want to proceed with the change. Click Yes if you do.

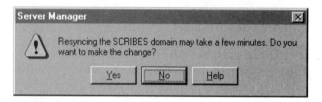

**FIGURE 16.12**

*Server Manager confirmation request for synchronizing a domain or a backup controller*

To synchronize just one backup domain controller with the primary domain controller, follow these steps:

1. Open Server Manager, and choose Servers from the View menu.

2. Select the backup domain controller you want resynchronized.

3. Choose Synchronize with Primary Domain Controller from the Computer menu.

4. In the dialog box that appears (which will look similar to the one in Figure 16.12), you will be asked to confirm that you want to proceed with the change. Click Yes if you do.

# Adding a Windows NT Computer to a Domain

To add a Windows NT computer (either a server or a workstation) to a domain, the computer must be authenticated to the primary domain controller. The easiest way to do this is, of course, during installation.

### During installation

During setup, you are asked to specify the security role of the Windows NT computer. With Windows NT Server, you can set up a domain controller (either primary or secondary) or a stand-alone server. With workstation, you can choose to make the computer part of a domain or part of a workgroup.

In order to join the domain, you have to enter a domain administrator's name and corresponding password. This is to prevent domain administrators from other domains from (inadvertently, we're sure) adding Windows NT computers to their domains.

### Using Server Manager

To add a computer to a domain, use Server Manager for the domain to which the computer is being added. Just follow these steps:

1. Choose Server Manager from the Administrative Tools menu.

2. Choose Add to Domain from the Computer menu to open the dialog box shown in Figure 16.13 on the following page.

3. Click the appropriate Computer Type option, and type a computer name of up to 15 characters in the Computer Name text box. (The computer name must be unique; it can't duplicate any other computer name on the network, and it can't be the same as any domain name on the network.)

4. Click Add, and the new computer is added to the domain.

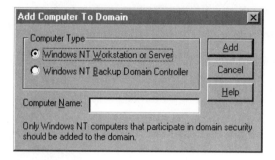

**FIGURE 16.13**

*Add Computer To Domain dialog box*

## Removing a Windows NT Computer from a Domain

If you need to remove a computer from a domain—to use it for other purposes, for example—that's also done through the Server Manager in the domain from which the Windows NT computer is being removed.

1. Open Server Manager, and select the name of the computer you want to remove.

2. Press Delete.

3. You'll see a dialog box message that warns you of the consequences of your action. Click Yes if you want to proceed with removing the computer from the domain.

- Trust relationships make cross-domain communication possible.

- Local groups can contain global groups, but they can't contain other local groups.

- Global groups can't contain other global groups or local groups.

- Global groups can't contain users from other domains; local groups can contain users from other domains.

- The fewer domains you have on your network the better if you want to save on administrative work.

- Calculate the acceptable size of your SAM database to determine how many domains you will need.

**WHAT'S NEXT?**

Now that you know how to get your domains to communicate politely, we'll move on in Chapter 17 to the subject of TCP/IP, the networking protocol that runs the Internet and probably your intranet as well.

# Chapter 17

# CHAPTER 17

## TCP/IP

Entire books have been written about TCP/IP and its many aspects, most of which we don't have to worry about as system administrators. But even though we don't need or want to know about the intricacies of programming a TCP/IP connection or what to expect as a return value from a *gethostbyname()* call, we do need to have a general understanding of TCP/IP, plus the ability to configure TCP/IP when that's required.

It's important to remember that TCP/IP is not a single entity; it's a suite of protocols in which each protocol has its own specialized function. The abbreviation TCP/IP stands for Transmission Control Protocol/Internet Protocol; these protocols are the core of the suite but are only two of the many included in the TCP/IP suite. What makes the TCP/IP suite so important is not any one of these protocols individually, but how all of the protocols fit together to get the job done.

Another important fact about TCP/IP is that it's not owned by anyone; no company controls it. IPX/SPX and NetBEUI are proprietary protocols developed and ultimately controlled by an individual vendor; TCP/IP, on the other hand, is an open standard controlled by the Internet Engineering Task Force (IETF) and by the users of the Internet itself in the form of Requests for Comments (RFCs). Anyone can submit an RFC for consideration and inclusion in the written definitions of the protocols and policies of the Internet and TCP/IP.

Virtually every type of computer and operating system in use today has available and supports TCP/IP as a networking protocol. They might be using some other proprietary protocol in addition to TCP/IP, but when it comes time to connect multiple computers running multiple operating systems across a variety of hardware and topologies, there's really only one way to get these—TCP/IP.

We covered some of the basics of TCP/IP and how to configure it in Chapter 7. In this chapter, we'll quickly review those basic concepts and then launch into the gory details of dealing with a complex, multidomain internetwork environment. We'll also take a sneak peek at the future of TCP/IP and what this will mean for your network capabilities. And finally, we'll do a quick review of the new administration tools that are included with Microsoft Windows NT Server version 4 for handling some of the less fun aspects of working with TCP/IP.

# IP

Internet Protocol (IP) is the core protocol of the TCP/IP suite. To quote RFC 791, "The Internet Protocol is designed for use in interconnected systems of packet-switched computer communication networks." It is not designed to provide any additional services beyond its primary function, which is to deliver a packet of bits (a "datagram") from point A to point B over any network "wire" it happens to encounter along the way.

**NOTE**

*We use the term "wire" very loosely in this discussion to indicate the physical network connection between two points. In fact, this wire could just as easily be a piece of optical fiber or even a radio or infrared wave. But in all cases it functions as the transmission "pipe" through which the packets travel.*

IP doesn't, in and of itself, know anything about the information in the datagram it carries, nor does it have any provision beyond a simple checksum to ensure that the data is intact or that it has reached its destination. These functions are left to the other protocols that are part of the TCP/IP suite.

# TCP

Transmission Control Protocol (TCP) is designed to be, in the words of RFC 793 (which is the defining RFC for this protocol), "a connection-oriented, end-to-end reliable protocol designed to fit into a layered hierarchy of protocols which support multi-network applications." Let's take a look at the words in this definition:

◆ **Connection-oriented** TCP provides for the communication of packets of bits between two points and connects them together, sending the datagram specifically from one computer or other device to another computer or device.

◆ **End-to-end** TCP packets have specific endpoints designated in the packet, and those packets are passed along the wire and ignored except by the actual endpoint of the packet and any device that needs to direct the packet.

◆ **Reliable** This is the key feature of TCP. When a program, such as ftp, uses TCP for its protocol, the TCP/IP suite itself takes responsibility for the reliability of the communication. It provides for interprocess communication to ensure that the packets that are sent not only get to the intended destination, but get there in the order in which they were sent. If a packet is missing, the protocol will communicate the necessary information back to the sending device to ensure that the packet is re-sent.

Because TCP has to create a reliable connection between two devices or processes, there is substantially more overhead associated with each packet that is sent than with the other, less reliable protocols included in the suite. But by the same token, when a programmer writes an application that uses TCP, he or she doesn't have to include lots of error checking and handshaking in the application itself.

## UDP

User Datagram Protocol (UDP) is a connectionless, transaction-oriented protocol designed for sending packets with a minimum of protocol overhead, as defined by RFC 768. It provides no guarantee that the packet was received by its intended recipient or that the information in the packet was received in the order in which it was sent. UDP is frequently used for broadcast messages, where there is no specific intended recipient (such as BOOTP and DHCP requests); but it also can be used for applications where the sender is willing to spend extra, internal overhead to ensure reliable delivery, which actually has the result of decreasing the overall overhead of the underlying protocol.

# Windows Sockets

Windows Sockets are a standard way of allowing applications programs to communicate with a TCP/IP stack without having to worry about the underlying variations in TCP/IP stack implementation. In the past there were many different vendors for TCP/IP protocol and applications suites running on MS-DOS–based computers, and each vendor had a slightly different version of the TCP/IP protocol and application suites. This made it extremely difficult to write an application program using TCP/IP that would work with all possible TCP/IP implementations. The Windows Sockets interface was designed to get around this problem by providing a uniform set of Application Programming Interface (API) calls that would remain the same, regardless of the underlying differences in the actual implementation of TCP/IP.

The original version of Windows Sockets (1.0) had a fair number of problems, which led to an upgrade (version 1.1) rather quickly after its initial implementation. Windows NT Server supports the current version of Windows Sockets (version 2.0); version 2 provides full compatibility with earlier versions at the same time that it provides improved functionality and support for additional features and expandability.

# RFCs

RFCs come in many different flavors, but all of them have the same intent and a somewhat similar format. Their purpose is to provide a way for a diverse group of people—the users of the Internet—to communicate and to agree on the architecture and functionality of the Internet. Some are official documents of the IETF; they define the standards of TCP/IP and of the Internet. Others are proposals that aspire to become standards. And other RFC documents fall somewhere in between—some are tutorial in nature, others are quite technical. But all RFCs are a way for the Internet—an essentially anarchistic entity—to be organized and to allow its users to communicate.

We won't attempt to list all of the RFCs here, nor do we expect that you'd want or need to read and understand them all. But you certainly should know where to go to find them and what some of the most important ones are. There are several places to go to find listings of RFCs; if you want to be absolutely sure you've got the most accurate and up-to-date information, use the official RFC site:

```
http://ds.internic.net/ds/dspg01.html
```

Our favorite site is this one:

```
http://www.cis.ohio-state.edu/hypertext/information/rfc.html
```

The RFCs at this site are organized and linked, which makes it easy to find the information you want. However, this site isn't nearly as current or up-to-date in its information as the official RFC site.

Table 17.1 is a list of some of the more important RFCs and their subject matter.

**Table 17.1**
**Some Key RFCs and Their Topics**

| RFC Number | Subject |
| --- | --- |
| RFC 791 | Internet Protocol (IP) |
| RFC 792 | Internet Control Message Protocol (ICMP) |
| RFC 793 | Transmission Control Protocol (TCP) |
| RFC 768 | User Datagram Protocol (UDP) |
| RFC 854 | Telnet Protocol |
| RFC 959 | File Transfer Protocol (FTP) |
| RFC 821 | Simple Mail Transfer Protocol (SMTP) |
| RFC 822 | Standard for the Format of ARPA Internet Text Messages |
| RFC 1117 | Assigned Numbers |
| RFC 991 | Official ARPA Internet Protocols |
| RFC 1034 | DNS - concepts and facilities |
| RFC 1035 | DNS - implementation and specification |

# IP Addresses

Your IP address is to the Internet or to other computers on your local network much the same as your street address is to your mail carrier. It identifies your specific computer using a simple, 32-bit addressing scheme. The scheme, which originated in the late 1960s and early 1970s, uses four octets, separated by dots, in the form $w.x.y.z$, which describes a combination of the network's address and the local machine's address on that network.

Networks are assigned one of three classes—A, B, or C. The classes divide the networks (sometimes referred to as *licenses*) according to their size and complexity. The license to use a range of IP addresses is controlled by the Internet Network Information Center (InterNIC). The InterNIC formerly was managed and controlled by the United States government, but it is now handled by a separate, commercial organization.

## Class A Networks

A class A network has an address that begins with a number from 0 through 127, which represents the first $w$ portion of the address and which describes the network itself; the remainder of the address is the address of the actual local device on that network. The class A address 127, however, is reserved for a specific function and isn't available for general use. This means there are 127 possible class A addresses in the world, and each one can contain more than 16 million unique network devices—this is, obviously, a pretty large network. There aren't very many networks of this size. All of the class A addresses were assigned a long time ago to entities such as the Department of Defense, Stanford University, and Hewlett-Packard.

### ◆ The Loopback Address

All IP addresses that begin with the network number 127 are very special. They are interpreted by your network card as a *loopback address*. Any packet sent to an address beginning with 127 is treated as if the destination address were the local device and the packet had arrived at its intended address. This means that packets addressed to 127.0.0.1 are treated the same as packets addressed to 127.37.90.17—both addresses are actually that of your current machine. The same is true for all of the other 16 million addresses in the 127 class A network. You, too, can have your very own class A network. Of course, you can only talk to yourself; but who cares when such *prestige* is involved?

## Class B Networks

A class B network has an address that begins with a number from 128 through 191, which represents the first $w$ portion of the address and which describes the network itself. The remainder of the address is the address of the actual local device on that network. There are approximately 16 thousand class B networks, each of which can have 64 thousand unique addresses on it. This is still a pretty large network. Most of the class B networks were assigned long ago to large organizations or companies, such as Rutgers University or Toyota Motor Corporation.

Many of the addresses in the class B address space have been broken up into smaller groups of addresses and reassigned. Large Internet service providers (ISPs), for example, use this technique to utilize the available address space more efficiently.

## Class C Networks

A class C network has an address that begins with a number from 192 through 223, which represents the first $w$ portion of the address and which describes the network itself. The remainder of the address is the address of the actual local device on that network. There are roughly 2 million class C networks, each of which can have a maximum of 254 devices on the network—enough address space for a small business network or a department network, but hardly enough space for a major corporate network.

## Class D and Class E Addresses

An IP address with a number from 224 through 239 for the first $w$ portion of the address is known as a class D address. It is used for multicast addresses. An IP address with a number from 240 through 247 for the first $w$ portion of the address is referred to as a class E address; this is space that is reserved for future use.

# Subnets, Gateways, and Routers

If every computer on the Internet saw every packet as it was transmitted, the overhead would be enormous—machines would be swamped in short order, and the entire Internet would have come to a grinding, screeching halt years ago. Obviously, a way to filter and route the packets was needed. Someone should be able to print to your network printer without disrupting other networks *and* still be able to reach any IP address on the Internet. And it should be possible to reach any IP address without having to know a whole lot about how to get there. Enter subnets, gateways, and routers.

## Subnets

A *subnet* is simply a portion of the network that operates like a separate network. It doesn't have to concern itself with what happens outside its specific portion of the network or "worry" that events in its portion will disrupt the rest of the network. A subnet is usually a separate physical piece of "wire" that has only one point of contact through a router or a bridge with the other areas of the network.

## ◆ IP Addresses for Networks That Will Never, Ever Be Connected to the Internet

Suppose you know that your internal, private network will never be directly connected to the Internet? It's not an unreasonable assumption. Can you then use any set of numbers for your computer? Well, you can—but no, you shouldn't. There is a special set of network addresses (defined in RFC 1918) reserved for just such a use. With these addresses, you can have access to a substantially larger address space than otherwise would be possible. Using them also protects the integrity of the Internet. There have been substantial problems when private networks have used regular class range addresses that already had been assigned to other organizations, and then the private network later connected to the Internet. Because the special address ranges are officially for private networks only, they are filtered automatically at routers, which protects the Internet.

The following special address ranges are the ranges provided for networks that will not be connecting to the Internet:

```
10.0.0.0 through 10.255.255.255 (a Class A network)
172.16.0.0 through 172.31.255.255 (16 contiguous Class B networks)
192.168.0.0 through 192.168.255.255 (256 contiguous Class C networks)
```

For example, if you have to or want to use TCP/IP for your network protocol but you need to create a test network or you otherwise know for sure that you won't ever be connecting your network to the Internet, use the addresses from this special address set.

To enable computers in one portion of the network to see and communicate directly with other computers in the same part of the network but not with computers in other parts of the network, we use a *subnet mask*. This is an address, again in the form *w.x.y.z*, that masks or blocks areas outside a specific area from sight. An example of a typical mask for a class C network would be 255.255.255.0. OK—that's nice. But what does it mean? Well, without going into a long treatise on binary numbering, it means that if, for example, your IP address is 192.168.222.17, the address at 192.168.223.25 will be hidden from you. You will be able to send a packet to that address only by first passing the packet to a gateway or router that knows where you are and also either where the other network is or whom to ask about where it might be. If, on the other hand, you want to send a packet to the printer at 192.168.222.129—no problem, you can see that address, so the packet goes straight to the printer.

A subnet works by letting you "see" only those portions of the IP address space that aren't masked by a number 1. A zero allows the respective portion of the address to be seen. For example, we have a typical class C address of 192.168.222.17 and our subnet mask is 255.255.255.0. Our machine can see only the portion of the address beyond the last "dot" in a destination address, as shown in the example in Figure 17.1.

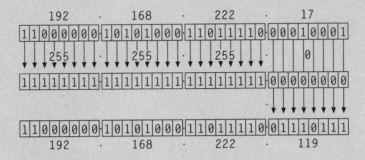

**FIGURE 17.1**

*An example of a subnet mask blocking portions of an IP address*

If you have an entire class of addresses assigned to you, it's relatively easy to figure out what your mask is; but if you are assigned only a portion of a class of addresses, you'll have to sit down with your binary-to-decimal conversion tables and figure out exactly what the correct subnet mask would be.

The important thing to know about this is that you can see any portion of an address that has a zero for the subnet mask, but you won't be able to see any portion of the address that has the number *255* in it. Remember, this is all actually done in binary. If you understand binary numbers, you can figure out what mask you need or what the mask you have is actually doing. If you're not comfortable with binary numbers, now's a good time to expand your comfort zone.

All of the subnet masks on a single portion of your network must be the same. If they aren't the same, you will have all sorts of weird problems. One computer, for example, might be able to send a packet to another computer; but the other computer might not be able to return the packet.

## Gateways

A *gateway* can be several different things on a network, but for the moment we're going to talk about it only in the context of subnets and routing. Remember, if your subnet mask is 255.255.255.0 and if the *y* portion of your IP address is 222, you won't be able to see an IP address on the network that has a *y* portion of 223. If you want to send a packet to the computer at this unknown address, the packet must be sent through a gateway.

A gateway is a physical device, usually a router but sometimes just another computer with more than one network card in it, that is physically connected to both portions of the network. It takes your packet from the 222 portion and sends it to the 223 portion. Thus, the device acts as a gatekeeper between the separate parts of the network, keeping the traffic from the 222 portion on the 222 segment and letting a packet through to the 223 segment only when it recognizes that the packet really belongs there.

## Routers

A *router* is a physical device that connects to more than one physical segment of the network; it sends packets between those segments as required. If it doesn't know where the packet goes, it knows where to ask for directions to the destination address, which is on another router. The router constantly updates its routing tables with information from other routers. If your network is part of the Internet, the router has to be able to handle a huge number of possible routes between locations and decide instantaneously the best way to get packets from one point to another.

---

### ◆ Routing Flaps

As the Internet has grown exponentially over the last few years, the technology for resolving addresses has been stressed to its limits—and sometimes past these limits. When a major router on the Internet goes down, even momentarily, all of the other routers on the Internet have to tell each other about it, and recalculate the best way to get to the various places that had used the failed router as part of the path. The result is large numbers of packets being passed back and forth just to maintain and update the information about available routes. What's worse, everyone is trying to do this at the same time. The result can be that traffic becomes so heavy the updates can't be made properly. The routers can't get the information through the traffic. And the whole Internet, or a large portion of it, comes to a virtual halt.

*(continued)*

---

So far, this kind of traffic jam hasn't occurred very often, but it is becoming more and more of a problem. The current technology in routers also is reaching its limit in being able to calculate the best route from all possible routes when a key router fails. Doomsayers would have us believe that the Internet will fail in the near future. We doubt it, but we are concerned nonetheless. The next generation of TCP/IP (known as IPng or IPv6) will help, as will new algorithms for how the calculations will be done. You can bet that there is a lot of money and energy being spent to come up with the best possible algorithm for handling this problem.

## Routing Protocols

Detailed information about how routing protocols work and about the algorithms that are involved in routing and address resolution are beyond what we can, or should, cover in this book. But it's useful to know what some of the protocols are, if only so that you can appear knowledgeable when the subject comes up in a conversation. The most commonly used TCP/IP address resolution protocols are these:

◆ **Address Resolution Protocol (ARP)** Maps the IP address to the physical hardware address (MAC address) of that IP address, permitting you to send something to an IP address without having to know which physical device it belongs to.

◆ **Reverse Address Resolution Protocol (RARP)** Maps the physical hardware address (MAC address) to the IP address, permitting you to determine the IP address when you know only the physical hardware address of the receiving machine.

◆ **Proxy Address Resolution Protocol (Proxy ARP)** A method for implementing subnets on older versions of TCP/IP, which don't "understand" subnetting. This protocol is defined in RFC 1027.

# Name Resolution

Well, all that stuff about addresses, numbers, and whatnot is interesting, but very few of us really want to have to deal with numbers for all of the sites we have to worry about, especially when numbers can change easily. Companies are continually upgrading the server equipment they use to run their Web sites, especially for the popular locations. Reconfiguring an entire machine to a different address is, at best, a royal pain, depending on what operating system is being used. It's easier to buy a new computer, give it a number on your network, build and test your Web page on an internal network, and then, when you're ready to go, put the new computer in place and change a line in your DNS entry; when the change propagates to the rest of the Internet, you're in business. And you don't need to worry about downtime because the original computer will be in place until after the new one is up and fully recognized.

So that's *why* one would rather deal with easy to remember names. Now we'll take a look at *how* names are handled in the TCP/IP and Internet world.

# Domain Name System (DNS)

As we said in Chapter 7, the Domain Name System was designed in the early 1980s, and became the official method for mapping IP addresses to names in 1984. Since that time there have been modifications to the overall structure of the DNS database and some of the ways it works, but the overall system is still remarkably similar to its original design.

## Domain name space

The *domain name space* is an expression that is sometimes used to describe the tree-shaped structure of all domains—from the root ("." or "dot") domain to the lowest level domain in the structure. This hierarchical structure separates each part of the domain name space with a dot, which lets you know where you are in the domain hierarchy.

The root domains are the first level of the tree below the root. They describe the kinds of networks that are within their domain in two or three letters. So we have ".com" for commercial networks, ".edu" for educational ones, and ".au" for Australian ones. As you can see, we have both functional root domains and geographical root domains.

### For More Information

*See RFC 1591 for an overall description of the Domain Name System and RFC 1034 and RFC 1035 for the actual specifications of the system. See Chapter 7 for more information about the structure of the Domain Name System tree.*

The Internet initially used a single, master file ("HOSTS.TXT") for domain names that was sent via ftp to everyone who had to be able to convert from numbers to names. This, obviously, generated enormous overhead, even when the Internet was still relatively small; with continued growth, the system would have become totally unworkable long ago. The DNS, however, is a distributed database that is expandable and extensible so that more information can be added as needed. It allows local administration of local names, while maintaining overall network integrity and compliance with standards.

It seems like everyone who runs a business these days wants to set up his or her very own domain. If you want your own domain name, how do you go about getting one? Who decides whether you get the name you want or knows whether someone else already has it? The InterNIC, of course. The process for getting a name is really quite simple:

1. Decide what name you'd like to have. Come up with several alternates and variants on it—you'll probably need them. The available short names are disappearing at a rapid rate, and many administrators are finding that they need to think up longer versions of preferred names to find one that isn't taken. And a really slick name with "net" or "internet" in it? Don't even think about it; they're *long* gone.

2. Do some research on existing names to find out if the name you want is already in use; try the variants as well, until you find one that hasn't been taken. The simplest and best way to do a name search is to go to the InterNIC registration home page and use "Whois" to see if someone is already using the name. The InterNIC address is:

   `http://rs.internic.net/rs-internic.html`

3. Create the necessary DNS records on your DNS server, or have your Internet service provider (ISP) do it. If you are connecting to the Internet through an ISP and if they will be the ones who maintain your DNS records, by all means let them do the dirty work and set up everything. You'll want to do your research first, of course.

4. Register the name with the InterNIC, using the same address as in step 2.

5. Pay $100 (U.S.) when the InterNIC sends you the bill, or you'll lose your right to the name. The fee is good for two years; after that you'll be billed $50 (U.S.) per year for the right to continue using the name. A word of warning: it used to be that domain names were free and forever, but no more. If you don't pay the InterNIC bill, you'll lose your domain name, and by the time you go to re-register it, chances are someone else will have grabbed it.

## From domain names to IP addresses

When you click on a link to "http://www.microsoft.com" and Internet Explorer tries to go there, what actually happens? How does it find www.microsoft.com? The short answer is that it asks the primary DNS server listed on the TCP/IP properties page at your workstation. OK. But how does the DNS server know this?

When a TCP/IP application wants to communicate with or connect to another location, it needs the address of that location. But it usually starts out knowing only the name, so it first has to convert the name to an IP address. The first place it looks is in the local cache of information containing names and the resolved associated IP addresses. After all, if you just asked about www.microsoft.com 15 minutes ago, why should the DNS server go through all the trouble of looking up that name again? The chances are that the IP address hasn't changed in this short span of time.

But suppose you haven't been surfing the net in the last couple of days and your DNS server doesn't have any recent information about www.microsoft.com? Well, if the DNS server doesn't know, it asks around to see if another server knows. It sends a special UDP packet out on the network (in this case, the Internet) and asks if any server recognizes the name. Ultimately, the query will get a response from one of the other DNS servers—even if the query has to go all the way to the authoritative DNS server for the root domain.

## For More Information

*For more information about the DNS, how it works, and how it is configured, see the* Microsoft Windows NT Server Resource Kit *from Microsoft Press or O'Reilly's* DNS and BIND *by Albitz and Liu.*

# DHCP

One of the problems that is facing many organizations using the Internet these days is how to handle intermittently connected computers, such as laptops and remote computers, in a limited IP address space—especially if the computers are mobile units. One answer to this problem is the DHCP.

DHCP allows you to set aside a block of IP addresses for computers that are connected only intermittently and then parcel out the addresses as they are required. This allows a mobile user to connect to the network whenever necessary and automatically be assigned an appropriate address that is based on the location of the computer from which the user is connecting. This means you don't have to pre-assign an address to a particular remote location that might be connected only one day a week when a dial-up user calls in. You also save on the total number of addresses required for your network.

There's a useful side benefit to DHCP as well. A system administrator can set up the DHCP server to provide all of the necessary configuration details to the client computer without the client or its user having to know anything about the details of TCP/IP. This can be a definite plus, even for permanently connected computers, because it leverages the skills of the relatively more skilled administrator. He or she has to set up the configuration information once on the server, and then a less skilled assistant can configure the machines on the network without having to know as much about TCP/IP.

**For More Information**

*See Chapter 7 for more information on DHCP.*

# WINS

The Windows Internet Name Service (WINS) is a way to map IP addresses to NetBIOS names. Although DNS provides all of the information about a computer name that most traditional TCP/IP applications will need to know, it actually provides too much information for what Windows NT needs most often—the NetBIOS name. DNS works off the *fully qualified domain name* ("server1.mycompany.com" or some such); but for Windows Networking, all Windows NT cares about is the NetBIOS name, which is usually something like "SERVER1." WINS provides the information Windows NT needs by mapping the IP address to the NetBIOS name. WINS' other advantage over DNS is that it is a dynamic protocol that can handle DHCP-assigned IP addresses.

In order to make WINS and Browsing work correctly when you are in an enterprise environment with subnets and multiple domains, there are a few tricks to keep in mind. We'll avoid the gory details of the subject and get to the heart of the matter: what it takes to make it work. For all of the technical details, see the *Microsoft Windows NT Server Resource Kit*.

There are three possible scenarios:

◆ A single domain across a subnet boundary

◆ Multiple domains within a subnet boundary

◆ Multiple domains across a subnet boundary

### ◆ "Browsing" vs. "browsing"

A definite source of potential confusion in any discussion about Microsoft networks is the subtle distinction between the word *"browsing"* as it is commonly used—to mean looking for or at the resources available—and as it is used in the Microsoft sense of the Computer Browser network service. It's easy to get confused, and we'll try to avoid that here by always referring to Browsing in initial caps when we mean specifically the Microsoft networking sense of the word.

## A single domain across a subnet boundary

In order to see the resources of the domain across a subnet boundary, with only TCP/IP as your protocol, you'll have to set up WINS servers on both sides of the router or else muck around with LMHOSTS files. We avoid LMHOSTS files like the plague. They are a pain to set up, and then they have to be edited manually every time there is a network change. And they don't work well with DHCP, where IP addresses can change.

In general, we think it's a good idea to put a backup domain controller on the far side of the router from your primary domain controller. The alternative to this arrangement is a lot more traffic across the router than you have to have—for example, every authentication request will have to pass through the router. So, the obvious choice is to make both the backup domain controller and the primary domain controller WINS servers. You don't have to do anything special for this to work because there is no other domain that has to be "declared" to Browsing.

## Multiple domains within a subnet boundary

To see and use the resources across a domain boundary when you have multiple domains within a subnet boundary, you'll have to set up a trust relationship between the domains. Also, you will want both domains to have WINS servers in them, but you don't need to do anything special with Browsing. You can set up and explicitly add the other domains to browse, but you don't have to do this for everything to work.

## Multiple domains across a subnet boundary

Ah, now we get to the tricky one. In order for everything to work here, you will have to set up everything just right. The Browsing packets won't cross a subnet boundary unless they know where they're going. To cross domain and router boundaries, you have to explicitly add the domains from the other side of the router that you want to browse. To do this, follow these steps:

1. Open the Network dialog box, and click the Services tab (Figure 17. 2).

2. Double-click Computer Browser, and you'll see the dialog box shown in Figure 17.3.

3. Add the domain(s) that are on the other side of a router boundary, and click OK. That's all there is to the browsing part.

Now, for WINS: set up WINS servers in each of the domains and establish the necessary trust relationships—and you're done.

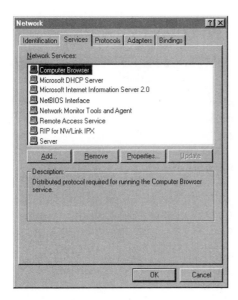

**FIGURE 17.2**

*Network dialog box showing Computer Browser service selected on the Services property sheet*

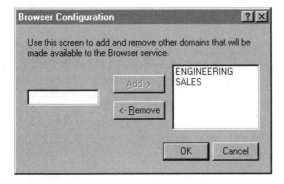

**FIGURE 17.3**

*Browser Configuration dialog box showing domains that are being added to Computer Browser*

# IPng (IPv6)

As we pointed out earlier in this chapter, the explosive growth of the Internet has greatly stressed its original design. Soon there simply will not be enough addresses for all of the computers and other devices that people want to hook up.

Several years ago, the IETF and others began working on solutions to the limitations of the 32-bit address space and the routing protocols in the current TCP/IP structure. The various proposed solutions have sorted themselves into a consensus on the next generation of IP, known as IPng or, more correctly, IPv6 (version 6 of the Internet Protocol). This was formally accepted by the IETF in December of 1994 and was documented in RFC 1752. It defines a 128-bit IP address space that is compatible with the current implementation of TCP/IP (version 4 or IPv4), but it provides for a greatly increased address space ($3 \times 10^{38}$!), as well as including additional information in the packets to provide for improved routing and handling of mobile devices.

The important thing to understand about IPng or IPv6 is that it is evolutionary, not revolutionary. We don't have to worry about waking up one morning and finding that we have to reconfigure every machine to support it. We can make the transition gradually because the protocol should be able to coexist in most situations with existing IPv4 implementations.

# Using the Administration Tools for TCP/IP

Windows NT Server provides several useful applications for administering the various parts of TCP/IP. Most of these you have already dealt with during the setup of TCP/IP, as discussed in Chapter 7; but there is still some ground to cover. Windows NT Server provides tools for setting up and managing a DNS server, a WINS server, and a DHCP server.

## DNS Manager

DNS Manager allows you to set up and manage a DNS server to resolve domain names to IP addresses locally and to maintain authoritative records for your own domains. It also allows you to administer multiple servers from the same application. If you have DNS server installed, you can open DNS Manager from the Administrative Tools (Common) menu off the Start menu.

### Adding a server

You can add a server to the list of DNS servers you administer. Choose New Server from the DNS menu. In the Add DNS Server dialog box (Figure 17.4), type the name or the IP address of the DNS server you want to manage in the DNS Server text box. The Windows NT Server DNS Administrator will attempt to connect to the server; and, if it is successful, it will display the statistics for that server as well as the types of records and zones maintained by the server.

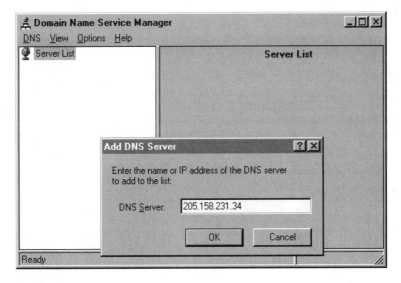

**FIGURE 17.4**

*Example of Domain Name Service Manager with an Add DNS Server dialog box showing the address of server that is being added*

**NOTE**

*Unfortunately, Windows NT Server DNS Manager only works with Windows NT DNS servers; you won't be able to use it to administer any other DNS servers you might be running. Too bad—it's a nice interface.*

## DNS server functions

From the DNS menu, you have several functions from which to choose:

◆ **Pause Zone** Takes the zone offline while you work on it.

◆ **New Zone** Allows you to add a zone, either as a primary or secondary server.

◆ **Add Domain** Allows you to add a new domain.

◆ **New Host** Allows you to add a new host and create the A record (and the PTR record, if you want) for the host.

◆ **New Record** Allows you to add a new record of any of the supported types for the host or domain selected.

- **Delete** Removes the selected item.
- **Update Server Data Files** Increments the serial number and updates the database.
- **Properties** Shows detailed properties for the selected item.

One important caveat here: when you make a change to the DNS records, make sure you choose Update Server Data Files. This will increment the serial number, letting other DNS servers know that you've made a change to the information and that they need to update their information, which is now out of date.

## Supported DNS records

Windows NT Server DNS supports a wide variety of DNS record types, including many that will become increasingly important as the world moves to IPv6.

- A Record (Address Record)
- AAAA Record (IPv6 Address Record)
- AFSDB Record (Andrews File System or DCE Record)
- CNAME Record (Alias Record)
- HINFO Record (Host Information Record)
- ISDN (ISDN Information Record)
- MB Record (Mailbox Name Record)
- MG Record (Mail Group Record)
- MINFO Record (Mailbox Information Record)
- MR Record (Mailbox Renamed Record)
- MX Record (Mail Exchange - "Smart Host" - Record)
- NS Record (Name Server Record)
- PTR Record (Pointer Resource Record)
- RP Record (Responsible Person Information Record)
- RT Record (Route-Through Record)
- TXT Record (Text Record)
- WKS Record (Well Known Services Record)
- X25 Record (X.25 Information Record)

# WINS Manager

WINS Manager allows you to set up and manage a WINS server to convert IP addresses into NetBIOS names, which you'll need to browse your network. If you have WINS Server installed, you can open WINS Manager from the Administrative Tools (Common) menu off the Start menu.

## Adding a server

You can add a WINS server to the list of WINS servers you manage. Choose Add WINS Server from the Server menu. In the WINS Servers list box of the WINS Manager window (Figure 17.5), by default, you'll see the primary and secondary WINS servers for the local computer. To add a server, type the name or the IP address of the server in the WINS Server text box. In the right pane of the WINS Manager window, you can see the current statistics for any WINS server that you select from the list.

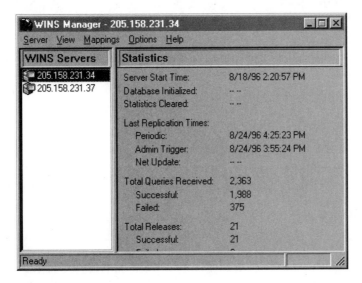

**FIGURE 17.5**

*Example of WINS Manager window showing the WINS servers for a local computer*

## WINS server functions

WINS Manager allows you to manage all of the WINS operations on multiple servers from the same application. These are the supported functions:

◆ **Add WINS Server** Allows you to add other WINS servers that you want to manage.

◆ **Delete WINS Server** Removes the selected WINS server from local management.

◆ **Detailed Information** Displays detailed statistics about the selected WINS server.

◆ **Configuration** Allows you to modify server configuration information, including expiration times, replication parameters, and logging.

◆ **Replication Partners** Allows you to add or delete replication partners and set options for the replication.

◆ **Show Database** Shows the full WINS database, including static mappings, as shown in Figure 17.6.

◆ **Initiate Scavenging** Purges the WINS database, and generally cleans it up.

◆ **Static Mappings** Allows you to add assigned names to fixed IP addresses manually.

All of these functions can be performed on multiple WINS servers, not just the one for which you are running the application; and, in fact, you can run WINS Manager from any Windows NT version 4 client.

### For More Information

*For additional information about WINS, see the* Microsoft Windows NT Server Resource Kit *from Microsoft Press.*

## DHCP Manager

DHCP Manager allows you to set up and manage a DHCP server to assign and manage IP addresses and their properties for DHCP clients. If you have DHCP server installed, you can open DHCP Manager from the Administrative Tools (Common) menu off the Start menu.

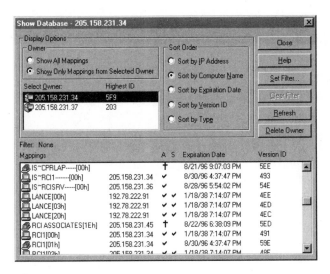

**FIGURE 17.6**

*WINS Show Database dialog box showing the NetBIOS-name-to-IP-Address mappings of a WINS server*

## Adding a server

You can add a DHCP server to the list of DHCP servers you manage. Choose Add from the Server menu. In the DHCP Server text box, type the name or IP address of the server you want to add, and then click OK.

## DHCP server functions

DHCP Manager (Figure 17.7 on the following page) allows you to administer all of your DHCP servers, and their properties and functionality, from a single location. These functions include the following:

◆ **Remove** Removes the selected server from the list of managed servers.

◆ **Create Scope** Creates a new scope for the selected subnet.

◆ **Scope Properties** Edits the properties for the selected scope, as shown in Figure 17.8 on the following page.

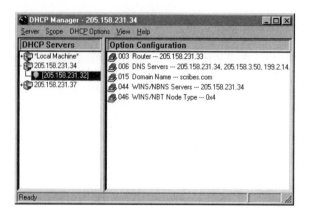

**FIGURE 17.7**

*Example of a DHCP Manager window*

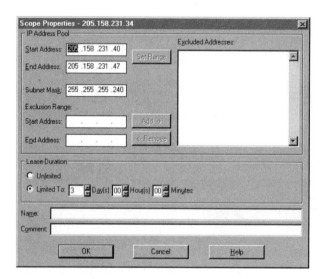

**FIGURE 17.8**

*Example of DHCP Scope properties settings*

- **Deactivate or Delete the Scope** Temporarily deactivates or re-activates a scope on the server or permanently deletes the scope.

- **Add Reservations** Adds reserved addresses for particular clients to the scope.

- **Active Leases** Shows all active client leases on the server, including reserved addresses, as shown in Figure 17.9.

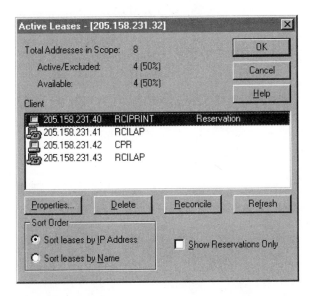

**FIGURE 17.9**

*Example of Active Leases dialog box in DHCP Manager showing active client leases for a server*

- DHCP Options

    - **Scope** Edits the configuration options for the selected scope.

    - **Global** Edits the global client configuration options.

    - **Default** Edits the default client configuration options.

The DHCP server allows you to preconfigure many options that would normally need to be set manually for a standard, fixed-address, TCP/IP device. With DHCP Manager you can set many of the options individually, for each scope, or globally. Individual clients can override the default settings, of course; but in most cases this will be neither necessary nor desirable, if you've set up your DHCP options correctly.

You can configure these options on a per scope, global, or default basis:

- Time Offset
- Router
- Timer Server
- Name Servers
- DNS Servers
- Log Servers
- Cookie Servers
- LPR Servers
- Impress Servers
- Resource Location Servers
- Host Name
- Boot File Size
- Merit Dump File
- Swap Server
- Root Path
- Extensions Path
- IP Layer Forwarding
- Non-Local Source Routing
- Policy Filter Masks
- Maximum DG Reassembly Size
- Default Time to Live
- Path MTU Aging TO
- Path MTU Plateau Table
- MTU Options
- All Subnets Are Local (for MTU)
- Broadcast Address
- Perform Mask Discovery
- Mask Supplier Option
- Perform Router Discovery
- Router Solicitation Address
- Static Route Option
- Trailer Encapsulation
- ARP Cache Timeout
- Ethernet Encapsulation
- Default TTL Option
- Keepalive Interval
- Keepalive Garbage
- NIS Domain Name
- NIS Servers
- NTP Servers
- Vendor Specific Info
- WINS/NBNS Servers
- WINS/NBT Node Type
- NetBIOS Scope ID
- XWindow System Font
- XWindow System Display
- NIS+ Domain Name
- NIS+ Servers
- Bootfile Name
- Mobile IP Home Agents

Whew! There is obviously a large number of options that you can configure for individual clients or DHCP scope. We recommend you set only things that you know need changing and not mess with things you're not sure about. You can add more later if you need to do so.

### For More Information

*For additional information about the various DHCP options, see the* Microsoft Windows NT Server Resource Kit *from Microsoft Press.*

## POINTS TO REMEMBER

- ◆ TCP/IP is not one protocol but a suite of protocols and applications.
- ◆ TCP/IP standards are set by the IETF.
- ◆ TCP/IP standards and proposed changes are published to the world in the form of Requests for Comments (RFCs).
- ◆ Windows NT Server provides tools for administering DNS, WINS, and DHCP servers.
- ◆ Use DHCP to simplify handling mobile, intermittently connected computers.
- ◆ IPv6 (IPng) is compatible with the existing IPv4 and will be implemented gradually over the next several years.

## WHAT'S NEXT?

In this chapter, we've covered the intricacies of TCP/IP and how it works. In Chapter 18, we'll cover setting up and maintaining remote access services so that your users can work at remote locations just as if they were connected locally to the network.

# CHAPTER 18

Remote Access Service

# CHAPTER 18

# Remote Access Service

The greatest growth sector in today's corporate environment is in the nontraditional area of telecommuting. Greater numbers of employees today are working at remote sites with access to the corporate computer or communication center (E-mail). Telecommuting, rather than the daily commute to the office, has become a norm in many companies. As a result, companies have seen their expenses go down, profits go up, and employee longevity increase. Being able to communicate with co-workers and having access to the data and the resources of the corporate network are essential to the remote user. Microsoft Windows NT Server version 4 provides these capabilities with RAS.

## Remote Node vs. Remote Control

Two types of remote access are available today—remote node access and remote control access. Both solve the problem of remote LAN access, although they have different capabilities and restrictions. The limitation both forms of remote connection have in common is that they are relatively slow compared to a direct LAN connection.

Remote node access treats the user's computer as an actual node on the network, extending the network connection either over telephone lines through a modem or by way of a router on an ISDN line or other specialized phone line. The network sees the remote computer as if it were a local connection; all processing is done on the remote computer. The remote node can perform almost any task from the remote location that a local node can perform. One of the main strengths of this type of remote access is that it is easy to learn—there are few differences in the way you access your data from a remote computer and from a computer in your office.

In remote control access, the remote computer takes control of a computer that is already attached to the network. In other words, the remote computer becomes just a remote monitor and keyboard for a LAN node. Processing is done on the host computer at the office rather than on the remote computer.

Remote node access has an important advantage over remote control access: simplicity. Working with split screens over two computers can be confusing for even the most seasoned computer user. The error rate in actions by the users is far greater with remote control access than with remote node access. Remote node access also reduces hardware costs. Because you can have a single RAS server providing network access for a large group of users, you save substantially over remote control access, which requires a local computer for each remote user.

Remote control access has another cost that particularly concerns system administrators—maintenance. Because there's no central point of administration, maintaining and supporting remote control computers can be a nightmare.

Windows NT Server's RAS provides a remote node service for users who dial in to the corporate computer network. A key benefit of using remote node access is that the full security system of your network applies to those who dial in remotely. The user who only occasionally works from a remote location sees the same resources he or she would normally expect to see when working at his or her office. The report for the president can be printed on the printer that services the president's office, even though the person printing the file could be calling in from anywhere in the world.

Once RAS has been installed and configured on a Windows NT server, anyone with the proper authorization and access codes can communicate with the office from any computer and modem in the world. It does not matter whether you are at home, in another city, or around the world; you can work as if you were sitting at your desk in the office. The goal is to make the process of connecting remotely as transparent to users as logging in from their desktops. The tough part is speed. A 28,800 bits per second (bps) modem is a lot slower than a network card.

## Basic Equipment Needs

Ideally, a separate computer works best for a RAS server. The number of remote access network users and remote mail users on your network will determine the type and amount of equipment you will require for a successful RAS server.

If you have only a few users who will want access to the office network or mail system, you can install a few simple modems on any Windows NT server. If your needs are likely to go beyond about a dozen or so remote users, you'll probably find that you want to use a separate, dedicated server to handle them.

The inclusion of TCP/IP and Point-to-Point Protocol (PPP) in Windows NT Server and Microsoft Windows 95 makes it feasible to have a single communications server for fax, remote mail, and remote access. In earlier remote access systems, a separate server was required for each protocol. This new flexibility allows even smaller companies to set up remote services that were once restricted to large companies and government agencies.

# Computer Hardware Requirements

A RAS server doesn't really require more than a basic workstation's hardware—a 486DX4/100 or a low-end Pentium with 16 MB of RAM should be sufficient, although 24 MB or 32 MB of RAM would be better. You can save a buck on hard drive space because you won't need much beyond the space for the operating system and a reasonable amount of room for temporary storage.

A key element in choosing the actual computer to use as your RAS server is the number of available ISA, Local Bus, or PCI slots that it has available for additional serial port boards, external routers, and network interfaces. Choose a computer that has plenty of spare slots to allow you to easily add additional interface cards as you need them.

# Connectivity Components

Network connectivity for your RAS server is easy—use whatever you used on the rest of the network. The difficult decision is what modems or routers to use. You need to provide for your current level of remote users and also make reasonable provision for growth. It's far better to plan for growth in remote access use at the outset than to try to patch things together later.

## Modems

The first choice you have to make is whether to use internal or external components. External modems and routers are always desirable, even in those cases where it's possible to use internal devices. Maintenance is easier, and resetting a stalled modem can be done by switching the modem off and on without rebooting the server.

The choice of speed for your modems will be based upon three factors:

◆ What is the slowest (and therefore the cheapest) access you can get away with? Keep in mind that the faster the access is, the more productive your users are.

◆ How much funding is available to accomplish the project?

◆ What types of phone lines are available to you—standard phone lines, ISDN, T1, or T3?

## Dedicated modems

You should plan on dedicating each modem to a single use. Although a modem might be capable of both FAX and data transfers, you should limit it to a single purpose. Use older, slower FAX modems for FAX, and keep newer, 28,800 bps or faster modems for remote access. ISDN and T1 modems or routers are even better choices for remote access where they are feasible. Having separate modems dedicated to inbound calls, outbound calls, and FAX will reduce the competition for resources.

### Shared modems

A shared modem is one that is configured to perform two or more functions, which can include inbound and outbound data transfer as well as FAX. This arrangement may be acceptable in a small, limited situation, but it has inherently more problems than a single-function modem.

### Routers and access servers

In a traditional network environment with multiple departments at one or more sites, the use of network routers is common and, in many cases, essential. The router can help divide the network into segments to keep traffic down. If you are connecting several sites, the routers act as traffic cops between the sites.

In addition to traditional routers, there are stand-alone, remote access routers available, such as the Ascend MAX/400, LANTRONIX LRS2, Shiva's LanRover Plus, Microcom's LANexpress 4000, and the JDS HYDRA 3000, that act exclusively as RAS servers. These devices take the burden of handling remote access off the computer running Windows NT Server and handle the entire process independently, giving your remote users transparent access to the resources of the network.

In large installations with multiple sites that are connected by a WAN, you probably will need more than one RAS server. You not only will need the remote access devices for your remote users but also at least two servers to connect the sites of your network as well.

## Software Requirements

A significant headache for the system administrator of any network that has remote users is the software licensing requirements. For every node on the network, local or remote, there must be software licenses to support the number of sessions that are active. The actual requirements will differ for different software packages. Some software companies allow the sharing of a single license by a workstation and a remote user as long as the actual user is the same person in each case and he or she has access to the network from only one place at a time. In other words, if you are logged on remotely, no one should be able to log on as you from your office workstation at the same time. Other companies require you to purchase two software licenses if you plan to use their program remotely as well as in the office. Still others just count the total number of concurrent users, regardless of their locations.

# RAS Installation and Configuration

The actual installation and configuration of RAS is a relatively simple task, but we can't emphasize enough the need to *plan* what you're going to do and how you're going to do it *before* you start the installation. These are the steps in the process:

1. Plan the connections.

2. Install RAS.

3. Create or modify the user accounts to permit remote dial-in.

4. Install and configure dial-out access and software.

## Planning Remote Access Connections

There are a number of things you'll want to plan. You need to know where your RAS server will be located and how you will connect to it. Will you be going through a central PBX or other switching system, or will you have a number of discrete, direct lines to your server? Or will you—as is more likely—have a combination of the two types of connections? You want to make sure, for example, that you will have access to your network in an emergency, even when the main phone system is down.

Will your phone lines be shared for incoming and outgoing calls, or will you be using dedicated lines for each type of call? Is your server in a secured area? Be sure you will have access to that area when it's time to install everything. And plan who will support and monitor the system while phone personnel are installing the lines. Will your modem bank need additional power outlets? Does each modem have its own power supply? In other words, think about the *physical layout* of the new setup to prepare for the installation.

What network protocols will you be installing? Which users will have remote access to the network? Will you be using a dialback to limit dial-in calls to known, safe sites? Will the callback be handled by the modems, or will the RAS server do the dirty work? In other words, think about the *logical layout* of the new setup to prepare for the installation.

Document the process. Identify each and every phone line, modem, network connection, and so on, that you work on. Write it all down and keep a log. Your life will be far, far easier later when you're trying to figure out what's what in a breakdown and everyone's going nuts.

## Installing RAS

The installation process for RAS is not a difficult procedure, but, again, be sure you've done your homework before you start. We covered the gory details of installing RAS in Chapter 7 (page 108) because some administrators will need RAS during the initial Windows NT Server installation to connect to the network. So we won't repeat that discussion here. After RAS is installed, however, you still have a couple of tasks to perform: you have to configure user accounts for users who will have dial-in privileges to permit remote access, and you have to add any dial-out software you will be using.

## Modifying User Accounts to Allow Remote Access

Before someone can use RAS for dial-in access to the network, dial-in access must be enabled explicitly for the specific user. The default is to have this permission disabled. You can't enable dial-in access for a group; you have to enable it either for an individual user or for *all* users at one time.

You can choose either of the two available options for managing user dial-in privileges—you can use User Manager for Domains (or the regular User Manager, if you're running in a non-domain environment), or you can use the remote access administrator (Remote Access Admin). Both of these utilities can be found on the Start menu under Programs, Administrative Tools (Common). We've already covered User Manager for Domains in Chapter 9, so we'll use the remote access administrator utility here to show you how it works. Open Remote Access Admin, and you will see a Remote Access Admin window that is similar to the one shown in Figure 18.1

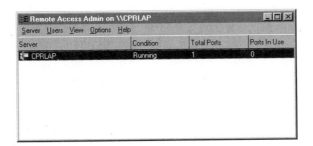

**FIGURE 18.1**

*Example of the Remote Access Admin window for a RAS server*

Now choose Permissions from the Users menu. You'll see a Remote Access Permissions dialog box that is similar to the one shown in Figure 18.2 on the following page. If you're running on a computer other than the primary domain controller, you'll see an informational message that reminds you all permissions are ultimately the responsibility of the primary domain controller and that your machine is running only a replicated version of the permissions database. You knew that, of course; but it's still a useful reminder. Click OK, and then you'll go to the Remote Access Permissions dialog box.

Select the user name of the account for which you are changing permissions, and make the necessary changes. RAS can be set to automatically call back the user,

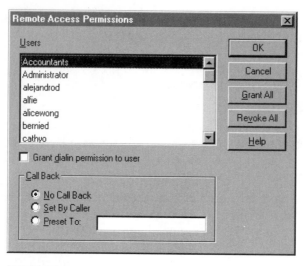

**FIGURE 18.2**

*Example of a Remote Access Permissions dialog box*

either to a preset number or to a number that is provided by the user when he or she calls in.

There are options here also for granting dial-in privileges to all users at one time, as well as removing them from all users at one time. Use these options with care—both are probably inappropriate in most situations. One deficiency in the way RAS handles permissions, in our opinion, is that you can't use a local group or global group to assign permissions. You must grant or revoke the permission on an individual basis. This can be a major pain if you have to administer a substantial number of users who change locations or job responsibilities fairly often.

After you've made all of the changes you want to make, click OK to return to the main Remote Access Admin window.

### ◆ Security and Callbacks

Allowing users to dial in to your corporate network is always a touchy subject for some sites—and with good cause. If you don't plan your security carefully, you open up your network to the world. There are many solutions to the security issue, including carefully crafted and maintained firewalls and Microsoft's PPTP. But one of the easiest and most foolproof security measures is a simple callback system in which the RAS server calls back remote users. If you set your callbacks to go *only* to expected phone numbers, you have a pretty sound way of ensuring that only authorized users have access to your network. You won't need to invest a lot of time, money, or resources in designing, setting up, and maintaining a firewall.

## Establishing Priorities for Outbound Access

The establishment of access priorities is essential. If you have a network with both incoming and outgoing traffic, you can easily end up with either one or the other locking up all of the available modems. We've found that it's generally best to dedicate several lines and devices for outbound traffic only and several for inbound traffic only. The rest of your remote devices can be configured for both.

# Connecting to the Outside

The chances are that after you have set up RAS and users can connect to your network from the outside, you'll hear gentle murmurings from them about wanting to connect from inside the company to the outside, specifically to the Internet. Here's where you'll need to plan carefully and to make some hard decisions about what kind of Internet access you're going to allow. It isn't the purpose of this chapter to deal with setting up firewalls or the security issues associated with having unsecured modem connections to the Internet. But you need to consider carefully the security implications for your network of having outside connections. They can't simply be ignored because security *will* be an issue if you don't find a way to provide outside access in a controlled manner.

Using RAS as a dial-out server is certainly one way to handle dial-out access. However, you're likely to need additional software to provide an adequate level of protection. And, in fact, you're probably going to need most of the packages we will discuss here, even if you set up an intranet.

## Web Browser

Probably first and foremost of the important software packages is a *Web browser*. The original browser was Mosaic, but its place in the market has been completely eclipsed by later Web browser offerings. Netscape Navigator is the dominant figure in this market. It's by far the most popular browser and has been the clear technology leader until recently. But with the release of Microsoft's Internet Explorer 3, Netscape's position of dominance is at least being threatened. Either of these Web browsers allows you access to Web pages and ftp sites throughout the world. Both provide a number of graphic image viewers that are built into their programs. Netscape also allows add-on programs to extend its capabilities, and many of these add-on products are now available. On the other hand, Internet Explorer supports ActiveX controls that allow third parties to add functionality to the program.

In addition, both Netscape Navigator and Internet Explorer have the ability to act as Internet E-mail clients, although this certainly isn't a required feature if you want access to Internet E-mail through Windows NT Server. There is already a perfectly adequate client in the Windows Messaging Inbox provided with Windows NT Server and an even more powerful client that is part of Microsoft Exchange Server.

# Internet Access Provider

When you have the necessary software packages ready, it is time to configure them with information about the local Internet service provider. For every system there are two possibilities to consider. One option is to have your own Internet server on-site. With your own servers, you maintain control over your own security and E-mail; and if you have a large number of accounts, this option can be as cost-effective as using an Internet service provider. However, the task of setting up and maintaining your own Internet server is not a trivial one and should be undertaken only after a careful analysis of the financial costs, including the cost of the skilled personnel you will need to maintain the operation.

The other option is to buy accounts from a local Internet provider. Regardless of the number of users you have who will need access to the Internet, you should be able to obtain an adequate number of IP addresses with your own domain name on your local provider's system. In some cases, you might have a set of IP addresses for external access to the Internet that are completely different from the ones you use for your internal network; in other cases, the addresses will be the same. However you handle the TCP/IP issues, you'll be able to integrate your internal E-mail system directly with Internet E-mail. Microsoft Exchange will allow you to handle your Internet E-mail in the same application as your Microsoft Mail, Microsoft Exchange, CompuServe Mail, and Lotus Notes Email. We expect to see Exchange clients for virtually every E-mail system as time goes on. To the user, the process is transparent; it allows someone to send and receive mail equally well to a Lotus Notes mail box or a UNIX E-mail system in the engineering department.

# Point-to-Point Tunneling Protocol (PPTP)

PPTP is Microsoft's new networking technology, which takes remote computing to the next level of development. PPTP enables clients to have access to their LAN via an Internet connection. One of the most obvious benefits of using PPTP technology is that the LAN administrator can reduce the number of modem pools for remote users. Using the established Internet connection shifts the workload to a stable multiprotocol component of your network, namely your Internet server. In addition to the decreased workload on your servers and gateways, PPTP offers an encrypted and secure transmission and the flexibility of working with any protocol, including IP, IPX, and NetBEUI.

The secret to the success of PPTP is that it treats your LAN as a virtual WAN, which can be supported through the Internet and other commercial services such as those provided by MCI and AT&T. You are no longer tied to voice long-distance-carrier rates; your local Internet service provider can become your long-distance carrier for data communications. And now with the advent of WebPhone, Internet Phone, Web Talk, and other similar programs, it is possible your Internet service provider could even become your voice long-distance carrier for interoffice communications, although it's still a bit early to go that route.

PPTP uses both the Password Authentication Protocol (PAP) and the Challenge-Handshake Authentication Protocol (CHAP) encryption algorithms for its security devices; this permits encrypted PPP links across the Internet. An additional benefit to using this technology is that you can use the Internet as the backbone for your remote IPX and NetBEUI network traffic. The installation of PPTP is fairly straightforward. Just follow these steps:

1. Open the Network dialog box, either from Network Neighborhood or the Network icon in Control Panel, and click the Protocols tab. Click Add.

2. In the Select Network Protocol dialog box that opens, select Point To Point Tunneling Protocol (as shown in Figure 18.3) and then click OK.

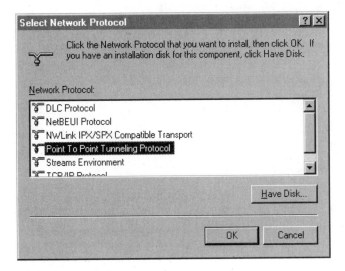

**FIGURE 18.3**

*Select Network Protocol dialog box showing selected protocol*

3. You'll be advised that the setup process needs to copy some Windows NT files. Make sure the correct path is shown, and then click Continue. (You will need the original Windows NT Server CD-ROM, unless you have made a source directory somewhere on your hard drive.) The necessary drivers will be copied to the WINNT\SYSTEM32 directory.

4. You'll then be asked to confirm the number of Virtual Private Networks. The default is one. Click OK to continue.

5. The next message demonstrates one aspect of how PPTP differs from other protocols (see Figure 18.4 on the following page): it requires that RAS be set up at the same time. Click OK.

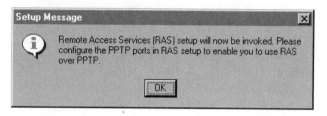

**FIGURE 18.4**

*Set up remote access confirmation message for PPTP installation*

6. The next dialog box shows the RAS setup. Any modems shown here are already set up for remote access—dial out only, receive calls only, or both. Click Configure to change the setup.

7. For the network administration, click Network and select the options you want from the Network Configuration dialog box (Figure 18.5).

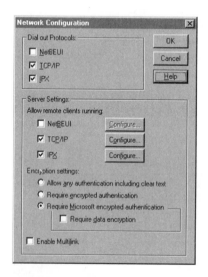

**FIGURE 18.5**

*Example of Network Configuration dialog box for PPTP installation*

8. Click Continue when you're finished. The necessary bindings will be configured. You will have to reboot the machine before the settings will take effect.

The enabling of PPTP for each network adapter in your computer can be done by following a few simple steps:

1. In Control Panel, double-click the Network icon; then click the Protocols tab.

2. Select TCP/IP Protocol, and click Properties.

3. On the IP Address tab, click Advanced to bring up the Advanced IP Addressing dialog box, which will look similar to the one shown in Figure 18.6.

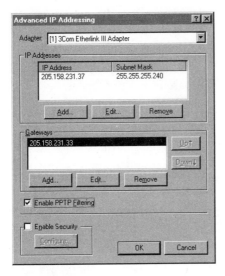

**FIGURE 18.6**

*Advanced IP Addressing dialog box showing the enabling of PPTP filtering for a network adapter*

4. In the Adapter drop-down list box, select the network adapter for which you want to specify PPTP filtering. The PPTP filtering settings in this dialog box are defined only for the network adapter you have selected.

5. If you want to enable PPTP filtering, select Enable PPTP Filtering. When you select PPTP filtering, you effectively disable the selected network adapter for all other protocols, and only PPTP packets will be allowed in. If this computer also must communicate with the LAN, it will require a second network adapter to do so. Clients outside the LAN can use PPTP to connect to this computer from across the Internet and, thus, gain secure access to the corporate network.

6. Click OK to return to the main TCP/IP screen. Click OK to accept the changes. The settings will take effect after you reboot the computer.

# RAS Maintenance and Troubleshooting

The more time you have invested in planning your server configuration, the less time you will have to spend maintaining and repairing it. And the time you spend maintaining the server will be saved many times over in reduced downtime, plus it will spare you the attendant yelling and carrying on that downtime inspires.

## Troubleshooting Problems

Good diagnostic skills are a requirement for network administrators and Help desk support specialists. Repairing a computer component is not difficult. The difficult task is diagnosing the problem and determining the *root cause* of that problem.

Hardware problems normally are solved by swapping parts. Software problems are a little more complex. They can be software bugs, or they can be conflicting software and hardware components. For a RAS server or any other computer with a modem, you must always be on the lookout for potential IRQ conflicts. And always be aware that new software packages introduced into the computer might change some of your RAS settings. You should make a complete backup of the registry before adding any new software to the server. (See Chapter 24 for details on backing up and restoring the registry.)

RAS problems tend to fall into three basic areas: failure to send or deliver a file or message, failure to receive a file or message, and access failure.

### Delivery

The most common delivery failures are E-mail messages that don't get to their intended recipient, files that aren't saved in the directory where the user thought he or she had saved them, and files that are corrupted in the process of being saved.

The usual delivery problem is a failure in translation from one service or type of mail to another. Typically, a user will be able to receive a message, but won't be able to send one, or vice-versa. Each type of mail service has its own peculiarities and quirks; translating those quirks is the job of the gateway program or Exchange Connector. Each gateway service has its own requirements and points of failure, but a careful reading of the logs created should point you in the direction of the problem. We can't urge you strongly enough to take delivery failures seriously and react to them promptly. The sense of frustration associated with outgoing E-mail problems tends to be less than the sense of frustration associated with incoming E-mail problems, but *any* E-mail problem tends to become very annoying, very quickly.

Another kind of delivery problem is file delivery, most typically misplaced files. A very difficult situation can arise when a user has logged on under another name or in a different domain and neglects to tell you that small fact. A user's desktop and directory structure may look exactly the same, but the reality is that the underlying root directory is completely different.

Another source of file problems is corrupted files that have been downloaded from the Internet. Typically this is a problem with files downloaded using ftp instead of a web browser. The default protocol for ftp transfers is ASCII, so trying to download a binary file with ftp usually doesn't produce any error messages. The resulting file might even appear to be the same size as the original file, but it is corrupted and not readable. Gently remind your users that they need to specify a binary file transfer for most file transfers, including word processing documents and spreadsheets—two types of documents they might not think about.

### Reception

Reception problems are restricted primarily to electronic mail connection errors, which normally are minor in nature and temporary because Microsoft Exchange is a stable mail system. Most errors occur when the LAN or Mail administrator is performing the required maintenance on the mail system. The only way to completely eliminate reception errors is to restrict access to the RAS server during mail system maintenance. The problem of address translation errors from one mail system to another also can be a source of grief, especially if either of the mail systems has recently had even a minor upgrade.

Remember to take all reports of lost or missing E-mail seriously. This is an area that gets users' attention quickly, and you need to respond equally fast.

### Access

Access problems will occur when the RAS server goes offline for any reason. Because the RAS server is an integral part of the network, it should have its own battery backup system to protect it from blackouts, power surges, and brownouts.

## Maintenance

Maintenance is essential to an effective communication system on your network. Remote users are completely dependent on its being available, and LAN users depend on it for access to the Internet for both external electronic mail and the World Wide Web. You should check the RAS server on a regular basis to verify that it is functioning properly. The frequency of your system maintenance will be determined by several factors:

◆ The total number of users on the network

◆ The number of remote users on the network

◆ The amount of traffic the RAS server handles

◆ The type of transactions that take place

The more remote users you have, the more likely it is that you will have problems on the RAS server's hard disk. Users who are simply querying a database or reading their mail aren't adding many files or using large amounts of disk space, but users who transfer large files or do most of their work at the remote location do use large amounts of disk space. You can keep problems to a minimum by providing as seamless an integration as possible, letting them use their normal home directories and system resources.

Regular backups are essential, as always. Make sure the RAS server is included in the network backup schedule, and also make sure any "public" directories on the RAS server are backed up regularly as well.

## Technical Tips and Solutions for RAS

The following tips and troubleshooting techniques will help improve the performance of RAS.

### Log files for RAS troubleshooting

One way to troubleshoot remote access problems is to tell the Windows NT server to create a log of everything that happens with remote access devices and the connections to these devices. To enable logging, you have to edit the registry.

Edit the registry by changing the value for logging to 1 (default = 0) in the following two registry keys:

HKEY_LOCAL_MACHINE\SYSTEM\CurrentControlSet\Services\RasMan\ Parameters

HKEY_LOCAL_MACHINE\SYSTEM\CurrentControlSet\Services\RasMan\ PPP

When you finish editing the registry, you'll have two log files in your RAS directory: DEVICE.LOG and PPP.LOG. The log files will appear the next time you start the RAS server in the \%SYSTEMROOT%\SYSTEM32\RAS directory.

**For More Information**

*You can find additional information about the registry in Chapter 24.*

### Failed connection to a RAS server

You might see the error message "Negotiation with PPP Server failed" after you install RAS. The solution is to set up the RAS server for using a PPP client. Several server settings should be enabled if the PPP client is to perform properly. You have to make sure both the server and the client are set to use the same type of authentication. We recommend that you always set them to require encrypted authentication for client access to your internal network.

This is the procedure for checking the type of authentication and setting up your clients to require encryption:

1. Double-click the Network icon in Control Panel to open the Network dialog box, and then click the Services tab.

2. Double-click Remote Access Service to get the Remote Access Setup dialog box, which will look similar to the one shown in Figure 18.7.

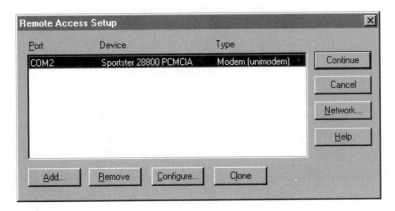

**FIGURE 18.7**

*Example of a Remote Access Setup dialog box*

3. Click Network to open the Network Configuration dialog box, which will look similar to the one shown in Figure 18.8.

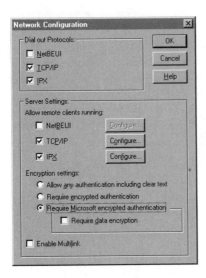

**FIGURE 18.8**

*Network Configuration dialog box showing the encryption settings*

4. If all of your clients are running Windows 95 or Windows NT, select Require Microsoft Encryption Authentication. This is the best authentication option when it's possible to use it. Otherwise, select Require Encrypted Authentication, which should work even for some non-Windows clients such as UNIX systems. (The non-Windows client computers will need to be set for CHAP authentication.)

## No server browsing capability from a RAS client

If a RAS client is not a member of a valid workgroup or domain on the network, the remote computer will not be able to browse the network from Explorer. You can configure a RAS client to belong to a workgroup on the remote network by changing its workgroup name to a workgroup name or domain name on the remote network. If you change the client workgroup name to a domain name on the remote network, the computer must have a machine account on that domain.

Even if a RAS client computer is not a member of a valid workgroup or domain, the client still can connect to servers directly using Explorer. In Explorer, choose Map Network Drive from the Tools menu and enter the share name directly by using the following syntax:

*\\servername\sharename*

## Access Denied error message

When a user connects to a remote network, the user name and the password entered in the RAS Authentication dialog box are used only to determine whether the account has dial-in permission. The information is not used by the remote network to check whether the user actually has permission to use the resources. Only when a user logs on to a client machine are the user name and password used to verify access to network resources—that is, RAS does not automatically log the user on to the remote network. You have a couple of options for working around this problem. You can have the user log on to the remote network after he or she has made the RAS connection. (Logging off and logging on will not hang up the RAS connection.) Another option is to create a local account that is the same as the account used to make the RAS connection; the user then logs on to the RAS client with this account.

♦   Map out a comprehensive RAS strategy.

♦   Verify your hardware requirements (and make sure you have the budget for them).

♦   Evaluate all of the connection options, including dedicated or shared modems.

♦   Do not even consider starting RAS until you have your security program in place.

♦   Maintain accurate logs of RAS problems; documentation of the solutions to problems that have come up also would be handy.

## WHAT'S NEXT?

In this chapter, we've covered setting up a RAS server and keeping it up and happy. In Chapter 19, we'll cover Microsoft's entry into the Internet/Intranet server arena, Internet Information Server (IIS). Unlike many servers that cost you large amounts of money beyond what you've already spent, IIS is included "in the box"—and it's a very good server indeed, especially for setting up and running a corporate intranet.

# CHAPTER 19

# CHAPTER 19

# Internet Information Server

Internet technology is not only the fastest growing area of computer technology, it's also the area of technology that is changing most rapidly. The same technology that is transforming the Internet is also providing the basis for "private networks" known as intranets. Armed only with the features included with Microsoft Windows NT Server version 4, you can create connections to the Internet, develop your own intranet, or both. In this chapter, we'll cover the Windows NT Server internetworking features and some of the ways you can use them.

Windows NT Server includes the Internet Information Server (IIS), a full-feature Internet server. With IIS, you can construct a World Wide Web server to display documents, graphics, sound, and even full-motion video to the world. In addition to providing these simple Web services, IIS provides ftp hosting services and a Gopher server, and it can link to a back-end database server to provide dynamic information as required. IIS also includes support for the Secure Sockets Layer (SSL) when a secure, encrypted connection is required.

The demand-based publishing technology that makes the Internet and World Wide Web such powerful and easy-to-use tools provides the same features and interface for internal corporate data in an *intra*net as opposed to an *inter*net. Here, the tight integration of IIS with Windows NT Server provides an even more powerful tool than a traditional network, with easy links to Microsoft SQL Server and full Microsoft Windows NT security.

## For More Information

*See Chapter 4, "Security Planning," for additional information on Windows NT security.*

When you use IIS as both an Internet and intranet server, you can perform a variety of tasks. For example:

◆ Publish a Web *home page* that provides current information about your department to the rest of the company, or information about your company to the rest of the world.

- Run a business, take orders, and create an online catalog.

- Create client/server applications that provide real-time information about current production numbers to other departments.

- Create a repository of up-to-date files that enable customers to download patches, updates, or even complete software programs using the ftp server.

- Publish older, plain-text documents from a variety of sources using the Gopher server.

# IIS Installation

You were offered the choice of installing IIS when you initially installed Windows NT Server. If you opted to do so, by all means skip ahead to the section "IIS as an Intranet Server." However, if you didn't install IIS then, you can do it easily now. You'll need to have TCP/IP configured before you begin the IIS installation, of course, but you should have that all taken care of by now. If not, see Chapter 7 and Chapter 17 for detailed information on configuring TCP/IP.

There is one important security matter to consider before you start the installation. You probably should install the home directories for the various services on an NTFS volume. The security of a FAT volume just isn't sufficient for running this sort of access, even on an entirely internal network. In addition, if you'll be using IIS as an external Internet server that is connected directly to the Internet, we strongly advise you to provide an additional layer (or layers) of security or a firewall between the server and your internal network.

When you installed Windows NT Server initially, an icon was added to the Administrator's desktop for running the IIS installation program. Double-click this icon to begin the installation. (You also can run the installation program from the Add/Remove Programs application in Control Panel.) Whichever way you decide to run the installation, you'll be presented (as shown in Figure 19.1 on the following page) with a list of components to install:

- **Internet Service Manager** The administrative tool for managing your IIS server

- **World Wide Web Service** The main Web server program

- **WWW Service Samples** Sample HTML, database, and ActiveX files

- **Internet Service Manager (HTML)** An HTML version of the administrative tools

- **Gopher Service** A publishing server that supports the hierarchical, distributed, text-based, Gopher service

- **ftp Service** A publishing server that supports the distribution of files using ftp

- **ODBC Drivers and Administration** Open Database Connectivity drivers that support connection to a database

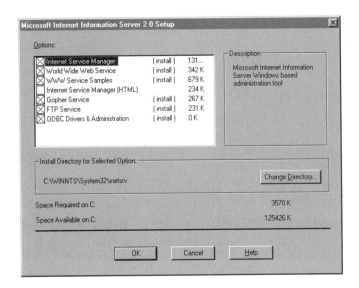

**FIGURE 19.1**

*The Internet Information Server installation screen*

## NOTE

*If you have already installed Microsoft SQL Server 6.5, do not use the IIS ODBC SQL Server drivers. The drivers that ship with SQL Server 6.5 are more recent. If you do install the ODBC SQL Server drivers that ship with IIS, you can reinstall the ODBC SQL Server drivers that ship with Microsoft SQL Server 6.5.*

By default, the HTML version of the administrative tool set is not installed. If you will be administering your server remotely, you might find the HTML version of Internet Service Manager a useful tool. Otherwise, you'll probably find it preferable to use the native Windows tools.

The default directory for IIS is %SYSTEMROOT%\SYSTEM32\INETSRV, although the default for the actual publishing services is under \INETPUB on the system drive. If you want to run your IIS installation in its own disk volume, now's the time to install it on its own disk volume. We tend to favor leaving the IIS program files in the default directory and then installing the actual publishing services on their own disk volume, where this is possible. Separating the IIS program files and the publishing services makes it easy to segregate the publishing services from the rest of your server's functions. However, if the sole function of the server is to act as your Web server, you might as well stick to the default directories.

Select the options you need, and click OK. The dialog box shown in Figure 19.2 will appear. From here, you can select the root directories for the various publishing services. Spend a few moments now thinking about where you want to install the root directories because it can be a nuisance to move the publishing services later.

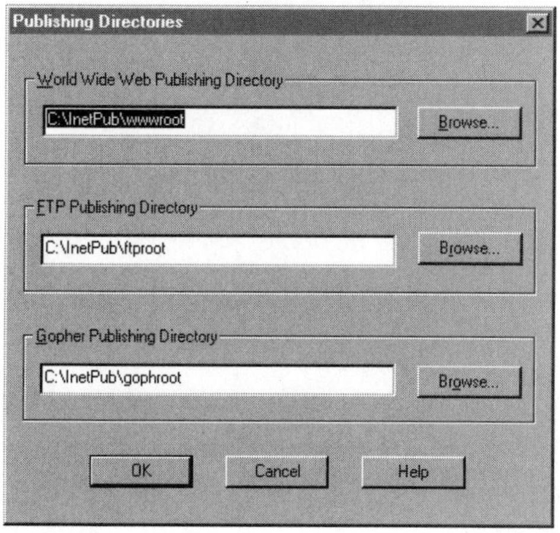

**FIGURE 19.2**

*IIS publishing service root directories*

After you have selected the location for your root directories, click OK to do the actual installation. The program will ask you whether you want to create new directories if they don't already exist. Click Yes to create them. The installation program will install the services you have selected and start them up. If you select ODBC Drivers and Administration, the program will prompt you for the available ODBC drivers. By default, the only OBDC driver is the one for SQL Server. If you've already installed SQL Server 6.5, do *not* install the IIS ODBC SQL Server driver; use the ODBC driver that ships with SQL Server 6.5.

The final step in the installation process is to test the server. From another computer on your network, start Internet Explorer and connect to the server you just set up. Because this is an internal network connection, you can shortcut the process by typing the name of the computer on which you just installed IIS in the address text box as shown in Figure 19.3 on the following page.

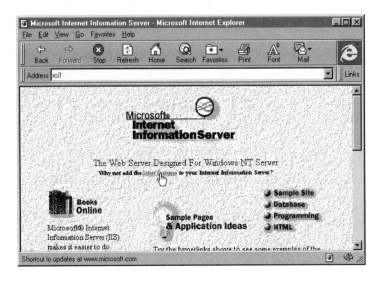

**FIGURE 19.3**

*Using the short version of the URL on an intranet*

**Tip**

*By default, IIS supports NetBIOS names as a shortcut for the home page of servers on an intranet. The full version of the URL (pronounced "earl"), however, would be*

http://<*fully qualified domain name*>

If you have a problem connecting to the server, try using the server's IP address instead of its name. This will narrow down the source of the problem; if you can connect with the server IP address but not with the server name, you will have to troubleshoot your name resolution subsystem. Start at the WINS server. If that appears to be OK, check the DNS server.

# IIS as an Intranet Server

The term *intranet* is relatively new and means the interconnected computers within an organization, regardless of operating systems, physical connection type, and so forth. This may be a simple Windows NT network with a half dozen workstations all connected together and all running the same operating system or a complex, world-wide enterprise network that runs a wide variety of operating systems connected via a variety of permanent, semipermanent, and intermittent networks using a variety of network protocols.

What distinguishes an intranet from the Internet is that the computers on an intranet are all part of a single organization. Furthermore, we generally assume that they are logically or physically isolated from the Internet. This isolation can be purely physical, with no portion of the network actually connected to the Internet—clearly the safest way to isolate your internal network, or the isolation can be a "logical" isolation—a firewall of some sort that permits legitimate use of the Internet from within the organization but shields the internal network from unauthorized external users.

As more and more organizations and corporate users experience the power and ease of use of the Internet, there is more pressure to leverage these same technologies to create an intranet within the organization. An intranet can provide an effective and efficient communication tool within an organization. Because it is a purely demand-based method of communication, it keeps network traffic to a minimum. Only those users who actually need a particular piece of information will download it and, then, only when they need it. The alternative—a traditional push system of updating files, memos, and information—requires that everyone who might possibly need a particular piece of information must get it sent to them, which is a much less efficient use of network resources.

IIS is ideally suited as an intranet server for two reasons:

◆    It supports a variety of protocols and programming languages.

◆    It takes advantage of the native Windows NT security features, which allow you to control access to sensitive areas of information easily at the same time you make the information readily available to those who need it.


IIS supports the ActiveX standard created by Microsoft. (Microsoft intends to transfer the standard to an independent group.) ActiveX allows software components to interact with client computers from a variety of operating systems without regard to the language or the operating system with which the object was created. ActiveX components can be:

◆    **Controls** Software components that run Web pages and provide interactive and user-controlled functions. ActiveX controls allow users to view animation, audio, and video without opening separate programs.

◆    **Scripting** A standard that provides a generic way for clients to execute scripts written in any scripting language, such as Visual Basic Script and Javascript.

◆    **Documents** An extension of OLE compound documents that supports using Web documents to open programs. It allows you to use non-HTML documents such as Excel or Word documents from within a Web browser such as Internet Explorer.

IIS also supports the Internet Server Application Programming Interface (ISAPI), which provide for significantly faster and more versatile connections than the Common Gateway Interface (CGI).

## ftp Service

Ftp service provides a platform-independent way of transfering files between computers. There are ftp servers and ftp clients available for virtually every operating system and hardware platform made in the last 20 years. IIS supports both anonymous ftp and traditional ftp, although it has a strong preference for anonymous ftp—and with cause. One of the problems with traditional, account-based (or user-based) ftp is that it requires you to send your password *unencrypted*. This is a "bad thing," obviously, although it might be perfectly acceptable in an intranet situation.

Anonymous ftp, on the other hand, assumes that everyone should have access to the files and that no user password information is actually passed. Modern Web browsers, such as Internet Explorer and Netscape Navigator, allow you to connect directly to an anonymous ftp server just as if it were another Web page. With IIS, all you have to do to make files available for downloading is place them in the FTPROOT directory. Figure 19.4 shows a simple example of a connection to an intranet ftp site using Internet Explorer and IIS. Type the URL in the text box in the form of ftp://<servername>, and you're in business. Any files in the directory become visible and available for downloading simply by clicking them. Meanwhile, Windows NT Server protects the rest of your server's file system by hiding any directories above the FTPROOT directory, masking them from prying eyes.

IIS also can be configured to permit uploads. The default is to have this set to "off," but you can change this by running Internet Service Manager and double-clicking the ftp server you want to change. Click the Directories tab to bring up the dialog box shown in Figure 19.5.

From here, it's easy to set a directory to allow uploads as well as downloads. It's a good idea to create a special directory for uploads separate from the regular download directory. Files are allowed to be uploaded only to this directory and are checked carefully for viruses and other problems before being made available to the rest of the network.

To make an upload directory, click Add and type the name of the directory in the Directory text box. If you haven't already created the directory, click Browse to locate where you want to put it and type the name of the directory in the New Directory Name text box. After you've added the directory, all you have to do is give the directory Write permission. For added security, you should remove the Read permission from the directory; this makes it impossible for users to see what's in the directory but they can still upload files to the directory. This configuration is

**FIGURE 19.4**

*Example of a connection to an ftp server*

**FIGURE 19.5**

*Using Internet Service Manager to set ftp directories*

shown in Figure 19.6, where we've created a special "incoming" directory for users uploading files to our server. The files in this directory cannot be seen because the Read permission isn't set, but users can upload files to it. The administrator then can check any uploads carefully before moving them into public view.

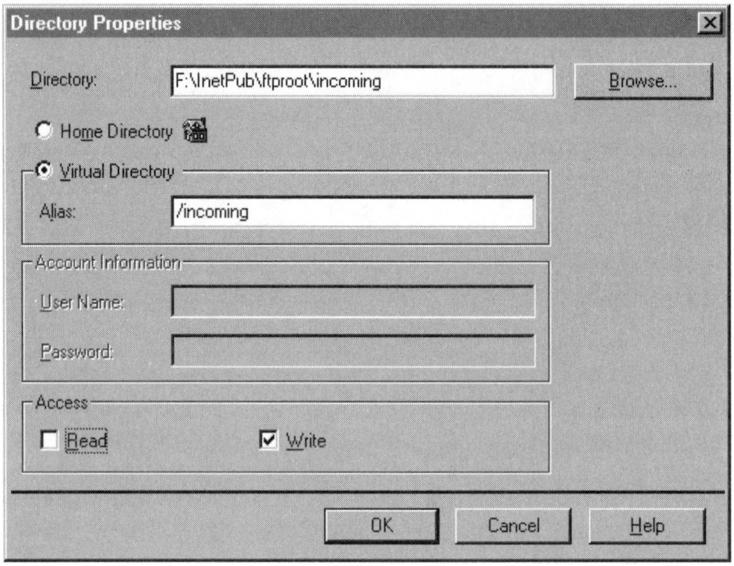

**FIGURE 19.6**

*Example of an an upload-only directory for the ftp server*

## Gopher Service

Gopher service is an older, text-only service that allows you to create a hierarchical, distributed database of text files that can be searched, viewed, and downloaded, without having to worry about where the files are located. It has been, in many ways, supplanted by the World Wide Web service; but it still has merit when you are searching, viewing, or downloading large amounts of text documentation that would be cumbersome to convert to HTML format. The federal government, for example, runs a number of Gopher servers. Other sources of useful Gopher documents are academic institutions. For a quick look at the breadth of information available for Gopher clients, open the URL:

http://galaxy.tradewave.com/GJ

This is a repository of some of the jewels of the "gopherspace," as the collection of interconnected Gopher servers is known.

# Internet Service Manager

Microsoft Internet Service Manager allows the management of remote servers over the Internet and provides a graphical means of displaying all IIS servers on your network. You can run Internet Service Manager from any computer connected through a network to your server—the IIS server, any workstation on the network, a remote location through RAS, or even a computer on the Internet. As a security measure, Windows NT Server grants only administrators the rights to run these administrative services.

To find all of the computers running IIS on your network, choose Find All Services from the Properties menu. To gain access to a single server, choose Connect To Server from the Properties menu.

You are able to configure the view of the information you are requesting by choosing the option you want from the View menu. These are the three available View options (the figures mentioned are on the following page):

◆ Report view (Figure 19.7)

◆ Service Type view (Figure 19.8)

◆ Server view (Figure 19.9)

From this administrative utility, you can control the services offered over the computer running IIS by pausing, stopping, and starting ftp, Gopher, and World Wide Web services. Internet Service Manager also permits you, as the administrator, to monitor sessions that are in progress, which makes it a great tool for monitoring the activity of end users who attempt to gain access to restricted areas of the network. In addition, you can generate daily logs to report activity on the network. The option is activated in the dialog box shown in Figure 19.10 on page 413. (To open this dialog box, click the service, and then click the Properties button.)

The logs generated by Internet Service Manager can be integrated into a SQL database. Every time an IIS service is accessed a log entry is recorded. Log entries contain the following information:

◆ Client IP address

◆ Client user name

◆ Date

◆ Time

◆ Service

◆ Computer name

**FIGURE 19.7**

*Internet Service Manager Report view*

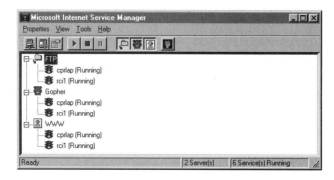

**FIGURE 19.8**

*Internet Service Manager Service Type view*

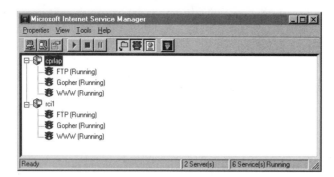

**FIGURE 19.9**

*Internet Service Manager Server view*

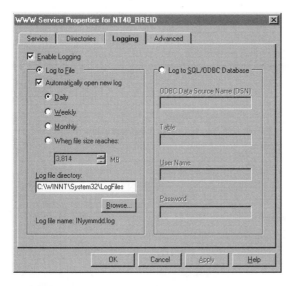

**FIGURE 19.10**

*Dialog box for configuring the use of logs to monitor Internet services*

- IP server address

- Processing time (ms)

- Bytes received

- Bytes sent

- Service status code

- Windows NT status code

- Name of operation

- Target of operation

Internet Service Manager also permits you to set up virtual directories. To the end user, files appear to be in the actual root directory where users would expect to find World Wide Web and ftp files. But in reality, these files can be located anywhere on the LAN. You use an alias to locate your files on any server in your system. Because the files are read-only, a department can maintain the security and accuracy of its documents by storing them on their own secure server and by sharing only the files with IIS. Figure 19.11 on the following page shows the dialog box that permits you to configure virtual directories on your network.

**FIGURE 19.11**

*Example of dialog box showing configuration of virtual directories in Internet Service Manager*

# Index Server: The Microsoft Search Engine

One of the key skills a user must develop is the ability to find items on the Internet. The easiest method of locating documents, addresses, and other information is to use one of the search engines that are available on the Internet. Two of the most popular and powerful of these are Yahoo and Digital's Alta Vista (Figure 19.12).

Microsoft Index Server is the search engine for IIS. Working in the background, Index Server automatically indexes the full text and properties of files on IIS. The operations performed by Index Server are automatic and have been designed in such a fashion as to not require maintenance once Index Server has been activated. It will automatically create indexes and then update them when you add new documents and Web pages to IIS. Another built-in feature is the automatic recovery of indexes that might be damaged if the power fails.

An additional feature of Index Server is language support, which allows end users to query documents in seven different languages. Documents written in Dutch, U.S. English, International English, French, German, Italian, Spanish, and Swedish can be searched by Index Server.

The search engine comes with a number of sample query forms that you can publish on your main search page. In addition, administrators have the ability to design

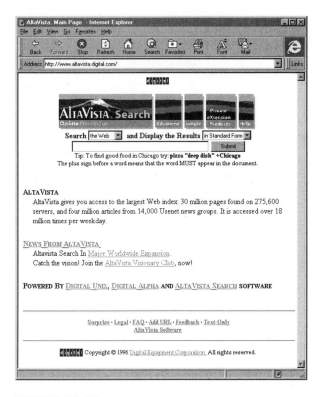

**FIGURE 19.12**

*The Alta Vista main page*

customized forms that allow the end user to set the conditions of his or her search. Figure 19.13 on the following page and Figure 19.14 on page 417 are two of the sample forms that are included with Index Server.

The search engine should be an integral part of your IIS; it's a service to those who have access to your Web server from the outside. It's an even more important service for users on an intranet because it allows them to search every document on the IIS for a particular phrase in a Word document, a statistical result in an Excel document, or any document that uses the corporate graphical image.

The search engine can run on the same computer as IIS. The only issues are making sure that there is additional hard drive space available for the indexes and additional RAM available to run all of the Windows NT utilities. For hard drive space, you should consider having about 250 MB free for indexes; for RAM, consider adding an additional 16 MB to run Index Server in the background with no loss of performance on your IIS.

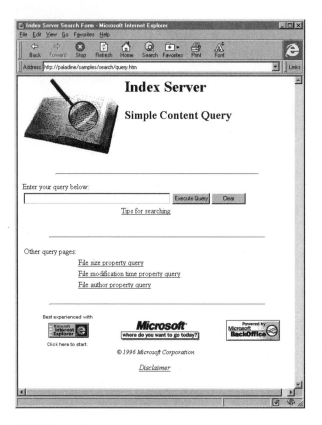

**FIGURE 19.13**

*Default text query form for Index Server*

The query tool in Index Server is extremely powerful. It can perform Boolean and Near Operator keyword searches in addition to standard text searches, which would place a word or words between double quotes (for example, "Microsoft BackOffice"). One of the more useful features of the search engine is that you can use wildcards. For example, if you set the criteria as comput*, the result of the search will include all pages and documents that have the prefix *comput*, such as "computer," "computation," "computing," and so forth. Another example of using the wildcard is to enter *blow**, which would yield pages that have words based on the same root as "blow," such as "blowing," "blown," "blew," and so forth.

Property value queries can be used to find the files that have property values that match the given criteria. The properties you can query include basic file information, such as the following:

◆ Filename

◆ File size

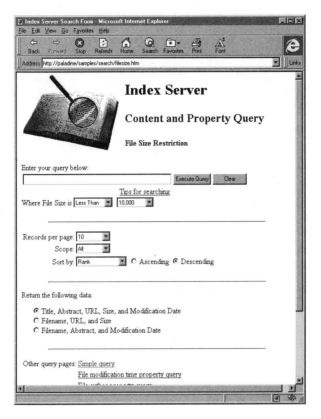

**FIGURE 19.14**

*Default properties query form for Index Server*

◆ ActiveX properties, including the document summary that is stored in files created by ActiveX-aware applications

There are two types of property queries: relational queries and regular expression queries. Relational property queries consist of an "at" character (@), a property name, a relational operator, and a property value. For example, to find all files larger than one million bytes, issue the query *@size > 1000000*. Regular expression property queries consist of a number sign (#), a property name, and a regular expression for the property value. For example, to find all .GIF files, you can issue the query *#filename *.gif*.

Table 19.1, beginning on the following page, is a list of the 40 property fields that can be queried with Index Server.

## Table 19.1
## Property Fields That Can Be Queried in Index Server

| Property Name | Description |
| --- | --- |
| Access | Last time the file was accessed |
| All | Everything |
| AllocSize | Size of disk allocation for the file |
| Attrib | File attributes |
| ClassId | Class ID of object |
| Change | Last time the file was changed |
| Characterization | Characterization/abstract of document (computed by Index Server) |
| Contents | Main contents of the file |
| Create | Time the file was created |
| DocAppName | Name of application owning the file |
| DocAuthor | Author of the document |
| DocCharCount | Number of characters in the document |
| DocComments | Comments about the document |
| DocCreatedTm | Time the document was created |
| DocEditTime | Total time spent editing the document |
| DocKeywords | Document key words |
| DocLastAuthor | Most recent user who edited the document |
| DocLastPrinted | Time the document was last printed |
| DocLastSavedTm | Time the document was last saved |
| DocPageCount | Number of pages in the document |
| DocRevNumber | Current version number of the document |
| DocSubject | Subject of the document |
| DocTemplate | Name of the template for the document |
| DocTitle | Title of the document |
| DocWordCount | Number of words in the document |
| FileIndex | Unique ID of the file |
| FileName | Name of the file |
| HitCount | Number of hits (words matching query) in the file |
| HtmlHRef | Text of HTML HREF |
| Path | Full physical path to file, including the filename |

| Property Name | Description |
| --- | --- |
| Rank | Rank of row (0 through 1000)—the larger the number, the better the match |
| SecurityChange | Last time security was changed on the file |
| ShortFileName | Short (8.3) filename |
| Size | Size of the file, in bytes |
| USN | Update sequence number (NTFS drives only) |
| Vpath | Full virtual path to the file, including the filename |
| Write | Last time the file was written |

# FrontPage: The HTML Design Tool

Microsoft FrontPage version 1 eliminates the need to know HTML, which makes designing and publishing Web pages easier than ever before. FrontPage consists of three components; the first two make up the client portion and the third is the server portion of the program suite.

◆ **FrontPage Explorer** A Web creation and management tool. This tool allows the Web designer to link pages and verify hyperlinks within a web. The Web designer can work from one of three views: link (Figure 19.15), outline, and summary (Figure 19.16 on the following page).

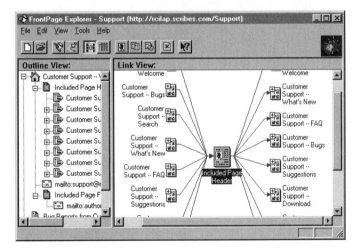

**FIGURE 19.15**

*Link View of FrontPage Explorer*

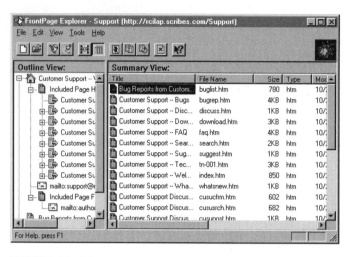

**FIGURE 19.16**

*Summary View of FrontPage Explorer*

◆ **FrontPage Editor** The WYSIWYG editing tool for writing HTML pages and forms (Figure 19.17). It's easy to design Web pages using clickable imagemaps, drag-and-drop creation of hyperlinks, and some simple typing of key text. Interactive functions can be added to a Web page using the WebBots (predefined tools, searches, and forms). FrontPage Editor includes an automatic document conversion tool that reads and automatically converts Rich Text Format (.RTF) and ASCII (.TXT) files to the necessary HTML format. Images in RTF files are converted to .GIF format. The inclusion of wizards and templates makes it easy to create Web pages.

◆ **The FrontPage Server** A basic, personal Web server that enables you to test your Web pages quickly and make them available to others (Figure 19.18). It includes extensions that add support for FrontPage-created pages to other servers.

The first page on your intranet Web site is likely to be a "Welcome" page that serves as a jumping-off point to other pages or to other departmental Web sites. It requires little training or experience to become a seasoned Webmaster if you use the tools provided in FrontPage. To design an intranet Web page, follow these steps:

1. Using FrontPage Explorer, create a new Web site by selecting one of the predesigned formats and providing the necessary information, such as the IP address and host name for the Web server, the name of the Web site, the name of the Web administrator, and, most important, the administrator's password.

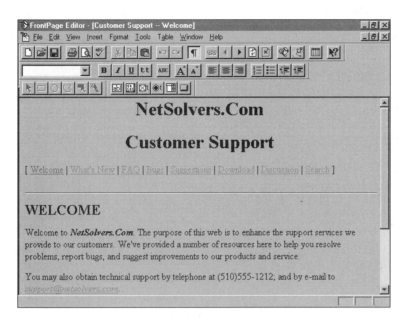

**FIGURE 19.17**

*FrontPage editor for creating a Web page*

**FIGURE 19.18**

*FrontPage Web server main page*

2. Verify the associations of the created pages with the Link and Summary views (Figure 19.15 and Figure 19.16).

3. Launch FrontPage Editor (Figure 19.19 on the following page), and fill in the areas where personal data and corporate data are identified.

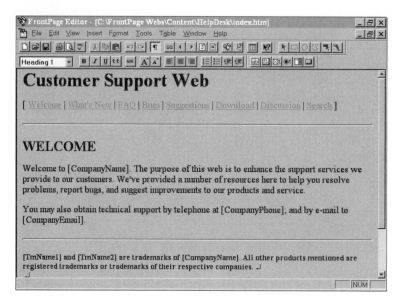

**FIGURE 19.19**

*FrontPage editor for creating a Web page*

4. Add appropriate graphic images, and select a background. If the white background of your images is too bold, you can make it transparent so that only the color scheme of the page background shows through. Click Make Transparent on the image toolbar; after the cursor changes to an eraser, click the white background of the image.

5. After you have saved your Web page, test it using the Web browser. Remember to start the Personal Web Server before you attempt to view your Web site.

6. After reviewing your Web site, you might want to add new pages and links. Additional pages can be created easily using FrontPage Editor; links between two pages can be established by using the Link view in Explorer. Click the new page, drag it to the page to which you wish to establish a link, and release the mouse button.

7. To enhance your Web page, you might want to define a clickable image. On the image toolbar, click the rectangle button to create a rectangular "hotspot" on your image. Holding the left mouse button down, complete the drawing of a rectangle on your image. When the mouse button is released, a Create Link dialog box will appear, in which you provide the requested information to complete the link.

8. To test your Web site, use your Web browser by supplying its URL.

# Internet Explorer:
# The Document Viewer and Locator

Internet Explorer (Figure 19.20) is a Web browser or, more specifically, a tool for exploring and for retrieving information on the Internet or on the corporate intranet. It provides a series of tools for finding, retrieving, and returning to materials on the World Wide Web that make these other activities as easy as opening a document on a diskette.

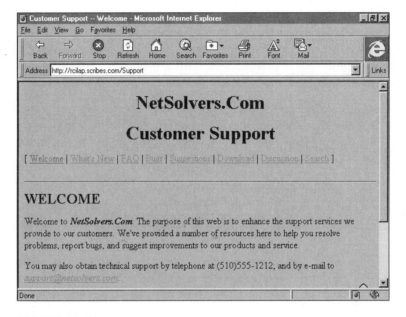

**FIGURE 19.20**

*The Internet Explorer tool main page*

As for any application, there is a set of rules (a syntax) that must be followed to use the program effectively. In Excel, if you use the wrong formula, you will get the wrong answer. The same is true for Internet Explorer; if you use the wrong syntax or wrong URL, you will never get where you want to go on the Internet or on the intranet.

URL syntax is a specific sequence—protocol, domain name, and path to the re-quested information. The protocol is the application that is used to gain access to information (for example, Hypertext Transport Protocol, commonly known as HTTP). Domain name is the name registered in the DNS. The path is the path on the server. The following list contains examples of URL syntax.

| Protocol | Domain Name | Path to Information |
|---|---|---|
| http:// | www.microsoft.com | /windowsnt |
| https:// (secure HTTP) | www.company.com | /products/orderform.htm |
| gopher:// | gopher.college.edu | /library/religion/index.htm |
| ftp:// | ftp.microsoft.com | /bussys/winnt/winnt-public/reskit |

Just as Word documents use the convention *FILENAME.DOC*, and programs use the convention *PROGRAMNAME.EXE*, the path to information determines whether the request is for a static HTML page, for a dynamic HTML page, or for a directory listing. Sometimes the path includes parameters or data that IIS will process before showing a dynamic page. Examples of request types are listed here:

| Type of Request | URL |
|---|---|
| Static HTML page | http://www.microsoft.com/backoffice/home.htm |
| ISAPI application | http://www.msn.com/custom/page1.dll?CUST=on |
| Internet database connector | http://www.microsoft.com/feedback/input.idc |
| CGI script | http://www.company.com/calculator/add.pl?2.2 |
| Directory listing | ftp://ftp.microsoft.com/bussys/winnt/winnt-public/reskit |

In all cases, the server replies with either an HTML page or an error message. If it replies with an error message, it might be that the server is down or that the requested URL cannot be found (which probably means that the URL has changed).

There are several important new features included with Windows NT version 4 and the Windows 95 version of Internet Explorer version 3:

◆ You can browse the Internet in safety and confidence. Internet Explorer provides support for Internet security to protect your privacy and your data.

◆ You can use Internet Explorer to read Internet newsgroups and to post newsgroup messages of your own.

◆ Performance improvements have made browsing the Internet faster. In addition, you can speed up the display of pages even more by turning off graphics, sounds, and animation.

◆ You can send an Internet shortcut using E-mail. When you choose Send To from the File menu and choose Mail Recipient from the resulting menu,

Internet Explorer opens your current E-mail program and pastes a shortcut to the current page into an E-mail message.

♦ It's much easier to return to your favorite Internet search page—just click the Search button on the toolbar. You can specify any page you want as your search page.

♦ You can choose what fonts will be used to display pages.

♦ The pop-up menu you see when you right-click a link contains the new command Save Target As, which enables you to download the page or picture indicated by the link without opening the item first.

♦ You can see the properties for the current page, the current item, and any links on a page. (To see the properties for an item, right-click it; then choose Properties from the pop-up menu.)

♦ Internet Explorer provides several new HTML authoring features, including the ability to add tables, sounds, video, or text marquees to a page.

## POINTS TO REMEMBER

♦ Is your network secure? If not, now is the time to develop a comprehensive security program for your network—before it is exposed to the world.

♦ Do your research first. Be sure you have all of your IP addresses and other related material ready before you begin the configuration process for IIS. Don't forget to order your registered domain name before going online.

♦ Make sure your network is working properly before you start this project. Verify the installation and the location of key components such as the SQL Server.

♦ Decide what network services you want to offer.

♦ Design some HTML pages before you implement IIS so that you have something ready to test and make available as soon as you are online.

## WHAT'S NEXT?

There's one last area to be covered in this section on enterprise solutions, and that's the integration of Novell NetWare and Apple Macintosh services with your Windows NT network. This is covered in Chapter 20, where we discuss coexisting (gracefully) with other network operating systems in the enterprise.

# CHAPTER 20

coexisting in the Enterprise

# CHAPTER 20

# Coexisting in the Enterprise

Once upon a time, and not so very long ago, network operating systems from different vendors would not even acknowledge each others' presence. True, they often would share the same cable plant, but each would see only its own resources without any way to share them with users of different network operating systems.

Today, things have changed so much that the dilemma isn't how to achieve interaction among the networks but how to choose from the many methods available to use! In this chapter, we'll explore the various ways your Microsoft Windows NT network can share its resources with Novell NetWare clients and make NetWare's resources available to the Windows NT clients, while making the process of sharing so simple it's virtually transparent to your users. We'll also look at the Windows NT Migration Tool for NetWare, which allows you to move easily from a NetWare network operating system (NOS) to a Windows NT NOS. In addition, we'll see how Apple Macintosh clients can be integrated easily into the Windows NT network.

## Services for Novell NetWare

In the following sections, we'll discuss the services for NetWare that are provided in Microsoft Windows NT Server version 4.

### Single-Point Logon

Directory Services Manager for NetWare (DSMN) allows you to synchronize user accounts from NetWare 2.*x* and NetWare 3.*x* servers into your Windows NT domain. DSMN extends directory service features for user and group account management from Microsoft Windows NT Server version 4 to NetWare servers. Then you can manage user and group accounts centrally when users have access to both servers running Windows NT Server and servers running NetWare. Each user has just one password for all servers to which he or she has access, regardless of which network operating system is being run on them; this password stays synchronized for all servers. No changes need to be made to the NetWare servers, although Novell's NETSYNC program must be removed if it is being run on them.

This is a selective process; you can move all users and groups or just a subset of users and groups from NetWare to Windows NT. Likewise, you can move all or just a subset of your Windows NT users and groups back to a NetWare server. This way, you can control access to all of the resources of the merged networks, which simplifies security procedures.

## Synchronization Manager

Synchronization Manager is the program you'll use to administer Directory Services Manager for NetWare. The Title bar shows your Windows NT logon domain. In the body of the window are listed the NetWare servers within the domain. An icon indicates whether a server is currently synchronized; the Description column lists the type, version number, and user count limit for each NetWare server.

## Adding a NetWare server to the domain

Before you add a NetWare server to a domain, you should back up the NetWare server's Bindery (using the Novell utility Bindfix) and decide which users will be synchronized between NetWare and Windows NT. Then proceed as follows:

1. Choose Add Server To Manage from Synchronization Manager's NetWare Server menu. Enter the name of the server, or select from the list; then click OK.

2. Enter the user name and password of the NetWare Supervisor, or a Supervisor-Equivalent user, and then click OK.

3. If you want to put all users and groups under Windows NT administration, choose Use Mapping File. Otherwise, pick Ignore Mapping File and specify the users and groups in the dialog box.

4. Do a Trial Run, which simulates the actions and produces a report without actually changing anything. This will point out any problems that should be overcome before continuing. Once that's done, click OK To Add Server.

5. At this point, be very careful which boxes you check so that you don't inadvertently change something you didn't want to change. In the Set Propagated Accounts On Server dialog box, you can determine which Windows NT accounts will be propagated back to the NetWare server. Select All if you want all users and groups propagated; otherwise, select the specific users and groups you want to propagate. If you want to keep some accounts as NetWare only, choose No in the delete accounts dialog box; otherwise, the accounts that were not moved to the Windows NT domain will be deleted.

## Synchronizing servers

NetWare servers are kept synchronized with the domain automatically, but it doesn't happen instantaneously. There might be times when it is necessary to force an immediate synchronization, such as when a user must be added or deleted immediately or when a server has been offline. On Synchronization Manager's NetWare Server menu, there are four choices for forcing synchronization.

The choices are as follows:

◆ **Synchronize Selected Server** Sends updated account information to the selected NetWare server; only account updates that have not yet been received by the NetWare server are sent.

◆ **Synchronize All Servers** Sends updated account information to all NetWare servers in the domain; each server receives only the account updates it needs.

◆ **Fully Synchronize Selected Server** Sends complete account information about all propagated accounts to the selected NetWare server; this command is used only when a server is extremely unsynchronized with the domain's directory.

◆ **Fully Synchronize All Servers** Sends complete account information about all propagated accounts to all NetWare servers in the domain; this command is used only when several NetWare servers are extremely unsynchronized with the domain's directory.

Other options on the NetWare Server menu allow you to choose when and where the Account Synchronization Database is backed up. You now can use User Manager to manage all of the NetWare and Windows NT synchronized users.

### For More Information

*See Chapter 9 and Chapter 10 for information about managing users and groups.*

Note that DSMN is an administrator's tool. Although it eases the administration of users and groups on your mixed network, it doesn't institute resource sharing by users. Let's look at what is needed to allow resource sharing.

## Using NetWare Resources

At the beginning of this chapter, we mentioned that there were several ways to achieve interaction between NetWare and Windows NT clients and servers. Nowhere is this more apparent than in the choices available for allowing Windows NT clients to use NetWare resources. Novell provides NetWare client software for MS-DOS, Microsoft Windows 3.x, Microsoft Windows for Workgroups, Microsoft Windows 95, and Microsoft Windows NT Workstation clients. Microsoft also provides NetWare client software for Windows 95 and Windows NT Workstation. By choosing to install one of these in addition to the Windows NT Server client software, a computer can be a client of both Windows NT Server and NetWare simultaneously. In addition, Windows NT clients can have access to NetWare server disks through NetWare gateway services installed on a Windows NT server.

Each of these methods has its good and bad points; which method you decide to use—or whether you decide to use a combination of two of them—will depend on the structure of your organization, the security model you are using, and the amount of time available for installation and maintenance.

## Novell client services

Novell provides three different forms of client services:

- **NETX** A 16-bit, real-mode network shell that sits on top of MS-DOS.

- **VLM** A 16-bit, real-mode MS-DOS redirector (for MS-DOS, Windows 3.*x*, and Windows 95).

- **Client32** A 32-bit, protected-mode client currently available for MS-DOS, Windows 3.*x*, and Windows 95.

The Novell redirector for Windows NT Workstation is similar to the VLM client. Novell has announced a version of Client32 for Windows NT for release in 1997.

Using these clients in conjunction with the necessary Windows NT client ensures full compatibility with NetWare, its utilities, and third-party applications written to the NetWare application programming interface. The downside is twofold: real-mode clients are inherently unstable in a protected-mode, multitasking environment; and the protected-mode client requires huge amounts of memory. In addition, configuring network cards can be tricky because the Novell real-mode clients want to see an IPX/SPX stack, while 32-bit clients want the newer Novell NetWare I/O System (NIOS) stack. It is possible to use the Windows NT Workstation NWLINK protocol or the Windows 95 IPX-compatible protocol, however.

### Tip

*Because it's possible to configure both NetWare and Windows NT Server clients to use the TCP/IP protocol, you might think this would be an easier choice. Unfortunately, the NetWare IP client is not compatible with the Microsoft TCP/IP stack, and vice versa. You can't have two TCP/IP stacks loaded at the same time, so there is no way to use TCP/IP to communicate with both servers.*

## Microsoft client services

Both Windows 95 and Windows NT Workstation version 4 ship with a Microsoft-provided client for NetWare that can be used to connect to NetWare 2.*x* or NetWare 3.*x* servers. Windows NT Workstation includes (and Windows 95 can add) the NetWare Directory Service to allow logging on to a NetWare 4.*x* server. Like the

Novell client, these would be loaded in addition to Windows NT Server client files for access to both networks. Microsoft clients are 32-bit, protected-mode clients and therefore more stable than Novell real-mode clients. In addition, they are far less memory-intensive because they share many of the same libraries needed by Windows NT Server client software, and they are better integrated with the protocols and drivers used by Windows NT Server clients. The drawback is that, although they support almost all published NetWare application programming interface calls, not all third-party NetWare applications will work properly if they use older nondocumented or rarely used Novell API calls.

## Gateway Service for NetWare

Both Microsoft and Novell clients must be installed on and configured for each client computer and user. This can be quite time-consuming in a large enterprise— or even in a medium-size one that has a small IS or computer operations staff. Ease of installation and maintenance is the strong point of this third method of access to NetWare resources.

Gateway Service for NetWare installs as a service on a Windows NT server. Computers without NetWare client software can connect to NetWare resources as if they were shared on a Windows NT Server computer. Administrators control which users can establish a gateway and the resources shared over the gateway. Users do not know that the resources are coming from NetWare because they use the familiar Windows NT networking commands and applications to gain access to them. The gateway translates the SMB (Server Message Block) Windows NT calls into NetWare NCP (NetWare Core Protocol) calls and forwards them to the NetWare server. It then receives the response, translates back to SMB, and replies to the client computer. In addition to being easy to set up and maintain, this service allows users at Windows NT workstations running non-Intel platforms access to NetWare resources—platforms for which Novell does not provide client services. Another benefit is that a large number of Windows NT Server clients can have access to the resources of a NetWare server that is licensed for a small number of users because there is only one connection to NetWare from the Windows NT server.

The major drawback to Gateway Service for NetWare is that it's harder to customize security on a user-by-user basis for NetWare resources. Each user profile must have a separate share set up on the gateway and, consequently, a separate drive letter, which limits the number of shares you can create. Because a Windows NT server must translate each request and response from SMB to NCP and back, access is noticeably slower if you use Gateway Service for NetWare rather than NetWare client software.

**Installation and configuration**   Installation of Gateway Service for NetWare could hardly be easier. Follow these steps:

1. Open Control Panel.

2. Double-click the NETWORK icon.

3. Click the Services tab. You'll see a dialog box similar to the one shown in Figure 20.1.

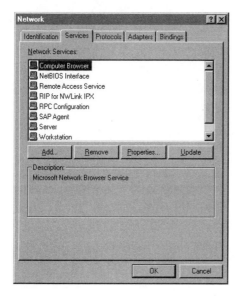

**FIGURE 20.1**

*Example of a Network dialog box Network Services list in Gateway Service for NetWare*

4. Click Add. After a moment, you'll see a list of additional available services. Select Gateway (and Client) Services for NetWare from the list, and then click OK.

That's it; it's installed. Of course, there's a little more work to do. Notice that Control Panel now includes a new icon called GSNW.

1. Double-click the GSNW icon to configure the gateway. The initial screen will look like the one in Figure 20.2 on the following page. Now specify the NetWare server that the Gateway Service will log on to.

2. Click the Default Tree And Context option button if the computer is a NetWare 4 server running Novell Directory Services; then type the tree name and context name in the respective text boxes.

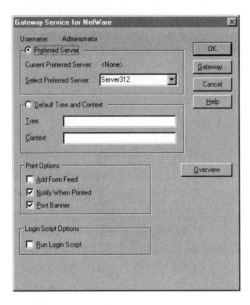

**FIGURE 20.2**

*Dialog box for configuring Gateway Service for NetWare*

**3.** If your server is a NetWare 3 server or if it is a NetWare 4 server running Bindery emulation and you want to connect in that context, click the Preferred Server option button. Select the NetWare server to which you will attach the service or type the name of the server in the combo box.

**4.** On the lower part of the screen, select the NetWare print options you want to use.

**5.** Click the Run Login Script check box if you want the NetWare logon script to run when Gateway Service first attaches to NetWare. Although most NetWare logon script commands have no effect on Gateway Service, you might use this logon script to capture information, run an application, or otherwise set up a NetWare environment for your clients.

**6.** If you now click Gateway, you can define one or more shares for your clients on the NetWare server, as shown in Figure 20.3. Note that everyone who has rights to Gateway Service will have access to any share you define and that each share also will take up one of the 26 available drive letters. You might need to reorganize the NetWare server directory structure to minimize the number of shares you need.

**NetWare server setup**   The NetWare administrator must create a user account and a group called NTGATEWAY for each gateway service. The user account must

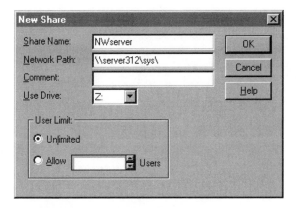

**FIGURE 20.3**

*Example of the dialog box for adding a share to Gateway Service for NetWare*

be a member of the NTGATEWAY group, and it must be granted access to the resources you want available to Windows NT clients. Therefore, to grant a Windows NT client access to a NetWare resource via Gateway Service for NetWare, the NetWare administrator must follow these steps:

1. Create a group called NTGATEWAY on the NetWare server.

2. Create a user for the gateway service being run; the user must be a member of the NTGATEWAY group for the service.

3. Assign rights for the resource to the user account for this service.

4. Create a share for the NetWare resource.

5. Grant the Windows NT user access to this shared resource.

## NetWare utilities

Most NetWare utilities will run on Windows NT workstations on which Gateway Service for NetWare has been installed. Consult the NetWare documentation for the specifics on the use of these utilities. The following MS-DOS–based utilities are known to work:

| | | | |
|---|---|---|---|
| chkvol | help | rconsole | settts |
| colorpal | listdir | remove | slist |
| dspace | map | revoke | syscon |
| flag | ncopy | rights | tlist |
| flagdir | ndir | security | userlist |
| fconsole | pconsole | send | volinfo |
| filer | psc | session | whoami |
| grant | pstat | setpass | |

The Windows NT command NET USE replaces the NetWare commands LOGIN, LOGOUT, ATTACH, and CAPTURE. Also, NET VIEW replaces NetWare's SLIST.

## NetWare-aware applications

Many NetWare-aware applications on Windows NT clients using Gateway Service for NetWare run as if they were running on a standard NetWare client. However, not all NetWare-aware applications are supported, and of those that are supported, many require special files supplied with either NetWare or Windows NT Server. The following files and services might be required for MS-DOS–based NetWare utilities and NetWare-aware applications if they are to be supported.

**NWIPXSPX.DLL**  Many applications written for 16-bit Windows that are NetWare-aware require NWIPXSPX.DLL from Novell. If you have used this application with another Windows-based operating system previously and are using the same computer for Windows NT, NWIPXSPX.DLL already exists on your system. If you start the application and it cannot find the file, use the Windows NT Find utility to search for the file on your hard drives. If you find the NWIPXSPX.DLL file, move it to the SYSTEM32 directory in your Windows NT directory. If you can't locate the NWIPXSPX.DLL file, obtain a copy from Novell and copy it to the SYSTEM32 directory in your Windows NT directory.

If you are running these applications on either the MIPS or Digital Alpha AXP platforms, you also will need NWIPXSPX.DLL. Copy the file to the SYSTEM32 directory in your Windows NT directory.

**Special requirements for MIPS and Alpha AXP platforms**  If a NetWare-aware application requires NWIPXSPX.DLL, you must have a copy of TBMI2.COM in the SYSTEM32 directory in your Windows NT directory to run the application on the MIPS and Digital Alpha AXP platforms.

1. In AUTOEXEC.NT, insert the following line immediately after the line that refers to vwipxspx:

   lh winnt\system32\tbmi2.com

2. Save the change to AUTOEXEC.NT, and then log off.

3. Log back on to your Windows NT Server computer.

**NETWARE.DRV, NWNETAPI.DLL, and NWCALLS.DLL**  NetWare-aware applications that use the NetWare API to send and receive NetWare core protocol (NCP) packets might require NETWARE.DRV and either NWNETAPI.DLL or, for more recent versions of NetWare, NWCALLS.DLL.NETWARE.DRV is installed in the SYSTEM32 directory in your Windows NT directory when you install Gateway

Service for NetWare. If you have previously used a NetWare-aware application with another Windows-based operating system on this computer, either NWNETAPI-.DLL or NWCALLS.DLL should already be installed on the computer.

If your application cannot find NWNETAPI.DLL or NWCALLS.DLL, make sure the appropriate file is installed on your computer and is in your computer's search path.

If you are running the application on a Digital Alpha AXP or MIPS platform or if you can't locate one of the .DLL files on your computer, contact Novell to obtain a copy of the appropriate file and then install it in the SYSTEM32 directory in your Windows NT directory.

If you aren't able to load the NetWare-aware application with the version of NETWARE.DRV that was installed with Gateway Service for NetWare, replace NETWARE.DRV with a corresponding file supplied by Novell (dated 10/27/92; file size = 126,144 bytes).

If you copied any of these files to your Windows NT server or if you modified the path statement during the current Windows NT work session, you must log off and then log back on for the changes to take effect.

## Which service should I use?

The first choice you have to make is whether you want client services or gateway service. If your choice is client services, you can choose either Novell client services or Microsoft client services. In some circumstances, it would be best to use a combination of gateway service and client services (again choosing either Novell or Microsoft clients). In Table 20.1 and Table 20.2, we have listed some, but by no means all, possible scenarios. It's very likely that your network will be a mixture of two or more of these scenarios, in which case you'll need to choose among or combine the solutions. Also factor in the number, workload, and expertise of your networking staff in your decision-making. Table 20.1 is a list of scenarios that are optimal either for client services or for gateway service; Table 20.2 is a list of scenarios that are optimal either with Microsoft clients or with Novell clients.

**Table 20.1**
**Client Services vs. Gateway Service**

| Scenario | Client Services | Gateway Service |
|---|---|---|
| Users' home directories are on a NetWare server. | X | |
| Users' home directories are on a Windows NT server. | | X |
| Applications are on a Windows NT server. | | X |
| Applications are on a NetWare server, but they can be used by all users. | | X |

*(continued)*

*Table 20.1* *continued*

| Scenario | Client Services | Gateway Service |
|---|---|---|
| Applications are on a NetWare server, but their use is restricted by user or by group. | X | |
| Users need access only to NetWare printers. | | X |
| Users need access only to files on a NetWare server that are shared among a large number of users. | | X |
| Users need access only to files on a NetWare server that are restricted by user or by group. | X | |
| Users are more familiar with NetWare utilities and commands than with those of Windows NT. | X | |
| Users are more familiar with Windows NT Server utilities and commands than with NetWare's utilities and commands. | X | |

## Table 20.2
## Microsoft Client Service vs. Novell Client Service

| Scenario | Microsoft Client Service | Novell Client Service |
|---|---|---|
| Client run on a non-Intel platform. | X | |
| Legacy NetWare-enabled applications are in use. | | X |
| Windows 95 peer services are in use. | X | |
| Microsoft File and Print Services for NetWare are in use. | X | |
| Client has a limited amount of RAM. | X | |

By looking at the combination of scenarios that exist in your organization, you should be able to decide on the best NetWare access solution for you. Let's look at another example to illustrate how client and gateway services can be mixed. If most of your users need access to NetWare printers and only a few small groups need access to files or applications on the NetWare server, you should install Gateway Service for the users who need printer access and then install client software for the few users who need file and application access.

# Sharing Resources with NetWare Clients

Now you need to look at access to resources from the opposite side of the coin: NetWare clients who want to use Windows NT server resources. As you learned in the preceding discussion, client services allow clients simultaneous access to NetWare and Windows NT resources. If you chose client services, there's nothing further you have to do now to share Windows NT resources with NetWare clients.

But if any of the following conditions apply, you should consider installing Microsoft's File and Print Servers for NetWare (FPNW):

◆ You are allowing users access to NetWare resources through Gateway Service for NetWare.

◆ Your Windows NT clients don't need access to NetWare resources.

◆ You're introducing a Windows NT server into a large, established NetWare network.

Although Microsoft chose not to distribute FPNW with Windows NT Server, it is available by purchasing the Microsoft Services for NetWare package, which includes Directory Service Manager for NetWare as well as FPNW. After you've installed FPNW on a Windows NT server, it looks just like a NetWare server to NetWare clients; no changes or additional software are required for them. The same NetWare utilities and commands can be used for access to resources on a Windows NT server that are used for access to resources on a NetWare server.

When you install FPNW, you create a SYSVOL directory, which can be located anywhere within the Windows NT server's directory tree. NetWare clients will see this as the root directory of the SYS: volume of the server. You can share other directory trees, hard drives, or CD-ROMs as additional volumes on the server. You also can limit the number of users who are allowed simultaneous access to any of these volumes.

## NOTE

*The volumes you create should be on an NTFS partition so that you can control file and directory permissions for the volumes and their contents.*

You will need to use User Manager for Domains to configure user accounts or add users who are to be allowed access to the volumes defined with FPNW; under the Maintain NetWare Compatible Login selection, you'll see that there are also other properties that can be defined for these users, including the following:

◆ Forced NetWare password expiration

◆ The number of Grace Logins (from 0 to "unlimited") allowed for users whose passwords have expired

◆ The number of concurrent connections to the server that the user can have

# Migration Tool for NetWare

It might be possible or desirable to move all of your NetWare-based users, files, and resources to Windows NT. If you're still running in Bindery mode, Microsoft's Migration Tool for NetWare makes this easy. If you convert your users and resources to Windows NT, you will simplify network administration and also save on support time and costs. Note that applications run as NetWare Loadable Modules (NLMs) cannot be migrated, although it might be possible to upgrade them to Windows NT Server–based applications or replace them with Windows NT Server–based applications that provide similar functionality—Novell GroupWise could be replaced by Microsoft Exchange Server, for example.

Using the migration tool to move NetWare users and resources makes it possible for you to do the following:

◆ Preserve most user account information.

◆ Control the transfer of user and group names.

◆ Set passwords for transferred accounts.

◆ Control the transfer of account restrictions and administrative rights.

◆ Select the folders and files to transfer.

◆ Select a destination for transferred folders and files.

◆ Preserve effective rights (the NetWare equivalent of permissions) on folders and files.

◆ Perform trial migrations to test how current settings will actually transfer information.

◆ Generate comprehensive log files that show in detail what happened during migration.

Although Migration Tool for NetWare can be run from any Windows NT server or workstation, you can migrate information only to a primary domain controller or backup domain controller. You also must be running the NWLINK protocol and Gateway Service for NetWare to migrate information. The protocol and service can, of course, be removed once the migration is complete. If you are more familiar with NetWare than with Windows NT, you should review Part One of this book before trying to migrate information to a Windows NT domain controller.

Table 20.3 and Table 20.4 on the following page show NetWare attributes, the Windows NT equivalents for these attributes, and the method of information transfer during migration for Windows NT servers with FPNW installed and for servers without FPNW.

**Table 20.3**
**Account Restrictions Transferred to a**
**Windows NT Server that Is Not Running FPNW**

| NetWare Account Restriction | Windows NT Equivalent (Without FPNW) | How Information Is Transferred |
|---|---|---|
| Expiration Date | Expiration Date | By individual user account |
| Account Disabled | Account Disabled | By individual user account |
| Limit Concurrent Connections | (None) | (Not transferred) |
| Require Password | Permit Blank Password | As policy for all accounts |
| Minimum Password Length | Minimum Password Length | As policy for all accounts |
| Force Periodic Password Changes | Password Never Expires | By individual user account |
| Days Between Forced Changes | Maximum Password Age | As policy for all accounts |
| Grace Logins | (None) | (Not transferred) |
| Allow User to Change Password | User Cannot Change Password | By individual user account |
| Require Unique Passwords | Password Uniqueness | As policy for all accounts |
| Station Restrictions | (None) | (Not transferred) |
| Time Restrictions | Logon Hours | By individual user account |
| Intruder Detection/ Lockout | Account Lockout | As policy for all accounts |
| User Disk Volume Restrictions | (None) | (Not transferred) |

**Table 20.4**

**The Additional Account Restrictions Transferred to a Windows NT Server that Is Running FPNW**

| NetWare Account Restriction | Windows NT Equivalent (with FPNW) | How Information Is Transferred |
|---|---|---|
| Limit Concurrent Connections | Limit Concurrent Connections | By individual user account |
| Grace Logins | Grace Logins | By individual user account |
| Station Restrictions | Station Restrictions | (Not transferred) |
| Login Scripts | Login Scripts | By individual user account |

We have noted here some important differences between the two operating systems for account restrictions migrated from NetWare to Windows NT Server:

♦ **Expiration Date** Both NetWare and Windows NT Server support expiration dates, after which an account cannot log on. Note that User Manager for Domains shows the last day an account is valid, and NetWare utilities show the first day the account is expired.

## NOTE

*NetWare accounts with expiration dates later than January 1, 2000, are given expiration dates of February 6, 2006, when migrated to Windows NT Server. Accounts with no expiration dates or with expiration dates of December 31, 1999, or earlier are not affected when they are migrated.*

♦ **Limit Concurrent Connections** NetWare supports limiting a user's concurrent network connections. Windows NT Server itself does not support this restriction, so this information is transferred only if the server to which information is being migrated runs FPNW.

♦ **Require Password** A password is not required on Windows NT Server when the account policy allows blank passwords.

♦ **Minimum Password Length** The NetWare default minimum is five characters; the Windows NT Server default is six characters.

◆ **Force Periodic Password Changes** The minimum interval at which a new password is required for an account. The NetWare default interval is 40 days; the Windows NT Server default is 42 days.

◆ **Grace Logins** The number of times a user can log on after his or her password has expired. Windows NT Server itself does not support this feature, so this information is transferred only if the server to which information is being migrated runs FPNW.

◆ **Require Unique Passwords** The number of different passwords required before the system allows the reuse of an old password. NetWare requires eight different passwords. The Windows NT Server default setting is five different passwords; the limit can be set from one to eight passwords.

◆ **Station Restrictions** The limit on the number of NetWare client computers from which a user can log on. The computers that a user can log on to are specified by their network and node addresses. Windows NT Server itself does not support this type of NetWare client restriction. FPNW provides a way for you to assign station restrictions to users, but existing station restrictions are not transferred by Migration Tool for NetWare. Windows NT Server supports a similar feature for restricting users to certain Microsoft client computers.

◆ **Time Restrictions** The limit on the hours during which a user can log on to the network. In NetWare, time restrictions are set in half-hour blocks; in Windows NT Server, they are set in one-hour blocks. When transferring time restrictions, the migration tool adjusts blocks set at the half hour to the whole hour. For example, if the NetWare restriction allows a user to log on between 7:30 A.M. and 7:30 P.M., the user will be able to log on between 7:00 P.M. and 8:00 P.M. on Windows NT Server.

◆ **Intruder Detection/Lockout** The limit on the number of unsuccessful logon attempts that are allowed before an account is locked for a specified amount of time. By default, NetWare allows seven attempts before locking the account; Windows NT Server (if intruder lockout is enabled) allows five attempts.

## Miscellaneous NetWare objects and restrictions

You also should be aware of the differences between NetWare and Windows NT Server operating systems with respect to individual and group account assignments; the differences are listed on the next page.

- **Supervisor account and Supervisor-equivalent accounts** On a computer running Windows NT Server, members of the Administrators group are functionally similar to a NetWare Supervisor. By default, when transferring user accounts, the migration tool does not add accounts that have Supervisor rights to the Administrators group. However, you can choose to do so.

- **Workgroup Manager and User Account Manager** Because user account administration is centralized on a Windows NT Server domain, there is no need to delegate account administration to individual users who have administrative power on a particular server. When transferring accounts, the migration tool does not grant any kind of Windows NT Server administrative rights to accounts that were Workgroup Managers or User Account Managers. The closest Windows NT Server equivalent to the NetWare Workgroup Manager and User Account Manager is the Account Operators group. Account Operators can create, delete, and manage user and group accounts (except administrative accounts and groups).

- **Console Operator** The closest Windows NT Server equivalent to the NetWare Console Operator is the Server Operators group. However, because Server Operators have greater power than Console Operators, the migration tool does not transfer NetWare Console Operators to the Windows NT Server Operators group. Unlike Console Operators, whose control can be restricted to a single server, Server Operators have abilities on every server in the domain.

- **Print Server Operator and Print Queue Operator** The NetWare Print Server and Print Queue Operators are equivalent to the Windows NT Server Print Operators group. The migration tool automatically adds users and groups who are Print Server Operators to the Windows NT Server Print Operators group. However, because adding Print Queue Operators to the Windows NT Server Print Operators group would grant them more authority than they currently have, Migration Tool for NetWare does not transfer users who are only Print Queue Operators to any Windows NT Server group.

## Migrating file and folder properties

Although NetWare and Windows NT have different types of Permissions, Migration Tool for NetWare will transfer folders and files and map their NetWare permissions to Windows NT permissions according to charts in Table 20.5 and Table 20.6.

## Table 20.5
## Migrated Folder Rights

| NetWare Folder Rights | Windows NT Server Folder Permissions |
| --- | --- |
| Supervisory (S) | (All) (All) |
| Read (R) | (RX) (RX) |
| Write (W) | (RWXD) (RWXD) |
| Create (C) | (WX) (not specified) |
| Erase (E) | (RWXD) (RWXD) |
| Modify (M) | (RWXD) (RWXD) |
| File Scan (F) | (RX) (not specified) |
| Access Control (A) | (P) (P) |

## Table 20.6
## Migrated File Access Rights

| NetWare File Rights | Windows NT Server File Permissions |
| --- | --- |
| Supervisory (S) | (All) |
| Read (R) | (RX) |
| Write (W) | (RWXD) |
| Erase (E) | (RWXD) |
| Modify (M) | (RWXD) |
| File Scan (R) | Does not map. |
| Access Control (A) | (P) |

## NOTE

*Windows NT has no equivalents for the NetWare Create for folders or for the File Scan for files; these rights are not migrated. Migrated folders and files are given Administrators Group ownership.*

## Planning for migration

Consider the following before migrating information to a Windows NT server:

◆ How will NetWare clients be given access to the Windows NT servers: by keeping Novell client software and installing FPNW on the Windows NT server, or by installing Windows NT client software on the former NetWare clients?

◆ What will your domain structure be? The time spent in planning is time saved in troubleshooting, especially if you are migrating a number of NetWare servers.

◆ If migrating more than one NetWare server to a single Windows NT server, in which order will they be migrated? Migration Tool for NetWare will merge NetWare volumes with the same name, but you must tell it how to handle the duplicate user names.

## Running Migration Tool for NetWare

The migration program is SYSTEMROOT\SYSTEM32\NWCONV.EXE on your Windows NT server, but it can be copied (along with LOGVIEW.EXE and their associated help files) to any workstation on the network and then run from there.

### CAUTION

*It is very important that all users be logged off and all files be closed on the two servers involved in a migration!*

1. Launch NWCONV, and the program will prompt you for the names of the NetWare server and Windows NT server involved in this migration and their paths (Figure 20.4).

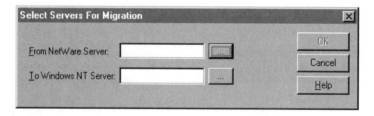

**FIGURE 20.4**

*Select Servers For Migration dialog box*

◆ **Bindery** The Bindery is the database that holds User and Group information in a NetWare 2.*x* or NetWare 3.*x* server. NetWare 4.*x* uses NDS, but it can establish a Bindery Context for users whose client software is not NDS-aware.

◆ **Bindery Context** Implemented in NDS as a gateway between non-NDS client software and the database itself. It looks like a NetWare 3.*x* Bindery to the software.

◆ **Bindfix** A utility to repair the Bindery, which also creates a set of backup files. The Bindery can be restored by running the Bindrest utility.

◆ **NetWare Core Protocol (NCP)** The protocol used between NetWare servers and clients and among NetWare servers. Microsoft's NetWare clients and File and Print Services for NetWare emulate NCP.

◆ **Novell Directory Service (NDS)** The database of user, group, file system, and other similar information in a NetWare 4 network; formerly called NetWare Directory Service.

◆ **NETSYNC** A NetWare Loadable Module that runs on a NetWare 3.*x* server and allows the NetWare 4 server NDS administration tools to synchronize a NetWare 3.*x* Bindery. Do not run NETSYNC if you are using Microsoft's Directory Services Manager for NetWare.

◆ **NetWare Loadable Module (NLM)** A program that runs on a NetWare server. (Just to confuse things, utilities that run with Novell's Client32 client software are also called NLMs.)

◆ **Supervisor Equivalent** Supervisor is the name of the administrative account on a NetWare 2.*x* or NetWare 3.*x* server. Any user can be made a Supervisor Equivalent, which grants the user the same privileges as the Supervisor account.

◆ **SYS:** The first volume on a NetWare server. Its name cannot be changed.

◆ **Volume** The largest disk space division on a NetWare server. A volume might be part of a physical disk or all of a physical disk, or it might span two or more physical disks.

2. After you have entered the first server that will migrate, you can include additional migrations in the same session by clicking Add in the Migration Tool for NetWare dialog box. (See Figure 20.5.)

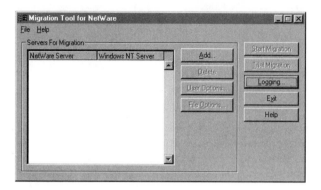

**FIGURE 20.5**

*Migration Tool for NetWare dialog box for adding servers to migration session*

3. Click User Options to specify how users and groups will be transferred. (This option is shown as disabled in the figure.)

4. Click File Options to choose the NetWare volumes to be transferred. (This option is shown as disabled in the figure.) For each volume, you can choose to transfer all or only some of the folders and files.

5. Now click Trial Migration. This will generate a log file of what would occur during a real migration, without actually transferring anything. Three log files will be created:

   ◆ The LOGFILE.LOG contains information on users, groups, and files, including the information that currently exists on the NetWare server.

   ◆ The SUMMARY.LOG presents an overview that includes the names of the servers that were migrated and the number of users, groups, and files that were transferred.

- The ERROR.LOG shows the information that Migration Tool for NetWare could not transfer as well as the information about system failures that prevented migration (for example, a lack of disk space).

6. Examine the log files to determine if the behavior was what you expected, and make any necessary changes to User Options and File Options. Then when you're ready, click Start Migration.

**NOTE**

*It isn't necessary to do the entire migration in a single session. Whenever you exit Migration Tool for NetWare, all selections are saved and then presented as defaults the next time the tool is started.*

# Services for Apple Macintosh

As mixed-platform environments have become more and more common, Microsoft has helped administrators a lot by offering Apple Macintosh Services for Windows NT, which makes it very easy to grant Macintosh users access to resources on a Windows NT network.

## Installing Services for Macintosh

Services for Macintosh is built into Windows NT, so it is fairly quick to install. Just follow these steps:

1. Inside Control Panel, double-click the Network icon.

2. Select the Services Tab, and then click Add.

3. Scroll down the Network Service list in the Select Network Service dialog box, and then double-click Services for Macintosh (Figure 20.6 on the following page). You'll be asked for the location of your Windows NT files; supply the CD and path. Click Continue.

4. Close the Network dialog box.

5. The AppleTalk Protocol Configuration dialog box will appear; select the desired Network.

6. Click OK, and then restart Windows NT.

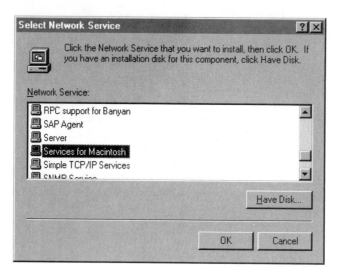

**FIGURE 20.6**

*Dialog box for installing Services for Macintosh*

# Authentication
# Services for Macintosh Clients

You can add Microsoft authentication to Macintosh clients so that they must have an account if they are to have access to Microsoft shared volumes. To do this, you will need to connect to a Windows NT server from a Macintosh computer.

1. Choose the Apple menu, and then select Chooser. Make sure that AppleTalk is active; then click the AppleShare icon. Select the AppleTalk zone on which the Windows NT server is located.

2. If you have selected the correct zone, the name of the Windows NT server will be displayed. Select the server, and then click OK.

3. You will be prompted to sign on. Choose to sign on as a Registered User. Fill in the name and password, and then click OK.

4. The program will prompt you to select a server. Choose Microsoft UAM Volume, and click OK. Then close Chooser.

5. Now double-click the Microsoft UAM Volume. When it opens, you will see an AppleShare folder. Select it, and then copy it to the System Folder. If the program asks whether you want to overwrite an existing

folder, select No. Open the existing AppleShare folder, and copy the Microsoft UAM file to the AppleShare folder in the System Folder manually.

6. Now when a Macintosh user connects to the Windows NT server, he or she will have the option of using Microsoft authentication to sign on.

## Managing Macintosh Users, Files, and Volumes

Fortunately, users on Macintosh clients can be managed with the User Manager for Domains just like other users. A little bit more is involved, however, when you manage Macintosh files and volumes on Windows NT Server. Note that if you create the volume on a CDFS volume instead of an NTFS volume, it will be read-only.

To create a Macintosh-accessible volume, follow these steps:

1. In File Manager, select the directory that you want to use as a Macintosh-accessible volume.

2. Choose Create Volume from the MacFile menu of File Manager. This will bring up the Create Macintosh-Accessible Volume dialog box.

3. Choose the volume name that you want. The path will be the location of the directory. By default, the volume doesn't require a password; if you want to password-protect the volume, you can provide one. Click OK to create the volume.

Now you will have a single volume where Macintosh files can be managed easily by both Windows NT and Macintosh users. The only difference is that the volume will appear as a mounted volume for Macintosh users and as a directory for Windows users.

## Data Transfer Between Macintosh and Windows NT Server

With Services for Macintosh installed, Windows NT users and Macintosh users can use the same shared volumes to transfer files with a minimum of hassle. On a shared volume, the files will look similar to Windows NT users and Macintosh users. As long as the volume is shared, the files can be transferred by Macintosh and Windows NT users.

Services for Macintosh is specially configured to translate file names. When a Macintosh user creates a file on a shared volume, the Macintosh file server scans the file name for characters that aren't accepted by NTFS and replaces them. Other than that, the filenames will be identical. Then Windows NT Server gives the files MS-DOS filenames for MS-DOS, Microsoft Windows 3.1, and OS/2 users who wouldn't be able to see the longer filenames. Similarly, NTFS and Windows 95 filenames (which can have up to 256 characters) are shortened to 31 characters for Macintosh users.

In the end, if users are working in a mixed environment on a day-to-day basis, the simplest thing to do is use filenames that will retain their meaning even after they are truncated. For example, if the only people using the network are Windows NT, Windows 95, and Macintosh users, users should try to limit filenames to 31 or fewer characters. If there are a lot of Windows 3.1 and MS-DOS users, users should try to create filenames according to the 8.3 naming conventions.

Note that on the Macintosh, all files are seen simply as generic Windows NT files by default; so a Macintosh user must know ahead of time what kind of application created the file. For example, a Macintosh user would know to open a Windows NT file that ends in .DOC with Microsoft Word or a file that ends in .TXT with Simple-Text. The only way the files can be handled automatically is if the Macintosh user is using PC Exchange, a System 7 Control Panel that can tell how to open a file by its file extension.

## Logging On with Macintosh to a Windows NT Network

A Macintosh logs on to a Windows NT network just as if it were logging on to any AppleShare volume. If you choose to install Microsoft authentication, then it will even use the same Windows NT authentication and password encryption.

## Macintosh Printing

With Services for Macintosh installed, Macintosh users can easily print to printers on the Windows NT network. One of the best things about using Services for Macintosh is that Macintosh users can print to non-PostScript printers that are connected to computers on the Windows NT network. On the Macintosh side, these printers appear to be the same as regular LaserWriter printers. On the Windows NT side, Windows NT users can print to LaserWriters that are hooked up to the AppleTalk network.

Services for Macintosh also lets you *capture* a printer. Capturing a printer means that a printer on an AppleTalk network will accept print jobs only from the Windows NT print server. This is very good for the administrator because it allows complete control over all of the printers from one location. It also ensures that users don't go through the print server or reset the printer, which could cause problems with the print spooler. In an environment where a lot of people will be using an Apple printer, it would be a good idea to capture the printer; it will save you a lot of time later on and help you to avoid problems with the print spooler.

## The Limitations of Macintosh on a Windows NT Network

A Macintosh user won't be able to set permissions for files and folders created from a Macintosh. Nor will the user have access to all of the shared volumes on Windows NT computers unless the shared volumes are set specifically to be Macintosh-accessible volumes. In addition, a Macintosh user can't run programs that are on the Windows NT network unless he or she has an MS-DOS expansion card that supports Windows NT.

### POINTS TO REMEMBER

♦ Directory Service Manager for NetWare allows you to administer NetWare servers as objects within a Windows NT domain; this allows the users a single logon to the network and the administrator a single point of administration for all network resources

♦ Gateway Service for NetWare is easy to install and maintain, but it's less granular from a security standpoint than using client services for access to NetWare resources.

♦ In almost all instances (the exception being the presence of legacy third-party NetWare-specific applications), the Microsoft Client for NetWare is easier to install, maintain, and use and is more robust than the Novell client software for the various client platforms.

♦ There is no Novell client for non-Intel Windows NT workstation clients.

♦ Although File and Print Service for NetWare is the easiest way to integrate a Windows NT server into an existing NetWare network, it isn't included in Windows NT Server and must be downloaded from a Microsoft ftp site or a World Wide Web site.

♦ Migration Tool for NetWare allows you to quickly and easily move all of your NetWare-server–based users, groups, folders, files, and other objects to a Windows NT server.

## WHAT'S NEXT?

In the next chapter, we move on to important administrative tools for monitoring your network. These tools, like Event Viewer and Performance Monitor, can help you locate problems ranging from the trivial to the catastrophic.

# Part Five

## Tuning, Maintenance, and Troubleshooting

# CHAPTER 21

# CHAPTER 21

## Monitoring the Network

A great many things go on in a network operation, much of it quite invisible to user and administrator alike. This is pleasant and desirable as long as everything is proceeding smoothly. However, when there's a pothole in the networking highway, it falls to the administrator to find out what's going wrong and why.

In this chapter, we'll talk about the tools in Microsoft Windows NT Server version 4 that enable you to look beneath the surface and monitor events on the network—and thus discover the source of the trouble.

## Event Viewer

From the standpoint of Windows NT Server, an event is an incident that has some potential interest. Most events, in fact, are of very little interest; your event logs can accumulate long lists of meaningless entries with only a few significant ones scattered among them. But when your system is behaving oddly, you'll suddenly find yourself interested in events that were never of interest before.

Event Viewer monitors three categories of events, which it then records in corresponding logs:

◆ **System events** Generated by the operating system and recorded in the systems log

◆ **Application events** Generated by applications and recorded in the applications log

◆ **Security events (formerly called audit events)** Generated by the operating system and recorded in the security log when an activity you select either succeeds or fails.

When you open Event Viewer, the default view is the system log. To view one of the other logs, just choose it from the Log menu. Figure 21.1 shows a system log.

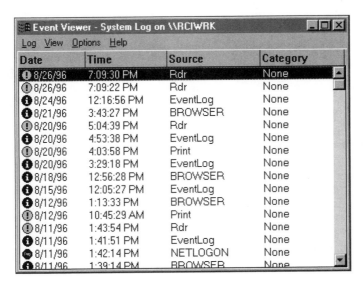

**FIGURE 21.1**

*Example of an Event Viewer system log*

## Logs

Log entries fall into one of five categories. You can tell which category a log entry belongs to by the identifying icon at the beginning of the entry.

Error    Warning    Information    Successful Security    Failed Security

After each icon is the data that relates to the event:

◆ The date and time of the event.

◆ The source of the event, which is sometimes a component of the system or a driver name.

◆ Category of the event—often NONE, but in the Security log the event is identified as Policy Change, Logon/Logoff, Privilege Use, or some other category.

◆ Event number assigned for each event.

## System Events

The events recorded in the systems log are divided into three categories:

- **Errors** Errors are system events that represent a possible loss of data or network functionality, which can be the failure of a driver or a system component to load during startup. This is the default screen in Event Viewer.

- **Warnings** Less serious than errors, warnings are nevertheless events that should be noted because some will indicate possible problems in the future. Warnings can be generated as a result of events such as a nearly full disk or a redirector time-out.

- **Information** The information category contains all events that aren't included in the Errors or Warnings categories. It can include events such as a synchronization between controllers or the successful loading of a database program.

To see more information about an event in the system log, double-click it. The example below (Figure 21.2) shows the details of a recorded error in the system log.

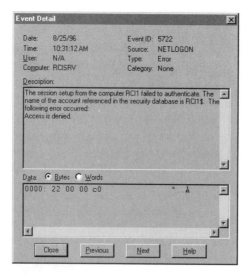

**FIGURE 21.2**

*Example of an error record in Event Viewer*

# Application Events

Application events are usually far fewer in number than other types of recorded events. They're logged by applications on the system and will vary widely. The example below (Figure 21.3) shows an "information" type of application event that was generated by running Exchange Server.

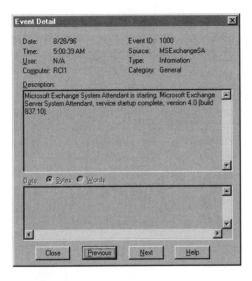

**FIGURE 21.3**

*Example of an application event record in Event Viewer*

# Security Events

Security events and the security log are probably of the most interest to an administrator. Settings for security events that are to be logged are set in User Manager for Domains. Choose Audit from the Policies menu to open the dialog box shown in Figure 21.4 on the following page.

As you can see, Windows NT Server can audit both successes and failures in all categories. In most circumstances, recording the event each time a user successfully logs on and opens a file will produce a system log of gargantuan proportions very quickly. Failures are of more interest to an administrator as a rule. However, you can change which items are to be audited at any point and for any length of time if it will help you pinpoint a problem.

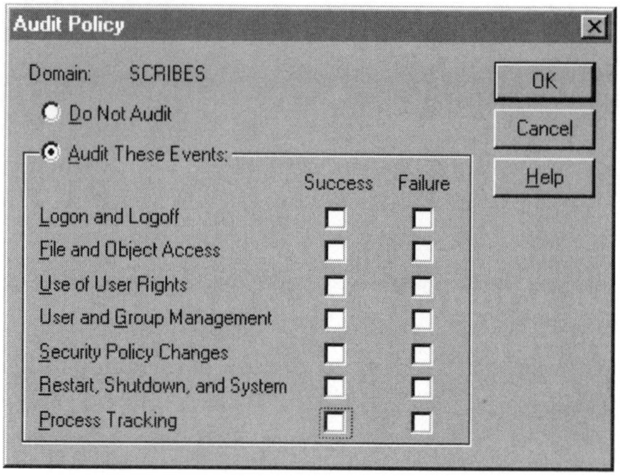

**FIGURE 21.4**

*Audit Policy dialog box*

## Event Log Filters

It only takes a few minutes to fill up an event log—particularly when it's the system log. So how do you sort through the dross to the presumed gold? Just open the log and choose Filter Events from the View menu to get the dialog box shown in Figure 21.5.

Here's how each of the fields in this dialog box can help focus your detective work:

♦ **View From and View Through** Use to narrow the events by date.

♦ **Types** Use to select the types of events you want to see.

♦ **Source** Use to choose events that are logged by a particular source, such as a driver or system component.

♦ **Category** Use to view all events of a particular classification.

♦ **User** Use to view all events that occurred while a particular user was logged on.

♦ **Computer** Use to view events for a particular computer.

♦ **Event ID** Use to view events of a particular ID in a category.

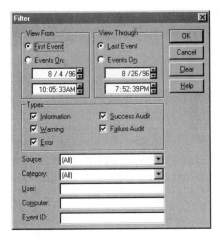

**FIGURE 21.5**

*Dialog box for filtering views of event records*

By judicious use of these fields—you might need a little Boolean algebra as well—you can wade through the morass of events in a log to find the points you're looking for. Bear in mind that until you understand how filtering works, you're bound to make a few false starts.

# Network Audits

To perform audits on your network, you'll need to first set the overall domain audit policy. Then you can set up particular file or folder audits or audit a printer. In the following sections, we discuss these subjects and also cover how to view the event log on another computer.

## Domain Audits

The basic audit policy for the domain is set in User Manager for Domains. You can refine the policy to audit specific files, folders, and printers; but you can't extend the auditing policy beyond what is configured here. To set the auditing ground rules for the domain, follow these steps:

1. Open User Manager for Domains.

2. Choose Audit from the Policies menu.

3. Click Audit These Events. Select the successful and unsuccessful events you want to monitor. When you're done, click OK.

## Folder and File Audits

Auditing who's doing what with a given folder (or even a single file) is set up under the Security tab of the folder or file. (The folders or files must be on an NTFS partition.) Just follow these steps:

1. Right-click the folder or file to be audited, and select Properties.

2. On the Security page, click Auditing.

3. If you've selected a folder, use the Replace Auditing On Subdirectories and Replace Auditing On Existing Files check boxes to specify the extent of the auditing.

   ◆ To apply auditing to a folder, existing subfolders, and all existing files, select both check boxes.

   ◆ To apply auditing to a folder and its files (but ignoring the subfolders), select Replace Auditing On Existing Files only.

   ◆ To apply auditing to a folder only (and ignoring all files and subfolders), clear both of the check boxes.

   ◆ To apply auditing to the folder and subfolders (and ignoring files), select Replace Auditing On Subdirectories and clear Replace Auditing On Existing Files.

4. Next, select the user whose files or folders you want to audit. Click Add to open the Add Users and Groups dialog box shown in Figure 21.6.

5. Select the groups or users whose use of the files or folders you want to audit. Click Add until all of the names are displayed in the Add Names box. Click OK when you're done to return to the Directory Auditing dialog box (Figure 21.7).

6. Select the events you want to audit; click OK to save the information.

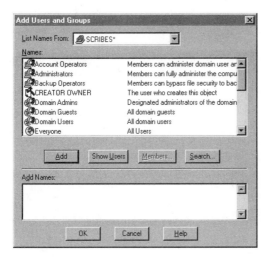

**FIGURE 21.6**

*Dialog box for selecting the groups and users you want to audit*

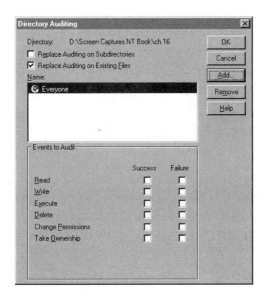

**FIGURE 21.7**

*Dialog box for selecting what events to audit*

## Printer Audits

Sad to say, there are folks who view an office printer as an opportunity to print free leaflets for their kid's dance recital or handbills in the hundreds for a garage sale. If you need to track down one of these culprits, you can do so by auditing the printer in question.

To configure auditing for a printer, follow these steps:

1. Open the Printers folder, and right-click the printer you want to audit. Select Properties from the pop-up menu that appears.

2. In the dialog box that opens, click the Security tab and then click Auditing.

3. Click Add in the Printer Auditing dialog box to open the Add Users and Groups dialog box.

4. Select the name of the individual or group whose activities you want to audit with respect to that printer, and click Add. When all of the names you want are displayed in the Add Names box, click OK.

5. Back in the Printer Auditing dialog box (Figure 21.8), select the events you want to audit. When you're done, click OK.

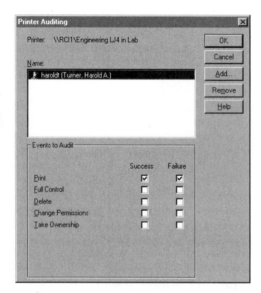

**FIGURE 21.8**

*Dialog box for selecting printing events to audit*

The results of the audit will show up in the Security log, which you can read in Event Viewer.

## Access to Nonlocal Event Logs

To see event logs on other computers, open Event Viewer and choose Select Computer from the Log menu. In the dialog box, double-click the computer whose Event log you want to view. The other computer's Event Viewer will open, and you, in your administrator's role, can manipulate the log as if it were your own.

# Event Log Configuration

By default, each of the event logs is limited to 512 KB. You can keep the logs smaller, or you can let them grow even larger, if you think you need that much information. To configure the event logs, follow these steps:

1. Open Event Viewer, and choose Log Settings from the Log menu.

2. In the Event Log Settings dialog box (Figure 21.9), select which log you want to change.

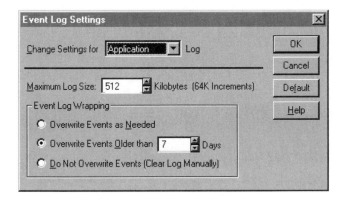

**FIGURE 21.9**

*Dialog box for selecting event log settings*

3. Set a maximum log size.

4. Select how you want a full log to be handled:

   ◆ **Overwrite Events as Needed** When the log gets full, the newest log entry will push out the oldest.

   ◆ **Overwrite Events Older than x Days** Retains the log for the number of days specified; the log will be maintained for that period of time, even if its size exceeds the number of KB chosen.

- ◆ **Do Not Overwrite Events** Retains all of the events and requires that the log be cleared manually; it will not clear itself automatically.

5. When you're done, click OK.

# Windows NT Diagnostics

The Windows NT Diagnostics tool is a way of looking at information about your computer that is otherwise hidden. Open Windows NT Diagnostics in the Administrative Tools menu to see a window like the one shown in Figure 21.10.

**FIGURE 21.10.**

*Windows NT Diagnostics dialog box*

Here's what you'll find on the various pages:

- ◆ **Version** The operating system version number, records of service packs installed, and the registered owner.

- ◆ **System** ROM BIOS and CPU information.

- ◆ **Display** Video information, including the video settings, video card manufacturer, video memory, and video chip type.

- ◆ **Drives** All drives connected to this computer listed by type or by name.

- ◆ **Memory** More than you ever wanted to know about memory. Of most interest is the actual physical memory (the amount of RAM installed and available) and the pagefile numbers. The pagefile space is the swap file, also known as virtual memory.

- ◆ **Services** The status of services on this computer. Click Devices to see the status of devices. To make *changes* to either of these lists, go to the Services icon or Devices icon in Control Panel.

- ◆ **Resources** A plethora of arcane information about IRQs, I/O Ports, Direct Memory Access channels, and so forth.

- ◆ **Environment** Useful information about the computer you're on (the processor type and various paths).

- ◆ **Network** Information about the network, including current network statistics.

# Performance Monitor

Performance Monitor is another tool that can help you determine just what's happening on your servers. It can present information as a chart, a log, or a report as well as send an alert to anyone on the network when an important event occurs.

Performance Monitor, when you first open it, is essentially a blank canvas. But when you delve a little deeper, you quickly see that it has enough levels of complexity to make you feel quite overwhelmed. However, if you remain calm (and we must *all* remain calm), you'll see that there are only a few settings you're likely to be interested in. The problems in your network that are most likely to show up are processors that are overburdened, memory that is too scant, and network hardware and software that aren't up to the job. When you begin your exploration, these are the three areas where you'd look first.

## Charts

When you open Performance Monitor, you're in Chart view. Choose Add To Chart from the Edit menu to open a dialog box with an immoderate number of choices. (See Figure 21.11 on the following page.)

> ◆ • **Tip**
>
> *In the Add To Chart dialog box, select an object and a counter; then click Explain for a description of what your choices mean.*

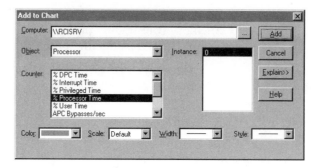

**FIGURE 21.11**

*Dialog box for adding functions to a chart in Performance Monitor*

A good indicator of whether a processor is overburdened is %Processor Time, which shows the percentage of time the processor is busy. Under the LogicalDisk object, the Average Disk Queue Length (the average number of reads and writes waiting on the disk) can show how long the line is to use the hard drive. Needless to say, the line should be very short indeed if you are concerned about the network's performance. Select the Memory object and then Pages/Sec, which will tell you how often the server is switching information from memory to disk. A high rate of switching means that the server is short of memory and, as a result, is running more slowly than necessary. Various statistics can be gathered to show patterns that you can use to diagnose your problem, as shown in Figure 21.12.

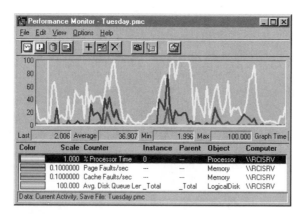

**FIGURE 21.12**

*Example of a Performance Monitor chart*

## Administrative Alerts

You also can use Performance Monitor to notify you (or someone else) when a specified event occurs on the network. Here's an example: assume you are setting up an alert that will go to the administrator whenever the processor on RCISRV is busy more than 50 percent of the time:

1. Open Performance Monitor, and choose Alert from the View menu.

2. Choose Add To Alert from the Edit menu to open the dialog box shown in Figure 21.13

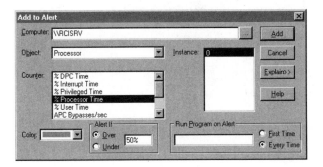

**FIGURE 21.13**

*Example of an Add to Alert dialog box in Performance Monitor*

3. Select an object, a counter, and the conditions for the alert under Alert If. (In Figure 21.13, we specified an alert if the %Processor counter went over 50 percent.) Click Add, and then click Done.

4. Choose Alert from the Options menu, and select what you want done with the alert:

   ◆ Open the Alert view of Performance Monitor.

   ◆ Log the event in the Application log (in Event Viewer).

♦ For a network alert, select the Send Network Message check box and provide the logon name of the person to be alerted in the Net Name text box.

♦ Select how often you want the alert updated.

5. When you're done, click OK.

Now, whenever the conditions for the alert are met, an alert will go out. Our preference was for the administrator to be notified over the network. When the conditions were met, the alert shown in Figure 21.14 was sent to the administrator.

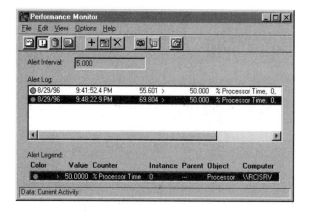

**FIGURE 21.14**

*Example of an alert notification in Performance Monitor*

## Reports

Performance Monitor also can produce lots and lots of numbers for those mind-numbing reports that management loves. You can log statistical information that can later be exported to a spreadsheet program and then graphed or otherwise displayed.

To log data in Performance Monitor, follow these steps:

1. Choose Log from the View menu, and then choose Add To Log from the Edit menu.

2. As you can see, you can add objects to the log—but only entire objects, not just one facet, as you can in Chart view. Select the objects you want, clicking Add after each selection. Click Done when you're finished.

3. Choose Log from the Options menu, and give your log a name. (See Figure 21.15.) Select how often you want the log updated. Click Start Log when you're finished.

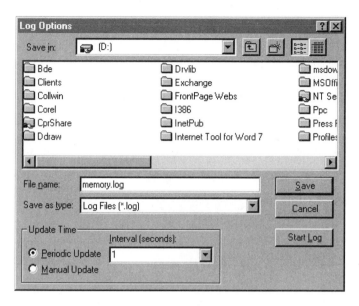

**FIGURE 21.15**

*Example of a Log Options dialog box showing the log name*

## POINTS TO REMEMBER

◆ Filtering the events that occur on your network can help you pinpoint the source of difficulties.

◆ Auditing files and folders is a useful way of gathering information about how resources are being used.

◆ Use Performance Monitor to track down hardware bottlenecks and then send alerts or generate logs for reports.

## WHAT'S NEXT?

From discussions about how to monitor and audit your network, we next move on in Chapter 22 to the subject of maintaining your file system for maximum stability and performance.

# CHAPTER 22

Disk Maintenance and Tuning

# CHAPTER 22

# Disk Maintenance and Tuning

One of the most important aspects of maintaining a server and providing a quality product to your customers—the end users—is a fast, efficient, and error-free file system. Of course, a substantial portion of that efficiency and freedom from worry for the users is provided by having a good backup strategy in place (and we'll talk in greater detail about backups in Chapter 23), but the best backup of all is the one you don't need!

There are several things you can do to both detect problems on your hard disk subsystems and protect yourself from the steady degradation of hard drive performance that can occur over time. Some of the tools you'll want or need are provided as part of Microsoft Windows NT Server version 4, but there are others that are not part of the package. You'll definitely want to look at some of the third-party alternatives as well.

## File System Maintenance

Preventive maintenance is always preferable to reactive maintenance. It's great to be able to recover a file system that's crashed, but it's even better to detect something amiss ahead of time. An efficiently laid out file system is also one that doesn't have to work as hard, which prolongs disk life and reduces the likelihood of having to use the backup tape you made.

Windows NT Server supports only two types of native file systems in version 4, the venerable FAT file system and NTFS, the file system Microsoft introduced in the original version of Windows NT. In most cases, we'd expect you to be running NTFS because it's a far more robust and secure file system than FAT, although it's not particularly faster than FAT except when you're dealing with very large files. NTFS also is much more appropriate for a server because it supports larger partitions without increasing the cluster size nearly as quickly as FAT does.

Let's take a quick look at the characteristics of the two supported file systems. We're not going to try to cover all of the details here, but we'll give you enough background to understand the strengths and limitations of each file system.

# FAT

FAT has been around since at least the inception of IBM PC-DOS and MS-DOS in 1981. It was designed to meet the needs of the original IBM PC—which had, if you were lucky, two floppy drives. Hard drives weren't even supported until the introduction of the IBM PC/XT.

The core of the FAT file system, and the source of its name, is a file allocation table that lists the starting point of each file on the disk—but *only* the starting point. FAT is even smart enough to keep a second version of the file allocation table on the disk just in case something goes wrong with the first one. Of course, it keeps the second version right next to the first version on the disk, which somewhat limits the robustness of this line of defense; but it's certainly better than having no second copy at all.

## Fragmentation of FAT file systems

When the operating system wants to read a file, it first checks the FAT for the address of the starting point and then reads a pointer at the end of the first file allocation unit of the file (also known as a *cluster*), which points to the next file allocation unit of the file, and so forth, until the system gets to the end of the file. If all units of the file are in order and on adjacent sectors of the disk, all is well—the file reads fairly quickly, with little chance of a loss or damage.

But as the file grows over time, it might not be able to fit in its original space on the hard drive anymore. Rather than go looking for a segment of the hard drive that will hold the entire file, the operating system tends to be lazy—it will write the old portion where it was before and then try to find another place to put the extra portion. This saves it from having to update the FAT for the old portion of the file.

As a file shrinks and grows over time, the result is a disk comprising many fragmented files. This seriously increases the time it takes for a typical disk access, which tends to read and write contiguous data sectors. The sectors now are no longer contiguous on the disk but spread all over. Fragmented files present another problem as well. It is considerably more difficult to recover a fragmented file that has been inadvertently corrupted or deleted.

Disk fragmentation is a well-understood process in a FAT-based file system, and MS-DOS and Microsoft Windows users have dealt with it for years. Originally, there were third-party solutions to defragment a file system; eventually, Microsoft recognized this need by including a limited defragmentation utility in all versions of MS-DOS from version 6 onward and also in Microsoft Windows 95.

## Cluster size and FAT volume size

Another serious problem for many applications is the way FAT file systems deal with the relatively large size of hard drives today. Remember that FAT was designed back when a high-end PC had just two floppy drives—and they were single-sided, 160 KB each!

Because of the FAT data design and table size, the pointer to the starting file allocation unit for each file is stored in 16 bits of storage space. As such, it can support only a maximum of $2^{16}$ (or 65,536) file allocation units because that's all the room it has for address space. So as the size of your hard drive grows, Windows NT (and all operating systems that support FAT file systems) has to compromise to support the larger size of the volumes—it can't increase the size of the pointers to the start of a file, so it increases the size of each cluster that makes up the file.

What this means in practical terms these days is this: if you have a modest hard drive of 1.2 GB and if you format it into a single partition using FAT, the smallest storage unit on the disk will be 32 KB in size. Yep. That means every single one of those little shortcuts you create in Windows NT will take up 32 KB of your hard drive space—not a pretty sight, and terribly wasteful. In addition, every time your hard drive wants to read that shortcut, it has to read all 32 KB, which is a definite slowdown in your disk access.

So what's the solution? Well, if you have lots of little files, you pretty much have to chop up your hard drive into smaller partitions to maximize your speed and storage utilization. A reasonable goal is to keep your maximum volume size under 512 MB. This will keep your cluster size down to 8 KB—still pretty large, but a reasonable tradeoff.

On the other hand, if your volume will be doing most of its job by storing a couple of large data files, you don't really need to worry about the size of the clusters; you can make the volume as big as you want. Well, actually, this is not quite true. The maximum size of a FAT volume is 2 GB, so once again you're kind of up against the limitations of the good old file allocation table. And this is to say nothing of FAT's limited ability to recover from problems or support advanced security features, plus a host of other problems we've already discussed in Chapter 8. Clearly, with modern hard drives growing in size and shrinking in cost almost hourly, FAT is coming close to the end of its effective life span in its current incarnation. Enter the Windows NT file system—NTFS.

### NOTE

*Microsoft is introducing an updated FAT file system called FAT32. This file system supports partitions larger than 2 GB and helps with the cluster-size problem, but it is not supported in Windows NT version 4. We recommend you avoid the FAT32 file system.*

# NTFS

Microsoft introduced Windows NT in 1993 and with it NTFS, an entirely new file system. NTFS was designed to overcome many of the deficiencies of FAT file systems and to provide a robust, secure, and recoverable file system that would meet the needs of a secure, enterprise operating system.

In NTFS, every portion of the file system is treated as a file. For example, a directory is simply a file that contains a description of the files within the directory. Even the Master File Table (MFT), which contains all of the metadata for the entire file system, is itself a file.

The MFT contains a record for each file, with the first 16 records reserved for its own use and the first record of this set of records reserved for the metadata of the MFT file itself. The second record points to the MFT mirror file, which contains the duplicate of the MFT that is used if the first copy becomes corrupted. Unlike the duplicate of the FAT, however, the MFT mirror file is located at the logical center of the disk, far away from the original file. The third record in the MFT is a log file that is used to facilitate recovery in the event of a system crash.

Starting with the seventeenth record in the MFT, each record describes an individual file or directory on the disk. If a file is small (roughly 1.5 KB or less), the entire file is contained within the MFT, making file access extremely fast. If the file is larger than will fit in the MFT, the MFT stores pointers to all portions of the file. This makes retrieval substantially faster than for FAT file systems, where each cluster has to be read to get a pointer to the next cluster. In addition, the likelihood of recovering data in the event of problems is substantially greater than with FAT.

## Fragmentation and NTFS

One of the promises made for NTFS is that it would be impervious to fragmentation. Unfortunately, this promise has not been realized. Although fragmentation is not a major problem and its impact is minimal on a file system that is not particularly full, fragmentation becomes more common and more of a problem as a file system gets closer to being full.

When Windows NT Server can fit an entire file into the MFT, it obviously won't get fragmented. If the file doesn't fit into the MFT, however, it will be written partially into the MFT and then as a contiguous *run* of data sectors on the disk, assuming there is room for a contiguous run. So far, so good. As the file grows, Windows NT Server will try to fit the file into a contiguous block; but when that isn't possible, it will split the file, writing part to one run and the rest to one or more additional runs. NTFS stores the metadata to locate these runs in the MFT, assigning sequential *virtual cluster numbers* to the data. These virtual cluster numbers are then mapped in the MFT to the actual locations on the disk where the data is stored.

Over time, especially as a volume fills up, the actual locations where data is stored on the disk become fragmented and spread around the disk. This doesn't materially increase the exposure to data loss in the event of corruption or disk failure because there is a complete mirror copy of the MFT in a different location; but it does make it much slower to read the entire file because the locations on the disk might require several head movements and waiting times while the disk rotates around to the necessary locations.

## Recoverability and logging

NTFS uses a transaction model for writing data to the disk, which ensures the ability to recover quickly in the event of a system crash or power failure. All changes to the file system are recorded in a log file before they are carried out and then marked as completed once they are finished. This enables the file system to recover by rolling back any transactions that hadn't been completed when the system comes back online. The rollback happens very quickly, typically in seconds, when the system comes back up, which provides a very fast recovery to full functionality. Furthermore, it ensures that the file system is not left in an indeterminate state.

### NOTE

*Unlike some fault tolerant file systems, the NTFS transaction model does not guarantee complete recoverability of user data in the event of a crash, only the integrity of the file system as a whole.*

## Cluster size and NTFS volume size

As we mentioned earlier, one of the concerns with FAT volumes is the increasing size of the clusters as the size of the volume increases. With NTFS, this is much less of an issue. You can choose an explicit cluster size when you format the volume. The choices are 512 bytes, 1 KB, 2 KB, 4 KB, 8 KB, 16 KB, 32 KB, and 64 KB per cluster; however, only cluster sizes up to 4 KB are supported if compression is used.

Normally, you should let Windows NT Server choose the appropriate cluster size, but if you know that a particular volume will contain, for example, only a few large database files, you can override the defaults when you format the volume by going to the command line and using the FORMAT /A:*<size>* option. But, frankly, we discourage it. The defaults are usually a good compromise.

# Disk Tools

Windows NT Server provides a graphical front end to the basic disk tools. You can format a volume, check its integrity, turn on compression (if it's an NTFS volume), or initiate a backup without taking your hand from the mouse. And if you have a defragmentation utility installed, you can even run that without leaving your mouse.

To get to these tools, right-click the drive icon in the Explorer window to bring up the pop-up menu shown in Figure 22.1. Choose Properties, and you'll see a dialog box something like the one in Figure 22.2.

**FIGURE 22.1**

*The right mouse button pop-up menu for a local volume*

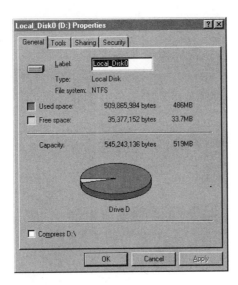

**FIGURE 22.2**

*Example of a disk Properties sheet for an NTFS volume*

This first tab on the drive properties sheet will show you some basic statistics about the volume you've selected. You can see the file system type, the label, the percentage of disk space used, and, if the volume you're inspecting is an NTFS volume, you'll see a little check box down in the lower left corner where you can turn on compression for the volume.

We haven't talked much about NTFS compression in this book, and there's a good reason why we haven't done so. We really don't see the point on a server system. With the price of hard disk space what it is today and given the role of a server, we think adding any overhead to the disk subsystem is a mistake. But if you really want to add compression, here's one way to do it. Click the Compress (*Drive*)\ check box, and you'll turn on file compression for that entire volume.

But disk maintenance is the subject of this chapter, so click the second tab (Tools) and you'll see the dialog box shown in Figure 22.3.

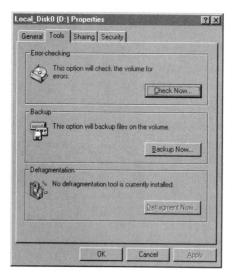

**FIGURE 22.3**

*The Tools page of the disk Properties sheet*

In most cases, the defragmentation option will be disabled, and you won't be able to defragment your drive. Microsoft chose, for reasons known only to the Windows NT developers, not to include a defragmentation application with Windows NT Server. We think this was a bad decision because we've seen more than enough evidence that fragmentation can get to be a serious problem over time even with an NTFS volume. And in many corporate environments, it's difficult to add separate utilities for such things without a substantial amount of justification. We don't make the decisions, however, so we'll simply point you to a couple of alternatives.

The most commonly used disk defragmentation program for Windows NT is Diskeeper from Executive Software. A limited version, called Diskeeper Lite, is available for free download from the Executive Software Web site:

```
http://www.execsoft.com
```

Diskeeper Lite is manual-only and has some limitations, but it does not expire and it's free. After you install it, the defragmentation option on the disk Properties sheet will no longer be disabled and you can defragment your NTFS and FAT volumes directly. If you want the version of this program that runs continuously in the background, you'll have to upgrade to the full version of Diskeeper, which is, of course, *not* free.

There are three buttons in the Tools page of the dialog box: the Defragment Now button (which is enabled when a third-party defragmentation program such as Diskeeper is used), the Backup Now button for starting the Windows NT Backup (NTBACKUP.EXE) program, and the Check Now button for checking the integrity of the file system on the volume. We'll cover NTBackup in the next chapter, so we'll skip that for now. But the button for checking a volume for errors deserves a moment's attention.

If your server is using a FAT volume (and every RISC-based server must use at least one small FAT volume), you'll want to check it regularly for errors. Even on an NTFS volume, it's probably a good idea to check for errors. You can click Check Now or simply run chkdsk from a command line. The result is the same, but we have to admit that clicking the Check Now button is a bit cuter. When you click Check Now, you'll see a dialog box like the one in Figure 22.4.

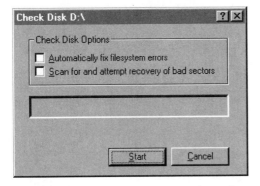

**FIGURE 22.4**

*Check Disk dialog box for detecting disk errors*

If you just want to do a quick check, don't select either of the options in the Check Disk dialog box; click Start. Windows NT Server will inspect the FAT or MFT to make sure there aren't any inconsistencies. If you want to have Windows NT Server also inspect the entire disk for bad sectors, click that option; if you're running from the command line, this is the equivalent of chkdsk /r. When you want Windows NT Server to fix any errors it detects automatically, click that option; this is the equivalent of running chkdsk /f from the command line. But to fix file system errors, Windows NT Server needs to run chkdsk when the machine first boots because it needs exclusive access to the disk while attempting repairs. You won't see the results of your efforts until the next time the system reboots. So if you do select this option, you'll see the message in Figure 22.5.

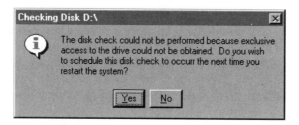

**FIGURE 22.5**

*Confirmation dialog box for disk inspection with automatic error correction*

Click Yes, and the next time you reboot your server you will have to wait a bit for it to come back up while the system performs an exhaustive check of the volume. Checking the volume can take anywhere from half a minute to several minutes, so you might want to plan for this if you suspect you might be on the longish side of that time frame.

## POINTS TO REMEMBER

♦ All disks, even NTFS volumes, are subject to file fragmentation.

♦ If the size of a FAT volume becomes very large, small files waste a substantial amount of space.

♦ You can use either a graphical version of the venerable chkdsk or the good old command-line version of chkdsk to check your file system for errors and to fix the errors it finds.

## WHAT'S NEXT?

In this chapter we've covered some ways to keep your disk healthy and to check its health. But the single best thing you can do to protect your files and file systems is to back them up. In Chapter 23, we'll cover all aspects of running Microsoft's NTBackup program to make sure you're covered in case of disaster.

# CHAPTER 23

Preventive Maintenance: Backups

# CHAPTER 23

# Preventive Maintenance: Backups

Microsoft Windows NT Server version 4 makes backups so easy that the only thing you have to remember is to change the backup tape. The Windows NT backup differs from all previous backup programs included with Microsoft Windows products in that it works only with tapes and does not permit the use of floppy disks. The size of files and databases these days makes backups to disks ridiculously slow and would require hundreds of floppies.

In this chapter, we will deal with the tools that come with Windows NT Server version 4 and with a third-party product. We'll look at a variety of scenarios and methods of performing backups. Finally, we will deal with the process of restoration, just in case you ever need it.

This is one of the most important topics in this book and one of the most important responsibilities of any network administrator. Applications can be replaced easily, but data is priceless.

## Backup Strategy

To develop a plan for backing up data, you need to consider these things:

◆ The equipment you need

◆ The best location for the tape drive

◆ The type of backup that should be implemented

## Required Equipment

The common media for backups and the only one used by Windows NT Backup is magnetic tape. Tapes have become popular because they offer great capacity for a minimal investment. Today there are three popular types of tapes:

◆ Quarter-inch cartridge (QIC)

◆ Digital audio tape (DAT)

◆ 8 mm cassette

As you prepare your backup strategy, invest some time in researching the best tape selection for your enterprise. In choosing a tape backup system, you should consider the following items:

- Does the drive provide error detection and correction?

- Does the drive offer data compression?

- Does the drive offer adequate capacity?

- Is the drive reliable?

- What is the cost of the tape media?

- What is the cost of the tape drive itself?

## Location Options

The location you choose for actual backups will depend a lot on what types of backups are being done. You have three basic options:

- **Server only backup** Only data files and applications on the actual server are backed up.

- **Local workstation backup** Here each workstation has its own tape backup and the responsibility of the backup is in the hands of the user.

- **Both server and workstation backups** This scenario has at least one individual in each department who is responsible for backing up all of that department's units. The server can be handled by the IS team or as a part of a departmental backup across the network.

You probably will use one of these approaches, but a lot depends on how much data needs to be preserved and the reliability of your team.

## Type of Backup

The capacity of your tape drive can be a factor in determining the type of backup you will implement on your network. There are five types of backup that can be performed on either the server or the workstation: normal, incremental, differential, copy, and daily.

- A *normal backup* archives all selected files and marks each as having been backed up. This method of backup allows for the fastest restoration because it has only the most recent files on it. It is also the method you would want to use at least once for all the contents of a hard drive, including the applications.

- An *incremental backup* archives only those files created or changed since the last normal backup. It also marks the files as being backed up. If you use a combination of the normal and incremental backups, you will have to restore the normal backup first and then any and all incremental backups to make sure you have restored the contents of the hard drive to its most recent status before the need for a restoration arises.

- A *differential backup* archives only those files that have been created or changed since the last normal backup. This method does not mark the files as backed up; it relies on the integrity of the last normal backup records. If you are using a combination of normal and differential backups, you need to restore the normal backup and only the last differential backup.

- A *copy backup* archives all selected files, but it does not mark the files as having been backed up. A copy backup is particularly useful if you want to back up files between a scheduled incremental backup and the last normal backup. By not marking the files, it allows the normal markings of an incremental backup to remain valid.

- A *daily backup* archives all of the selected files that have been modified on that day, but it does not mark the files as being backed up.

## Tape Rotation Plan

Always have at least two emergency replacement tapes on hand in case one tape breaks. Tapes have a recommended life span; don't plan on using any tape beyond that time. Some tapes can last much longer than their recommended life spans, but a damaged or worn out tape will cause you problems beyond bearing if you're in a situation where you need to restore the tape and it won't work. So replace your tapes on a regular (and conservative) schedule.

The first plan for rotating tapes involves four sets of tapes. Each set is used in a twelve-week schedule, and ten tapes are required for each set. (See Figure 23.1.) A different tape is used each day. On Monday through Thursday, an incremental backup is performed each day. On Friday, a normal backup is made. At the end of the second week after the normal backup is finished, the first week's normal backup tape is stored off-site in a secure place. At the end of the third week, the normal backup tape from the first week is returned, and the second week's normal backup tape is taken off-site. This procedure continues through a twelve-week cycle, at which time the complete twelve-tape set is stored off-site in a secure location and a new set of tapes is started.

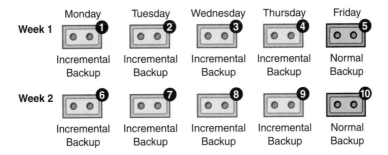

**FIGURE 23.1**

*Schedule for one tape set in the 12-week, 10-tape backup plan*

The second tape backup plan requires 19 tapes, which will cover all of the backups for an entire year (Figure 23.2). Four tapes are used for incremental or differential backups on Monday through Thursday. Three of the tapes are used for a normal backup on each of the first three Fridays of a month. The remaining 12 tapes are used for normal backup on the fourth Friday of each month. The twelve fourth-Friday backup tapes are stored off-site in a secure place.

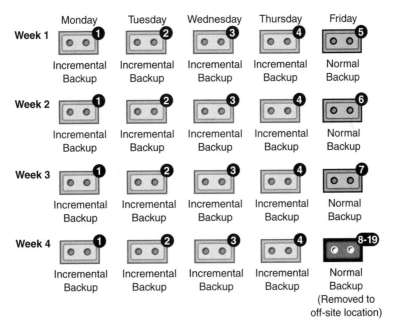

**FIGURE 23.2**

*A four-week cycle in the annual 19-tape backup plan*

# Server Backups

On a network that is server-based—that is, the applications are run from the server, or the data is stored centrally—a server backup strategy is best. In this scenario, the tape drives are attached directly to the server, and the backup is run at a scheduled time. No one has to be present to perform the backup because it's an automatic operation. But if your total data is greater than the capacity of the tape cartridge, a change of tapes will be required to complete the backup. This can be overcome if there are multiple tape drives on a large-capacity server. Each tape drive operates as a separate service on Windows NT and can be configured individually to back up different portions of the hard drive. For example, one tape drive can be configured to back up the applications portion of the hard drive, while a second tape drive handles only areas dedicated to data files.

A server-based backup has several advantages over a client-based backup. One advantage is that fewer tape drives are required; another advantage is that, normally, one person can be responsible for managing the backup.

There are also several disadvantages to the server-based backup plan. The backup procedure—and restoration, if it's ever needed—is much slower than a client-based local backup. Network traffic can increase dramatically the amount of time required to perform a backup. It's best that you carefully schedule the server-based backup for times when network traffic is at its lowest level. An ideal backup time is the middle of the night, when it's likely that no clients would be on the network and fewer applications would be running. One of the biggest disadvantages of a server backup, however, is that unless you make backups at the client level as well, you will not have any backup for client registries and event logs.

# Client Backups

A client-based backup is typically more expensive to support than a server-based backup because it requires many more tape drives and cartridges. However, the advantages of such a plan include much faster backup, quicker restoration times, and fewer network resources committed during a lengthy backup procedure. An additional benefit is that you have a backup of local registries and event logs, which are important to the health of the client connection to the network.

# Server Backups plus Client Backups

A more balanced approach is to use a combination of the server-based and client-based backup methods. The server-based backup works well for centrally stored data; the client-based backup is essential for maintaining accurate images of a client computer. You should have a portable tape backup unit for each department to use to maintain a backup of its client computers (Figure 23.3). In this scenario, the administrator corps is responsible for the central server backup of shared data and shared applications.

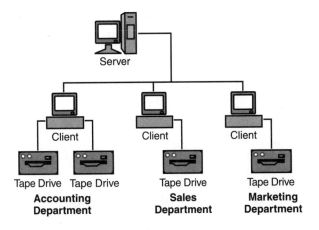

**FIGURE 23.3**

*Example of a client-based backup plan*

# The Windows NT Backup Tool

There are administrators who will need to use backup tools provided by third-party vendors because of their special network needs and because Windows NT Backup (NTBACKUP.EXE) is simply a basic backup utility with a minimum number of advanced options. However, Windows NT Backup can do the following things for you:

◆ Perform all five types of backup.

◆ Place multiple backup sets on a single tape.

◆ Span multiple tapes with both backup sets and files.

◆ Create a batch file to automate repeated backups of complete drives or selected directories.

◆ Save a log about the events associated with a backup.

◆ Back up and restore both local and remote files on an NTFS or a FAT partition.

◆ Select files for backing up and restoring by volume name, directory name, or individual filenames.

◆ Run a verification of the integrity of the backup to ensure reliability.

Windows NT Backup follows rules that protect system security and data integrity. Some file types are not backed up automatically when you run Windows NT Backup:

◆ Files you do not have permission to read. Only persons with backup privileges can copy files they do not own.

- Paging files. (These are temporary files used for virtual memory.)

- Registries on remote computers. Windows NT Backup backs up only the local registry.

- Files exclusively locked by application software. Windows NT locks two types of files: event logs and registry files. However, Windows NT Backup supports the backup of all files that are part of the operating system.

If Windows NT Backup encounters a file that is open in share/read mode, it backs up the last saved version of the file.

## Working with Windows NT Backup

On a Windows NT computer, only administrators and backup operators have default privileges to back up files that they do not own or have access to (secured files). Other users can back up only those files to which they have read access. Windows NT Backup enables users to restrict access to backup tapes through software. Only an administrator, the creator of the tape, or someone with restore privileges can restore a restricted tape. Do not restrict access to tapes that were created for file-transfer purposes.

Reserve backup and restore privileges for those few individuals who have regular responsibility for backing up your network. Large sites might want to create two groups of backup operators: one group with backup privileges only, the other with backup and restore privileges. Notice that backup privileges enable administrators and backup operators to bypass the protection provided by normal file permissions. Also, note that granting restore privileges enables a user to ignore normal file permission conflicts during restoration and to overwrite existing files; so use caution in granting these privileges.

You can back up files only on a drive to which you normally have access. Otherwise, you need to be logged on as a member of either the Administrators or the Backup Operators group.

The Backup Information dialog box for Windows NT Backup (Figure 23.4) is where you set a variety of options for the backup you want to make. The initial configuration of the hardware is in the Tape option in Control Panel. It's here that you can select or detect the type of tape drive hardware installed on your server. You also can select the best device driver for your tape drive.

Each time you start Windows NT, it checks automatically for your tape drive hardware. When you activate Windows NT Backup, it initializes the hardware and prepares it for use. As we mentioned earlier, it is possible to have more than one tape drive on a server. To select which tape drive you want to use, choose the Hardware Setup command from the Operations menu.

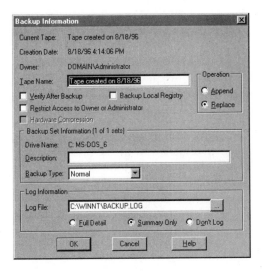

**FIGURE 23.4**

*Backup Information dialog box for configuring a Windows NT backup*

The following bulleted list describes the information and options of the backup configuration dialog box in Figure 23.4.

◆ **Current Tape** The current tape's name is shown here unless it is blank, it has an unrecognized format, or there is no tape loaded.

◆ **Creation Date** The date the original backup set was created or the date when it was last replaced is displayed here.

◆ **Owner** The owner of the tape (whoever put the first backup set on the tape) is displayed here.

◆ **Tape Name** You can use up to 32 characters to create or change a current tape name.

◆ **Append** This operation adds the backup set(s) to the end of the last backup set on the active tape. Tape Name and Restrict Access To Owner Or Administrator are unavailable with this operation.

◆ **Replace** This operation overwrites all of the information on the tape. However, if you do not confirm the choice, another message gives you the option of appending instead.

◆ **Verify After Backup** You can select whether or not to perform a verification comparison of the files written to the tape and the files on the disks.

◆ **Restrict Access to Owner or Administrator** You can designate the tape as "secure." Only the tape owner or a member of the Administrators or Backup Operators group can read, write, or erase the tape using Windows NT Backup. To restore it on another computer in the same domain, you must be logged on with the same user account name for that domain. Members of the Administrators or Backup Operators group can read, write, or erase a tape on any computer and in any domain.

Figure 23.5 shows a Windows NT Backup in progress. But just what steps were necessary to get to this point? Let's take a quick look at the sequence of events necessary for performing a backup.

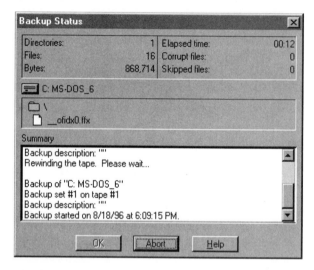

**FIGURE 23.5**

*Example of a Backup Status dialog box*

## Performing a Backup

As soon as you launch the Windows NT Backup application, it scans for the presence of a tape device. If it finds any conflicts with what has already been recorded in the Device Registry, it will prompt you to go to the Install Tape Device icon in Control Panel. It's here that you can install the proper device driver for your tape drive hardware. If there are no hardware conflicts, the startup sequence will scan the inserted tape cartridge for its contents.

You can back up only the drives on your local computer and network drives or directories for which you have sufficient privileges. You also must have the appropriate privileges for the restoration process. Those who have Administrator rights or Backup rights have access to any and all drives that are available on the network.

The menu bar offers the most commonly used commands in the Operations and Select menus. The options that are available in these menus are listed in Table 23.1.

**Table 23.1**
**Commonly Used Commands in the Operations and Select Menus**

| Command | Description |
|---|---|
| Backup | Launches a backup of any and all selected files from the drives accessible to the computer. |
| Restore | Launches a restore of either the selected tape or backup set that has been selected or both. You also can select a single file to restore from a backup. |
| Catalog | Launches a search for backup sets on the installed tape. |
| Erase Tape | Wipes clean the contents of a tape cartridge. |
| Retension Tape | Performs maintenance of the tape by tightening the tape so that it does not slip over the heads when making or restoring a backup. |
| Eject Tape | Simply ejects the installed tape from the tape drive. |
| Format Tape | Formats the tape cartridge, erasing the contents to make the tape appear new. |
| Hardware Setup | Confirms which tape drive is installed and permits you to choose which drive to use if there is more than one tape drive installed on the server. |
| Check | Allows you to select a drive, directory, or file to be backed up. |
| Uncheck | Removes the drive, directory, or file that had been previously selected for a backup. |

The command options provided under the Tree, View, and Window menus function as they do in Explorer. They simply allow you to view the drives, directories, and files in a variety of ways.

To select the directories of files you want to back up, double-click the Drives icon. This opens up a secondary window that looks like Explorer. To select the whole drive for backup, click the check box next to the Drives icon. To deselect the entire drive, clear the check box. Click the check box for any directory or file you want to include in this backup. When you are ready to begin the backup, close this window.

As you prepare to launch the backup you have defined, give it a name (up to 32 characters) and select the type of backup you are going to perform: normal (full) or incremental.

The final decision you have to make is whether you want to create a log of the backup procedure. We recommend that you make a Full Detail log if it's your first complete backup of data. The Summary Only option suffices for subsequent backups. These are your log options:

◆ **Full Detail**  You make a complete log of all transactions, including the names of all the directories and files that are backed up and the status of each.

◆ **Summary Only**  You log only the most important pieces of information, including the loading of a tape, the starting and ending of a backup, and any skipped files.

◆ **Don't Log**  You do not create a log file.

You are now ready to start the backup. The amount of time that is required will vary according to the amount of data you are attempting to back up, the speed of the computer, and the resources available for the backup. We recommend you shut down as many processes as possible before beginning the backup; this will speed it along. It's possible to continue your work on the computer while the backup process is minimized and running in the background, although the process will take much longer. A word to the wise: don't use any of the applications you have selected for your backup. Remember, Windows NT Backup skips over open files; you don't want to miss any important application files in your backup.

## Automating Backups with Windows NT Backup

Windows NT Backup allows you to set up and run backups from either batch or command files. Because Windows NT Server includes a scheduler, it's easy to set things up so that your backups run automatically during periods of relative inactivity on the system, which keeps user frustration and inconvenience to a minimum.

The command line syntax for Windows NT Backup is this:

```
ntbackup op path [/a] [/b] [/d "text"] [/e] [/hc:{off|on}]
    [/l "filename"][/r] [/t {opt}] [/tape:{n}] [/v]
```

You also have two other options that can't be used in batch files because they require user input: [/nopoll], which causes the tape to be erased, and [/missingtape], which specifies that a tape is missing from a backup set and restoration should treat each tape as a separate entity. Table 23.2 is a list of the available options and what they mean.

**Table 23.2**
**Windows NT Backup Command Line and Batch File Options**

| Parameter | Choices | Explanation |
|---|---|---|
| *op* | backup | Performs a backup, using the parameters that follow to control the process. |
| | eject | Ejects the tape. (Valid only with /tape parameter.) |
| *path* | drives and directories | Specifies drives and directories. Individual files and wildcards are not supported from a command line backup. |
| /a | | Backup sets append to the end of the tape automatically. When more than one drive is specified under *path* but /a is omitted, the tape will be erased and then the first drive will be written, with each of the remaining drives appended after. (Default is *off*.) |
| /b | | Backs up local registry files. (Default is *off*.) |
| /d | *"text"* | Adds a description of the backup set to the tape for easier identification later. |
| /e | | Logs exceptions only. |
| /hc: | on | Uses hardware compression. (Valid only if supported by the drive type.) |
| | off | Doesn't use hardware compression. |
| /l | *"filename"* | Logs filename and path. |
| /r | | Restricts access based on permissions. (Not valid and ignored if /a is enabled.) |
| /t | Normal | Performs full, normal backup of the drives and directories specified. Archive bit is set off. |
| | Incremental | Backs up only the files that were modified or added since the last incremental or normal backup. Archive bit is set off on backed up files. |
| | Differential | Backs up only the files that have changed or been added since the last full, normal backup. Archive bit is left alone. |
| | Copy | Performs full backup of the drives and directories specified. Archive bit is left untouched. |
| | Daily | Backs up all files that were changed or added today. |
| /tape: | *n* | Uses tape drive *n*, where *n* is a number from 0 through 9. Default is the first drive (drive 0). |
| /v | | Does a full verification of the backup. |

You can use the Windows NT Server scheduler program to automatically execute a batch file that will back up all files on your hard drive, including the local registry. The scheduler has, shall we say, a less than friendly command line interface, modeled after the UNIX "at" command but not nearly as forgiving. The syntax of Windows NT Server's "at" command is:

```
at [\\computername] time [/interactive] [/every:date[,...]
    | /next:date[,...]] command

at [\\computername] [[id] [/delete] | /delete [/yes]]
```

This lets you set up a command to execute automatically every Thursday, for example, or next Sunday, or the first of every month, and so forth. Table 23.3 shows what these different options mean.

**Table 23.3**
**Command Line Options for the "at" Command**

| Parameter | Explanation |
| --- | --- |
| \\computername | Allows you to schedule the commands that are to be run on another computer in the domain. (Default is the current computer.) |
| time | The time of day to run the command. (Accepts AM/PM or Military format.) |
| /interactive | Allows the job to interact with the desktop of any user logged on when the command executes. |
| /every:date[,...] | Runs command on the next matching date and every matching date thereafter until canceled. (Date can be a day of the week or a day of the month.) |
| /next:date[,...] | Runs command on the next matching date. (Date can be a day of the week or a day of the month.) |
| command | The command file (.BAT or .CMD) to be run at the specified time. |
| id | The ID number of the job to be deleted. |
| /delete | Deletes the job ID specified, or, if no ID is specified, deletes all jobs on the specified computer |
| /yes | "Don't bother asking me to confirm the deletion, just do it." |

By combining the "at" command with a batch file, you can create an automatic backup set of three batch files that does a full backup every Sunday and differential backups every other day of the week. The backups are verified automatically, and the tape is ejected after the backup is complete to make sure you don't accidentally overwrite the tape. The first batch file (possibly named FULLBACK.BAT) does the full backup of your C: and D: drives (including the registry), overwriting anything on the tape. It also does a full verification and logs the results to C:\TEMP-\FULL.LOG, and, finally, ejects the tape when done. Such a batch file would look something like the following:

```
@echo off
ntbackup backup C: D: /v /b /l "c:\temp\full.log" /t normal
ntbackup eject
```

The second batch file (possibly named DIFFBACK.BAT) does the daily differential backups and would look something like the following:

```
@echo off
ntbackup backup C: D: /v /b /l "c:\temp\diff.log" /t differential
ntbackup eject
```

The third batch file uses a pair of "at" commands to run the other two batch files. The "at" commands would be:

```
at 3AM /every:Sunday c:\bat\fullback.bat
at 3AM /every:M,T,W,Th,F,S c:\bat\diffback.bat
```

## Third-Party Tools

There are many alternatives to using the basic Windows NT Backup application that comes with Windows NT. One of the most powerful and popular is Backup Exec by Arcada (see Figure 23.6 on the following page), one of the oldest third-party backup providers. Another is Cheyenne's ArcServe, better known in the Novell NetWare world, but now building solutions for Windows NT Server as well.

Backup Exec is fully configurable and can be run as a service under Windows NT Server version 4. Because it's a service, you can control its operation through the scheduling module and thus schedule the backup for the most appropriate time on your network.

Scheduling is one of the most difficult areas to coordinate for backing up applications and data. If your network is essentially shut down after 5:00 P.M., performing a backup is an easy task. It's when you have around-the-clock operations that it becomes more difficult—you have to perform backups of live applications and live data. It might be necessary to shut down an application and close its data file at a regularly scheduled time, so that an accurate backup can be made of the data. Figure 23.7 on the following page is an example of the advanced configuration dialog box for Backup Exec.

A key issue for any backup across a Windows NT network is the matter of network privileges. As a Windows NT service, the backup application is assigned to a particular network account. It's likely that the backup application will be associated

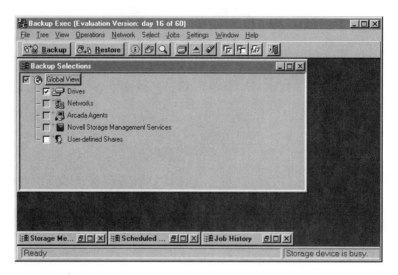

**FIGURE 23.6**

*Backup Exec dialog box showing configuration options*

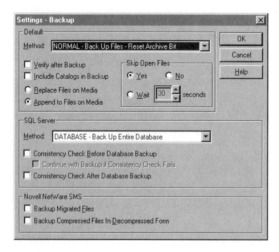

**FIGURE 23.7**

*Advanced options in Settings-Backup dialog box in Backup Exec*

with your account as Administrator. It can, however, have its own account. No matter to which account the backup application is linked, it must have administrative rights for access to all areas of the network. If any area of the network is not granted to the backup account, that area will not be backed up to tape. So careful planning is necessary here to prevent major gaps in backing up vital data. Figure 23.8 illustrates a backup in progress using Backup Exec.

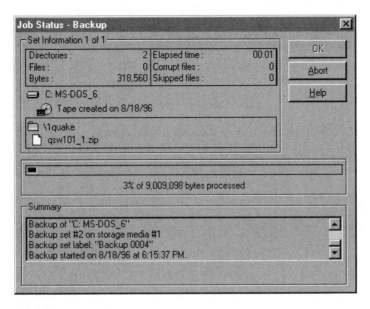

**FIGURE 23.8**

*Job Status-Backup dialog box showing Backup Exec in action*

Most third-party backup applications include a special module that works hand-in-hand with Microsoft SQL Server. Before you can activate the backup of any or all of your SQL databases, you must have administrative rights or be a database owner for the databases you want to back up.

# Protecting the Enterprise

The key to minimizing the effect a disaster can have on your data and applications is to implement an effective enterprise storage management solution. Simply put: plan for disaster, and design a network that can be restored quickly and easily.

In today's corporate world, it's assumed that most organizations have more than one network operating system and possibly multiple client platforms running on the network. As network administrator, you want, ideally, to have a single solution that can provide data protection for all of the platforms, as shown in Figure 23.9 on the following page. Windows NT Server version 4 provides that capability, assuming you are using the NTFS format on your server drives. (This is the default and normal format for Windows NT Server version 4.)

Windows NT Backup copies files only from computers that can be established as logical drives. The connection to the drives must be complete before a backup session begins. It also should be noted that Windows NT Backup does not work with MS-DOS or Microsoft Windows 3.1 workstations.

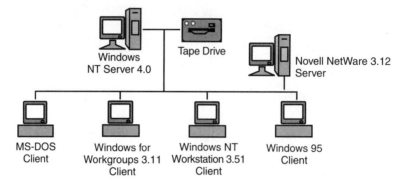

**FIGURE 23.9**

*Multi-operating system backup configuration*

# Recovering and Restoring

A disaster recovery plan is a necessity for anyone who uses a computer—from the individual who relies on his or her computer to conduct business to the largest multinational corporation. No one is exempt from the possibility of disaster. What is really important is whether or not you are ready to deal with data corruption or hardware failure.

By the time you have made it to this part of the chapter, you have read about a number of schemes that, if followed, will provide you with secure data that can be restored to a damaged system. Your readiness will be tested one day when you least expect it. Developing a backup plan, implementing it, and keeping up with it are all essential to the successful restoration of a single computer or an entire corporate network.

Backed-up information is useless if it can't be restored. Windows NT provides a Restore command to provide access to tapes, backup sets, and files for restoring as needed.

Restoration policies for everyday maintenance, not to mention for emergency recovery, are as important as backup policies. Practice ahead of time on spare drives, though, so that you don't risk overwriting real data. You also should do trial restorations periodically to find out whether files have been backed up properly. Trial restorations check for possible hardware problems that don't show up with the software or whose symptoms are not easily recognized. For that reason, keep a backup status log and check it regularly for error messages.

When you want to restore a large number of files, you need to consider what type of backup you used. If you did differential or incremental backups, restore the selected files from the most recent normal backup first. Then restore files from all subsequent incremental backups of those files. Last of all, restore the most recent differential backup performed after the last incremental backup.

You can restore the current tape, one or more backup sets, or individual files. Open the Tapes window, and make your selections the same way you would for a backup.

All catalog information is maintained on the corresponding tape for that backup set. Family sets have the information on the last tape in the backup. The tape name appears in the left panel of the Tapes window to the right of each tape icon. The following information is shown in the right panel of the Tapes window:

◆   The drive that is backed up

◆   Backup set number

◆   Tape number and what number it is within a set of tapes

◆   Backup type

◆   Date and time of backup

◆   Backup description

When you insert a tape to restore information, only the information about the first backup set is displayed in the right panel. To restore the entire tape, you must first load the tape's catalog to display the complete list of other backup sets on the tape. Otherwise, when you select an entire tape, you are really selecting only those sets that are already displayed. To know which files are in each backup set, you must load the individual catalogs for each set.

As a safety measure, Windows NT Backup restores all files except the following:

◆   Tape files that are older than a disk file. If a file that is being restored already exists on disk and the disk file is newer than the tape file, the Backup program asks you to confirm replacement.

◆   A file to be restored to a directory for which you do not have access or a file for which you do not have write access. These conditions do not apply if you have restore privileges.

# Emergency Restoration—New Hard Drive

In the event of the complete destruction of a hard drive as a result of hardware failure, you will have to reinstall Windows NT Server version 4 on the replacement drive. Once you have done this, configure the tape drive.

To restore the local registry, restore the last complete normal backup and any subsequent incremental backups. Completing a normal restoration will also restore the File Security Settings for all of the directories. This information will be restored only to NTFS partitions and not to FAT partitions.

## POINTS TO REMEMBER

- ◆ Develop a backup strategy.
- ◆ Develop a comprehensive disaster recovery plan.
- ◆ Invest in the best equipment you can afford and in adequate supplies for your enterprise.
- ◆ Test your equipment and procedures.
- ◆ Once you start implementing your backup plan, stick with it every day.

## WHAT'S NEXT?

In this chapter, we've covered the options for backing up and restoring data. In Chapter 24, we'll discuss the methods of modifying and preserving the configuration information maintained in your computers' registry files.

# Chapter 24

# The Registry Database

# CHAPTER 24

## The Registry Database

## Introduction to the Registry

The registry was first introduced in early releases of Microsoft Windows as a method of storing file-type associations and maintaining information used by other applications for object linking and embedding (commonly known as OLE). The original release of Microsoft Windows NT (version 3.1) expanded the registry concept considerably.

During the initial design of Windows NT, developers determined that users desperately needed a method for consolidating and simplifying the tasks of maintaining and configuring hardware and software information and also the tasks of maintaining and configuring the options users needed for their computers. A new, hierarchical registry database was designed that would provide users with a central repository for all hardware and software configuration information that was local to the computer. This database also would contain configuration information for each user who logged on to the computer; the ability to maintain a separate information file for each user was a big improvement over the "one size fits all" approach used previously. More important, the new design makes it possible for users to log on to different computers on the network and have their configuration settings and preferences follow them around to whatever computers they happen to be using on the network.

In the new database, all of the various configuration files that users have been required to manage over the years were essentially eliminated. There was no longer a need to maintain an AUTOEXEC.BAT, CONFIG.SYS, WIN.INI, SYSTEM.INI, or any of the many other configuration files found on your hard disk. Best of all, Windows NT still had support for some of the older configuration files, making the migration to Windows NT a little easier (see the sidebar "What Areas Are Not Supported?")

When Microsoft Windows 95 was released in August, 1995, users found that it, too, had moved to a new registry database that is very similar to the Windows NT registry database. Although the Windows 95 registry database is structured very closely along the lines of the Windows NT registry, there are differences between the two, including how they are stored on the disk. Fortunately, although the registries of the two operating systems are not compatible, the API that developers use for access to them is. As the applications users have come to depend on over the years migrate to 32-bit code, you can expect the various configuration files they use to disappear as this information is migrated to the registry.

# The Registry Structure

The new registry database consists of six major divisions, which are called *hives*. Each hive consists of numerous *keys*, which divide the pieces of configuration information into different categories. The keys, in turn, are subdivided into *subkeys* that further separate the information into more narrowly defined categories. And the subkeys also can be divided into another, lower level of subkeys if required. At the next level below the subkeys are *values*, each of which is assigned a name and can be set to store a specific piece of configuration information called *the value's data*. You can see that the registry structure resembles the concept of directories and files on your hard drive, with the keys and the subkeys corresponding to directories and the values corresponding to files.

The six hives are called HKEY_LOCAL_MACHINE, HKEY_USERS, HKEY-_CLASSES_ROOT, HKEY_CURRENT_USER, HKEY_DYN_DATA, and HKEY-_CURRENT_CONFIG. Of these six, only two—HKEY_LOCAL_MACHINE and HKEY_USERS—are really hives. The other four divisions are actually pointers to information in the first two hives; they were created because access to the information they point to is required frequently by many different applications. The sole reason for the existence of HKEY_CLASSES_ROOT, HKEY_CURRENT_USER, HKEY_DYN_DATA, and HKEY_CURRENT_CONFIG is to make it easier for developers and applications to gain access to that information. Because these four hives just point to keys contained in the hives HKEY_LOCAL_MACHINE and HKEY_USERS, you can change entries in the registry by directly modifying the entries in HKEY_LOCAL_MACHINE and HKEY_USERS or by changing the entries by using the pointer hives for quick access to the configuration entries. The end result is the same—either method will update the desired entries.

# The HKEY_LOCAL_MACHINE Hive

The HKEY_LOCAL_MACHINE hive is used to store information about the hardware, software, and users that are specific to the computer on which the registry database is located. There are five keys in it: HARDWARE, SAM, SECURITY, SOFTWARE, and SYSTEM.

The HARDWARE key contains information about all of the hardware currently installed on the computer. It's divided into four subkeys called DESCRIPTION, DEVICEMAP, OWNERMAP, and RESOURCEMAP, which contain all of the options and configuration settings for the hardware that is installed on the computer.

The SAM key and SECURITY key are used to store information about all of the users, local groups, and global groups that are created on the local computer. By default, this information is protected from access by any user (including administrators). To modify information contained in the registry keys you have to use the administrative tools provided with Windows NT Server. User Manager for Domains allows you to modify most of this information and is the preferable method for making changes in the SAM and SECURITY keys.

The SOFTWARE key contains the file-type-to-program associations and the keys for application vendors whose software you have installed. When you install application software for a new vendor, the vendor's installation program should create a key under SOFTWARE with the vendor's name and, below that, one subkey for each of the vendor's products you have installed. Under a product subkey, you will find the settings that are specific to the computer on which the product is installed.

The SYSTEM key contains the settings for the system software components that are installed on the computer. These include information and configuration settings for the drivers required for the devices installed in the computer, settings and startup information for the services that are installed, and setup information from the Windows NT installation.

The SYSTEM key is divided into six subkeys: ControlSet001, ControlSet002, CurrentControlSet, Clone, Select, and Setup. The device drivers and services settings are stored under the ControlSet001, ControlSet002, and CurrentControlSet keys. Windows NT generally maintains two copies of this information, the current settings and the last-known good boot settings that were successful. This is done to protect the computer from changes that render the system inoperative. ControlSet001 and ControlSet002 are the current and the last-known good settings, and CurrentControlSet is actually just a pointer to the control set that was last used to start the computer. The names of the ControlSet001 and ControlSet002 keys might vary, depending on how new system software is installed, but there always will be two keys, unless the settings that were just used to boot the computer caused a failure. The last three characters of the key names are always a sequential number. CurrentControlSet always points to the control set in use; the other ControlSet always will be the last-known good settings that were booted. The Clone key is reserved and is currently unused.

The Select key is used to store which ControlSet key is the current control set and which ControlSet key is the last-known good control set. After a successful boot, ControlSet001 and ControlSet002 should contain the same information. Changes made to the system software during the current boot are made to the control set that is pointed to by the CurrentControlSet key. If there are problems when the system is rebooted to put the changes into effect, the user can return to the last-known good boot settings, which will revert to the old control set settings.

The last key is Setup, which is used during Windows NT installation and setup. It's used to continue with the GUI portion of the Windows NT installation, after the text mode portion of the installation is complete and the system has rebooted.

## The HKEY_USERS Hive

The HKEY_USERS registry hive is used to store information that is specific to the users who log on to the computer. Under the HKEY_USERS hive you will find two keys: .DEFAULT and a key whose name is the SID of the currently logged on user. When a new user logs on to the computer for the first time, his or her registry key is populated with the information contained in the .DEFAULT key; this makes it easy to set up common defaults for new users by modifying the .DEFAULT key's registry settings. The second key contains the configuration settings that are specific to the user currently logged on to the computer.

◆ **Security Accounts Database**

When a Windows NT administrator assigns privileges or permissions to a user account or to a group account, he or she is assigning those privileges and permissions to the user or to the group account's SID. Fortunately, all Windows NT administrative tools allow an administrator to reference the user accounts by user name instead of by SID. (Remember that deleting a user account and immediately creating a new account with the same name does *not* re-establish the deleted account. Once an account is deleted there is no way to re-establish the same account unless you restore the security accounts database for the computer. Short of that, you have to create a new account and reset all the permissions the user had in the original account.)

Under the key for the currently logged on user you will find ten subkeys:

◆ **AppEvents** Contains information on the names of all the system and application events that can have a sound assigned to them and which sound files to play when those events occur.

◆ **Console** Contains the settings used for the command prompt and the default settings used by all console applications.

◆ **Control Panel** Contains subkeys for all Control Panel applets and under each subkey, the settings for the applets.

◆ **Environment** Contains the environment variable settings that are user-specific. For system-specific environment settings refer to the SYSTEM\CurrentControlSet\Control\Session Manager\Environment subkey under HKEY_LOCAL_MACHINE.

◆ **Keyboard Layout** Stores the current keyboard layout that is in use and also the information for other keyboard layouts that have drivers installed.

◆ **Network** Contains information for the network drives that have been permanently mapped.

◆ **Printers** Contains information on the printers currently installed and on the network printers that are permanently connected.

◆ **SOFTWARE** Contains a subkey for each vendor's software that you have installed. When you install application software for a new vendor, the vendor's installation program should create a key under SOFT-WARE with the vendor's name; under that key, the installation program should then create a key for each of the vendor's products you have installed. Under each of the product keys, you will find the settings and options that the currently logged on user has selected for that product.

◆ **UNICODE Program Groups** Used to store the settings for the Personal Program Groups that the currently logged on user has created in Program Manager. This subkey is for backwards compatibility with previous versions of Windows NT that used the Program Manager shell instead of the Explorer shell.

◆ **Windows 3.1 Migration Status** Used when Windows NT is installed into the same directory as a previous installation of Windows 3.1 or Microsoft Windows for Workgroups. It's used to determine whether Windows NT should migrate the user groups and INI file settings from the previous installation to the Windows NT installation.

### The HKEY_CLASSES_ROOT Hive

The HKEY_CLASSES_ROOT registry hive is a pointer to the Software\Classes key located in the HKEY_LOCAL_MACHINE hive. This key contains the registry information that was stored in the original Windows 3.1 registry.

### The HKEY_CURRENT_USER Hive

The HKEY_CURRENT_USER hive is a pointer to the key that represents the currently logged on user under HKEY_USERS. As you will recall, the other key in this hive is .DEFAULT.

The HKEY_CURRENT_USER hive was created to allow software applications to easily store application configuration settings that are specific to the user, without having to jump through the hoops required to determine the user's SID. An application only needs to reference this hive to set and retrieve the configuration settings for the current user.

### The HKEY_DYN_DATA Hive

This hive is being reserved for a future iteration of Windows NT and currently is not used.

### The HKEY_CURRENT_CONFIG Hive

The HKEY_CURRENT_CONFIG hive is a pointer to the SYSTEM\CurrentControlSet\Hardware Profiles\Current subkey located in the HKEY_LOCAL_MACHINE hive. This hive will not be used much in Windows NT version 4; but it's there to set the stage for the Plug and Play support that is planned for the next version of Windows NT and to support the new hardware profiles that exist in Windows NT version 4. So far, the video driver information is the only information maintained there. This information allows the user to configure different hardware profiles to use different video resolutions, which will be quite useful for the users of laptops that have a docking station on their desktops.

## Windows NT Registry Data Types

Each piece of information that is stored in the registry is assigned a name. The name doesn't have to be unique to the entire registry, it only has to be unique to the registry key or subkey under which the value name is created. The data associated with the name is assigned a data type that describes the kind of information stored in that registry entry. There are currently twelve data types supported by the Windows NT registry, although only five of these are used frequently. Table 24.1 on the following page lists all of the data types supported by the Windows NT version 4 registry and gives a brief description of their use. The most commonly used data types are marked with an asterisk.

**Table 24.1**

**Types of Data Used in the Registry**

| Type of Registry Data | How Data Is Used |
|---|---|
| REG_NONE | Used when none of the other types of data are applicable. At present, this type of data doesn't appear to be used in the registry. |
| REG_SZ* | Used to store a Unicode null terminated string. It's commonly used throughout the registry to store character data. |
| REG_EXPAND_SZ* | Also used to store a Unicode null terminated string but allows the string to contain environment variable references. It's commonly used throughout the registry to store character data that contains environment variables. API functions allow developers to expand the environment variable portions of a string to their current values. |
| REG_BINARY* | Used to store binary data in any form. It's commonly used throughout the registry. |
| REG_DWORD* | Used to store a 32-bit number. It's commonly used throughout the registry. |
| REG_DWORD_LITTLE-_ENDIAN | Used to store a 32-bit number in little endian format; it's just another name for the REG_DWORD data type. In little endian format, the most significant byte of a word is the high-order byte. This type of data is available for RISC-based machines that store DWORD values in both endian formats. |
| REG_DWORD_BIG-_ENDIAN | Used to store a 32-bit number in big endian format. In big endian format, the most significant byte of a word is the low-order byte. This type of data is available for RISC-based machines. |
| REG_LINK | Used to store a Unicode symbolic link. At present, this type of data does not appear to be used in the registry. |
| REG_MULTI_SZ* | Used to store an array of null terminated strings. The array is terminated by an additional null character. This type of data is commonly used throughout the registry when more than one character string needs to be stored in a single registry entry. |
| REG_RESOURCE_LIST | Used to store a resource list, which is a data structure used to describe the computer's hardware configuration. This type of data is used to store many of the entries in the HKEY_LOCAL_MACHINE\HARDWARE\RE-SOURCEMAP subkey. |
| REG_FULL_RESOURCE-_DESCRIPTOR | Also used to store a resource list. This type of data is used to store many of the entries in the HKEY_LOCAL-_MACHINE\HARDWARE\DESCRIPTION subkey. |
| REG_RESOURCE-_REQUIREMENTS_LIST | Used to store the options or requirements from the items in a resource list. |

# Windows NT Registry Files

The registry is made up of many files. In the versions of Windows NT prior to version 4, all of the files that made up the registry are stored in the %SYSTEMROOT%\-SYSTEM32\CONFIG directory. (%SYSTEMROOT% is an environment variable set up during the installation of Windows NT; it points to the directory where Windows NT was installed). The registry settings that are specific to each Windows NT user account are stored in a file that uses the user account name as part of the filename.

Windows NT version 4 follows this same scheme with a few exceptions. All files, with the exception of the registry settings that are specific to each user account, are still stored in the %SYSTEMROOT%\SYSTEM32\CONFIG directory. In Windows NT version 4, a new directory has been added to its directory structure and is called %SYSTEMROOT%\PROFILES. This new directory has multiple directories under it, one for each Windows NT user account that has been defined to the Windows NT security accounts database. The directory names are the names of the user accounts. In each of these user account directories you will find a file called NTUSER.DAT. The registry information specific to each user is stored in the user's directory in the NTUSER.DAT file. The new directory structure also adds subdirectories under each of the user directories for things like Application Data, Desktop, Favorites, NetHood, Personal, PrintHood, Recent, SendTo, Start Menu, and Templates.

Table 24.2 lists all of the files that are used to make up the Windows NT version 4 registry and gives a brief description of what the files are used for.

**Table 24.2**
**Files That Make Up the Windows NT Version 4 Registry**

| Registry File Name | How the Registry File Is Used |
| --- | --- |
| DEFAULT | The default settings used to create a new user profile for a user who logs on to the computer and doesn't have a defined profile. |
| SAM | The local security information for user accounts and group accounts on the computer. On a domain controller, it also contains the domain security information. |
| SECURITY | The local security information for user rights, password policies, and group memberships on the computer. |
| SOFTWARE | The local application software configuration database for the software that is installed on the computer. |
| SYSTEM | The local system database that controls the system boot process, drivers, services, and general operating system options. |

*(continued)*

*Table 24.2* continued

| Registry File Name | How the Registry File Is Used |
| --- | --- |
| SYSTEM.ALT | A complete copy of the SYSTEM registry file that is kept in sync and that is used as a fallback if a hardware or software error occurs during an update of the SYSTEM registry file. |
| DEFAULT.LOG | A transaction log used to stage changes to the HKEY_USERS\.DEFAULT subkey. |
| SAM.LOG | A transaction log used to stage changes to the HKEY_LOCAL_MACHINE\SAM subkey. |
| SECURITY.LOG | A transaction log used to stage changes to the HKEY_LOCAL_MACHINE\SECURITY subkey. |
| SOFTWARE.LOG | A transaction log used to stage changes to the HKEY_LOCAL_MACHINE\SOFTWARE subkey. |
| SYSTEM.LOG | A transaction log used to stage changes to the HKEY_LOCAL_MACHINE\SYSTEM subkey. |
| DEFAULT.SAV | A backup copy of the HKEY_USER\DEFAULT subkey that is used during the GUI part of Windows NT setup. |
| SOFTWARE.SAV | A backup copy of the HKEY_LOCAL_MACHINE\SOFTWARE subkey that is used during the GUI part of Windows NT setup. |
| SYSTEM.SAV | A backup copy of the HKEY_LOCAL_MACHINE\SYSTEM subkey that is used during the GUI part of Windows NT setup. |
| USERDIFF | The settings that are applied to all users the first time they log on after Windows NT has been upgraded. |
| NTUSER.DAT | The settings, options, and preferences specific to user accounts that define their work environments. Each user account that is defined has this file in his or her profile directory (the HKEY_CURRENT_USER hive of the registry). |
| NTUSER.DAT.LOG | A transaction log used to stage changes to the HKEY_CURRENT_USER hive. Each user account that is defined has this file in his or her profile directory. |

# Backing Up the Registry

Although the new Windows NT registry structure provides many new benefits to computer users, it also puts them at greater risk because all of their configuration information now is dependent on the registry. This makes it more important than ever to maintain a consistent set of backups of your system. Unlike the registry files in Windows 95, the Windows NT version 4 registry files are open at all times during the operation of Windows NT; therefore, you can't just copy the files to a safe location periodically as you can with Windows 95.

Microsoft currently provides two methods for backing up the registry. The first method is to use the Windows NT Backup program which comes with Windows NT. Although the Windows NT Backup program is not as robust as many of the third party products, the price is right; and it has proven to be an adequate backup tool. This method will require a computer whose registry will be backed up to have a local tape drive supported by Windows NT. It also requires Windows NT Backup to be run on that computer. (You cannot back up the registry of a remotely connected computer with Windows NT Backup.) Because most Windows NT Server installations contain gigabytes of installed data and applications, this should not pose much of a problem; tape is currently the most economical method of backing up large volumes of data.

The second method of backing up the registry is to use the REGBACK program available in the *Microsoft Windows NT Server Resource Kit,* which you can buy directly from Microsoft or from other resellers.

### NOTE

*The* Microsoft Windows NT Server Resource Kit *is a* must have *for system administrators. The kit comes with many useful utilities and the resource kit books contain information that you're not going to find anywhere else.*

## Using Windows NT Backup

There are two ways of backing up the Windows NT registry using Windows NT Backup. The first is to run Windows NT Backup interactively and select the appropriate options you desire to perform the backup. To do this, start Backup by clicking the Start button on the taskbar; choose Programs from the Start menu, choose Administrative Tools (Common) from the Programs menu, and then choose Backup from the Administrative Tools (Common) menu. A Windows NT Backup window, similar to the one shown in Figure 24.1 on the following page, will appear.

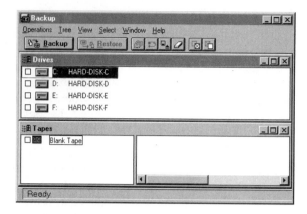

**FIGURE 24.1**

*Backing up the registry with Windows NT Backup*

The Windows NT Backup program's main window contains two windows. The first window, Drives, provides a list of the available drives from which you can select the directories and files to back up. The second window, Tapes, lists the backup volume sets contained on the current tape (if this tape was used previously to perform a backup).

In order to back up the Windows NT version 4 registry using Windows NT Backup, you must select either the drive on which Windows NT was installed or at least one file or directory on the drive on which Windows NT was installed. Be aware that although the local registry backup option includes the registry information specific to the computer on which the backup is being performed, it does *not* include the registry information specific to each of the user accounts on this computer. To back up the registry information for all the user accounts defined on the computer, include the PROFILES directory that is located in the Windows NT directory in your backup. This will back up all the information that is specific to each of the user accounts defined on the computer.

After selecting the directories and files to back up, click Backup on the toolbar. A Backup Information dialog box similar to the one shown in Figure 24.2 will appear. This dialog box allows you to specify backup options. If you are backing up multiple drives, a scrollbar will be displayed in the Backup Set Information area of the dialog box. Scroll to the backup set that will include the Windows NT drive, and select the Backup Local Registry option in the upper half of the dialog box. (This option will be grayed out until you scroll to the backup set containing the Windows NT drive.) Select any other options you want. Click OK to start the backup process.

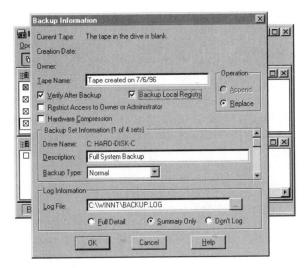

**FIGURE 24.2**

*Specifying the backup options for Windows NT Backup*

The second way of using Windows NT Backup to back up the registry is to run Windows NT Backup from a command prompt and specify all of the desired options on the command line. The following batch file listing can be used to back up registry information for the computer and registry information specific to all of the user accounts defined on this computer. (Note that the batch file is a single command and should appear on one line; it has been broken here to fit on the book page.)

```
@ntbackup backup %SystemRoot%\system32\config %SystemRoot%\profiles /a /v /d
    "Reg BU" /b /t normal /l "c:\reg.log" /e
```

You can expand this batch file to perform daily backups for the computer by adding additional drives or directories to the above batch file (after the "backup" keyword).

## Using REGBACK

The REGBACK program provided in the *Windows NT Server Resource Kit* provides another way of backing up the registry, one that allows you to back up the registry to disk. This can be very useful if you want to do a quick backup of the registry before you install new software.

The current version of REGBACK is the one that's included in the *Microsoft Windows NT Server Resource Kit*.

Note that when you run REGBACK on a Windows NT version 4 installation, it backs up both the registry information that is specific to the computer *and the registry information that is specific to the currently logged on user*. It does not back up the registry information for any other users.

Because the user-specific registry information is stored in the %SYSTEMROOT%\-PROFILES\%USERNAME%\NTUSER.DAT file in Windows NT version 4 instead of in the %SYSTEMROOT%\SYSTEM32\CONFIG\%USERNAME% file as it was in previous versions of Windows NT, you must use a different form of the REGBACK command to back up the registry information specific to the currently logged on user under Windows NT version 4.

When you run REGBACK, you must specify the directory where you want to store the backup registry files. One suggestion is to create a directory to hold the directories of the registry backups you want to maintain. For example, let's create a C:\REGBU directory to hold the registry backup directories. In the C:\REGBU directory, create a separate directory for each new registry backup. Use the following format for backing up registry information specific to the computer to one of the directories in the C:\REGBU directory:

```
c:\>regback c:\regbu\Monday
```

When you execute this command, you will see messages on the screen that indicate the progress of the registry backup; they will look similar to these messages:

```
saving SECURITY to c:\regbu\monday\SECURITY
saving SOFTWARE to c:\regbu\monday\software
saving SYSTEM to c:\regbu\monday\system
saving DEFAULT to c:\regbu\monday\default
saving SAM to c:\regbu\monday\SAM
***Hive = \REGISTRY\USER\S-1-5-21-522347448-489971457-886967795-1000

Stored in file \Device\Harddisk1\Partition1\WINNT\Profiles\joe\Ntuser.dat
Must be backed up manually

regback <filename you choose> users
    S-1-5-21-522347448-489971457-886967795-1000
```

(Note that the preceding two lines are a single command and should appear on one line; it has been broken here to fit the book page.)

The last four lines of screen output are the ones that identify what needs to be done to back up the currently logged on user's registry information. To back up that information, use the command format indicated by the last message on the screen. To easily identify to which user account the registry information belongs, we recommend you use a filename that is the same as the user account name. For example, to back up the registry information for the user account in the example above, use the command format below. (Note that this is a single command and should appear on one line; it has been broken here to fit the book page.)

```
regback c:\regbu\Monday\joe.dat users
    S-1-5-21-522347448-489971457-886967795-1000
```

After executing this command, you will see messages on the screen that indicate the progress of the registry backup; they will look similar to these messages:

saving S-1-5-21-522347448-489971457-886967795-1000 to c:\regbu\Monday\joe.dat

The long number in the preceding command specifies the SID of the user account whose registry information you want to back up. The SID will be displayed in REGBACK screen output; you also can obtain it by logging on to the computer that has that account and then looking at the second key under HKEY_USERS using the registry editor. (See "Introduction to the Windows NT Registry Editor" and "Introduction to the NEW Windows NT Registry Editor" for information about how to do this).

**Tip**

*The REGBACK examples we've used in this discussion back up all registry entries specific to the computer and all registry entries for the currently logged on user but **not** registry entries for other users. Therefore, backing up registry entries for each user who has an account defined on this computer would require a separate execution of the REGBACK command for each user account, specifying the user's SID as the user account to back up. With a large number of users, this would be unwieldy and time consuming. Although REGBACK works well for a single user and one computer, the best method to use for handling a large number of users is the Windows NT Backup program. Select the Backup Local Registry option in the Backup Information dialog box and include the %SYSTEMROOT%\-PROFILES directory in the regular backup schedule.*

# Restoring the Registry

Microsoft currently provides two methods of restoring the registry. The first is to use Windows NT Backup, which comes with Windows NT version 4. This method requires that you have a local tape drive supported by Windows NT installed on the computer whose registry you want to restore and that you run Windows NT Backup on this computer. (You can't restore the registry of a remotely connected computer with Windows NT Backup.) The second method of restoring the registry is to use REGREST, which is available in the *Microsoft Windows NT Server Resource Kit.*

## Using Windows NT Backup

Windows NT Backup does not provide you with command-line options for backing up the registry; you can restore the registry only by using the GUI interface. To restore a registry that was backed up with Windows NT Backup, insert the tape that contains the registry backup and start the Windows NT Backup program. A Windows NT Backup program window similar to the one shown in Figure 24.3 will appear.

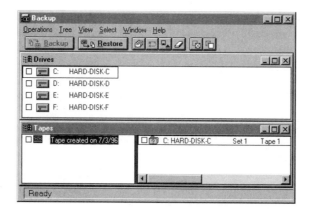

**FIGURE 24.3**

*Restoring the registry with Windows NT Backup*

The Windows NT Backup program's main window contains two windows. The first, Drives, is used during the backup process to specify what you want to back up. The other window, Tapes, lists the backup volume sets contained on the current tape; in this window you specify which items you want to restore.

The Tapes window has two panes: the left pane lists the tapes on which you have previously created backup volume sets, and the right pane lists the backup volume sets for the tape that is selected in the left pane. Windows NT Backup initially displays only the first backup volume set in the right pane; to see a list of all backup volume sets on a tape, double-click the tape you want in the left pane. A Catalog Status dialog box will appear while the information on the backup volume sets is obtained from the tape. After all of the information has been obtained from the tape, the right pane of the Tapes window will display a list of all backup volume sets on the tape, as shown in Figure 24.4.

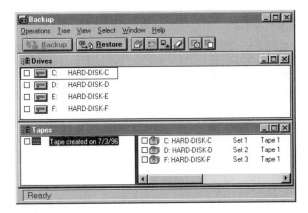

**FIGURE 24.4**

*Example of a list of backup volume sets on a tape in Windows NT Backup*

Double-click the backup volume set in the right pane that contains the version of the registry that you want to restore. The tape will be read again to obtain the list of directories and files that are contained in the selected backup volume set. After the list has been obtained, another window opens to display the contents of the selected backup volume set in a directory tree format, as shown in Figure 24.5.

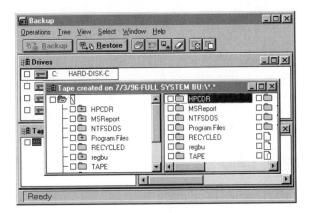

**FIGURE 24.5**

*Displaying the contents of a backup volume set in Windows NT Backup*

To restore the registry you must select at least one file to restore, because the option to restore the registry is disabled until you select a file to restore. (We hope Microsoft will address this issue in a future version of Windows NT.) Use the window that is displaying the contents of the backup set to select the files you want to restore, and click Restore on the toolbar.

The Restore Local Registry option of Windows NT Backup does *not* restore the registry information that is specific to the user accounts; it restores only the information that is specific to the computer and the default user. To restore information for a specific user account, the %SYSTEMROOT%\PROFILES directory must have been included in the backup set. To restore the registry information for a specific user account, you have to restore the NTUSER.DAT file in the profile directory for that user. The user's profile directory is located in %SYSTEMROOT%\PROFILES.

The Restore Information dialog box will appear, as shown in Figure 24.6. Select the Restore Local Registry option, and then click OK to begin the restore. The Restore Status window will open and show the progress of the restore. When the restore is complete, a Backup dialog box will display a message that indicates the active files won't be usable until the computer is restarted. Click OK; shut down and restart Windows NT. After rebooting, the restored registry settings now will be in use.

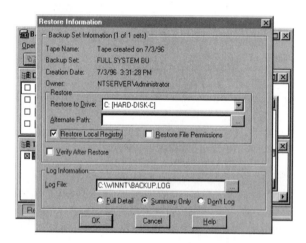

**FIGURE 24.6**

*Specifying the restore options for Windows NT Backup*

## Using REGREST

The REGREST program provides another method for restoring the Windows NT registry. It's available in the *Microsoft Windows NT Server Resource Kit* and is the restore counterpart of the REGBACK program.

When you select the Restore Local Registry option in the Restore Information dialog box or when you specify restoring the NTUSER.DAT file for the currently logged on user, Windows NT cannot restore the files immediately because they are currently in use by the operating system. To restore these files, Windows NT temporarily renames the registry files to REG*xxxxx* and the registry log files to REG*xxxxx*.LOG. The *xxxxx* in these filenames is a sequential number that does not cause a filename conflict with a file already on the hard disk. The next time you reboot Windows NT, the restored registry files will have their correct names and will have replaced the versions previously in use. This process is transparent to the user.

The REGREST program that comes with *the Microsoft Windows NT Server Resource Kit* works fine with Windows NT version 4 but, like the REGBACK program, requires you to perform an additional step to restore the registry information for the currently logged on user.

After the backup of the local registry and the backup of the currently logged on users registry information is complete, as described in "Using REGBACK to Back Up the Registry," we have the following files in our C:\REGBU\MONDAY directory:

```
SAM
SYSTEM
DEFAULT
SECURITY
SOFTWARE
JOE.DAT
```

When you run REGREST, you must specify the name of the directory that contains the registry files you want to restore. You also must specify a name for the directory to which you want to save the current registry files. For our example, let's create the C:\OLDREGBU directory to hold the registry files that are currently in use. To restore the registry files in the C:\REGBU\MONDAY directory, you would use this command:

```
c:\>regrest c:\regbu\Monday c:\oldregbu
```

For the REGREST program to restore the registry successfully, both the directory containing the registry files you want to restore *and* the directory where you want to store the backups of these registry files *must* be located on the partition on which Windows NT version 4 is installed. The reason for this has to do with how REGREST actually restores the registry. It does not copy the files you are restoring to the correct location; instead, it *renames* them in place on the partition. If you do not have the registry files on the same partition on which Window NT is installed, you must move the registry backup files to the Windows NT partition or the REGREST program will fail.

After executing the preceding command, you will see messages on the screen that indicate the progress of the registry restore; these messages will be similar to the following messages:

```
replacing SECURITY with c:\regbu\Monday\SECURITY
replacing SOFTWARE with c:\regbu\Monday\SOFTWARE
replacing SYSTEM with c:\regbu\Monday\SYSTEM
replacing.DEFAULT with c:\regbu\Monday\DEFAULT
replacing SAM with c:\regbu\Monday\SAM

***Hive = \REGISTRY\USER\S-1-5-21-522347448-489971457-886967795-1000
Stored in file \Device\Harddisk1\Partition1\WINNT\Profiles\joe\NTUSER.DAT
Must be replaced manually
regrest <newpath> <savepath> users
    S-1-5-21-522347448-489971457-886967795-1000
```

(Note that the preceding two lines are a single command and should appear on one line; it has been broken here to fit the book page.)

```
You must reboot for changes to take effect.
```

The last five lines of the screen output are the ones that identify what needs to be done to restore the registry information for the user whose registry information was backed up previously. To restore the registry information for that user, use the command format indicated in the second to the last message on the screen. For example, for our previously backed-up user information, use this command format:

```
c:\>regrest c:\regbu\Monday\joe.dat c:\oldregbu\joe.dat
    users S-1-5-21-522347448-489971457-886967795-1000
```

(Note that the preceding two lines are a single command and should appear on one line; it has been broken here to fit the book page.)

After executing this command, you will see messages on the screen that indicate the progress of the registry restore; these messages will be similar to the messages shown below. (Note that this is a single command and should appear on one line; it has been broken here to fit the book page.)

```
replacing S-1-5-21-522347448-489971457-886967795-1000
    with c:\regbu\Monday\joe.dat


You must reboot for changes to take effect.
```

After the registry files have been restored successfully, you should shut down the computer and then restart it so that Windows NT can use the restored registry files.

# Registry Editor REGEDT32

REGEDT32.EXE is the name of the registry editor utility that has been provided with Windows NT since Windows NT first was released in 1993. Microsoft did not create an icon for it in Program Manager for earlier versions of Windows NT, and it has continued this practice in Windows NT version 4. The most likely reason for this is protection for you: it makes it less easy to inadvertently mess up your system—because if you modify the registry incorrectly, you can render your system inoperable. Our best advice is that you make sure you have adequate and recent backups of the registry before you attempt to make any changes to it.

## Using REGEDT32

To run the REGEDT32 utility, click the Start button. Choose Run, type *REGEDT32*, and then click OK. You also can start the utility from a command prompt by typing *REGEDT32*.

> **Tip**
>
> *If you find yourself using REGEDIT32 frequently, you might want to create a shortcut to it on your desktop or place it on the Start menu.*

When you run the REGEDT32 utility, the main program window will look similar to the one shown in Figure 24.7 on the following page. Inside this window, you will see five windows: two of them are for registry hives HKEY_LOCAL_MACHINE and HKEY_USERS; the other three are for the pointers HKEY_CURRENT-_CONFIG, HKEY_CLASSES_ROOT, and HKEY_CURRENT_USER.

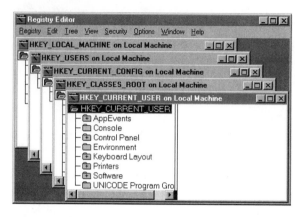

**FIGURE 24.7**

*The Windows NT registry editor utility REGEDT32*

Each of the windows displays its piece of the registry in a tree-like structure, much as File Manager displays the directories and files on your hard drive. The windows are divided into two panes—the left pane, which displays the registry keys and subkeys, and the right pane, which displays the registry values and their contents for the registry key that has been selected in the left pane of the window.

In front of each key is a folder icon that can be blank or can contain a plus sign (+) or a minus sign (–). If the folder icon is blank, it means the key does not contain any subkeys. If the folder icon has a plus sign, it means there are subkeys under the key but the key hasn't been expanded yet. If the folder icon is a minus sign, it means there are subkeys under the key and that the key already has been expanded.

The REGEDT32 main program window has six primary menus: Registry, Edit, Tree, View, Security, and Options. (The Window and Help menus are standard menus.) Each of the menus is described in the following sections.

## Registry

- ◆ **Open Local** Opens the hive windows for the local computer's registry. By default, this is performed when you start the REGEDT32 program.

- ◆ **Close** Closes the hive windows for the computer's registry. If the currently open window is one of the registry windows for the local computer, all five windows will close. If the currently open window is one of the windows for a remote computer's registry, the two windows displaying the remote computer's registry will close.

- ◆ **Load Hive** Temporarily loads a registry hive into the open registry hive being displayed. This option is available only when the current window displays either HKEY_LOCAL_MACHINE or HKEY_USERS for the local computer or for a remote computer's registry. One use of this option is to modify the registry entries for another user. After loading the hive for another user account, it will appear as a separate key in HKEY_USERS. You now can view or modify the registry information for that user. After you have finished working with that user's registry information, unload it from the registry. For more details on loading the registry hives for other user accounts, see "Registry Tips and Tricks" at the end of this chapter.

- ◆ **Unload Hive** Saves modifications that were made to a previously loaded hive to disk and unloads the hive from memory. This option should be used only for registry items that you have previously loaded with Load Hive.

- ◆ **Restore** Restores a hive previously saved to disk. When you restore a hive, the current hive is overwritten with the restored hive's information. These changes are a permanent replacement for the hive's information.

- ◆ **Save Key** Saves all of the items in a registry key and its subkeys to a file. The registry information is saved to the filename that you specify in binary format. The file may later be loaded back into the registry with the Load Hive menu option or with the Restore menu option.

- ◆ **Select Computer** Connects to another computer to display and modify its registry hives. After you select this menu item, a dialog box will appear that allows you to select the computer from a list of computers or to type the desired computer name. Be sure to precede the computer name with two backslashes if you type it. After you have selected the computer, two additional windows will open, one to display the HKEY_LOCAL_MACHINE hive and another to display the HKEY_USERS hive for the computer selected.

- ◆ **Print Subtree** Prints the currently selected registry key, all of this key's subkeys, and all of the values contained in the subkeys.

- ◆ **Printer Setup** Permits the selection of a particular printer and the specification of printer options for that printer.

- ◆ **Save Subtree As** Saves the currently selected registry key, all of this key's subkeys, and all values contained in the subkeys to a text file.

- ◆ **Exit** Closes the registry editor program.

## Edit

- **Add Key** Adds a new subkey to the currently selected key. REGEDT32 will prompt you for the key name and the class name of the new key.

- **Add Value** Allows a new value to be added to the currently selected key. REGEDT32 will prompt you for the key name and the type of data. The REGEDT32 registry editor supports only the most commonly used registry data types: REG_BINARY, REG_DWORD, REG_EXPAND_SZ, REG_MULTI_SZ, and REG_SZ.

- **Delete** Removes the currently selected item. If a key is selected, it deletes the key, all of this key's subkeys, and all of the values contained in the subkeys. If a value is selected, only that value is deleted.

- **Binary** Displays the binary editor for REGEDT32 to allow modification of the selected binary value. (A binary value also can be modified by double-clicking the desired binary value.)

- **String** Opens the string editor for REGEDT32 to allow modification of the selected string value. The string editor is used to modify REG_EXPAND_SZ and REG_SZ values. (A string value also can be modified by double-clicking the desired string value.)

- **DWORD** Opens the DWORD editor for REGEDT32 to allow modification of the selected DWORD value. (A DWORD value also can be modified by double-clicking the desired DWORD value.)

- **Multi String** Opens the multi-string editor for REGEDIT32 to allow modification of the selected REG_MULTI_SZ value. (A REG_MULTI_SZ value also can be modified by double-clicking the desired REG_MULTI_SZ value.)

## Tree

- **Expand One Level** Expands the currently selected key to display the next level of subkeys under it.

- **Expand Branch** Shows all of the subkeys under the currently selected key.

- **Expand All** Expands all subkeys for the currently open registry window.

- **Collapse Branch** Closes the tree levels for all of the subkeys in the currently selected registry key.

## View

♦ **Tree and Data** Displays both the left pane (tree information) and the right pane (values and data) information in the currently open registry window.

♦ **Tree Only** Displays only the left pane (tree information) in the currently open registry window.

♦ **Data Only** Displays only the right pane (values and data) information in the currently open registry window.

♦ **Split** Allows you to move the bar that separates the left pane and right pane to adjust the size of the panes.

♦ **Display Binary Data** Displays the currently selected value in binary format in read-only mode.

♦ **Refresh All** Updates the registry information displayed for all registry windows associated with the currently open registry window.

♦ **Refresh Active** Updates the registry information displayed for the currently open registry window to show any changes that have been made to the registry entries.

♦ **Find Key** Displays a dialog box that allows you to locate a registry key in the currently open registry window.

## Security

♦ **Permissions** Displays the currently selected registry key granted to defined user accounts and group accounts and allows modification of the access to this key. At this time, the access required for specific registry keys is not well documented; therefore, you should proceed with caution if you modify a registry key's security settings.

♦ **Auditing** Permits auditing of additions, changes, and deletions to the currently selected registry key.

♦ **Owner** Displays the name of the owner of the currently selected registry key and allows modification of this ownership.

## Options

♦ **Font** Displays the Font dialog box which is used to select the font to be used in registry windows.

- **Auto Refresh** Displays registry updates immediately in all registry windows. Auto refresh is turned off when you view another computer's registry hives.

- **Read-Only Mode** Changes all registry keys and values in all of the displayed registry windows to read-only. No changes are allowed to any of the registry keys or values in read-only mode.

- **Confirm on Delete** Displays a dialog box whenever you delete a registry key or value that prompts you to confirm your choice to delete this key or value.

- **Save Settings on Exit** Saves the window positions, window sizes, and font selection currently in use so that they are used each time you run REGEDT32.

## Advantages of REGEDT32

The REGEDT32 program provides several features that are not readily available anywhere else unless you develop your own application using the Win 32 Software Development Kit (SDK) available from Microsoft. These are some of the features:

- The ability to view and modify security permissions on registry keys

- The ability to audit the access, additions, changes, and deletions of registry keys

- The ability to take ownership of a registry key, if the appropriate security permissions have been set

- The ability to connect to, view, and modify the registry settings of another computer on the network, if the appropriate security permissions have been set

- The ability to load and modify a registry hive that has been previously saved to disk and is currently not loaded in the registry

- The ability to display the data type of each value along with the value's data contents

In most cases, the person using these functions must be the administrator of the computer whose registry is being accessed or modified or be a member of the local Administrators group on the computer.

## Disadvantages of REGEDT32

Despite the many advantages of the REGEDT32 program, there are areas where it could be improved. The biggest weakness of REGEDT32 is the limited search capability of the Find function; it can search only the registry of a specific registry key. This is significant because you frequently will want to search the registry for a specific value's name or for a specific piece of information in a value's data.

Another weak area of REGEDT32 is the program's interface. Rather than resembling the look and feel of the new Windows NT user interface, it still resembles the look and feel of the older Windows 3.1 interface. Although this isn't a major disadvantage, it does mean that the nicer, new features, such as context menus and right-mouse-button support, are not available.

# Registry Editor REGEDIT

When Windows 95 was released, users found a new and much improved registry editor called REGEDIT.EXE; this registry editor is now a welcome addition to Windows NT version 4, although some of the functionality of the Windows 95 version will not appear in Windows NT until a subsequent iteration is produced at a later time. However, most of the core improvements introduced in Windows 95 are in Windows NT version 4.

## Using REGEDIT

The obvious place to look for the new registry editor, REGEDIT, would be in Administrative Tools (Common); but as for the REGEDT32 program, there's no icon for REGEDIT on the Start menu. Most likely this is because of the dangers involved in making changes to the registry. It cannot be stressed enough how important it is to have a reliable backup process in place and have recent backups of the registry stored safely on disk before you attempt to make any changes to the registry.

To run the new REGEDIT utility, click the Start button. Choose Run, and type *REGEDIT.* Click OK. You can also start REGEDIT from a command prompt by typing *REGEDIT.* If you find yourself using this utility frequently, you might want to create a shortcut to it on your desktop or place it on the Start menu.

When you start REGEDIT, it will display its main program window, shown in Figure 24.8 on the following page. Unlike the REGEDT32 program, however, REGEDIT doesn't display each of the registry hives in its own window; instead, it uses a display similar to Windows NT Explorer. The window is divided into two panes: the left pane displays the names of the computers to which you are connected with their respective registry hives listed under them, and the right pane displays the registry values and their contents for the registry key currently selected in the window's left pane.

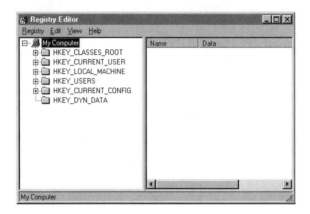

**FIGURE 24.8**

*The new Windows NT registry editor utility REGEDIT*

REGEDIT's main program window has four menus: Registry, Edit, View, and Help, which provide access to all of the program's functions. The entries on the first three menus are described in the following sections.

### Registry

♦ **Import Registry File** Imports a REGEDIT4 format text file into the registry.

♦ **Export Registry File** Exports all or a selected part of the registry to a REGEDIT4 formatted text file. This file can be easily edited with any text editor and re-imported back into the registry.

♦ **Connect Network Registry** Will allow you to connect to another computer's registry to view and modify its registry entries. Unfortunately, it's not functional at this time and isn't scheduled to be fixed until a future version of Windows NT.

♦ **Disconnect Network Registry** Disconnects the previously made connection to another computer's registry.

♦ **Print** Prints the entire registry of the selected key, all of the key's subkeys, and all of the values contained in the subkeys.

♦ **Exit** Closes the registry editor program.

### Edit

- **Modify** Edits the value currently selected in the right pane of the window. (This entry appears only when a value is selected in the right pane of the window.)

- **New item** Creates a new subkey of the currently selected key or a new string, binary, or DWORD value for the currently selected key.

- **Delete** Deletes the currently selected item. If a key is selected, it deletes the key, all of the key's subkeys, and all of the values contained in the subkeys. If a value is selected, only that value is deleted.

- **Rename** Changes the name of the currently selected key, subkey, or value.

- **Copy Key Name** Copies the fully qualified name of the selected key or subkey to the clipboard.

- **Find** Searches the entire registry for the specified character string. Key names, subkey names, value names, and their data all can be searched for the character string specified.

- **Find Next** Finds the next occurrence of the previously specified character string.

### View

- **Status Bar** Toggles the display of the status bar at the bottom of the REGEDIT window. The status bar can display the description of the currently selected menu command or the path to the currently selected registry key.

- **Split** Moves the splitter bar that separates the left pane and right pane to adjust the size of the panes.

- **Refresh** Updates the registry display to reflect changes that have been made to the registry by another program.

## Advantages of REGEDIT

REGEDIT has several major advantages over the older REGEDT32 utility in features that greatly enhance the ease of gaining access to the registry and modifying it. These are the most significant advantages:

- A vastly improved Find feature that can search the key names, value names, and value data for specified search criteria.

- The ability to limit which areas the Find feature should search. Key names, value names, and value data all can be individually included or excluded from the search.

- The ability to import a REGEDIT4 format text file into the registry.

- The ability to export the entire registry, a specific registry hive, or a specific registry branch and all of the entries it contains to a REGEDIT4 format text file.

- A much-improved interface that provides all of the nice features of the new user interface, such as context menus and right-mouse-button support.

## Disadvantages of REGEDIT

Despite the significant advantages of the new registry editor, there are several areas in which it needs improvement.

- Even though the Registry menu contains the Connect Network Registry and Disconnect Network Registry items, REGEDIT can't connect you to the registry of another computer.

- Although the import and export features provide methods for saving and restoring registry information to and from a REGEDIT4 format text file (a very useful and powerful feature), there is no method of loading the registry information of a currently unloaded registry hive, such as the registry hive of a user who is not currently logged on.

- The data type of each value is not displayed along with the value's data contents, so you must invoke the editor for the data value to have the data type displayed.

In spite of these disadvantages, the new registry editor is a very welcome addition to Windows NT. Microsoft chose to include it because of the significant features it does provide. It is likely that the missing functionality of REGEDIT will be addressed in a future version of Windows NT, and we probably will see the two registry editors merged into a single application.

# Registry Tips and Tricks

In this section, we will provide you with a few tips and tricks for working with the Windows NT registry. Note that to perform the tasks described in this section you should log on to the computer that is being modified as the administrator of that computer or as a user that is a member of the local Administrators group.

## Installing New Software

We recommend that you perform a backup of the registry before you install any new software. This backup provides you with a recovery option if something goes wrong during the software installation and, as a result, the registry information is corrupted or if the changes you make to the registry produce undesirable results.

To perform a complete registry backup for the local computer and also back up the registry information for *all* user accounts on the local computer, use a batch file (which uses the Windows NT Backup program that comes with Windows NT). When the backup is complete, Notepad will be launched to display the log file that is created during the backup.

```
@Echo Off
REM
REM Backup the local computer's registry information and the
REM registry information for all user accounts on the local
REM computer using NT Backup.
REM
ntbackup backup c:\winnt\system32\config c:\winnt\profiles /a /v /d
    "Registry BU" /b /t normal /l "c:\bu.log" /e
```

(Note that the preceding two lines are a single command and should appear on one line; it has been broken here to fit the book page.)

```
notepad c:\bu.log
```

The batch file described below will perform a complete registry backup for the local computer and also will back up the registry information for a single user account (that you specify) on the local computer using REGBACK. Note that you *must* modify this batch file to specify the SID for the user account that you want to back up and that the account specified must be for the currently logged on user. To determine the SID for a currently logged on user, run REGEDIT and expand the HKEY_USERS hive. One of the two subkeys will have the SID for the currently logged on user as its name. (The other key is always the .DEFAULT subkey.) Modify the batch file where noted to specify this number for the user account you want to back up. (This batch file assumes that the *Microsoft Windows NT Server Resource Kit* has been installed and added to the path so that REGBACK can be located.)

```
@Echo Off
REM
REM Backup the local computer's registry information and the
REM registry information for the specified user account on
REM the local computer using the REGBACK program from the
REM Windows NT Server Resource Kit.
REM
if.%1==. goto NoDir

REM Check to make sure the specified directory exists
if not exist %1\nul goto NotExist

REM Back up the local computer's registry information
regback %1
if ErrorLevel 2 goto RegFail

REM Back up the registry information for the specified user
REM account on the local computer.
REM
REM The next command must be modified to specify the user accounts
REM SID that you want to back up.
regback %1\NTUSER.DAT users s-1-1-12-123456789-1234567890-1234567890-
    1234
```

(Note that the preceding two lines are a single command and should appear on
line; it has been broken here to fit the book page.)

```
if ErrorLevel 1 goto URegFail

goto End

:NoDir
Echo No directory specified to backup the registry to.
goto End

:NotExist
Echo The directory specified does not exist.
goto End

:RegFail
Echo Error backing up the local computer registry information.
goto End

:URegFail
Echo Error backing up the specified user's registry information.
goto End

:End
```

# Adding to the Right-Click Menu

You can use the method described below to add an item to the right-click menu for file types that are not currently associated with any application. It provides a convenient way to add your favorite text file editor to this menu.

1. Start REGEDIT.EXE by clicking the Start button. Choose Run, and type *REGEDIT*. Then click OK.

2. Locate the HKEY_CLASSES_ROOT hive, and click the plus sign in the icon in front of the name to expand the hive.

3. Locate and expand the Unknown subkey of HKEY_CLASSES_ROOT by clicking the plus sign in the icon in front of the name.

4. Click the shell subkey.

5. Now right-click the shell subkey. Choose New from the pop-up menu, and then choose Key from the New menu.

6. Enter the name of your text file editor as the name for the registry subkey. Press Enter.

7. Right-click the registry subkey that was just created for your text file editor. Choose New from the pop-up menu, and then choose Key from the New menu.

8. Enter *Command* as the name of the new subkey. Press Enter.

9. Double-click Default in the right pane of the program window to modify the default entry for the Command subkey that you just created. Enter the fully qualified path to your text file editor, followed by a space and %1. Then click OK. For example, to use Notepad you might enter:

```
c:\winnt\notepad.exe %1
```

After you have made this change, you can right-click any file whose type is not associated with an application and launch your favorite text editor with that file loaded. The change will affect all users who log on to the computer because the change is made to the registry information for the computer and *not* to the registry information for the currently logged on user.

# Server Name Display

The .DEFAULT subkey settings are used by the computer when there is no user currently logged on to the computer as well as when a new user logs on for the first time. Although individual users can specify which screen saver and options they want to use, you must modify the registry directly to set the default screen saver and options to use when no user is logged on to the computer. The default screen saver is used to display the name of the computer. You can use the method described below to identify your servers easily when there are multiple servers in a common location or when you're using a switch box for a group of computers that allows them to share a monitor, keyboard, and mouse.

1. Start REGEDIT.EXE by clicking the Start button. Choose Run, and type *REGEDIT.* Then click OK.

2. Expand the HKEY_USERS hive in the left pane of the window by clicking the plus sign in the icon in front of HKEY_USERS.

3. Expand the .DEFAULT subkey by clicking the plus sign in the icon in front of its name.

4. Expand the Control Panel subkey by clicking the plus sign in the icon in front of its name.

5. Select the Desktop subkey by clicking Desktop.

6. Locate SCRNSAVE.EXE in the right pane of the window, and double-click it to modify it.

7. The Edit String dialog box will appear. Modify the Value Data text box to specify the SSMARQUE screen saver. For example, if you installed Windows NT in the C:\WINNT directory, you then would type the following:

```
c:\winnt\system32\ssmarque.scr
```

8. Click OK to save your changes.

9. Locate ScreenSaveTimeOut in the right pane of the window, and double-click it to modify it.

10. The Edit String dialog box will appear. Enter 60 in the Value Data text box to specify the number of seconds the screen saver waits before starting. Then click OK to save your changes.

11. Select the Screen Saver.Marquee subkey of Control Panel by clicking it in the left pane of the window.

12. Locate Size in the right pane of the window, and double-click it to modify it.

13. The Edit String dialog box will appear. Enter *36* in the Value Data text box to specify the desired size. Then click OK to save your changes.

14. Locate Speed in the right pane of the window, and double-click it to modify it.

15. The Edit String dialog box will appear. Enter *1* in the Value Data text box to specify the desired speed. Then click OK to save your changes.

16. Locate Text in the right pane of the window, and double-click it to modify it.

17. The Edit String dialog box will appear. Enter the name of the computer in the Value Data text box to specify the string that the screen saver will display. Then click OK to save your changes.

The SSMARQUE screen saver now will display the computer name when no user is currently logged on to the computer.

# Viewing a Remote Registry

The method described below can be used to load the registry hive of another user whose account is on the computer but who is not currently logged on. An administrator uses this technique when he or she needs to modify registry settings on such an account.

1. Start REGEDT32.EXE by clicking the Start button. Choose Run, and type *REGEDT32*. Then click OK.

2. Choose HKEY_USERS On Local Machine from the Window menu.

3. Select the HKEY_USERS hive by clicking HKEY_USERS in the left pane of the window.

4. Choose Load Hive from the Registry menu.

5. In the Load Hive dialog box, switch to the directory where Windows NT is installed; then open the Profiles directory located in the Windows NT directory.

6. Open the directory for the user account that you want to load by double-clicking on that user's directory.

7. Click the NTUSER.DAT file located in the user's directory, and then click Open.

8. A dialog box will appear that prompts you for a Key Name. Type the name of the user account that you are loading, and then click OK.

9. The user's registry information now will be available as a subkey under HKEY_USERS. You can view and modify the registry settings as desired.

After you have finished working with the user's registry hive, you *must* unload the hive so that it's available to the user if he or she wants to log on to the computer. To unload the user's registry hive, follow these steps:

1. Select the subkey in the HKEY_USERS hive that was previously loaded by clicking the subkey entry.

2. Choose Unload Hive from the Registry menu.

3. A warning message will be displayed that asks you if you want to continue. Click Yes to unload the user's registry hive.

## POINTS TO REMEMBER

◆ The registry in Windows NT is a method for storing type associations and for maintaining information used by other applications for object linking and embedding.

◆ Each piece of information that is stored in the registry is assigned a name. The name used doesn't need to be unique to the entire registry; it needs to be unique only to the registry key or subkey in which the value name is created.

◆ Data associated with a name is assigned a data type that describes the type of information stored in that registry entry.

◆ Two registry edit programs are included with Windows NT Server: the older REGEDIT32 and the newer REGEDIT.

◆ Always back up the registry before you install new software.

## WHAT'S NEXT?

Windows NT Server is justly renowned for its stability and robustness, but even the most fault tolerant system can be made even safer. In Chapter 25, we move on to how to create that extra margin of safety for your system and how to cope when even the best laid plans go awry.

# CHAPTER 25

# CHAPTER 25

## Disaster Recovery

Bicycle riders wear helmets even though they ride carefully and hope they never, ever need that helmet to perform its job. But as the saying goes, "There are only two kinds of riders, those who've crashed and those who haven't...yet."

Well, as system administrators, we sincerely hope we will never need to use our verified backups and emergency repair disks. But we keep them because there are only two types of networks, those that have experienced disaster and those that haven't...yet.

In this chapter, we'll cover emergency preparedness as well as the actual recovery process. We'll discuss creating a disaster recovery plan, with standardized procedures to follow in the event of catastrophe. We'll show you how to make a Microsoft Windows NT Emergency Repair Disk, what to change in your recovery procedures if you're using a mirrored boot partition, and how to handle the replacement of a server in the event that the worst happens.

## Preparing a Disaster Recovery Plan

It is an unfortunate fact of life that network systems do crash occasionally and that almost no one's reaction to these disasters is predictable. Even the most level-headed system administrator can and does get flustered when the system has crashed, the users are screaming, the boss is asking every five minutes when the problem will be fixed—and the server won't boot. You can reduce your stress levels and prevent mistakes by planning for disaster recovery before the disaster occurs.

To be really prepared, you need to plan for as many eventualities as you can. Figure out as many of the possible breakdown scenarios as you can, and practice what to do for each one. Write down all the steps you will need to follow for each scenario. It's very important to have a written set of standard procedures for recovering a system when it fails. This process is the same as planning emergency procedures for a fire, and you do it for the same reason—not because you view fires or system failures as inevitable but because the reality is that fires and system crashes *do* happen.

Start by trying to list all the possible ways that your system could fail. If you have a team of people responsible for supporting the network, get them together to help in the process. The more people you have involved in the brainstorming, the more ideas you'll get and the more procedures you can develop and practice.

When you have put together a comprehensive list, get some of the people in the group involved in creating the recovery procedures. Initially they should outline the main steps for each recovery procedure, without going into detail. When the outlines are finished, get the group together again and go over each of the procedures, smoothing the rough edges. As you refine the outlines, *listen* to the feedback from the group to be sure you didn't miss any critical steps. When you feel confident you've actually captured the essence of the procedures, it's time to test them and to document them completely.

Depending on the size of your group, you'll probably want to break it up into smaller teams of two or three people to test and document individual recovery procedures. As you create the documentation, write down *everything.* What seems obvious to you now while creating the procedure will not necessarily seem at all obvious six months or a year from now when you suddenly have to implement it. In addition, you can't be sure that *you* will be the one who will have to use it.

Keep copies of the current version of your emergency procedures in several places so that you can get at them no matter what the emergency or where you are when it happens. Then keep the procedures up to date! This seems like an obvious point to make, but keeping procedures up to date is actually not that easy to do. Systems change over time, and the procedures to recover them have to change as well. You'll also have to make sure that all of the distributed copies are updated. We like to keep the master copy of our emergency procedures in a secure directory on the mirrored boot partition, with a version control system in place to check them out and back in. (Version control software works like an electronic library. Users can check files in and out; no modifications are permitted to a file that is checked out.) When your Windows NT server won't boot—which pretty much defines an emergency for most system administrators—haul out the standardized disaster recovery procedures you've created, and follow them step by step.

# Recovering from a Disaster

The important thing to keep in mind about recovery procedures is that you want to take a minimalist approach; always try the least invasive and least drastic steps first. If they succeed, you'll have the greatest amount of recovered information and the least amount of impact on the network and on your users—which, of course, is the point of the recovery effort. In the following sections, we'll discuss, in order from the least drastic action to the most drastic action, the recovery methods available to you.

## The Last Known Good Menu

If you make a change to your system, you can inadvertently create a configuration that doesn't allow you to boot the system. The easiest and usually the best recovery tool in this situation is available when you begin the rebooting process. You'll see a message that says:

Press spacebar NOW to invoke Hardware Profile/Last Known Good menu

Pressing the Spacebar will get you a menu of possible logon choices that will let you, in many cases, simply bypass that last, ill-advised change. But be forewarned: you also will be eliminating any changes you've made to your system since the configuration was last saved. This might be a problem if you want to go back to the original configuration, which is always one of the options. In addition, many changes you made to the system won't be reflected in this recovery option, so you might not always have a good configuration to go back to. Even if you have made a change that is captured by the system as an option, you might still have problems. When you have successfully logged on to a system after a configuration change, Windows NT Server assumes that the configuration is good—and it might not be.

You also can use the Last Known Good Configuration menu option to recover your system if your server has multiple hardware configurations. Although this isn't terribly likely with Windows NT Server, it certainly isn't uncommon in some situations, such as when Microsoft Windows NT Workstation is loaded on a laptop.

## Hardware Profile Copy

If you want to be sure you've got yourself covered before you begin to make a major hardware change, first create a new hardware profile that's a copy of your current hardware profile. Then boot into the new profile, and make the changes you want to make. If something doesn't work quite as you'd hoped, you can still return to your previous configuration.

To create a copy of your current hardware profile and make that the preferred boot option, follow these steps:

1. Right-click the My Computer icon in the upper left corner of the desktop.

2. Choose Properties to bring up the System Properties dialog box.

3. Click the Hardware Profiles tab to bring up the dialog box shown in Figure 25.1.

4. Select the current hardware profile, and click Copy. Type the name for the new configuration in the To text box.

5. If you want to make the new profile the preferred boot option, select it, and then click the upward-pointing arrow next to the list box to move your new hardware profile to the top of the box.

6. Decide whether you want Windows NT Server to choose the new hardware profile automatically (after a delay) when you boot up or you want

the system to wait indefinitely until you choose the hardware profile by selecting the appropriate option.

7. Click OK. The new configuration will be saved, and your startup options will be set.

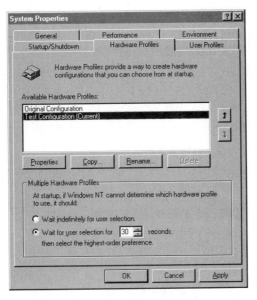

**FIGURE 25.1**

*Hardware Profiles tab of the System Properties dialog box*

## Emergency Repair Disk

When you first installed Windows NT Server, the installation program prompted you to create an Emergency Repair Disk (ERD). We hope you followed our advice and let the installation program create that disk. But the ERD is useful only if you've kept it current. Most systems are the products of a constant evolutionary process; your ERD is going to be able to bail you out of a mess only if it has the information about your current setup stored on it.

So exactly what is on the ERD? The files on the ERD are the hives of the registry, along with copies of the MS-DOS subsystem initialization files (AUTOEXEC.NT and CONFIG.NT) and the Security Accounts Manager database. Whenever you make a major change to your system, it's a good idea to make a fresh copy of the ERD before *and* after you make the change. This provides a fallback position if something goes wrong. When something doesn't work right, you can restore the previous configuration quickly.

So what's a major change? Adding, removing, or otherwise modifying the hard drives or their partitions, file systems, configurations, and so forth. For example, any time you change the hard drive configuration, you definitely want to make a fresh ERD before and after the change. The addition of a new component to your server, such as Microsoft Exchange Server or Microsoft SQL Server, and changes from Control Panel also are situations where you want to refresh the ERD both before and after the change.

Also keep in mind that it's a good thing to have a backup of your ERD; always keep an ERD from at least one generation back. We also like to keep the original ERD that was created during the installation as a kind of ultimate fallback position.

When you create a fresh Emergency Repair Disk, you will need to use a floppy disk that you don't mind having formatted because RDISK.EXE, the program that creates the ERD, always formats the floppy disk. To create the ERD, follow these steps:

1. Insert a 3.5-inch, 1.44-MB floppy disk in the A: drive.

2. Choose Run from the Start menu.

3. Type *rdisk*, and click OK to bring up the dialog box shown in Figure 25.2.

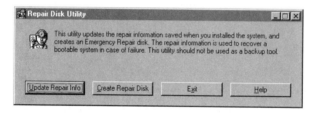

**FIGURE 25.2**

*Repair Disk Utility dialog box*

4. Click Update Repair Info to bring up the confirmation dialog box shown in Figure 25.3. Click Yes to update the repair information. Running rdisk will overwrite any previously saved information. When you are doing an update after a major change, you can skip this step until you're sure the change is stable and desirable. Click No if you want to skip it.

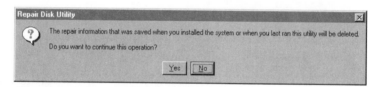

**FIGURE 25.3**

*Emergency Repair Disk update confirmation dialog box*

5. After the repair information has been updated, the system will prompt you to create an Emergency Repair Disk, as shown in Figure 25.4. Click Yes to make the disk.

6. Store the disk in a safe and secure place.

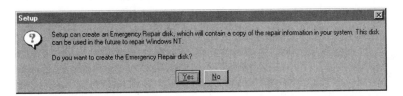

**FIGURE 25.4**

*Create Emergency Repair Disk confirmation dialog box*

If you want to back up the user accounts and file security, run rdisk with the /S switch instead of running rdisk alone in step 3. This will bypass the initial screen (Figure 25.2) and its confirmation step and go directly to the update of the repair directory information. After it has saved your current configuration, it will prompt you to make the ERD in the dialog box shown in Figure 25.4. When you have the freshly formatted floppy disk in the A: drive, select Yes; then click OK. The information will be saved on the floppy disk.

Note that although the Emergency Repair Disk is a useful and necessary tool, it is *not* a bootable disk. Nor is there room on it for both the boot files and the repair information files.

## Emergency Boot Disk

If your system won't boot, you can use the initial installation disks to boot it or you can use an Emergency Boot Disk, which, in many situations, will get you up and running substantially quicker.

### ◆ Why MS-DOS Boot Disks Won't Help

More than one person new to Windows NT has accidentally deleted or corrupted a key file required to boot Windows NT and then tried to recover the file by using an old MS-DOS boot floppy disk. It doesn't work too well, unfortunately, especially if your file system is NTFS and the files you need to get your hard drive back to booting on its own aren't on an MS-DOS floppy disk. When you install Windows NT Server, it modifies the system's boot sector to look for and run a file named "NTLDR." When you format a floppy disk under MS-DOS, even when you make it a system disk, the NTLDR file doesn't get created because MS-DOS doesn't know anything about Windows NT.

You can use the emergency boot floppy disk to boot from and get directly into your existing Windows NT partition, even if a critical file in your system partition has accidentally been deleted or corrupted.

The boot disk you're about to create is *not* generic for every Windows NT Server machine. But if you have a fairly standard configuration across several machines, this disk will work, for example, for all machines that use the same partition and disk controller as their Windows NT boot partition.

### Creating a Windows NT boot floppy disk: x86 version

Insert a floppy disk into the A: drive; then from the command line or from Explorer, format the floppy disk. Remember, this floppy disk must be formatted under Windows NT. After the disk is formatted, copy the following files on to the floppy disk from the root directory of the system partition:

◆ NTLDR

◆ NTDETECT.COM

◆ NTBOOTDD.SYS (if present)

◆ BOOT.INI

The file NTBOOTDD.SYS will be present only if you're using a SCSI controller that doesn't use its BIOS to control the boot process. If NTBOOTDD.SYS is not on the boot partition, you don't need it.

### Creating a Windows NT boot floppy disk: RISC version

To create a Windows NT boot floppy disk for RISC-based machines, follow the same procedure as for x86-based computers except that you have to copy a different set of files from the root directory to the floppy disk. These are the files:

◆ OSLOADER.EXE

◆ HAL.DLL

On RISC-based systems, the information stored in nonvolatile RAM is the equivalent of the information stored in the BOOT.INI file on an x86-based computer. You'll have to modify the boot selection menu to add an option that will point to the floppy disk. The Advanced RISC Computing (ARC) name you'll use for the SYSTEM-PARTITION on the floppy disk is this:

```
scsi(0)disk(0)fdisk(0)
```

Set the necessary values for:

- OSLOADER: The pointer to the floppy disk you've just created

- OSLOADPARTITION: Your primary partition (unless you're running mirrored boot partitions, in which case you'll want to point to the secondary mirror partition)

- OSLOADFILENAME: The path to the \SYSTEMROOT directory

### ◆ ARC Naming Conventions

Understanding how the hard drives and partitions are named on your system is not a trivial task, unfortunately. To provide a uniform naming convention across multiple platforms, Microsoft uses a fairly arcane designation for all disks and partitions on your computer.

ARC is a generic naming convention that can be used the same way for both Intel x86–based and RISC-based computers. The convention describes the adapter type and number, the disk number, the rdisk number, and finally the partition number. The format takes this form:

*<adaptertype>(x)disk(y)rdisk(z)partition(n)*

where *<adaptertype>* can be either "scsi" or "multi." Use "multi" for all non-SCSI adapters and for those SCSI adapters that use a BIOS, which are most adapters used with x86 processors. The value $x$ is the adapter number, starting at zero. The value $y$ is the SCSI ID of the disk for SCSI adapters. For "multi" this value is always zero. The value $z$ is always zero for "scsi" and is the ordinal number of the disk for "multi," starting at zero. Finally, the partition number $n$ is the number of the partition on the target disk; partition numbers start at one, with the number zero reserved for unused space on the disk.

## Emergency Boot Disk for a Mirrored Boot Partition

We all know that hard drives have gotten much more dependable in recent years. The general rule is that if they last the first couple of months, they should last at least as long as the computer. The problem, of course, is that just as soon as you become totally dependent on the system, Murphy comes along and smiles on you. The point of having a mirrored boot partition is that you really, really don't want to have trouble. And if you do have problems, you can get back on line quickly: if your boot disk crashes, you need to switch quickly to running off the mirror while you get a replacement for the boot partition.

However, to do this, you need an emergency boot floppy disk to get into the system. To create an emergency boot floppy disk, follow the procedure we outlined in the preceding section but add one more step. For an Intel x86 processor, you have to edit the BOOT.INI file on the floppy disk to change the ARC name of the boot partition so that it points to the secondary mirror partition rather than to the primary boot partition. For example, if you have a pair of Adaptec 2940 adapters and have duplexed your boot drives using the SCSI BIOS to boot off the primary partition on the first hard disk, you might have a line like this in your BOOT.INI:

    multi(0)disk(0)rdisk(0)partition(1)\NTS40="Windows NT Server"

You would need to change that line to read as follows:

    multi(1)disk(0)rdisk(0)partition(4)\NTS40="Windows NT Server"

## Restoring a Failed Server

So the worst has happened. You've had a total crash of a server. You've replaced the failed hard drive, and you have a backup tape for restoring lost files. But you have to get back to the point where you can at least boot before you can restore the files from the tape.

1. The first step is to reinstall Windows NT Server on the new disk. After you have the basic system installed, you can restore the registry and partition information from the Emergency Repair Disk or from the tape, whichever is most current.

2. Restart the server from the boot disk; select the Repair option if you're going to be using an ERD to repair your downed server. (The Repair option will allow you to restore your partition information and much of the registry.)

3. After the Emergency Repair Disk has done its best, you can restart the server and restore the rest of your lost data from your most recent normal backup tape. The tape drive has to be a locally attached drive, not a networked tape drive. Make sure you select the Restore Local Registry option to recover the rest of your registry information.

4. Restart the server, and you're ready to go.

This whole process can take a significant amount of time. In an environment such as manufacturing or some other production operation, where the server *must* be available on a continuous basis, you might not be able to take so much time. The best solution in this situation is to prepare for such an eventuality by mirroring, or better yet duplexing, the system disk. This will allow you to get back up and running in the minimum amount of time.

**For More Information**

*Mirroring and duplexing hard drives are covered in Chapter 8.*

## Creating and Using a Recovery Drive

A somewhat cheaper alternative to mirroring the drive is to keep a smallish external recovery drive (100-MB minimum). This is an excellent way to recycle an older, small drive that's not really good for much else. You can even use the external recovery drive for several servers if you set it up as a portable device.

To create the recovery drive, install Windows NT Server on the drive, configuring your swap file to be on that drive. Make sure that the installation includes the tape driver you will be using. Create a bootable Windows NT recovery disk following the procedure outlined on page 551 through page 553, and edit the BOOT.INI file on the disk so that it points to the SCSI address of the recovery drive.

When a system failure occurs, simply attach the recovery drive to the server and boot off the emergency boot disk that points to the recovery drive. (This is the disk you created as part of your emergency preparations.) If the recovery drive has sufficient user accounts and software to keep your system running, you can run off the recovery drive until you're able to schedule a full-scale repair or replacement of the failed drive. When you are ready to take the system down and replace the failed drive, all you need to do is restore your backup tape to it and restart the server. You can even do the restore in the background while you continue to run off the recovery drive, if necessary.

### POINTS TO REMEMBER

◆ Plan ahead for disaster. Under extreme stress, people make mistakes and forget important steps. So create standardized recovery procedures, and keep them up to date.

◆ Always use the least invasive repair procedure first. There are better ways to ring the doorbell than shooting it with a bazooka.

◆ Always make a fresh Emergency Repair Disk before you install a new software package or make any major change to your system.

◆ After you install Windows NT Server, make an emergency boot disk that will let you bypass corrupted boot information.

# Appendixes

# APPENDIX A

# Navigating the Interface

If you're not acquainted with Microsoft Windows 95, the look of Microsoft Windows NT Server version 4 might come as a bit of a surprise. Windows NT now uses the Windows 95 user interface, which means that a lot of things not only look different but also work in a new way. The Windows 95 user interface is designed to be "explorable," that is, you can figure out a lot of it just by poking around. The purpose of this appendix is to give you a quick start and save you as much of that poking-around time as possible.

## Mouse Skills

The key to using Windows NT Server efficiently is sitting right there on your desk—namely, your mouse or trackball. Windows NT Server, like Windows 95, is very "mousy" compared to some other operating systems. In fact, you scarcely have to touch the keyboard at all for most basic operations.

### Mouse Trick #1

First of all, the right-hand button on the mouse (right mouse button) is used *everywhere.* In fact, it's not too much of an exaggeration to say that you can place the mouse pointer almost anywhere and press the right mouse button, and something will happen. Usually, a menu of options appears, such as the one shown here:

**NOTE**

*If you're a keyboard kind of person, you still can use the keyboard if you like. A list of keyboard commands and shortcuts can be found in Appendix B.*

The contents of the menu will vary, depending on whether you're pointing at a file, a *folder* (the Windows 95 term for a directory), a control such as a list box or button, or an icon that represents some type of hardware.

There might be occasions when you're looking at a dialog box full of settings and you haven't a clue what some of them mean. Place your mouse pointer on the text and press the right mouse button (right-click). If you see a box that looks like the one here,

> What's This?

you can click it and get a window that contains an explanation of the feature. There's usually enough information presented in the window to spare you the necessity of consulting the Help files.

## Mouse Trick #2

Here's another way the mouse behaves differently than it did in earlier versions of Windows NT. When you want to open a menu, left-click the menu name once. Slide the mouse pointer (do *not* hold the mouse button down as you do this) to the item you want to choose, and then left-click one more time. Although the old method still works, holding the mouse button down as you move the pointer should be limited to situations in which you're actually dragging and dropping an object.

Notice that when you do want to drag an object, the type of operation that is carried out will depend on whether you're using the left mouse button or the right mouse button.

| Mouse Button Used to Click and Drag | Where Object Is Dragged | Result |
| --- | --- | --- |
| Left mouse button | Within a drive | Object is moved. |
| Left mouse button | Across drives | Object is copied. |
| Right mouse button | Anywhere | A menu of choices appears: Move Copy Create Shortcut |

As you can see, the right mouse button is by far the easiest to use. When you use the left mouse button, you must remember where the object is relative to your drive(s). If you get in the habit of using the right mouse button, you can be saved from that necessity.

# Shortcuts

Shortcuts are one of the primary benefits of the new Windows 95 user interface, but they're not completely self-explanatory. We mention them here so that you can learn a little about them and the part they play in your interactions with the computer.

A shortcut is a very small file that functions as a "pointer" to another file, to a folder, or to a program. For example, a shortcut allows you to have as many "copies" of your printer as you want—in as many locations as you want. Of course, a shortcut to the printer isn't really a copy of the printer, just another icon that serves as a pointer to the printer. You also can have a shortcut to your word processor in as many locations as necessary and use only a small amount of disk space for each location. Another advantage of using a shortcut is that when you're done with it, you can delete the shortcut with impunity. Deleting the shortcut has no effect on the original object.

Shortcuts are identifiable by the small arrow in the lower left corner of the icon, as shown in this example:

When created, the shortcut icon also will have the label "Shortcut To," followed by the name of the object. A shortcut can be renamed to make the label more manageable. To rename a shortcut right-click the name and choose Rename from the menu.

The Create Shortcut option is available in several places:

◆ On an object's pop-up menu

◆ From some drop-down menus

◆ On the desktop (shown in Figure A.1)

**FIGURE A.1**

*Desktop pop-up menu with Create Shortcut option*

# Start Button

The default screen in Windows NT Server is a mostly blank desktop with a taskbar at the bottom and two icons in the upper left corner. Fortunately, there's an obvious signal where you should begin—a Start button at the left end of the taskbar. Left-click the Start button once to open a menu. Initially, only a few basic options will be available, but they are enough to get you going. Here's what you'll see:

## Programs

Slide the mouse pointer to Programs. You'll get a cascading menu that includes all of the programs currently installed, as well as access to a command prompt, administrative tools, accessories (mainly applets of various types), and a few other entries depending on how your server is set up. This is an example of what you will see:

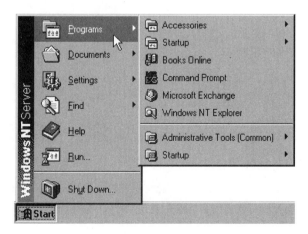

Slide the mouse pointer to items with right arrows to see their cascading submenus.

## Documents

Windows NT Server remembers all of the files you have worked on and puts them on this menu.

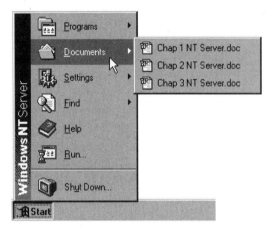

If you want to clear the Documents menu, you can do so by following these steps:

1. Right-click a blank space on the taskbar, and choose Properties from the pop-up menu.

2. Click the Start Menu Programs tab in the Taskbar Properties dialog box.

3. Click Clear in the Documents Menu section.

To clear the menu selectively, you'll need to find a folder named Recent, located in your profile folder. For example, if you're logged on as user Administrator, look for the Recent folder under WINNT\Profiles\Administrator. Items in the Recent folder are shortcuts only, so they can be deleted without affecting the actual files.

## Settings

The Settings menu item provides access to the Control Panel settings, the Printers settings, and the Taskbar settings, as shown in the example on the next page.

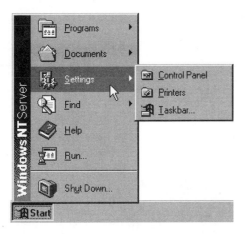

## Find

The Find program is a handy one. It allows you to search for files, folders, or even a particular piece of text. You also can use Find to search for a specific computer on the network. As you can see from the tab headings in the example, you can search by name and location or by the date modified.

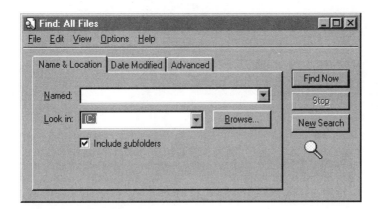

The Advanced tab provides the option of searching for a particular word or text phrase. Advanced tab menu options allow you to make your search letter-case sensitive or to save the results of a search.

The really nice thing about Find is that once you locate the file you want, you can just double-click the file to open it or you can drag the file to another location. In other words, the file or list of files displayed at the end of a search is "live," and you can act on it accordingly.

**Tip**

*To launch a search of the current folder, press the F3 key.*

## Help

The Help files in Windows NT version 4 are much improved over those in the earlier versions of Windows NT. The files are a lot more searchable, for one thing. When
you first select Help, you'll get a dialog box like the one shown in Figure A.2.

**FIGURE A.2**

*Help Topics dialog box*

The Contents and Index tabs of Help Topics are pretty straightforward. There is a
new feature in the form of the Find tab. You can use Find to search all or a part of
the Help files for a particular word or text phrase. This can be really nice when you
know the term you want but you haven't a clue where the documentation authors
might have filed it. The first time you use the Help Topics Find tool, Windows NT
Server builds a database of Help files for future searches. You can choose one of
three options:

◆ Minimize database size. With this option, not all Help files will be included in the database, but all of the ones that are likely to have useful
information will be included.

- Maximize search capabilities. With this option, all of the Help files will be included in the database. It's the most thorough approach, but it can make searches a little slower if either your processor or your hard drive is slow.

- Customize search capabilities. With this option, you can choose which Help files will be included in the database.

After Windows NT Server builds the Help file database, you can use Find to make very sophisticated Help searches.

## Run

Those who love the command line will find an oasis here. Choose Run, and you will get a dialog box like the one shown here:

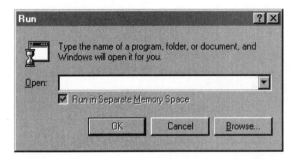

You can type in the name of any program you want to launch. You'll have to include the path, but if you like this kind of hands-on operation, you won't mind at all.

### Tip

*If you left-click the Down arrow in the Run dialog box, you get a drop-down list of all the recent programs you've run from this box. You also can use the Browse button to look around for the program you want.*

## Shut Down

This option is for shutting down your computer before turning it off, restarting the computer, or logging on as a different user.

# Taskbar

The taskbar is new to the Windows NT user interface. By default, it is located at the bottom of the screen when either Windows NT Server or Windows NT Workstation boots up. To change the location of the taskbar, click any blank spot on the taskbar and, holding the mouse button down, drag the taskbar to the top or to either side of the screen.

The taskbar displays all of the active programs. Each active program has a button on the taskbar. Even if the program window you want is buried under several other windows, you can click the corresponding taskbar button and the desired program window pops to the front. By default, the taskbar is always on top.

To change taskbar settings, right-click a blank space on the taskbar and choose Properties from the pop-up menu. A Taskbar Properties dialog box will appear (Figure A.3). Click the Taskbar Options tab. To customize the taskbar functions, choose from the options shown. When you select an option, you will see a preview of the results in the top half of the dialog box.

**FIGURE A.3**

*Taskbar Properties dialog box*

## Tip

*If you right-click the taskbar, you can open Task Manager and also cascade, tile, or minimize all active program windows. Unfortunately, there's no easy way to close all open programs. The fastest way probably is to minimize all windows and then right-click each program button and choose Close from the menu.*

# Desktop Icons

Only two icons are always present on the default desktop of Windows NT Server, the My Computer icon and the Recycle Bin icon. (You might see other icons as well, depending on the options you chose when installing Windows NT Server version 4.) You will add other icons as you decide what programs are most important to you and how you want to configure your desktop.

## My Computer

If you double-click the My Computer icon, you will see the icons for all of your drives, plus folders for Control Panel and Printers. This isn't the only way to get at your drives, but the My Computer icon does have a number of handy features:

◆ If you right-click on My Computer,

  ◆ You can access the Find program quickly.

  ◆ You can map a network drive for this machine.

  ◆ You can choose Properties for a look at your computer's system variables, virtual memory settings, and hardware profiles.

◆ If you double-click the My Computer icon and choose Options from the View menu, you can select on the Folder tab whether you want single-window or separate-window browsing. "Single window" means that as you go from folder to subfolder to subsubfolder, only one window is open at a time. "Separate window" means that all of the parent folders stay open as you go from folder to folder.

> **Tip**
>
> *If the name My Computer doesn't suit your taste, right-click the My Computer icon; choose Rename from the menu. Type a new name in the text box that's more to your liking. This won't change the name of your computer on the network; it will just change the label under the icon on your desktop.*

## Recycle Bin

The Recycle Bin, as you might imagine, is where old deleted files go before they die. Despite the program's name, deleted files aren't recycled. The Recycle Bin just gives you a nice margin of safety that wasn't available in previous versions of Windows NT Server (unless you had another program that provided it). When you delete a file, you have days or even weeks (depending on how you set things up) to change your mind and retrieve the file from the bin before it's deleted permanently.

Here are the important facts to know about the Recycle Bin:

◆ The Recycle Bin can't be deleted or renamed.

◆ Each user's Recycle Bin is secure. It can't be shared or accessed over the network.

◆ Only files deleted from a local hard drive are moved to the Recycle Bin. If you delete files from a floppy disk or a network drive, the files are permanently deleted.

◆ Only files deleted using Windows NT Server are sent to the Recycle Bin. If you delete files using another program, such as a word processor, the files are not stored in the Recycle Bin; they are permanently deleted. So caution is advised when deleting files.

To configure the Recycle Bin, right-click the icon below and choose Properties.

## Property Sheets

In previous versions of Windows, including Windows NT 3.5*x*, it was sometimes a real pain to find out how to change the settings for a file, a program, or a piece of hardware; you had to memorize where critical settings were to be found. Now there's only one rule to remember:

Right-click the object on the screen, and choose Properties.

When you choose Properties, you open what's called a property sheet. Property sheets vary, of course. Some files will have several pages and many options in the property sheet; other files will have only one page and very few options. Figure A.4 is an example of a property sheet for a simple graphic file.

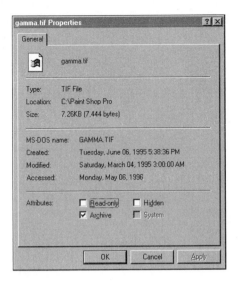

**FIGURE A.4**

*Example of a graphic file property sheet*

Property sheets are valuable repositories of information about files, programs, and devices. So when you find yourself with a program or a piece of hardware that isn't working the way you want it to work, refer to the rule on the preceding page. As a matter of fact, you might apply that rule to just about every aspect of Windows NT Server version 4. When you want to know more about *anything* in Windows NT Server, right-click whatever it is you want to know more about and see what appears.

# Desktop Settings

If you're fond of a certain type of postmodern austerity, you'll like the default Windows NT Server desktop. Others might find it a tad boring. However, you can have your desktop as plain or as fancy as you want it to be.

Remember, you can use the entire screen area of your monitor in Windows NT Server. You can have many folders, a few folders, or no folders. You can have all of your programs on menus that fold out of the Start button menus, or you can have program icons on the desktop itself, where you can open them by double-clicking the icons. Even better, you can choose screen colors, text fonts, and desktop wallpaper from among many available options.

Here's how to get at all the settings that affect the desktop. Move the mouse pointer to a blank space (of which there's a muchness) on the screen, and click once with the right mouse button. Choose Properties from the pop-up menu, and you're there. (See Figure A.5.) Each tab in the Display Properties window contains the properties for each of the desktop settings.

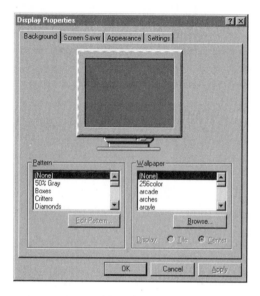

**FIGURE A.5**

*Property sheets for configuring desktop settings*

### NOTE

*The availability of these settings in the system doesn't change the administrator's ability to restrict user choice and configure users' desktops. See Chapter 9 for more information.*

## Background

The Background sheet is where you choose the wallpaper and background pattern settings, much as you choose Desktop settings in Microsoft Windows NT 3.51 and Microsoft Windows 3.11. Use Browse to locate the files you can use as wallpaper.

Any files that are bit maps (.BMP) or device-independent bit maps (.DIB) can be used as wallpaper.

## Screen Saver

If you're using a screen saver, whether one that comes with Windows NT Server or one from some other package, you can adjust the settings under this tab. All of the installed screen savers are listed in the Screen Saver drop-down list.

Click Preview to get a full-screen view of the screen saver you have selected. Move your mouse in any direction or press any key on the keyboard to return to Display Properties.

## Appearance

The Appearance settings also are similar to Desktop settings in Windows NT 3.51. Use one of the many color combinations listed under Schemes, or create your own color combination.

Click any of the elements in the window at the top of the Appearance page, and a description will appear in the Item box. You can change the size or the color or both. If there's a font that can be changed, the one currently in use will be displayed in the Font box.

# Settings

Of all the desktop Display properties, Settings has the most options. (See Figure A.6.) Here's where you can change the resolution and the number of colors shown on your screen, as well as the drivers for your video hardware.

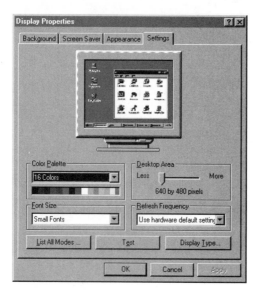

**FIGURE A.6**

*Display settings*

Screen displays are described in terms of their resolution—that is, the number of dots on the screen and the number of colors displayed at the same time. The choice of screen resolution is made using the slider under Desktop Area and is determined by the hardware you have. You can't make your monitor and video card display a higher resolution than is built into them. Left-click List All Modes to see what display options are available on your system.

The Display Type button on the Settings page is used when you're changing either your display adapter (video card) or monitor, or when you want to use a video driver other than the one Windows NT Server currently is using. Left-click Display Type; you'll see a window like the one in Figure A.7. To change either the adapter or the monitor, left-click Change and follow the instructions.

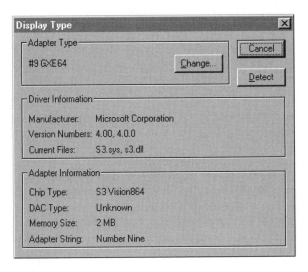

**FIGURE A.7**

*Display Type dialog box*

# Final Note

The most difficult thing about learning the new Windows interface is "unlearning" the way you did things in previous versions of Windows. Once you get past that hurdle, you'll find the new look is more than skin deep—in fact, it's an interface design that makes the system much easier and faster to use.

# APPENDIX B

# Keyboard Shortcuts

Even though Microsoft Windows NT version 4 is even more "mousy" than earlier versions of Microsoft Windows, you still can do practically everything from the keyboard. Of course, you probably can't be bothered memorizing all of the keyboard combinations, but you might want to consider retaining a few of them in your memory bank (the one in your head), particularly if there are actions that you perform repeatedly and if you find the mouse too clumsy to use for them. The following list includes the most useful (and, in many cases, undocumented) keyboard shortcuts.

| KEY | ACTION |
| --- | --- |
| F1 | Opens Help. |
| F2 | Allows renaming of the selected file or folder. |
| F3 | Opens the Find program. |
| F4 | Opens the drop-down list in the toolbar. Press F4 a second time, and the drop-down list will close. |
| F5 | Refreshes (or updates) the view in the active window. |
| Tab or F6 | Moves the focus from the drop-down window in the toolbar to the left pane, to the right pane (in Windows NT Explorer), and back again. |
| F10 or Alt | Puts the focus on the menu bar. To move between menus, use the Left ($\leftarrow$) and Right ($\rightarrow$) arrow keys. The Down arrow ($\downarrow$) key will open the menu. |
| Backspace | Moves up one level in the folder hierarchy. |
| Right arrow ($\rightarrow$) | Expands the highlighted folder. In Explorer, if the folder is already expanded, it will move to the first subfolder. |
| Left arrow ($\leftarrow$) | Collapses the highlighted folder. In Explorer, if the folder is already collapsed, it will move up one level in the folder hierarchy. |
| Alt-Esc | Moves the focus between open applications. Hold down the Alt key and press Esc. Each press of Esc moves the focus to another application. Applications on the taskbar, once they are highlighted, are activated by pressing Enter. |

| Alt-Tab | Opens a window in the middle of the screen; icons in the window represent all open files and folders. (See the illustration at the end of this list.) Hold down the Alt key and press Tab to move the cursor from item to item. Release Alt to switch to the corresponding file or folder. |
|---|---|
| Alt-Shift-Tab | Moves the cursor through the open items in the opposite direction from Alt-Tab. |
| Ctrl-Esc | Opens the Start menu. |
| Alt-F4 | Closes the current application. If no application is open, this will activate the Shut Down window. |
| Alt-Spacebar | Opens the Control Menu of the active window. (It functions the same as clicking the icon at the extreme upper left corner of the application or folder window.) |
| Spacebar | Toggles the choice when the selection cursor in a dialog box is selected. |
| Tab | Moves the selection cursor to the next choice in a folder or dialog box. |
| Shift-Tab | Moves the selection cursor in the opposite direction from Tab. |
| Shift-Print Screen | Copies the current screen to the Clipboard, from which the screen contents can be pasted into Paint or another graphics application. |
| Alt-Print Screen | Copies the active window to the Clipboard. |

# APPENDIX C

# The OSI Reference Model

As with most emerging technologies, the early days of networking were characterized by strictly proprietary hardware and software. No one agreed on any particular method of building and implementing networks. That meant you could choose to buy your network only from IBM, DEC, Burroughs, or a few others. This was a momentous decision to make because after that, you were locked in. Nobody else's equipment or software would work with yours. You had to buy everything from the original vendor, and if they didn't happen to have a product that you really, truly wanted, you were just out of luck.

In an attempt to cut across this entirely proprietary universe, the International Organization of Standards (ISO) developed a standard to make possible open systems that could communicate with one another no matter who manufactured them. Today, there still are a lot of proprietary systems, and they don't always communicate with one another as well as we might hope. But what they do have in common is the Open Systems Interconnection (OSI) reference model, which provides a framework for the organization of network components. It can provide a clearer picture of how the components relate to one another.

The OSI reference model consists of seven layers (Figure C.1). Each layer has a specific task and relates only to the layers adjacent to it. The main idea is to have independent standards for the different layers so that a change in one layer would not cause changes in the other layers. In the layered approach, it is possible to use different network hardware without changing the existing application programs.

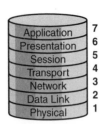

**FIGURE C.1**

*The OSI reference model*

To arrive at the layers, the ISO applied the following principles:

◆ A new layer would be created only when a different level of abstraction is needed.

◆ Each layer would have a clearly definable function.

◆ Each layer's function would define internationally standardized protocols.

◆ Information flow across layer boundaries would have to be minimal.

◆ The number of layers would have to be kept as low as possible while keeping distinct functions in separate layers.

The seven layers in sequence from bottom to top are as follows: physical, data link, network, transport, session, presentation, and application.

Data is passed down the stack as it is sent to the network and passed up the stack as it's received. The sending and receiving machines use a common protocol for each layer of the communication. The collection of protocols is called a *protocol stack*.

The OSI reference model is useful because every networking protocol stack is based, in some regard, on the OSI structure. None of the protocols you encounter will fit the model exactly, but there's always enough correspondence to help you understand the relationship among the parts—and certainly enough to get you started if you want to delve deeper into the technical core of networking.

# Physical Layer

The physical layer deals with how data signals are transmitted on the network cable or other transmission medium—in effect, the mechanical and electrical procedures. It is oblivious to whether the signal is made up of digital bits or is in analog form. Protocols used at the physical layer are ISO 2110, IEEE 802, and IEEE 802.2.

# Data Link Layer

The data link layer transmits information that has been organized into low-level logical units called *frames*. It then waits for acknowledgment that the frames were received and retransmits any frames that were lost. This layer performs the access methods known as Ethernet and Token Ring. Protocols used by this layer are SLIP, CSLIP, MTU, and PPP.

# Network Layer

The network layer builds on the connection made by the data link layer. It adds a unit of information called a *packet*. The network layer handles routing (the process of delivering packets through an internetwork) and congestion control. It's the highest layer of the OSI model that understands the network's topology—that is, the physical configuring of the machines, type and length of cabling, and so forth. Examples of network protocols that are supported by Microsoft Windows NT Server version 4 are IPX and IP.

## Transport Layer

The transport layer builds on the error-control mechanisms in the lower layers. It's the last stop for making sure the necessary corrections are made in the sending and receiving of packets. The transport protocols supported by Windows NT Server version 4 are SPX and TCP.

## Session Layer

The session layer deals with two-way communications between nodes. When a dialog between nodes begins, a session is initiated. A good example of this is when a workstation connects to a Windows NT server. Rules are established as to how the two will communicate and which protocols will be used. NetBIOS is an example of a session protocol.

## Presentation Layer

The presentation layer handles how data is represented, such as how data is formatted, how lines of characters are to be shown, or whether data is encoded. Although the presentation layer is not always implemented in a protocol, SNMP is an example of a presentation protocol supported by Windows NT Server.

## Application Layer

The application layer handles information transfer between two network applications, including remote file services, message handling for E-mail, and remote database access. Many of the services in this layer are called application programming interfaces (APIs), which are implemented as programming libraries that are used to write applications. Protocols at the application layer include DNS, tftp, BOOTP, MIME, and FINGER.

### NOTE

*The TCP/IP protocol architecture has fewer layers (either four or five); there's no universal agreement. The functions performed still start at the application layer and end at the physical layer (or vice versa). But some layers are combined, and the layers overlap somewhat more than in the "strict" OSI model.*

# Glossary

# GLOSSARY

**Address**  Code by which the Internet identifies a specific user. The format is *username@hostname*, where "username" is the user's name, logon name, or account number and "hostname" is the name of the computer or Internet provider that you are using. A host name can consist of a few words separated by periods.

**Address resolution protocol**  A TCP/IP protocol that provides IP-address–to–MAC-address resolution for IP packets.

**Anonymous ftp**  A program for using ftp to log on to another computer to copy files when you don't have an account on that computer. When you log on, enter *anonymous* as the user name and your address as the password. This gives you access to publicly available files. (*See also* File Transfer Protocol.)

**Associate**  To logically connect files having a particular extension to a specific program. When you double-click a file with this extension, the associated program opens, and the file you clicked also opens.

**Audit policy**  A network system policy that defines the type of security events that are to be logged. It can be defined for a server or for an individual computer.

**Authentication**  Verification of the identity of a user or computer process. In Microsoft Windows NT, this involves comparing the user's security identifier (SID) and password to a list of authorized users on a primary domain controller or backup domain controller.

**Backbone**  A high-speed line or a series of connections that form a major pathway within a network. The term is relative because a backbone in a small network is likely to be much smaller than many non-backbone lines in a large network.

**Backup domain controller (BDC)**  A Windows NT domain server that stores a backup of the database from the primary domain controller (PDC). The backup domain controller database is synchronized automatically with the copy of the database on the primary domain controller. A backup domain controller also authenticates users when they log on and can be promoted to a primary domain controller if necessary.

**Binding**  A software connection between a network card and a network transport protocol (such as TCP/IP).

**Controller**   In a Windows NT Server domain, the server that authenticates users who are logging on and maintains the master database and the security policy.

**Conversations**   Two-way connections between two applications that alternately transmit and receive data.

**Daemon**   A background program that runs unattended, gathering information or performing other kinds of tasks.

**DNS name servers**   Servers that contain information about part of the Domain Name System database. These servers make computer names available to queries for name resolution across the Internet.

**Domain**   1. In Windows NT, a group of computers that share a security policy and a user account database. 2. On the Internet, a TCP/IP network domain. (*See also* domain name.)

**Domain controller**   A server in a domain that accepts user names and passwords from users logging on to the system and initiates their authentication.

**Domain name**   The unique name that identifies an Internet site. A given computer may have more than one domain name, but a given domain name points to only one computer. It's also possible for a domain name to exist but not to be connected to an actual machine. This is often the case when a group or business wants to have an Internet E-mail address without having to establish a real Internet site; an Internet service provider's computer handles the mail on behalf of the listed domain name.

**Domain Name System (DNS)**   A distributed database that provides a hierarchical naming system for identifying hosts on the Internet. DNS differs from WINS in that DNS is a static configuration. WINS is a fully dynamic configuration. (*See also* Windows Internet Name Service.)

**Dynamic Data Exchange (DDE)**   Communication between processes. When programs that support DDE are running at the same time they can exchange data by means of conversations.

**Dynamic link library (DLL)**   A program module that contains executable code and data that can be used by various programs. The DLL is used by a program only when the program is active. DLL is unloaded when the program that has been using it exits.

**Enterprise**   A term that is used to encompass all of a business operation, including all remote offices and branches.

**Environment variable**   A variable that contains a string of environment information, such as a drive, a path, or a filename associated with a symbolic name. The System option in Control Panel or the Set command from the Windows NT command prompt can be used to define environment variables.

**File allocation table (FAT)**    A file system used by MS-DOS that basically consists of a table that keeps track of the file size and location of files on a hard drive.

**File Transfer Protocol (ftp)**    A tool for transferring one or more files from one computer to another over a network or telephone line.

**Finger**    A program that displays information about someone on the Internet. On most UNIX systems, this command tells you who is logged on right now. On most Internet hosts, it tells you the name and the last time that a person logged on (and possibly some other information that is based on the person's Internet address).

**Firewall**    A protective filter for messages and logons. Firewalls are used by organizations connected directly to the Internet to prevent unauthorized access to their networks.

**Fully qualified domain name (FQDN)**    An Internet domain name that includes the names of all network domains leading back to the root. For a university in the United States, an example of a fully qualified domain name is this one from the University of California at Berkeley:

```
german.modlangs.ucberk.edu
```

A commercial enterprise could have a fully qualified domain name such as this:

```
accts.finance.dataflointl.com
```

**Gateway**    A device used to connect networks that are using different protocols so information can be passed from one network to another.

**Global account**    A normal Windows NT user account in that user's home domain. On a multiple-domain network, it's better for each user to have a single account in only one domain (the home domain) and to be allowed access to other domains only through domain trust relationships.

**Global group**    A group of users in Windows NT that contains accounts from only its home domain. However, a global group can be granted permissions and rights for servers, both in its home domain and in trusting domains, and it can be a "member" of local groups.

**Gopher**    A menu-driven tool that allows a user to find information on remote computers. Telnet is usually used to connect with a Gopher server, where menus are available for browsing.

**Graphic Interchange Format (GIF)**    A file format used to store graphics images.

**Hive**   One of six sections of the registry on your hard disk. Each hive is a discrete body of keys, subkeys, and values that record configuration information for the computer. Each hive is a file and can be moved from one system to another, but it can be edited only by using Registry Editor.

**Home domain**   Domain in which a user account or group account resides.

**Host**   Any device on a network that uses TCP/IP. Also, a computer on the Internet that you can log on to. You can use ftp to retrieve files from a host computer on the Internet. Other programs (such as Telnet) allow you to connect to and use an Internet host computer.

**HOSTS file**   A local ASCII text file that maps host names to IP addresses. Each line represents one host and starts with the IP address, which is then followed by one or more spaces and then the host's name.

**Hypertext**   A system of writing and displaying text that makes it possible for the text to be linked in many ways. Hypertext documents can contain links to related documents, such as documents referred to in footnotes. Hypermedia also can contain pictures, sounds, and video.

**Hypertext Markup Language (HTML)**   A system used for writing pages for the World Wide Web. HTML allows text to include codes that define fonts, layout, embedded graphics, and hypertext links.

**Hypertext Transfer Protocol (HTTP)**   The method by which World Wide Web pages are transferred over the network.

**Internet**   1. (Internet) The world-wide collection of interconnected networks that all use TCP/IP and that evolved from the ARPANET of the late 1960s and early 1970s. The Internet connects roughly 70,000 independent networks into a vast global network. 2. (internet) Any large network that is made up of a number of smaller networks.

**Internet Control Message Protocol (ICMP)**   A protocol that is used to report problems encountered with the delivery of data, such as an unreachable host or an unavailable port. It's also used to send a request packet to determine whether a host is available; if the receiving host is alive and functioning, it sends back a packet. (*See also* Ping.)

**Internet Explorer**   Microsoft's Windows-based, WinSock-compliant program for browsing the World Wide Web.

**Internet Protocol (IP)**   The transport layer protocol that is used as a basis of the Internet. IP enables data to be divided into discrete packets of information for routing from one network to another and then to be reassembled from these packets at the destination.

**Internet Relay Chat (IRC)**   A system that enables Internet users to talk with each other in real time over the Internet.

**Intranet**   A network of interconnected computers within a specific organization.

**IP address**   A unique four-part number separated by periods (for example, 165.113.245.2) that identifies a machine on the Internet. Every machine on the Internet has a unique IP number; if a machine does not have an IP number, it is not really on the Internet. Most machines also have one or more domain names that are easier for people to remember.

**IPX/SPX**   Transport protocols used in Novell NetWare networks.

**Java**   A programming language similar to C and C++ that is used to design applets in Web pages.

**Kernel**   The part of the Windows NT executive that manages the processor. The kernel performs thread scheduling and dispatching, interrupt and exception handling, and multiprocessor synchronization.

**Leased line**   A telephone line that is rented for exclusive 24-hour access between your location and another location.

**Listserv**   A family of programs that manages Internet mailing lists by distributing the messages that are posted to the list and by adding and deleting members automatically when a user sends an E-mail message to subscribe to or be removed from the list.

**LMHOSTS file**   An ASCII text file that maps IP addresses to host names within a specific network; similar to HOSTS—to remember which is which, remember LMHOSTS as LAN Manager HOSTS.

**Local account**   A user account in Windows NT that can be used on an individual computer without logging on to a domain.

**Local Area Network (LAN)**   A group of computers connected with a communications link and usually located close to one another (for example, in the same building or on the same floor of a building) so that data can be shared among them.

**Local group**   A group of users in Windows NT that can be granted permissions and rights for servers that are in its home domain. For Microsoft Windows NT Workstation, a group that can be granted permissions and rights only for its own workstation. Local groups in Windows NT Server and Windows NT Workstation can contain both user accounts and global groups from the home domain and also from trusted domains.

**Logon (also login)**   The account name used to gain access to a computer system. Unlike a password, the logon is not a secret.

**Log on (also log in)**    To identify oneself to the authenticating computer; for example, "Log on to CompuServe, and then go to the Travel forum."

**Logon script**    Typically a batch file that executes when a user logs on. It's used to configure a user's initial environment. A logon script can be assigned to multiple users.

**MAC address**    A unique, 48-bit number assigned to network interface cards by the manufacturer. MAC addresses are used for mapping in TCP/IP network communication.

**Member server**    A computer that is running Windows NT Server but is *not* a domain controller. Member servers make resources such as files and printers available to other computers on the network. A member server does not authenticate logons or maintain a security database.

**Mirror**    1. Two partitions on separate hard drives that are configured so that they contain identical data. If one drive fails, the partition on the other hard drive still contains valid data, and processing can continue. 2. An ftp server that "mirrors" another ftp server—it provides copies of the same set of files as the other ftp server. Some ftp servers are used so often that other servers are set up to mirror them and spread the ftp load to more than one site.

**Modem (MOdulator/DEModulator)**    A device that enables a computer to transmit data over a telephone line to another computer. Modems convert the computer's digital signals into analog waves that can be transmitted over standard voice telephone lines. Modem speeds are measured in bits per second (bps) or kilobits (thousands of bits) per second (Kbps). For example, 28.8 Kbps and 28,800 bps are the same thing—28,800 bits per second.

**Multitasking**    A mode of operation that makes a computer appear to run more than one program at the same time. Each program is allowed to run for a brief amount of time before the next program is loaded into the processor. Programs are switched in and out of the processor so quickly that it appears the computer is working on them all at once. The stability of a multitasking system depends on how well the various programs are isolated from one another.

**Multithreading**    The simultaneous running of several processes (also known as threads) within a program. Because several threads can be processed in parallel, one thread does not have to finish before another one can start. (*See also* thread.)

**Named pipe**    An interprocess communication that allows one process to send data to another process either remotely or locally.

**Name resolution**    The process of mapping a name to its corresponding address.

**NetBIOS Extended User Interface (NetBEUI)**    A small and fast network protocol that requires little memory but can't be routed. Remote locations linked by routers can't use NetBEUI to communicate.

**Netlogon service**   Accepts logon requests from any client and provides authentication from the Security Account Manager accounts database.

**Network**   Two or more computers connected by a communications link in order to share resources.

**Network News Transfer Protocol (NNTP)**   A protocol designed for the distribution, inquiry, retrieval, and posting of news articles on the Internet.

**Newsgroup**   On the Internet, a distributed bulletin board system about a particular topic. Usenet News (also known as Netnews) is a system that distributes thousands of newsgroups to all parts of the Internet.

**Node**   A computer on the Internet, also called a host. Computers that provide a service, such as ftp sites or places that run Gopher, are also called servers.

**NT file system (NTFS)**   The native file system for Windows NT. It supports long filenames, a variety of permissions for sharing files, and a transaction log that allows Windows NT to finish incomplete file-related tasks if the operating system is interrupted.

**Packet**   A chunk of information sent over a network. Each packet contains the destination address, the sender's address, error-control information, and data.

**Page**   1. A document, or collection of information, available via the World Wide Web. A page may contain text, graphics, video, and sound files. 2. A portion of memory that the virtual memory manager can swap to and from a hard drive.

**Paging**   A virtual memory operation in which pages are transferred from memory to disk when memory becomes full. When a thread accesses a page that's not in memory, a page fault occurs; the memory manager then uses page tables to find the page on disk and load it into memory.

**Peer-to-peer**   A type of network in which two or more computers can communicate with each other without the need for any intermediary device. On a peer-to-peer network, a computer can be both a client and a server.

**Ping**   A network management tool that checks to see if another computer is alive and functioning. It sends a short message to which the other computer responds automatically. If the other computer does not respond to the ping, you usually cannot establish communications with it.

**Point of Presence (POP)**   A physical site in a geographic area where a network access provider, such as MCI, has equipment to which users connect. The local telephone company's central office in a particular area is also sometimes referred to as their POP for that area.

**Point-to-Point Protocol (PPP)**   A protocol that provides router-to-router and host-to-network connections over a telephone line (or a network link that acts like a telephone line)—similar to SLIP.

**Post Office Protocol (POP)**  A system by which a mail server on the Internet allows you to download your mail to your PC or Macintosh. Most people refer to this protocol with its version number (POP2, POP3, and so on) to avoid confusing it with Point of Presence.

**Primary domain controller (PDC)**  A Windows NT domain server that authenticates users logging on to the domain and also maintains the security policy and the master database for a domain.

**RAID (Redundant Array of Inexpensive Disks)**  A range of disk management and striping techniques for implementing fault tolerance.

**Registered file types**  In Microsoft Windows, associated file extensions are usually called *registered* file types.

**Remote access service (RAS)**  A service that allows users to dial in from remote locations and gain access to their networks for file and printer sharing, E-mail, scheduling, and SQL database access.

**Replication**  A service that enables the contents of a directory (designated as an export directory) to be copied to other directories (called import directories) on network computers.

**Requests for Comments (RFC)**  Documents that provide a way for a diverse group of people—the users of the Internet—to communicate and agree on the architecture and functionality of the Internet. Some RFCs are official documents of the Internet Engineering Task Force (IETF), which defines the standards of TCP/IP and the Internet; other RCFs are proposals for new standards or documents that fall somewhere in between—some tutorial in nature, others quite technical in nature.

**Router**  A special-purpose computer (or software package) that handles the connection between two or more networks. Routers look at the destination addresses of the packets passing through them and decide which route to use to send them.

**Security Accounts Manager (SAM)**  Manager of all security rules and information in Windows NT Server and Windows NT Workstation.

**Security ID (SID)**  A unique number assigned to every computer and user account on a Windows NT network. A SID is never reused.

**Serial Line Internet Protocol (SLIP)**  A protocol used to run IP over serial lines or telephone lines using modems. This protocol is rapidly being replaced by the Point-to-Point Protocol (PPP).

**Server**  A computer that provides a service to other computers on a network. A file server, for example, provides files to client computers.

**Simple Mail Transfer Protocol (SMTP)**  A protocol used to transfer E-mail messages between computers.

**Socket**   An endpoint to a connection. Two sockets form a complete path for a bidirectional pipe for incoming and outgoing data between networked computers. The Windows Sockets API is a networking API for programmers writing for the Windows family of products.

**Synchronize**   To replicate the domain database that is loaded on the primary domain controller to one or all of the backup domain controllers in a domain. The system performs this automatically, but the administrator can also do this using Server Manager.

**Telnet**   The program used to log on from one Internet site to another. The Telnet program gets you to the logon prompt of another host.

**Terminal**   A device that allows you to send commands to another computer. At a minimum, this usually means a keyboard, a display screen, and some simple circuitry. Usually you will use terminal software in a personal computer—the software pretends to be (emulates) a physical terminal and allows you to type commands to another computer.

**Thread**   An executable entity that belongs to one (and only one) process. In a multitasking environment, a single program can contain several threads, all running at the same time.

**Transmission Control Protocol/Internet Protocol (TCP/IP)**   The protocol that networks use to communicate with each other on the Internet.

**Trust relationship**   A security term meaning that one workstation or server trusts a domain controller to authenticate a user logon on its behalf. Also, and more commonly, it means that a domain controller in one domain trusts a domain controller from another domain to authenticate users who are logging on to this domain from the other domain.

**Uniform Resource Locator (URL)**   The standard format for specifying addresses of resources on the Internet that are part of the World Wide Web. An example of an URL is this address:

```
http://www.capecod.net/~fcollege/index.htm
```

The most common way to use an URL is to enter a Web browser program, such as Microsoft Internet Explorer or Netscape Navigator.

**UNIX**   A computer operating system designed to be used by many computer users at the same time (a "multiuser" system) with TCP/IP built in. It is the most common operating system for servers on the Internet.

**User account**   A user's access to a Windows NT machine. Each user account has a unique user name and security ID.

**User profile**   Information about and the access restrictions for a user account.

**Viewer**   A program used by Gopher, WAIS, or WWW client programs to display files that contain graphics or video files or to play files that contain sounds.

**Virtual Reality Markup Language (VRML)**   A system used for writing pages for the World Wide Web. VRML allows your Web page to include codes that define animations and 3D graphics.

**Wide Area Network (WAN)**   Any Internet or intranet network that covers an area larger than a single building or campus. (*See also* Internet, Local Area Network, Network.)

**Windows Internet Name Service (WINS)**   A name resolution service that converts computer names to IP addresses in a routed environment.

**Windows Socket (WinSock)**   A standard interface used for Windows-based programs working with TCP/IP. You can use WinSock if you use SLIP to connect to the Internet.

**World Wide Web (WWW)**   A hypermedia-based system for gaining access to information on the Internet.

**Workstation**   In Windows NT, a computer that is running the Windows NT Workstation operating system. In a wider context, "workstation" is used to describe any powerful computer optimized for graphics or computer-aided design (CAD) or any of a number of other functions requiring high performance.

# Index

# INDEX

Note: An *italic* page-number reference indicates a figure or table.

emergency restoration to new disks, 505–6

equipment. *See* hardware

ERD (Emergency Repair Disk), 88, 124, *124*, 549–51, *550, 551*

error checking for disks, 483–84, *483, 484*

event logs

    access to nonlocal event logs, 467

    categories of entries, 459

    configuring, 467–68, *467*

    data in entries, 460

    filters, 462–63, *463*

    system, *459*

Event Viewer

    application events, 458, 461, *461*

    event logs

        access to nonlocal event logs, 467

        categories of entries, 459

        configuring, 467–68, *467*

        data in entries, 459

        filters, 462–63, *463*

        system, *459*

    introduced, 316, *317*, 458, *459*

    security events, 458, 461, *462*

    system events, 458, 460, *460*

Everyone local group, 208, 209, 261, 336

Exchange. *See* Microsoft Exchange

extended partitions, 120, 126

---

**F** ∿∿∿∿∿∿∿∿∿∿∿∿∿∿∿∿

FAT. *See* File Allocation Table (FAT)

FAT32 file system, 478

File Allocation Table (FAT)

    cluster size and volume sizes, 478

    fragmentation and, 477

    introduced, 477

    partitions and, 60–62, 63

File and Print Services for NetWare (FPNW), 322, 439

file attributes, 53

file audits, 464, *465*

filenames in MS-DOS, 251

file permissions

    adding users from another domain to share permissions, 336–37, *337, 338*, 339, *339*

    assigning, 264, *264*

    available permissions, 53, *54*, 259, *260*

    cross-domain groups and, 339–43, *340, 342*

    Everyone group and, 336

    how permissions work, 260–61

    introduced, 249, 258–59

    special access, 264, *265, 266*

    types, 53, *54*, 259, *260*

files

    backing up (*see* backups)

    data, 55

    document, 55

    File and Print Services for NetWare (FPNW), 322, 439

    library, 54

    managing Macintosh users, files, and volumes, 451

    ownership and, 266–67, *267*

    program, 54

    registry, 515, *515–16*

file security, 52–53, *53–54*, 54–55, *55*

file server hardware, 42

file systems

    FAT (*see* File Allocation Table (FAT))

    FAT32, 478

    High Performance File System (HPFS), 62

    maintaining

        FAT, 477–78

        introduced, 476

        NTFS, 479–80

    NTFS (*see* NT file system (NTFS))

    selecting, 60–62

Find option, 563–64, *563*

folder

    audits, 464, *465*

    defined, 559

    migrating file and folder properties, 444, *445*

    typical arrangement, *55*

Microsoft Windows NT Server 4.0, *continued*

NetWare services and (*see* Novell NetWare services)

reinstalling, 72, 84–85

server tools (*see also* User Manager for Domains)

installing, 314–15, *315*

removing, 322–23, *323*

things server tools can't do, 321

using Event Viewer, 316, *317*

using Server Manager, 318, *318, 319*

transfer of data between Macintosh and, 451–52

upgrading from earlier versions, 72, 84–85

Windows 95 considerations, 72–73

workgroups versus NT Server networks, 14–15

Microsoft Windows NT Server Resource Kit, 517, 519, 524, 525

Migration Tool for NetWare

introduced, 440–43, *441, 442*

migrating file and folder properties, 444, *445*

miscellaneous NetWare objects and restrictions, 443–44

planning for migration, 446

running, 446, *446,* 448–49, *448*

.mil domain, 104, *104*

mirrored boot partitions, 147, 553–54

mirror sets (RAID 1)

breaking, 145–47, *146, 147, 148*

creating, 142–45, *143, 144*

defined, 121

introduced, 64, 142

mixed administration, 48–49, *49*

modems

dedicated, 384–85

installing, 110–12, *110, 111, 112, 113*

Install New Modem wizard, 110–11, *110, 111*

introduced, 384

shared, 385

mouse skills, 558–59

MS-DOS

attaching device names to logical printers, 237

boot disks, 551

disk partitions and, 121–22, *122*

filenames in, 251

share names in, 251

multiple domains

management tasks, 328–29

need for, 343–45

multiple-master domain model, 28–30, *29*

multiprocessor support of Windows NT, 6

multitasking, 7

multithreading, 7

My Computer icon, 567

## N

name resolution

Bootstrap Protocol (BOOTP) and, 105–6

Domain Name System (DNS), 103–4, 364–66, 370–73, *371*

Dynamic Host Configuration Protocol (DHCP) and, 105–6, 366–67, 374–79, *376, 377*

HOSTS files, 105

introduced, 102, 363–64

LMHOSTS files, 105

NetBIOS and, 102

Windows Internet Naming Service (WINS), 104–5, 367–68, *369,* 373–74, *373, 375*

names

server, 87, 540–41

user, 157

NCP (NetWare Core Protocol), 447

NDS (Novell Directory Service), 447

NetBIOS Extended User Interface (NetBEUI) protocol, 64, 65, 107–8

NetBIOS naming convention, 102

.net domain, 104, *104*

NETLOGON share, 253

netmask, 100

NETSYNC, 447

NT Server. *See* Microsoft Windows NT
   Server 4.0
NTUSER.DAT.LOG registry file, *516*
NTUSER.DAT registry file, *516*
NWCALLS.DLL, 436–37
NWIPXSPX.DLL, 436
NWNETAPI.DLL, 436–37

## O

object linking and embedding (OLE)
   technology, 300
one-way trust relationships, 22–23
Open Systems Interconnection (OSI) reference
   model
   application layer, *576*, 578
   data link layer, *576*, 577
   introduced, 576–77, *576*
   network layer, *576*, 577–78
   physical layer, *576*, 577
   presentation layer, *576*, 578
   session layer, *576*, 578
   transport layer, *576*, 578
.org domain, 104, *104*
OSI model. *See* Open Systems Interconnection
   (OSI) reference model
ownership, 266–67, *267*

## P

Packet INternet Groper (PING), 99
packets
   connectionless, 98
   defined, 577
PAP (Password Authentication Protocol), 391
parity, 140
partitions
   defined, 120
   extended, 120, 126
   introduced, 121–22, *122*
   mirrored boot, 147, 553–54
   planning, 62–64
   primary, 120, 122, *123*, 124–26, *124*, *125*

Password Authentication Protocol (PAP), 391
passwords. *See also* administration; audits;
      security
   changing, 56
   choosing, 56
   managing
      Account Lockout, 159, 181
      introduced, 179, *180*
      setting password rules, 180
   new users, *156*, 158, *158–59*
   number assigned to each user, 50
PDC. *See* primary domain controller (PDC)
peer-to-peer networks, 14–15
Performance Monitor
   administrative alerts, 471–72, *471*, *472*
   charts, 469–71, *470*
   introduced, 469
   reports, 472, *473*
permissions
   defined, 182, 248
   directory
      assigning, 261–63, *262*
      available permissions, 53, *53–54*, 259, *259*
      how permissions work, 260–61
      introduced, 249, 258–59
      special access, 264, *265*
      types, 53, *53–54*, 259, *259*
   file
      adding users from another domain to
         share permissions, 336–37, *337*, *338*,
         *339*, *339*
      assigning, 264, *264*
      available permissions, 53, *54*, 259, *260*
      cross-domain groups and, 339–43, *340*,
         *342*
      Everyone group and, 336
      how permissions work, 260–61
      introduced, 249, 258–59
      special access, 264, *265*, *266*
      types, 53, *54*, 259, *260*
   groups and, 198
   ownership and, 266–67, *267*
   printer, viewing or changing, 241–43, *241*,
      *242*

## Charlie Russel

Charlie Russel is Lead Database Administrator for a software development company. Prior to this position, he was the systems administrator of a combined Microsoft Windows NT/UNIX network at a large automotive manufacturing plant for more than a decade. He has written several books, including *ABCs of Windows NT Workstation 4.0* and *Murphy's Laws of DOS*, and is coauthor with Linda L. Gaus of *SCO OpenServer: The Windows Network Solution*.

## Sharon Crawford

Sharon Crawford is a former technical editor who now writes full-time, specializing in books and magazine articles related to the high technology industry. She has written *ABCs of Windows 95, Your First Modem*, and *Managing Your Personal Finances with Quicken* and is coauthor with Andy Rathbone of *NT Workstation 4.0 for Dummies*. She also is a member of ClubWin, an online Windows 95 support group, and is the Technology Advisor for the Working From Home forum on CompuServe.

In addition to the books they have written individually, Charlie Russel and Sharon Crawford have coauthored numerous books on operating systems. Their titles include *Upgrading to Windows 95, OS/2 for Windows Users, Voodoo UNIX*, and *Murphy's Laws of Windows*.

Charlie and Sharon live in Northern California with six cats and hope to have time to plant a garden *next* year.

The manuscript for this book was prepared and submitted to Microsoft Press in electronic form. Text files were prepared using Microsoft Word 7.0 for Windows 95. Pages were composed by Microsoft Press using Adobe PageMaker 6.0 for Windows 95, with text in Palatino and display type in Emigre BaseNine. Composed pages were delivered to the printer as electronic prepress files.

**Cover Graphic Designer**
Gregory Erickson
Tim Girvin Design, Inc.

**Interior Graphic Designer**
Pam Hidaka

**Interior Graphic Artist**
Michael Victor

**Desktop Publishers**
Sandra Haynes
Dick Carter
Jeffrey Brendecke

**Principal Proofreaders**
Patricia Masserman
Deborah Long

**Indexer**
Foxon-Maddocks Associates

# Keep things **running** smoothly around the **Office.**

These are *the* answer books for business users of Microsoft® Office 97 applications. They are packed with everything from quick, clear instructions for new users to comprehensive answers for power users. The Microsoft Press® *Running* series features authoritative handbooks you'll keep by your computer and use every day.

**Running Microsoft® Excel 97**
**Mark Dodge, Chris Kinata, and Craig Stinson**
**U.S.A. $39.95**  ($53.95 Canada)
ISBN 1-57231-321-8

**Running Microsoft® Office 97**
**Michael Halvorson and Michael Young**
**U.S.A. $39.95**  ($53.95 Canada)
ISBN 1-57231-322-6

**Running Microsoft® Word 97**
**Russell Borland**
**U.S.A. $39.95**  ($53.95 Canada)
ISBN 1-57231-320-X

**Running Microsoft® PowerPoint® 97**
**Stephen W. Sagman**
**U.S.A. $29.95**  ($39.95 Canada)
ISBN 1-57231-324-2

**Running Microsoft® Access 97**
**John L. Viescas**
**U.S.A. $39.95**  ($53.95 Canada)
ISBN 1-57231-323-4

Microsoft Press® products are available worldwide wherever quality computer books are sold. For more information, contact your book retailer, computer reseller, or local Microsoft Sales Office.

To locate your nearest source for Microsoft Press products, reach us at www.microsoft.com/mspress/, or call 1-800-MSPRESS in the U.S. (in Canada: 1-800-667-1115 or 416-293-8464).

To order Microsoft Press products, call 1-800-MSPRESS in the U.S. (in Canada: 1-800-667-1115 or 416-293-8464).

Prices and availability dates are subject to change.

**Microsoft**®Press

# DEVELOPING APPLICATIONS WITH MICROSOFT OFFICE 95 is a must-read for anyone interested in Office 95 application development.

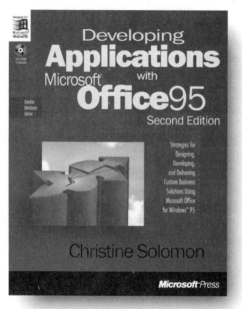

**U.S.A.** **$39.95**
U.K.  £37.49 [V.A.T. included]
Canada  $53.95
ISBN 1-55615-898-X

## Learn to build mission-critical applications with the powerful tools in Microsoft® Office 95.

DEVELOPING APPLICATIONS WITH MICROSOFT OFFICE 95, Second Edition, is a highly readable account of how to design, develop, and deliver customized business systems with Microsoft Office for Windows® 95. Every phase of the process is explained, from choosing which tools to use to designing a good GUI to providing end-user training and support. Christine Solomon, a Microsoft Solution Provider with years of experience in Office application development, writes eloquently on issues such as how and why to include the user in the development process, how to turn power users into programmers and programmers into power users (and why that's so important), and how to roll out and support an application so that the successfully designed application is perceived as successful by its users. The book's companion CD features case studies drawn from the author's work with Fortune 500 companies, fully functional sample applications, and sample code to illustrate key points.

# How to **build** groupware applications in **less than** a **day.**

With this results-oriented, step-by-step guide and Microsoft® Exchange, you can do it. In fact, with this volume, even nonprogrammers can learn to quickly create professional-quality mail-enabled groupware applications. And Visual Basic® programmers can give those applications more power. The secret for customizing Microsoft Exchange is in three built-in components—public folders, the Exchange Forms Designer, and Visual Basic for Applications. This book shows you how to put them to work. Get BUILDING MICROSOFT EXCHANGE APPLICATIONS. And start saving time.

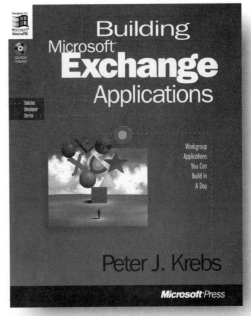

| U.S.A. | **$39.95** |
| --- | --- |
| U.K. | £37.49 [V.A.T. included] |
| Canada | $54.95 |
| ISBN 1-57231-334-X | |

**Microsoft** Press

# Make your presence **felt** on the **Internet** or within your own **intranet.**

**T**his book is not about developing Web site content (although it touches on it). BUILD YOUR OWN WEB SITE shows you how to publish your content on the Internet or your corporate intranet using Microsoft® Windows NT® Server and Microsoft Internet Information Server—even if you have little or no programming or networking experience. In this helpful guide, you will find everything you need to know about:

- How the Internet or an intranet works
- Why Windows NT Server is the platform to choose
- How to calculate choices of hardware, connections, security, bandwidth, and routing
- How to set up your system, maintain security, create content, and observe Internet etiquette
- How to configure your system, deal with maintenance issues, and plan for the future
- How to become an Internet service provider

BUILD YOUR OWN WEB SITE also familiarizes you with hot new technologies such as Java and ActiveX™.

**If you're ready to establish your organization on the Internet or to set up your own intranet, BUILD YOUR OWN WEB SITE is the smart place to start.**

| | |
|---|---|
| U.S.A. | **$29.95** |
| U.K. | £27.99 [V.A.T. included] |
| Canada | $39.95 |
| ISBN 1-57231-304-8 | |

Microsoft Press® products are available worldwide wherever quality computer books are sold. For more information, contact your book retailer, computer reseller, or local Microsoft Sales Office.

To locate your nearest source for Microsoft Press products, reach us at www.microsoft.com/mspress/, or call 1-800-MSPRESS in the U.S. (in Canada: 1-800-667-1115 or 416-293-8464).

To order Microsoft Press products, call 1-800-MSPRESS in the U.S. (in Canada: 1-800-667-1115 or 416-293-8464).

Prices and availability dates are subject to change.

***Microsoft*** *Press*

# Register Today!

## Return this
## *Running Microsoft® Windows NT® Server 4.0*
## registration card for
## a Microsoft Press® catalog

U.S. and Canada addresses only. Fill in information below and mail postage-free. Please mail only the bottom half of this page.

1-57231-333-1A     ***RUNNING MICROSOFT® WINDOWS NT®***     *Owner Registration Card*
                   ***SERVER 4.0***

_____

NAME

_____

INSTITUTION OR COMPANY NAME

_____

ADDRESS

_____

CITY                                          STATE          ZIP

# **Microsoft**®*Press*
## *Quality Computer Books*

For a free catalog of
Microsoft Press® products, call
## 1-800-MSPRESS

NO POSTAGE
NECESSARY
IF MAILED
IN THE
UNITED STATES